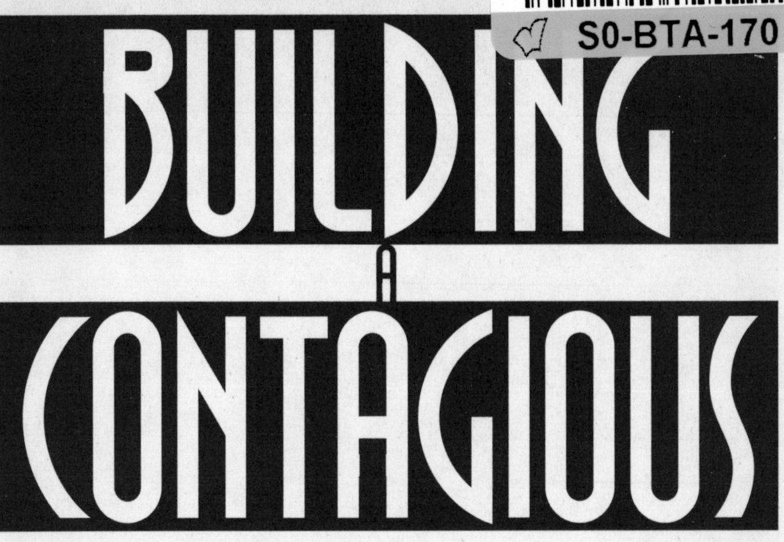

BUILDING A CONTAGIOUS CHURCH

REVOLUTIONIZING THE WAY WE VIEW AND DO EVANGELISM

MARK MITTELBERG

WITH CONTRIBUTIONS BY BILL HYBELS

ZondervanPublishing
Grand Rapids, Michigan

A Division of HarperCollins*Publishers*

Building a Contagious Church

International Trade Paper Edition

Requests for information should be addressed to:
ZondervanPublishingHouse
Grand Rapids, Michigan 49530

ISBN 0-310-23200-7

Interior design by Melissa Elenbaas
Printed in the United States of America

00 01 02 03 04 05 06 /❖ DC/ 10 9 8 7 6 5 4 3 2

Endorsements for *Building a Contagious Church*

I couldn't recommend a book more enthusiastically than I endorse *Building a Contagious Church*. Imagine a city where the churches are outwardly focused on reaching their neighborhoods. This is good news indeed.

Luis Palau
International Evangelist
Author of *God Is Relevant*

Mark has done all of us a great service. Based on indispensable biblical values, he has opened new windows for our witness in an increasingly hostile environment. If you want to tell the Good News effectively ... this is your book.

Dr. Joseph M. Stowell
President, Moody Bible Institute
Author of *Loving Christ*

This is a wonderful manual on local church evangelism. It is both well-researched and well-written, providing a practical framework for doing evangelism. But most important, it comes from the heart of Mark Mittelberg, who is passionate about reaching unbelievers. You can't read this book without having your heart stirred to share the gospel. It's *contagious*!

Rick Warren
Senior Pastor, Saddleback Valley Community Church
Author of *The Purpose-Driven® Church*

Mark Mittelberg has got it together. With invigorating winsomeness yet uncompromising frankness, he tells how to relate the offense of the gospel to lost people. Following these guidelines, any church will come alive to evangelism.

Robert E. Coleman
Director of the School of World Mission and Evangelism,
Trinity International University
Author of *The Master Plan of Evangelism*

Building a Contagious Church is an evangelistic *tour de force* that will greatly help any church or ministry that is serious about fulfilling the Great Commission. Entire leadership teams and outreach committees should read and discuss this powerful book—and then put its principles into action.

John C. Maxwell
Founder of The INJOY Group
Author of *Developing the Leaders Around You*

Mark Mittelberg has done it again. He has written a book that many of us have been waiting for. This book is one of the finest and most practical books I have ever read on the subject of local church evangelism. It should be of great help and encouragement to every pastor and local church leader who reads it.

Dr. Paul A. Cedar
Chairman, Mission America
Author of *A Life of Prayer*

This book does the impossible. It lays out a coherent plan for congregations to spread the Good News while giving countless examples of real churches doing it well. What encouragement! What inspiration! What motivation! It's, well, contagious!

Marshall Shelley
Editor, *Leadership*
Author of *Growing Your Church through Evangelism and Outreach*

Every church leader *must* read this powerful book! Implement its thoroughly biblical strategy—as Mark and I have done together for many years—and watch God infuse your church with fresh evangelistic fervor and effectiveness. Who knows how many will find Christ as a result?

LEE STROBEL
TEACHING PASTOR AT SADDLEBACK VALLEY COMMUNITY CHURCH
AUTHOR OF *THE CASE FOR CHRIST* AND *THE CASE FOR FAITH*

What I love about this book is that Mittelberg provides not only strategies and practical help for churches who want to get off the dime and become evangelizing centers—but he urges us to not forget the absolute necessity of prayer and dependence upon the Holy Spirit. His love for God and his heart for the lost bubbles over on every page!

REBECCA MANLEY PIPPERT
AUTHOR OF *OUT OF THE SALTSHAKER & INTO THE WORLD*

You are holding a road map for churches looking for the road that leads outwardly. No matter what your congregation's size, this book will illuminate the way out! I'm studying it with all my leaders.

STEVE SJOGREN
FOUNDING PASTOR, VINEYARD COMMUNITY CHURCH, CINCINNATI, OHIO
AUTHOR OF *CONSPIRACY OF KINDNESS*

Mark Mittelberg is passionate about evangelism. He is passionate about the local church. And in his outstanding book, *Building a Contagious Church*, Mark shows us how the most effective evangelism takes place in the local church. This book needs to be read because it is biblical, because it is practical, and because the principles will lead churches to make an eternal difference in the lives of millions of lost and unchurched people around the world.

THOM S. RAINER
DEAN, BILLY GRAHAM SCHOOL OF MISSIONS,
EVANGELISM, AND CHURCH GROWTH
AUTHOR OF *EFFECTIVE EVANGELISTIC CHURCHES*

Mark Mittelberg attacks a sleeping giant with this book, and he is right on the mark. While most evangelism training focuses on convincing Christians to evangelize, this book seeks to convince and equip *the church* to reach the lost. He is right! We won't have one without the other.

LON ALLISON
DIRECTOR, BILLY GRAHAM CENTER, WHEATON COLLEGE

Pastors, ministry leaders, and entire congregations who have a passion for reaching lost people will greatly benefit from the proven principles and practical applications identified in this book.

STERLING W. HUSTON
DIRECTOR, NORTH AMERICAN MINISTRIES,
BILLY GRAHAM EVANGELISTIC ASSOCIATION
AUTHOR OF *CRUSADE EVANGELISM AND THE LOCAL CHURCH*

A tremendous guidebook for young preachers who are beginning new ministries. Personally, I wish it had been written forty years ago. I heartily recommend it to everyone involved in Christian service.

BILLY KIM
PRESIDENT, FAR EAST BROADCASTING COMPANY, KOREA
PRESIDENT, BAPTIST WORLD ALLIANCE

We desperately need contagious churches maximizing outreach that expands the borders of God's kingdom! Mittelberg offers a courageous approach to church-based evangelism that's compelling and doable for all.

Stephen A. Macchia
President, Vision New England
Author of *Becoming a Healthy Church*

Few churches or Christians need one more lecture on evangelism. But we all need a road map for sharing our faith in an increasingly postmodern world. My friend and colleague, Mark Mittelberg, gives every reader of *Building a Contagious Church* an incredibly practical guide for understanding God's great love for lost people and how we can strengthen our church's capacity to extend his love to them. Skip the books on evangelism theory. This is the book that will give you hope that God still wants to work through your church to draw lost people to himself.

J. David Schmidt
President, J. David Schmidt and Associates
Coauthor of *The Prospering Parachurch*

Finally, here it is—a step-by-step manual for turning ordinary churches into fired-up, contagious ones! Based on proven biblical principles God has used over the years here at Willow Creek and in other places, no church should be without this road map for effective evangelism.

Garry Poole
Director of Evangelism, Willow Creek Community Church
Coauthor of the *Tough Questions* curriculum for seeker small groups

---

One of the most critical issues facing the church is how do we help our people succeed at "walking like Jesus walked, becoming a friend of sinners"? This book will greatly help leaders mobilize their ministries toward outreach. You will find many practical insights for breaking out of ingrown "church-ianity" and becoming balanced in evangelism and discipleship.

Dr. Dann Spader
Founder and Director, Sonlife Ministries
Author of *The Everyday Commission*

Willow Creek Community Church is the most important apostolic experiment in the United States in this generation. *Building a Contagious Church* represents twenty-five years of serious reflection within this experiment. Thousands of church leaders will read this book and discover ways their church can reach out more effectively.

George G. Hunter
Professor of Church Growth, School of World Mission and Evangelism,
Asbury Theological Seminary
Author of *Church for the Unchurched*

Mark Mittelberg reminds us that high-impact evangelism has its greatest fruit when it overflows out of the heart of a contagious church. Every church leadership team needs to work through this book together.

Gene Appel
Senior Pastor, Central Christian Church,
Las Vegas/Henderson, Nevada
Coauthor of *How to Change Your Church (Without Killing It)*

Learn from one of America's great success stories about local church evangelism. Using stories and illustrations, Mark does a masterful job of sharing the lessons learned by Willow Creek Community Church as they created a "Contagious Church," beginning with their own leadership team. Regardless of the size, setting, or style of your church, this book will provide a renewed sense of purpose for your evangelism program.

BOB BUFORD
FOUNDING CHAIRMAN, LEADERSHIP NETWORK
AUTHOR OF *HALFTIME* AND *GAME PLAN*

Ouch! As with any inoculation, this hurts a bit. But I am sure an epidemic of Contagious Churches has begun. Read this book now and avoid taking your church to the Emergency Room later! Thanks, Mark. I am reassured that with God's help we can finish up the Great Commission.

TOM YOUNGBLOOD
VICE PRESIDENT, U. S. FIELD MINISTRIES,
INTERNATIONAL BIBLE SOCIETY

Building a Contagious Church gives any church or ministry an excellent process for reaching the lost. Mark has been very helpful in stimulating InterVarsity's recent "evangelism revolution." We've been applying his 6-Stage Process on campuses for a couple of years—it works! Now it's great to have his ideas in print!

RICK RICHARDSON
NATIONAL EVANGELIST, INTERVARSITY CHRISTIAN FELLOWSHIP
AUTHOR OF *EVANGELISM OUTSIDE THE BOX*

Over thirty years ago my late husband Paul Little taught Christians how to give away their faith. In *Building a Contagious Church,* Mark Mittelberg teaches whole churches how to give away their faith and reach more and more lost people for Christ. This is an awesome book!

MARIE LITTLE
AUTHOR AND FORMER INTERVARSITY STAFF WORKER

Building a Contagious Church is one of the most refreshing books on evangelism I have read in years. At once biblical, inspirational, motivational, and educational, this book is destined to become a classic.

LYLE W. DORSETT
PROFESSOR OF EVANGELISM AND SPIRITUAL FORMATION,
WHEATON COLLEGE AND GRADUATE SCHOOL
AUTHOR OF *A PASSION FOR SOULS*

To my wife, Heidi, and our two children,

Emma Jean and Matthew.

Your love, encouragement, patience,

and prayers throughout this entire project have

meant more than words can say

ACKNOWLEDGMENTS

This book would have never been written without the strength and grace of God, as well as the love, support, encouragement, and prayers of many faithful friends and family members. I am indebted to numerous people, including:

My wife, Heidi, for your unwavering support from the day we wrote down the initial outline to the recent morning when you helped me organize the final edits—you've cheered me on all along the way like nobody else could. Matthew, for your faith-filled prayers each night, and Emma Jean, for your sweet words of encouragement each day. In addition, thanks to all three of you for your enduring patience, and the inspiring posters and notes to cheer me along the way.

Lee Strobel, for your ideas, advice, and input—and faithful friendship that never changes, whether we live near or far! Bill Hybels, for your support, the ministry opportunities you've opened for me, your modeling of a contagious Christian life, as well as the several messages used in this book. Don Cousins, for strong influence early in my ministry that has shaped my thinking and approach in many important ways.

Karl and Barbara Singer, for extraordinary help and a home away from home where I could get so much writing done. Kevin and Sherry Harney, for researching and collecting stories from contagious churches all over the country, your fervent prayers, and the inspiring e-mail and voice mail messages. Rickey Bolden, for encouraging me to take the first steps and for spurring me on throughout the process. Laura Dorans, for your undying support and assistance. Brad Mitchell, for constantly unleashing your encouragement gift on me.

Jack Kuhatschek at Zondervan, for genuinely caring, understanding, and helping to shape the book, as well as Dirk Buursma, for passionate commitment to making every word and detail right, and Stan Gundry, for believing in and supporting this project from the beginning.

Jim Mellado and the leadership team of the Willow Creek Association, for your enthusiasm about this ministry resource and your support during the many steps of its development. The team also includes Gary Schwammlein, Sharon Swing, Steve Bell, Tripp Stegall, and Joe Sherman (who initially helped prompt me to develop this tool), as well as former leadership team members, John Williams and Wende Lindsey-Kotouc. You've all been a great encouragement.

The friends and ministry colleagues who prayed and gave a wealth of support in a variety of ways and at various stages, including Garry Poole, Russ and Lynn Robinson, Paul Braoudakis, Bob Gordon, Judson Poling, Wendy Seidman, Cathy Burnett, Christine Anderson, Doug Yonamine, Tammy Burke, David Hannah, Tom and Robin Smith, Mindy Thompson, Lynn Norum, Larry and Rosemary Estry (especially the middle-of-the-night prayers!), Marie Little, Renee McMurry, Kari Lesser, Ashley Podgorski, Jeff Johnson, Rob and Tone Gorman, Mark Edwards, Bill Conard, Mark Miller, Steve Pate, Gary and Sheri Kingsbury, Jen Barr, Kimberly Knoll, Larry O'Reilly, Bob and Julie Harney, Tom and Nancy Vitacco, Chad Meister, Tom Youngblood, Stan Kellner, Bryan Hochhalter, Wanda Fogarty, Nancy Grisham, Lon Allison, Rick Richardson, Brad Smith, Dann Spader, Marc Harrienger, Dave and Sandy Gelwicks, Ron Seyk, Lance Murdock, and Rich and Mary Verlare.

Finally and especially, thanks to my wonderful family members who prayed for this project and encouraged me throughout, including my parents, Orland and Ginny Mittelberg; my grandmother, Effa Mittelberg; my sisters, Kathy and Lisa; my brother, Gary; and my father- and mother-in-law, Hillis and Jean Hugelen.

CONTENTS

FOREWORD

As I sit in my office and reflect on the evangelistic fervor I see day after day around Willow Creek Community Church, I can hardly contain my enthusiasm. Thousands of people invited their seeking friends to a recent outreach musical, hundreds more went through evangelism training—*again*—to sharpen their skills in sharing their faith, small groups for people investigating Christianity are multiplying at a dizzying pace, and we celebrated the baptism of more than a thousand new believers last year alone.

As I gaze out my window, I can see preparations being made at our pond for yet another baptism service, when we will see multitudes of freshly redeemed people from all walks of life publicly declaring their newfound faith in Jesus Christ.

I've said it time after time, but I can't help marvel once more: There's nothing like the local church when it's working right. And when churches are fully engaged in fulfilling their redemptive potential, the lost get found, the spiritually confused find truth, and lives are changed in this world and for eternity. Tell me: What other endeavor on the planet is so worthy of our time and effort?

All church leaders want to experience what it's like to be involved in an evangelistically active congregation, where every Christian is purposefully reaching out to their spiritually lost friends, neighbors, colleagues, and family members. However, the truth is that zeal for the Great Commission has grown tepid in many churches, and pastors are often uncertain about how they can lead the charge toward a new era of effective outreach.

That's where this powerful and practical book comes in. It is nothing short of a field-proven blueprint for reigniting the evangelistic fire in churches where hearts have stopped burning brightly for those outside of God's family.

This book has not been written by an academic theorist but by an active practitioner who speaks out of firsthand knowledge about evangelism in the local church. Mark Mittelberg joined our staff in 1987 as our first evangelism director, and he spearheaded the development of a plan to equip our entire congregation for personal evangelism. Not only has he trained thousands of people himself, but he also invented and built a whole new kind of evangelism team, which continues to flourish today. What's more, he has innovated a number of ministries and events to seize the attention of seekers and lead them to Christ.

This book distills these developments, as well as lessons learned through interactions with other churches, into a thoroughly biblical, step-by-step process that is described through colorful stories and helpful illustrations. Frankly, I hope every church leader carefully and prayerfully studies these principles—and then summons the courage to move ahead in the power of the Holy Spirit.

After all, there's too much at stake to settle for the status quo. Lost people matter to God—and I hope you will do everything you can to apply what you learn in this book to build a contagious church that will reach them with the life-changing and eternity-altering gospel of Jesus Christ.

BILL HYBELS
SENIOR PASTOR, WILLOW CREEK COMMUNITY CHURCH
JUNE, 2000

INTRODUCTION

If you have a passion for reaching lost people with the love and truth of Christ—

- If you would like to develop and expand that passion—
- If you care deeply about fulfilling the Great Commission and want to help your church or ministry become more effective in that endeavor—

this book is for you!

It doesn't matter whether your church is large or small, old or new, urban or suburban, upscale or downscale, high church or low church. You may be seeker-focused, seeker-friendly, seeker-neutral—or you may not even like the term *seeker.* You may be traditional, contemporary, or somewhere in between. You may be mainline, evangelical, fundamentalist, denominational, independent, conservative, progressive, or one of a hundred other labels. Perhaps you are a church that disparages labels altogether.

You may be a pastor, a ministry staff member, a volunteer leader, a Sunday school teacher, a small group leader. Maybe you are a parent concerned about keeping your kids in the faith. Or perhaps you are a regular church member who cares deeply about the effectiveness of your church. What matters most is that you have a love for God, a commitment to the truth of Scripture, and a growing heart for the people in your community who don't yet know Christ. If that's you, and if you would like to expand your heart for lost people and express it in practical ways, then read on!

This book presents proven approaches and transferable principles for raising the evangelistic temperature in yourself and in your entire church. It offers strategies for training all of your members to naturally communicate their faith. It gives guidance for developing and deploying members who have latent evangelism gifts. It also presents numerous ideas for high-impact outreach ministries and events that will build on the full range of diverse personalities and evangelistic styles God has built into your congregation.

Regardless of where you're starting from, I'm confident that in the power of the Holy Spirit you can take significant steps toward making your ministry more outwardly focused and evangelistically fruitful. My prayer for you is the same as the apostle Paul penned two thousand years ago in Colossians 4:5 for the earliest followers of Christ:

Be wise in the way you act toward outsiders
and
make the most of every opportunity.

Together, let's commit to doing whatever it takes in each of our own community settings, utilizing all of the gifts, resources, and team members God has provided, to build a highly contagious church.

— *Mark Mittelberg*

PART 1

A CONTAGIOUS PLAN

Organizations of all kinds, and churches in particular, have a dangerous tendency to stay so busy dealing with day-to-day programs, pressures, and problems that, over time, we lose track of what we are trying to accomplish. Before we know it, we have slipped into thinking, "Mission statements, values, strategies—who has time to worry about such things when we're already working overtime just trying to keep up?" But unless we step back and examine our overall direction, how can we know whether or not our efforts are taking us where we want to go?

One thing's for sure: Without intentional planning, decision making, and leadership—and a whole lot of course corrections along the way—a church or ministry will never experience sustained evangelistic fruitfulness. This is not something churches drift into on their own. No, *building a contagious church only happens on purpose!* A carefully developed plan, along with supporting values and action steps, must be in place before a church can become truly effective at reaching lost people for Christ.

Thus, the three chapters in part 1 are about reestablishing our redemptive mission (chapter 1), reinforcing our evangelistic values (chapter 2), and reinstating a practical outreach strategy (chapter 3). Combined, we'll have a pretty good initial picture of what a contagious church looks like.

Building this kind of church is going to take focus and hard work. But as we, by God's grace, reach increasing numbers of family members, friends, neighbors, and coworkers, we'll know for certain that it is worth our every effort!

1

EVANGELISM AGAINST THE ODDS

WHAT ARE WE TRYING TO DO?

"Listen, I've taken my questions to a pastor, a priest, and a rabbi. Not one of them was able to give me any good reasons to believe in God. In fact, they've just congratulated me for thinking it through so carefully. One of them even told me I'd given *him* some things to think about! I've spent a lot of time and energy on this, so don't think you're going to easily sway me into believing that your ideas are right."

So energized was the discussion between this young Jewish businessman and my pastor friend that a church usher actually stepped in to try to break up the "fight." But as soon as he did, both of them protested. "It's okay," my friend assured the usher, "we're both just very passionate about this."

"Not only that," added this intense seeker, "I can't tell you how refreshing it is to finally find a place like this where people seem to actually care about logic and truth. This is fantastic!" This man, like so many others today, was highly interested in discovering what is real in the spiritual realm, and he was eager to talk about it.

We see it all around us. From cover stories of national newsmagazines, to titles of best-selling books, to themes of television programs and movies, to songs on the music charts—people are hungry for information about God.

Spiritual interest is at a high level in our culture but so is bewilderment about what to believe and whom to trust. The good news is that although there is growing suspicion of organized religion, many men and women, like this Jewish businessman, are still willing to turn to an ordinary church like yours or like mine in the hope that they might—just might—find some answers there.

The question is, are we prepared to help them? Are we becoming the kind of people—and are we building the kind of churches—that will be able to assist them in embarking on spiritual journeys that will eventually bring them to Christ?

Evangelism. It's one of the highest values in the church—and one of the least practiced.

We all believe in it. I don't think I've ever met anyone who genuinely believed in the Bible but didn't believe in evangelism. When you embrace the truth of God's Word, it's pretty difficult to discount its call to reach lost people. It's on our bulletins, in our hymns, and throughout our creeds. It's posted on our marquees and peppered throughout our statements of faith. It's emphasized in our theology books, praised in our seminaries, and encouraged in our pulpits. Most Christian leaders list it as one of their ministry's top priorities. There is little ambiguity or doubt that evangelism is central to what we're supposed to be about.

The irony is that while many of us are in churches and denominations that have a rich heritage and strong reputation for evangelism, in many cases, precious little is actually happening. Let's be honest: in most ministries very few lost people are being reached for Christ.

Yet the words of Jesus in the Great Commission are seared in our minds: "Go and make disciples of all nations, baptizing them in the name of the Father and of the Son and of the Holy Spirit, and teaching them to obey everything I have commanded you. And surely I am with you always, to the very end of the age" (Matthew 28:19–20). This mandate was given for all churches of all time, so it includes every one of us who is a part of those congregations.

Since we all agree that we are supposed to be carrying out the Great Commission, why aren't we doing more about it? Studies show that most Christians don't have very many—if *any*—friendships with non-Christians. The majority of church members can no longer quote the words in John 3:16 about God's great love for the world, much less articulate a clear gospel illustration. A mere fourteen percent of pastors claim that their churches are heavily involved in evangelism. Only one out of three churches ever trains its people in evangelism.[1]

We may talk a good game, but our actions speak louder than our words. Do we really care about lost people? Do we sincerely believe that knowing Christ is the best way to live and the only way to die? Are we convinced that everyone we know, without exception, needs to find the forgiveness, friendship, life, and leadership Jesus offers? Do we truly believe in hell, and that our friends and family members will end up there if they don't trust in Christ before they die? Do we *really* believe that? If so, are we willing to take risks to warn them? And are we willing to invest our time and energy in developing churches that will attract, challenge, and teach them to step across the line of faith?

Do we sincerely believe that knowing Christ is the best way to live and the only way to die?

Jesus has commissioned us to become persuasive communicators of his love and truth. That is, he asks us to become contagious Christians and to build contagious churches that will do everything necessary, through the guidance and power of the Holy Spirit, to bring more and more people to him. If you know and love Christ, I'm confident that your spirit is saying, "Yes, that's right. I long to become that kind of Christian and to be a part of that kind of church. I really want to impact people's lives and eternities!"

We were made to fulfill the Great Commission. I believe evangelizing is the primary reason God left us here on the planet. We can spend all of eternity worshiping God, learning from his Word, praying to him, and encouraging and edifying one another. But only here and now do we have the chance to reach lost people for Christ. What a privilege and what an adventure!

THE NEED FOR CONTAGIOUS CHURCHES

What will it take to have the widespread impact we were made to have?

Personal, relational evangelism plays a vital role. That's why I wrote *Becoming a Contagious Christian* with Bill Hybels and later developed the *Becoming a Contagious Christian* training course with Lee Strobel and Bill Hybels.[2] We wanted to equip ordinary believers to communicate their faith naturally and effectively. People come to Christ one life at a time—and usually through the influence of one or two authentic Christians who have built genuine relationships with them. All believers can and should have that kind of impact on the people around them.

But we need more than enthusiastic and equipped individual believers. We also need the synergy of biblically functioning, outwardly focused, evangelistically active churches—and we need lots of them. We need churches that proactively partner with their members to reach increasing numbers of people who are far from God. We need churches that are convinced that "the gates of hell shall not prevail against [them]" (Matthew 16:18 KJV), and really act like it. We need *contagious* churches.

I believe in the importance of contagious churches for two reasons. First, I know from experience how hard it is to do effective evangelism outside the context of a contagious church. Second, I know the advantages and the joy of doing outreach in tandem with a contagious church.

The Limitations of Lone Ranger Evangelism

When I committed my life to Christ at age nineteen, God immediately implanted in me a desire to lead my friends to him. I was more than willing to talk to them about my faith. I gave them books and tapes about the Christian faith, led evangelistic Bible studies, organized outreach events, and even brought contemporary Christian music groups to my town to perform concerts as a platform for evangelism. In fact, some friends and I started a ministry that promoted numerous concerts over a five-year period in an effort to reach our non-Christian friends. It was an exciting spiritual venture but somewhat misunderstood in the rural reaches of northern North Dakota in the late '70s and early '80s!

I became known among my Christian friends for what they kiddingly referred to as "car evangelism." I would routinely invite spiritually receptive people to go for a ride so we could discuss spiritual matters or hear a tape about Christianity. We would often end up driving long distances along the back roads of Dakota listening to recorded gospel presentations on the cassette deck and then talking about what we had listened to. Unorthodox perhaps. And sure, it burned up plenty of fuel. But, hey, gas was cheap back then—and many of those people made commitments to Christ and are still serving him today!

There was, however, a downside. This kind of outreach was isolated and independent. For many of the people I was trying to reach, I was the singular link in the spiritual chain. To the degree that a few like-minded buddies and I could sustain our efforts, we had impact. But many times people fell through the cracks. Why? Because we were a ragtag, loosely organized team, and we weren't tightly integrated into a local church that could support or follow up on our outreach efforts.

Yes, we all were involved in various churches. But at the time, most of those churches were inwardly focused and had limited vision or energy for reaching outsiders—especially when it came to some of the newer, more innovative approaches we were beginning to take. The churches didn't know what to make of us, and we didn't know how to work with them. As a result, there was no natural handoff of seekers who wanted to go on to the next level in their search, or of new believers who needed to grow in their freshly found faith. These people related to our style of communicating and teaching, but they had a difficult time connecting with the culture of the traditional churches. In fact, at times it seemed easier to lead people to Christ than to get them into a church! Consequently, my friends and I found ourselves independently inventing solutions, piecemealing together the elements necessary to hold people in the fellowship and to keep them taking steps forward in their walk with Christ. We were feeling the pain of trying to be contagious Christians apart from the collaboration and support of a contagious church. God blessed many of our efforts, but the long-term results were limited compared to what could have been.

The Power of Church-Based Evangelism

What a difference my wife, Heidi, and I experienced when years later we moved to the Chicago area and became part of a body of believers who were learning to be a contagious church! The things we had been trying to do in isolation—personal evangelism, creative outreach events, discipleship, Bible teaching, relevant worship, and much more—were all being done under the roof of this single local church. What evangelistic power and potential!

When we or other church members would build friendships with non-Christians, we now had a place to bring them to experience a relevant church service. When seeker friends asked spiritual questions, we could turn to seminars, classes, teachers, tapes, and other available tools for help. When they finally made a commitment to Christ, the church had a built-in course of action whereby they could find community, growth, and accountability in a small group.

Then those new believers could learn to exalt God in worship services. They also had the opportunity to take classes to discover personal spiritual gifts and engage in meaningful service. They had a church where they could invest their time and resources in a way that would help expand God's kingdom. All of this was available at the same place that helped bring them to faith in Christ in the first place!

Heidi and I rejoiced as we watched God produce fruit in our new church. People were—and still are—coming to Christ frequently. Testimonies of conversions are common, baptisms of new believers are numerous, and expectations of evangelistic impact are expanding.

There's a synergistic "one-two punch" when individual contagious Christians do relational evangelism in partnership with a well-led contagious church that prioritizes outreach. So, what about your church? I don't care what brand your church is, what flavor it is, what color it is, how old it is, what neighborhood it is in, or how financially solvent it is. I just love the power and potential of contagious churches that hold to the message of Christ and take whatever risks are needed to reach lost people.

Jesus promised, "I will build my church; and the gates of hell shall not prevail against it" (Matthew 16:18 KJV). Why are the vast majority of churches *not* growing, or growing almost exclusively through transfers of Christians from other churches and through births of babies within their own congregations? Why are so many churches actually losing ground, not even reaching people at the rate the population around them is growing? Why are many churches actually shutting down and closing their doors forever? Many Christians seem content when a church "holds its own" and merely maintains its membership and budget numbers. Could that really be what Jesus had in mind when he gave us the Great Commission? I don't think so. It's certainly not an example of a contagious church.

Bill Hybels recently spoke about this to a group of church leaders in Europe:

> If you went to the airport, and there were no airplanes landing, and there were no airplanes taking off, you'd say, "There's a problem!" If you went to the train station, and there were no trains coming and no trains leaving, you'd say, "There's a problem!" So why is it that we can be a part of churches that go on year after year with almost no truly unchurched people coming to faith in Christ, and with very few people really becoming more Christlike, and yet think there's no problem. Friends, if that describes your church, *"There's a problem!"*

By its very nature and purpose, the church ought to be a contagious place that is "infecting" more and more outsiders with the Christian faith. In fact, there ought to be an epidemic of people trusting in Christ. Why isn't this happening?

CLARIFYING THE MISSION

A major part of the problem is that many churches have been around so long that they've lost sight of the primary purposes for which they were created in the first place. Simply asking members the question, "What are we trying to do?" will often evoke blank stares or puzzled looks that seem to say, "We're not trying to *do* anything—we're a *church,* for goodness' sake!"

On the other end of the spectrum, some people will respond with an entire laundry list. "Oh, we're here to fulfill God's plan, you know, to teach people and build up the body of Christ, and to worship and grow, and teach young people about God, and help needy people in the community, and to send missionaries overseas." These aren't bad goals, but they're ordered by a stream of consciousness, not by a clear sense of mission or priority. And, you may have noticed, evangelism usually falls to the bottom of the list if it's on the list at all.

By its very nature and purpose, the church ought to be a contagious place that is "infecting" more and more outsiders with the Christian faith.

Some churches try to justify their lack of activity in the area of evangelism by pointing to their other areas of strength. "We're a *teaching* church; if you want an *evangelistic* church, you should check out the one at the other end of town." Or others will say, "Sure, we believe in outreach, but *our* emphasis is praise and worship. This is a great place to get close to God each week."

There is nothing wrong with churches developing strengths in particular areas. Often this is a result of God's specific calling and gifting of individual leaders and congregations. But when these strengths are developed to the *exclusion* of other basic aspects of what a biblically functioning church is supposed to be like, then there's a real problem. It's like a man saying, "Sure I neglect my kids—but, hey, I'm a great husband to my wife!" Anyone can see the imbalance in this. Jesus gave us our universal mission statement in the Great Commission, and any church that neglects any aspect of it—including the "make disciples" part—is disregarding his divine mandate.

Churches state their evangelistic mission in different ways. My church says we're trying to "reach irreligious people and turn them into fully devoted followers of Christ." Calvary Church Newport Mesa in Southern California is working "to help people who are saying 'No!' to God say 'Yes!' to God in every stage and facet of their lives." Central Christian Church in Las Vegas, Nevada, wants "to connect the unconnected to Christ and *together* grow to full devotion to him." I was recently at a conference at an Episcopal church in Jacksonville, Florida. On brightly colored signs posted all over the office and classroom doors—as well as over the drinking fountain—were the words: "St. John's Cathedral: a parish congregation committed to community outreach and diocesan leadership in proclaiming the Gospel of Jesus Christ." I heard about another church that has a mission statement that simply reads, "Our main thing is keeping the main thing the main thing"—and then it spells out what the "main thing" is in terms of evangelism and discipleship.

The leaders of InterVarsity Christian Fellowship realized several years ago that they had been emphasizing the back half of the Great Commission (discipleship) and to some degree neglecting the front half of the Great Commission (evangelism). So their leaders have been working hard and making some bold moves to raise the value of evangelism and bring greater balance to their ministry. In 1998 they took one of their most visible and important steps by adopting a new mission statement that says they're working to form "witnessing communities" on every campus. This term "witnessing communities" has become a rallying cry in their ministry. It constantly reminds them of the evangelistic aspect of their work, and it is resulting in some reprioritizing of staff time and reallocation of financial resources. The results? The number of students coming to Christ through InterVarsity is going up, and there's a sense of excitement and optimism that this is only the beginning.

Contagious churches result when leaders know what they're trying to build and who they're trying to reach—and then work tirelessly and prayerfully to fulfill their objectives.

What about your church or ministry? Is your mission clear? Is it aligned with the Great Commission? Is it known by your people and in the minds of your leaders? Is it concise and memorable? (Leadership expert Peter Drucker says that if you can't print your mission statement on the back of a T-shirt, it's too long!) Is it the active criterion by which you make decisions about where your ministry will invest its time, energy, and money? Can you articulate it now?

We must not fool ourselves. Churches will never become contagious by chance. Contagious churches result when leaders know what they're trying to build and who they're trying to reach—and then work tirelessly and prayerfully to fulfill their objectives.

If your mission isn't clear, or if it isn't clearly evangelistic, I'd strongly urge you and your fellow church leaders to draft one that is and then begin to communicate it—*and to live by it.*

THE SPIRITUAL CHALLENGE

Before we move on to chapter 2 and discuss the values needed to support a church in its evangelistic mission, we need to address what is likely to be our greatest challenge: A very real spiritual enemy, Satan, would rather keep us busy doing anything in the world other than building a contagious church. Satan knows all about our call to reach lost people. He understands that our efforts in this area are designed to expand God's kingdom and diminish his, so he tries to keep us tangled up in sin and selfish preoccupations. In fact, the seemingly mild sin of self-centeredness is, in my opinion, Satan's greatest weapon against evangelism.

Satan's more subtle tack is to keep us engrossed in things that are not bad but are of lesser importance. Trivial matters. The tyranny of the urgent. The squeaky wheels. Maintenance over mobilization. The good over the best. The temporal over the eternal. Anything—except reaching lost men, women, and children for Christ.

Just try to walk against the wind by building a contagious church, and you'll soon discover what I mean. It's a real fight. True, the battle is not all with the evil one—there are also internal struggles and sometimes conflict with people who don't understand the mission. But there is a spiritual war just the same. Ephesians 6:12 makes this very clear: "For our struggle is not against flesh and blood, but against the rulers, against the authorities, against the powers of this dark world and against the spiritual forces of evil in the heavenly realms."

Being aware of the presence and purposes of the enemy gives us a profound realization that we need to seek God daily for wisdom, guidance, and strength. A biblical strategy is essential. Great training is core. Discovering our unique evangelism style is something every Christ-follower should do. But if we fail to pray, if we fail to fight the spiritual battle, if we don't hit our knees and enter the conflict at this level, we will miss the power and blessings of God. If we want to be contagious Christians and to build a contagious church, prayer must be woven into the very fabric of *all* we do.

REASONS FOR CONFIDENCE

The good news is that God really is on our side! Take to heart verses like the following: "If God is for us, who can be against us?" (Romans 8:31). "Submit yourselves, then, to God. Resist the devil, and he will flee from you" (James 4:7). "The prayer of a righteous man is powerful and effective" (James 5:16). "I can do everything through him who gives me strength" (Philippians 4:13). And "I am not ashamed of the gospel, because it is the power of God for the salvation of everyone who believes" (Romans 1:16).

God will help you face any problems, challenges, resistance, or misunderstandings that you might encounter along the way, whether natural or supernatural. I pray that he will also use what is on the pages ahead to raise your excitement and vision for what he can do through you and your church.

One of the most influential writings of our generation is *Experiencing God: Knowing and Doing the Will of God* by Henry Blackaby and Claude King.[3] Its central theme is that God is always at work—he's a dynamic, active God—and our job is to find out what he's up to and join him. When we do that, we *know* he'll use us, because we're simply signing up for the things he was doing in the first place!

This brings us back to where we started. Evangelism is God's idea. Jesus said his mission is "to seek and to save what was lost" (Luke 19:10). Before leaving, he told his followers, "As the Father has sent me, I am sending you" (John 20:21). He left us here to reach lost people—people who matter deeply to him. He assures us in his Word that he is patient with those outside his family, "not wanting anyone to perish, but everyone to come to repentance" (2 Peter 3:9). So when we partner with him, as individuals and as churches, we know he'll use us, because we're simply joining him in his great redemptive campaign.

Still, that's easier to say than it is to do. The obstacles are real. The odds seem stacked against us. But let me end by telling you about a real-life church that had, humanly speaking, very little going for it.

THE LITTLE CHURCH THAT COULD

Mount Carmel Community Church—the name sounds impressive. But the church is located in Glennville, California, a town with an entire population of 130 people!

Here's the picture: two restaurants, one elementary school, a post office, and a church. The church was founded in 1866. When Rev. Harrell Knox joined them in 1984 they were meeting in a small chapel building with a steeple and a bell. They had a weekly attendance of fifteen (that's fifteen *people,* not families or "giving units"). What's worse, the church had a poor reputation due to disputes that had spilled over into the community. This was hardly a candidate for becoming a highly contagious church!

Undaunted, Knox began to cast a vision for reaching unchurched people through the ministry of their little church. "Our target audience," said Knox, "is every person in the five-hundred-square-mile area of Kern and Tulare county—all five hundred of them!"

The members of Mount Carmel began to build relationships with the nonchurched people in their community. They knew they had to win back these people's respect and earn their trust. They started praying for these neighbors as well as for their church and its efforts to reach those who didn't know Christ.

When the leaders felt the church was ready, they launched a few outreach events. After mustering all of their talent and abilities, they found they could do four events a year—Christmas, Easter, Fourth of July, and an event at the end of Vacation Bible School in the summer. "These events are a total church effort," Knox reports. "Over ninety percent of the people serve, and more than twenty-five percent of the church budget is invested to make them happen!"

Being relevant to the local community called for diversity in programming and musical styles. They've used a Dixieland jazz band, a gospel rock group, a swing band, and an African-American vocal group. This wide range of music is appreciated in the region, and it is used in the outreach events along with original drama sketches, media, and a spoken biblical message.

The results of this church's evangelistic leadership, relationship building, strategic investing, and risk-taking seeker events? Today Mount Carmel has eighty to one hundred people in attendance. Over 300 people from the surrounding area came to a recent Christmas program. And of the 500 people they are trying to reach, 350 have been touched through one or more of their programs.

On a more personal level, Roger, Ann, and their family have been impacted for eternity. Pastor Knox reports the following:

> Roger and Ann attended a seeker event at the urging of their daughter (a young church member) and others in the church who had befriended them. But then that year Rochelle became forever "sweet sixteen" in a terrible accident, and the church ministered to the family in their grief.
>
> The family began to tear apart, due in part to Roger's heart attacks and his chronic alcoholism that sprang from not knowing how to deal with the grief. Krisha, the next daughter, continued to come to church and to request prayer for her daddy and the family.
>
> Miraculously God has touched their family, and Roger has prayed to receive the forgiveness and leadership of Christ. Today they are faithful members of the church, and God is using their story to bring others to himself.

YOUR CHURCH CAN TOO

Don't you want to get in on that kind of meaningful ministry? You can! It's worth the effort, it's worth the risks, it's worth the discomfort, and it's worth the investment. It's worth nailing down a strong, memorable mission statement with evangelism at its core and then communicating it and putting it into action in every way possible.

In the next chapter, we'll discover the biblical values that will support your church's mission to reach lost people—like the Jewish seeker I mentioned at the beginning, or like your son or daughter, brother or sister, father or mother, aunt or uncle, niece or nephew, friend, neighbor, or coworker. Perhaps they've heard the truth and seen it lived out in your life but haven't yet made it their own.

Maybe, just maybe, the combined efforts of you and the other members of a contagious church—*your church*—is what will be used by the Holy Spirit to break through to them and help them join God's family for all eternity.

It'll all be worth it then!

To Consider and Discuss

Building a contagious church that reaches unchurched people will require intentional and sustained effort as well as strong prayer support. The first key is to make certain all of your leaders and members understand that evangelism is central to what you're working to accomplish.

1. If you take nothing else away from this chapter, hear the challenge to articulate a mission statement that has evangelism at its heart. Do you have a statement that clearly states your intention to reach people outside of God's family? If not, start there. If you do, is the language up-to-date? Does it speak in terms that are both biblically sound and personally compelling? Is it concise enough to be remembered?

   After making any adjustments needed (if any) to your current statement or forming an entirely new one, write it down here:

____

____

____

____

2. Once you have a mission statement that prioritizes the value of evangelism, it must be communicated. Print it, preach on it in your worship services, and teach on it in your classes and small groups. Make it known in as many forums as possible. Jim Mellado, the president of the Willow Creek Association, says, "When you think you're about to reach communication overload, you're probably just getting close to the level of awareness you'll need among the church members."

   The goal is to reach the point where you can ask any regular attender, "What is this church trying to do?" and have him or her answer reflexively, "Oh, we're trying to reach unchurched people and turn them into fully devoted followers of Christ" (or whatever your mission is). Your mission statement needs to be embedded into your culture this strongly before it will begin to be a guiding principle in the daily decisions and actions of your church.

   What are some of the primary ways you and the other leaders can better communicate your mission statement to the broader church body?

3. Make the fulfillment of your mission a matter of personal and public prayer. Ask God to work in you and in the broader team of leaders to make you the kind of people—and your church the kind of place—that he can use to reach more and more people. Request his power, wisdom, and protection so you can defeat the schemes and counter the attacks of the evil one. Ask God—even right now, whether alone or with your group—to help you build a truly contagious church that will reach lost people.

2

EVANGELISTIC VALUES IN A SECULAR WORLD

WHY ARE WE TRYING TO DO THIS?

Jim had a passion for God, a love for people, and a burden to communicate the gospel. But he wrestled with the question of how to bring the message of Christ into a setting that seemed so far from him. How could he help people see and embrace the truth when they had so little biblical understanding? The barriers seemed insurmountable. The task appeared virtually impossible.

Even with all of the obstacles in front of him, Jim knew he had to try. God had given him a vision to make a difference in the lives of these men and women. So try he did! In fact, he went to great lengths to relate to their culture—lengths that would probably make you or me feel very uncomfortable. Following the example of the apostle Paul, he took bold risks to "become all things to all people.... for the sake of the gospel" (1 Corinthians 9:22–23 NRSV).

What kinds of risks? For starters, he shaved his head right down to the skin—that is, except for the patch of hair he grew long. Not only that, he began wearing it in a pigtail and even dyed it a different color, all in an effort to fit in with the fashions of the people he wanted to reach! He also gave up his familiar business attire and began to dress like them. He even changed his eating patterns and started to dine in the style of the ones he cared so much about. Further, he worked hard to learn their vocabulary, in the hopes that he would be able to effectively convey biblical teachings in their everyday street language. He read their papers, studied their ideas, and went out of his way to discover and build on whatever areas of common ground he had with them.

Jim didn't do this all from a distance. No, he actually moved into the neighborhood with these people. He lived close to them, became their friend, and spent extended periods of time talking with them, getting to know them, playing with their children—all of this in spite of their non-Christian lifestyles and, in almost every case, their outright rejection of his message.

What did other church leaders think of all of this? Did they celebrate Jim's tenacious commitment to reaching these unchurched people? Did they rally around him and support his courageous efforts? Did they uphold him in prayer and find ways to encourage him and spur him on in his bold evangelistic pursuits?

Not even close!

On the contrary, they mostly misunderstood, misrepresented, and even openly maligned him. The very people who should have supported and helped him turned their backs on him and his ministry. In many ways he had to continue his efforts by himself, with the backing of just a few close friends who shared his vision.

Jim paid the price of loneliness, weariness, and discouragement, along with criticism from much of the church. He also lived with the daily rejection of most of those he wanted to reach. And he did this year after year.

Jim saw the task, faced the opponents, followed the vision, and by the grace and help of God, fulfilled his calling. Jim is an extraordinary example of doing the work of evangelism in a difficult situation. His life is a powerful illustration of evangelism against the odds. And today, generations later, countless people from the neighborhoods he worked so hard to reach now know and serve Jesus Christ as their Forgiver and Leader.

Jim—or as he's more widely known, James Hudson Taylor—is the man who more than a century ago gave up everything to build a ministry called China Inland Mission. More than anyone else, he is credited with turning so many in that nation to faith in Christ. And today he is regarded widely as one of the greatest pioneers of the modern missions movement.

Is it worth taking risks to reach lost people with the love of Jesus? Is it right to proclaim the gospel in ways that break a few paradigms, push back a few boundaries, and ruffle a few feathers? If you aren't sure, you might want to ask the hundreds of thousands of Chinese Christians who have been touched, directly or indirectly, by Hudson Taylor's risk-taking, God-honoring ministry.

Jesus said,

> Suppose one of you wants to build a tower. Will he not first sit down and estimate the cost to see if he has enough money to complete it? For if he lays the foundation and is not able to finish it, everyone who sees it will ridicule him, saying, "This fellow began to build and was not able to finish."
>
> Or suppose a king is about to go to war against another king. Will he not first sit down and consider whether he is able with ten thousand men to oppose the one coming against him with twenty thousand? If he is not able, he will send a delegation while the other is still a long way off and will ask for terms of peace. In the same way, any of you who does not give up everything he has cannot be my disciple.
>
> LUKE 14:28–33

Jesus presents two principles here that apply to our task of building a contagious church: First, like Hudson Taylor, we need to be completely sold-out to the mission to which God has called us. We must keep our hands open and our hearts warm before him, willingly doing whatever he asks in order to build and expand his church.

Second, we need to get an accurate understanding of the task at hand. We must have a clear vision of what it is going to take to "build the tower" and "win the war" by fulfilling the assignment God has given us. Hudson Taylor looked long and hard at the unchurched culture of nineteenth-century China, and he aligned his mission, values, and strategy to fulfill God's call to reach this unreached group. The result? Church historian Ruth Tucker declared in her book *From Jerusalem to Irian Jaya,* "No other missionary in the nineteen centuries since the apostle Paul has had a wider vision and has carried out a more systematized plan of evangelizing a broad geographical area than Hudson Taylor. His sights were set on reaching the whole of China, all four hundred million people, and it was to that end that he labored."[1]

For those of us who have our sights set on reaching secular people in our increasingly post-Christian society, we must step back and figure out what our own mission field's cultural landscape looks like. We need to know what we're up against. We also need to determine what values will have to be reinforced in ourselves and in other church leaders so that we can effectively embark on this evangelistic adventure. These are the goals of this chapter. I will paint a picture of the secular landscape and discuss seven essential values that will undergird all of our outreach efforts. These values are vitally important, and they need to be owned and supported by the broad leadership of a church before initiating new outreach ministries and events. So we'll start with values, and then in the next chapter we'll look at how those values can be expressed through a practical, step-by-step evangelistic strategy.

VALUE #1: PEOPLE MATTER TO GOD

Stay with me here! I know that when you hear the words "People Matter to God" you're tempted to say, "I've got this one down—let's skip to the more advanced principles." But hear me: *This belief is the hardest one to fully absorb into our value system.* It's also the most difficult value to build into those around us.

Those of us who have been in the church for a long time, myself included, get very adept at affirming a statement like this and then completely ignoring it in our daily lives. When we hear it, we run an instantaneous internal litmus-test program that concludes, "Of course, John 3:16—'God so loved the world'—this is a value that passes my theological filter. I agree with it."

We agree with it, but we don't own it. We slot it into our minds right next to other biblical truths like "David was king," "Moses parted the Red Sea," and "Ruth was a Moabite." We nod our heads in intellectual approval and move on to other topics.

So please slow down and read carefully what I write next, for it has life-and-death implications: *What we do with every other concept in this book will directly depend on the degree to which we own and apply this first value.* People matter to God. Do you believe this to the very core of your being?

What we do with every other concept in this book will directly depend on the degree to which we own and apply this first value.

A friend of mine says that when this value really takes root, it dramatically affects our checkbooks and calendars, because those are the places where it expresses itself in daily life. We ought to be able to look back and say, "Here's where I've spent time and energy trying to reach people outside the family of God." We should be able to open up our checkbook ledgers and say, "Here's where I've invested my resources to help make evangelism happen through supporting the church's outreach efforts; buying Bibles, books, and tapes to give to spiritual seekers; spending money to take a nonbelieving friend out to breakfast or lunch; or inviting non-Christians into my home." These are investments that flow out of a heart that says genuinely, "People matter to God and they matter to me too."

When you start trying to rearrange the priorities in your life—or in your church's life—this value will be tested immediately. The question naturally arises, whether aloud or below the surface: How *much* do people matter to God? Without announcing themselves or asking for anyone's permission, other values start competing with and crowding out this first one.

It's clear from the biographies of Hudson Taylor that he constantly had his resolve challenged in this way. When loneliness set in, when criticism flowed from fellow missionaries, when resistance and threats came from the very people he was trying to reach, he would start to reconsider what he was doing and why he was giving up so much to make it happen. He may not have put it in these terms, but certainly he was tempted to ask, "How much do these unchurched Chinese people matter to God?" Thankfully, he kept his head clear and his heart warm, and he faithfully stuck to his priority of reaching these people who mattered so much to God.

Hudson Taylor followed the example of Jesus. Remember in John chapter 4, where Jesus broke a Jewish custom by traveling through the heart of Samaria? Then, completely ignoring the rules of political correctness, he risked his reputation by talking openly with a sinful Samaritan woman. This was scandalous behavior for any Jewish man and even more so for Jesus, because he was a rabbi. What could he have been thinking?

I'm confident that Jesus was thinking about how much this wayward woman mattered to the Father. He felt a holy love and concern for her and her people. In fact, he lingered at the well long enough to allow this broken woman to bring her friends down to meet him. Then Jesus spent more time teaching them. He even altered his plans—making last-minute adjustments to his ministry calendar—so that he and the disciples could stay and minister in Samaria for two more days. And the text tells us that "because of his words many more became believers" (John 4:41).

That is only one of numerous examples from Jesus' life that reveals how *much* people matter to God. But we can't stop there. Ephesians 5:1 tells us to "be imitators of God, therefore, as dearly loved children." We need to do whatever it takes to gain God's heart toward those outside the family. We need to make sure they matter to us the way they matter to him.

Like Jesus, we need to see every person as someone who was created in the image of God and who is loved by him. We must always remember the Spirit's inspired words: "He is patient . . . not wanting anyone to perish, but everyone to come to repentance" (2 Peter 3:9). It doesn't matter how old they are, what color they are, what country they're from, how much money they have, how much education they have, what job they hold, or even how flagrant their sins are. They have great value in God's eyes, and their repentance will bring "rejoicing in the presence of the angels of God" (Luke 15:10). Bill Hybels puts it in practical terms when he says, "You've never locked eyes with anyone who doesn't matter to the Father."

As leaders we need to keep on cultivating this value in our own hearts. Then once it has taken deep root in our hearts, we need to do all we can to instill it into other believers around us. We'll look in-depth at ways we can do this in later chapters.

Figure 2.1

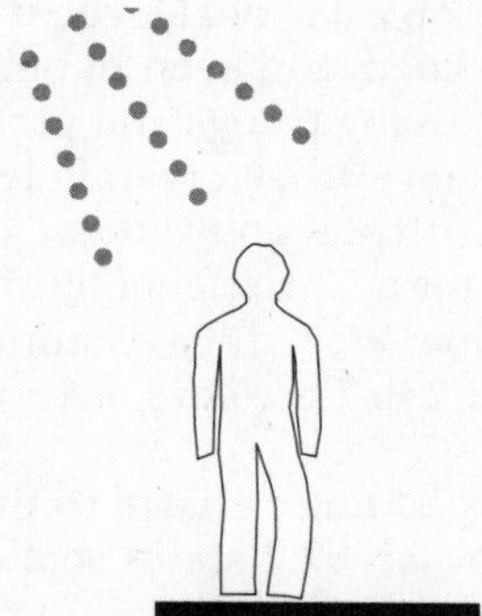

Figure 2.1 has the beginnings of a drawing that we'll expand throughout this chapter and in other parts of the book. This simple figure represents someone in your life who, although he or she doesn't yet know God, matters deeply to him.

VALUE #2: PEOPLE ARE SPIRITUALLY LOST

After going into the home of Zacchaeus and helping him receive salvation, Jesus declared that his mission was "to seek and to save what was lost" (Luke 19:10). Jesus doesn't use the word "lost" here in a derogatory way but as a simple statement of truth about those who have not yet found him and his grace.

The truth that people are spiritually lost is the core of this second value. Contrary to the prevailing belief that "I'm OK, you're OK," the Bible gives us a very different picture. Romans 3:9–12 spells out the real situation when it tells us,

> Jews and Gentiles alike are all under sin. As it is written:
>
> "There is no one righteous, not even one;
> there is no one who understands,
> no one who seeks God.
> All have turned away,
> they have together become worthless;
> there is no one who does good,
> not even one."

That is not a pretty picture. But it is one we had better understand and deal with if we are serious about our call to build outwardly focused contagious churches.

Applying this passage on a personal level, it means that our friends at work, in the neighborhood, and even in our families are *not* okay simply because they do loving things and perhaps engage in sincere religious activities. We have to be crystal clear on this: No matter how "good" people are, if they don't know Christ as Forgiver and Leader, they are headed for a Christless eternity. The Bible is unwaveringly consistent on this: We "all have sinned and fall short of the glory of God" (Romans 3:23). Therefore, *everyone* we know needs to know and follow Christ.

This can be shown by adding a chasm to the drawing (Figure 2.2), which illustrates what Isaiah 59:2 states so clearly: "Your iniquities have separated you from your God."

Figure 2.2

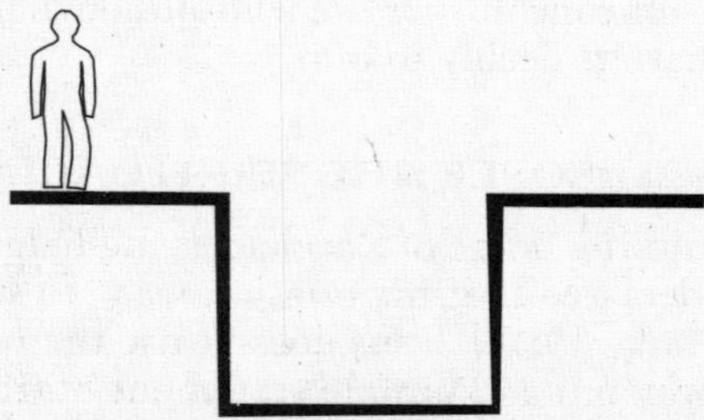

VALUE #3: PEOPLE NEED CHRIST

Here again, modern thinking militates against clear biblical teaching. People will sometimes challenge us with statements like these: "Who are *you* to say that you're right and everybody else is wrong? Everybody has their own truth and their own views of God. What does it matter if they approach it a little differently from you or use other names for God? What matters is that they're sincere in what they believe, and that it works for them in their lives. We should all practice our religions in ways that respect the views of others, and we should never impose our personal beliefs on anybody else."

Add to that challenge the fact that in some corners of Christendom belief that Christ is the only way to God is being systematically undermined. An insidious form of religious pluralism is seeping into the church, which says that there really might be multiple paths to God. Further, some preachers and teachers are playing down the importance of the biblical teaching of the substitutionary atonement of Christ (that his death was a necessary payment for our sins). Attacks are being launched from both inside and outside the church against the biblical conviction that all people need to know Christ.

Against these kinds of backdrops, Jesus said plainly, "I am the way and the truth and the life. No one comes to the Father except through me" (John 14:6). Peter added that "salvation is found in no one else, for there is no other name under heaven given to men by which we must be saved" (Acts 4:12). He also explained that "Christ died for sins once for all, the righteous for the unrighteous, to bring you to God" (1 Peter 3:18). Paul capped it with his simple declaration, "Christ Jesus came into the world to save sinners" (1 Timothy 1:15).

Like it or not, we have an unpopular message, and we have been commissioned to present it boldly. But while it may be unpopular, it certainly is good news to people who are lost and headed for a Christless eternity.

We have to keep our thinking clear and our hearts strong. People need to hear the message of the cross of Christ because "it is the power of God for the salvation of everyone who believes" (Romans 1:16). To expand our drawing (Figure 2.3), I'll add the cross over the chasm as the bridge that leads us back to God.[2] However, for reasons I'll soon explain, I'll only shade it in right now.

Figure 2.3

Before I introduce the fourth value, I need to comment on the first three. These values certainly are not new. This is standard Christian thought that has been taught in various ways for two thousand years. But it was important for us to review it and to move it from being mere head knowledge to genuine, heartfelt values.

It is also important to point out that the picture is not yet complete for reaching people in our secular culture. A few decades ago, this may have been enough, at least in the United States, because reality was pretty much the way it looks in the diagram. The vast majority of people in American society lived up close to the chasm and had at least some understanding that they were sinners who had rebelled against God and needed his forgiveness. They had memories, even if distant and fading, of Sunday school classes, Bible stories, and lessons about Jesus dying on the cross. Most people shared sort of a collective church consciousness. They may not have acted on what they knew, but they probably felt at times like they should.

Event-Oriented Evangelism

A few decades ago, evangelism could be very direct and hard-hitting. Its function was to remind people of what they already knew and challenge them to act on it by trusting in Christ. It could all happen in a single, high-impact event, such as an evangelistic meeting or an intense one-on-one spiritual conversation. In fact, not only *could* this happen in a single encounter, it probably *should* happen that way. If the person already understood the message and was simply trying to decide whether or not to get off the fence, then why not try to help him or her make the right decision right away? Whenever people have a good grasp of the problem of sin and the need for a Savior, a direct, event-oriented evangelistic approach is the natural way to go.

The Expanding Spiritual Landscape

The problem is that people in our culture have *moved.* They no longer live close to the chasm where they can look over the edge and see the depth of their sins. They don't realize how far away God is or where the bridge can be found. In fact, many are so far back that, from their perspective, there doesn't appear to be a chasm at all. Like hikers in the mountains who are walking toward the towering peak, it looks like getting to the destination will be an easy stroll. They severely underestimate the distance, the valleys, and the obstacles.

Notice how I've portrayed this in Figure 2.4. The spectrum is much wider than previously portrayed, and people are further away than we had originally thought—and they're continuing to move in the wrong direction.

Figure 2.4

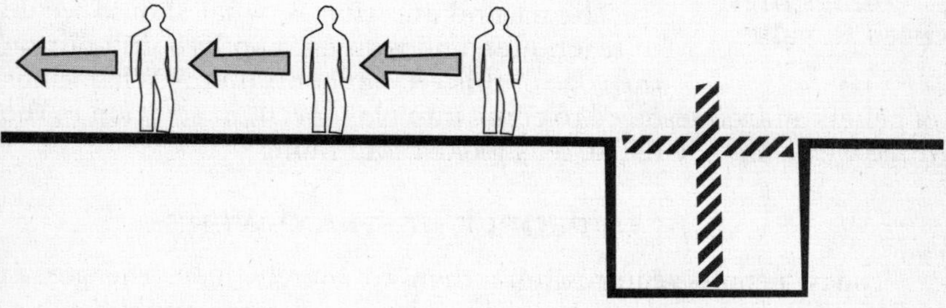

The term we use to describe this is *secularization.* People in our culture have gradually taken steps away from Christian beliefs, values, and morals. So when we say, "God cares about you and wants to forgive you and give you eternal life," many will respond, "Oh, yeah? Which God? There are so many options in the smorgasbord of deities these days. And what have I done that is so bad that I need forgiveness? I'm no murderer! And why should I look to your God for *eternal* life when he, she, or it can't even take care of all the starving children in the world who may not make it through *this* life?"

Have you ever noticed what happens when a Christian stands up on a television talk show and advocates a biblical viewpoint on the sanctity of life or on God's plan for keeping sex within marriage? They have to duck quickly before people start throwing things at them! At a minimum, they usually get booed or laughed back into their seat.

People get hostile. They scoff. They scorn. They ask, "How can anyone still believe *that?* I thought those ideas died with the Victorian age!"

All of this is happening in a country where a few decades ago couples couldn't rent an apartment without a marriage certificate and proof that they attended a local church. It was not that long ago that abortion was murder, pregnancy outside of marriage was a scandal, pornographers were outlaws, homosexuality was an embarrassment, musicians who used drugs were an outrage, and public school teachers who refused to lead prayers and post the Ten Commandments soon found themselves unemployed. Times have changed!

People don't think the way they used to think, believe the things they used to believe, or value the things they used to value.

Call it what you want—*secular, postmodern, post-Christian.* Whatever the label, people don't think the way they used to think, believe the things they used to believe, or value the things they used to value.

The natural question is, what should we do to reach men and women who live way out on the edge of this secular continuum? What kinds of beliefs and values need to come into play? Well, in addition to the three we've already listed, let's look at four more.

VALUE #4: PEOPLE NEED ANSWERS

Today people require more than to merely have the gospel *declared* to them. They also need to have it *defined* and *defended.* They don't merely need to decide whether to follow Christ—they need to know who Christ is and what it means to follow him.

As I mentioned above, as soon as the topic of faith comes up, many people have a list of doubts and concerns pop into their minds. "How can I be sure God even exists?" "If he does exist, how could I ever know what he is like?" "There are so many religions, how can I have confidence any of them is really true?" "With all of the bad examples out there, why should I trust any religious teacher or organization? Can't I just worship God by myself, out in the woods?" "If God really cares about us, why would he let me go through so many awful things in my life?"

These and similar questions form what I call *intellectual roadblocks* that prevent persons from taking steps forward in their spiritual journey. (Adding to our drawing, I'll insert a couple of these roadblocks, like brick walls, into our picture. See Figure 2.5.) If we want to help people move toward Christ, we are going to have to proactively address their issues and show that the Christian faith is built on a foundation of truth and can be trusted wholeheartedly. As Paul boldly put it, "We demolish arguments and every pretension that sets itself up against the knowledge of God, and we take captive every thought to make it obedient to Christ" (2 Corinthians 10:5).

Figure 2.5

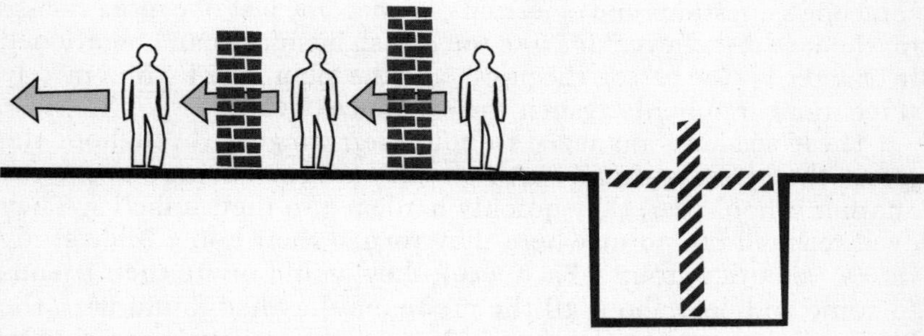

The importance of following through with this scriptural principle became clear to me a while back when I got a telephone call from a high school student who started the conversation by saying, "I used to be a Christian."

With that one little statement he certainly had my undivided attention! "What do you mean, you *used* to be a Christian?" I asked.

This young man proceeded to tell me that he attended another church but had been given my name as someone to talk to as sort of a last-ditch effort to deal with his growing doubts about the Christian faith. In fact, at one time he had led a Bible study at his home where other students would come and learn from Scripture and discuss their faith. But when questions started to come up that none of them could answer, he and a friend went to their church's youth leaders for help.

"You'll just have to have more faith," the students were told. "If you'd pray more, God would make it all clear to you." For obvious reasons, these responses didn't satisfy them. In fact, they only contributed to the students' growing suspicion that maybe there weren't any good answers, and that perhaps the whole Christian faith was one grand leap of faith supported only by years of tradition, with one generation blindly passing it on to the next.

The clincher came when the students went to their church's Bible camp that summer and again raised some of their honest concerns. They were dumbfounded when the leaders told them that these were inappropriate questions to even put into words, and that they had best keep quiet before they infected the rest of the students at the camp with their doubts and skepticism.

The late Walter Martin, author of *The Kingdom of the Cults* and an early pioneer in reaching people in aberrant religious groups with the gospel, once said during a radio program, "When we fail to answer someone's questions and objections, we become just one more excuse for them to disbelieve." It's like the Jewish businessman I mentioned in chapter 1—the pastor, the priest, and the rabbi were for him merely three more arguments against the existence of God.

These students managed to hold their tongues throughout the rest of their time at camp. But when they got back home and entered another school year, they quickly hardened in their unbelief. They even reached the point where they turned their home Bible study into a "skeptics group." Each week they would invite their friends to come and hear about all the problems they had found with the Bible and the reasons why they had given up on Christian teachings. Like an infection, their doubts were spreading to more and more students.

Needless to say, I was highly motivated to talk to this young man. I invited him to come and talk with me face-to-face about his questions. We set the date, and I cleared the calendar to provide plenty of time. When he and his friend arrived, I found them to be sincere and persistent in their search for truth. We spent the afternoon discussing their issues and looking at the Bible, logic, and outside evidence to see whether the Christian faith is built on fact or fiction. At the end of this first visit together, I sensed a softening in them.

Before leaving, the student who had initially called me on the phone invited me to come and speak to his skeptics group. It was an offer I couldn't refuse. I told him I'd be honored to meet with them but that, just as he'd done that day, I'd like to bring a friend with me. A week later Lee Strobel and I went to their skeptics group ready for some evangelistic action!

We had a wonderful time. Lee told the story of how he'd formerly been a skeptic and an atheist. He detailed some of the evidence that had persuaded him that the Christian faith is true.[3] Then we spent a couple of hours answering whatever questions they felt like raising. Within weeks, one of the two young men recommitted his life to Christ, and the other one received Christ for the first time.

I could tell many other stories of young people, middle-aged people, and older people who have been greatly helped when they have found solid answers to their spiritual questions. They have used different language and focused on a variety of issues, but, as members of a culture that has drifted further and further from the Christian worldview, they needed a clear response to their perplexing objections.

We are not trying to substitute answers for the gospel. We're simply trying to "give an answer to everyone who asks [us] to give the reason for the hope that [we] have" (1 Peter 3:15). We do this to clear the way for people to get back to the central message of the cross of Christ (as Figure 2.6 illustrates). This is where the real power lies—the "power of God for the salvation of everyone who believes" (Romans 1:16).

Figure 2.6

VALUE #5: PEOPLE NEED COMMUNITY

Have you noticed a common thread in many of the popular television sitcoms of recent years? Whether it be *Cheers, Friends, Frasier, Home Improvement,* or *Seinfeld,* the glue that holds the stories together is the interaction between a tight-knit circle of friends. A major attraction to these shows, in addition to the humor, is the feeling that there is some level of genuine acceptance and connectedness. This comes across in the lyrics to the *Cheers* theme song: "Sometimes you wanna go . . . where everybody knows your name, and they're always glad you came. You wanna be where you can see our troubles are all the same. You wanna be where everybody knows your name." This song has been highly popular in our culture (proven by the fact that you'll be humming it for the rest of the day). But what do the words indicate the person is really looking for?

I believe he's craving the kind of deep, relational connection that can be found fully only in the church of Jesus Christ. Interestingly, even though this song is several years old, it's still relevant today. During a recent ministry season, our church's high school ministry team used it as a theme song to open every service!

Many of the people we are trying to reach, especially those from the younger generations, come from broken homes. They have felt the pain of living in a fragmented family. They know what it feels like to be isolated and alone. They long for deeper community of some kind. They are attracted to whatever source seems to be able to give it, even in the absence of truth. I think this explains why many of the cults, sects, and world religions are growing so quickly. Often their teachings are illogical and even outlandish, but they offer a sense of family and community that people desperately desire. Consequently, many people put their minds on pause for the sake of seeing their relational needs met.

A few years ago I got to know one of the leaders of a local Mormon church. The man told me he had a Protestant background. When I inquired why he had switched to Mormonism, he said he was attracted by their strong social and family programs as well as by the friendships he had made within the group. Incredulous, I asked how he had dealt with such major contradictions to the Christian beliefs he had grown up with (such as the Mormon doctrine that there are many gods, and that the God of this world was once a man, and that we can someday in eternity become gods ourselves). His answer jolted me. "Oh, those things used to bother me, but I was able to get used to them," he said. "There were just too many other things that felt right."

To this day I've had a hard time comprehending how someone can "get used to" such blatantly unbiblical teachings. But it opened my eyes to the fact that a desire to be part of a close-knit community can carry a person a long way—whether in the right or wrong direction. We were designed by God to be in community with each other. The question for us is, how can we expose outsiders to genuine biblical fellowship—the "community of oneness" that Christ commissioned and prayed for in John 17? When we do, when we bring non-Christians into a context where "two or three come together" in Jesus' name, and he is there with them (see Matthew 18:20), they will be warmed and drawn in, both by the human relationships and the divine Presence.

I like what Dieter Zander, coauthor of *Inside the Soul of a New Generation,*[4] said when we met to talk about reaching people from the age-group commonly referred to as Generation X (born between 1965 and 1980). He explained that today's spiritual seekers want more than logic and truth. They want to "test-drive" the faith. They do this by hanging around the family first—before joining it. As Dieter put it, "We used to view conversion as the gateway to fellowship; now we view fellowship (using the term more broadly) as the gateway to conversion."

In his book *A Peculiar People: The Church As Culture in a Post-Christian Society,* Rodney Clapp says that evangelism must be understood today "not simply as declaring a message to someone but as initiation into the world-changing kingdom of God. It is not enough to think of evangelism as proclamation. We must understand it once again as the earliest Christians did, as 'the persuading of people to become Christians and take their place as responsible members of the body of Christ.'"[5] Later he adds that we should "recognize that we are inescapably communal creatures. . . . Community may be jostled, deprived, squeezed, but it is as persistent and hard to kill as a rattlesnake. We want it too much; it is too much, without remainder, what life worth living just is."[6]

I'll convey this innate human desire for community by adding a small group of people next to our unchurched friend on the diagram (Figure 2.7). This illustrates the need all people have for community and our responsibility to build churches where true community can flourish.

Figure 2.7

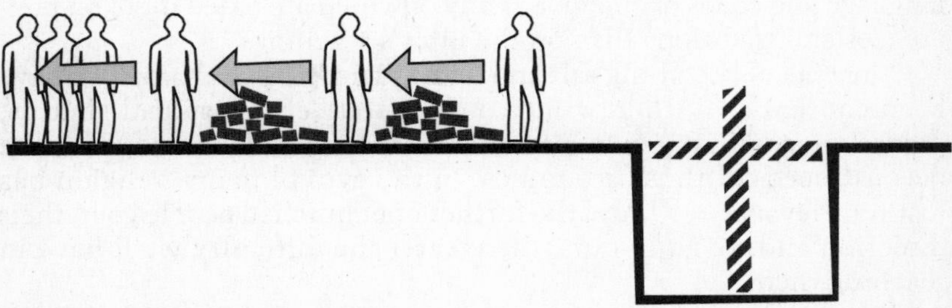

As we shore up our evangelism-related values, we need to be thinking of ways to provide people with opportunities to get a taste of genuine Christian community. Once outsiders discover what it feels like to be on the inside, among believers and in the presence of God, many of them will be highly motivated to respond to the gospel and become members of his family.

VALUE #6: PEOPLE NEED CULTURAL RELEVANCE

When we send missionaries to a foreign land, they must first do language and culture studies so they will be able to clearly communicate Christ to the people they are hoping to reach. This is true whether they are a Hudson Taylor going to China, a William Carey going to India, or a David Livingstone going into the heart of Africa.

The job of the missionary is to communicate the complete gospel message—without altering it or compromising it in any way—in the context of the culture he or she has been called to reach. The missiologist's term for this is *contextualization.* The amount of study and effort required to prepare a person for this task can be enormous.

While it is obvious we need to prepare a foreign missionary in this way, we often overlook the fact that *we* have to do the same kind of work if we're going to be effective right here at home. We wrongly assume that because we grew up here; because we know these people as neighbors and friends; because we speak the same language, wear the same clothing, and drive the same cars, then there must not be any real distance or barrier between us and them.

In virtually every case, we're dead wrong. We overlook the fact that our friends and neighbors live in a culture that is growing more secular and less Christian. We forget that they don't know what we know, value what we value, or trust what we trust. We also fail to realize that our church world is also a culture unto itself, and that we have tended to become increasingly insular. We have developed our own in-house language and codes of conduct, many of which are based more on preferences and traditions than on the Bible's teachings.

"Instead of becoming salt and light," said Billy Graham, "we have been content to withdraw into our separate ecclesiastical ghettos, preoccupied with our own internal affairs and unconcerned about the deepest needs of those around us. In the eyes of many, religion has lost its relevance . . ."[7] And the further nonchurched people go in their direction and we go in ours, the greater the difficulty we'll have in reaching them.

Let me illustrate this by expanding our drawing (Figure 2.8). First, I'll remove the shaded-in cross from the chasm. Why? *Because that's not the chasm the cross fills!* There's a wider and deeper chasm to the right, even further from where unchurched people live. That's the *sin* chasm, and it's the abyss that only the cross of Christ can bridge. God is way over on the right side, and between the sin chasm and the people we want to reach is the gap we have been describing in this section, which I'll now label as the *culture* chasm.

Figure 2.8

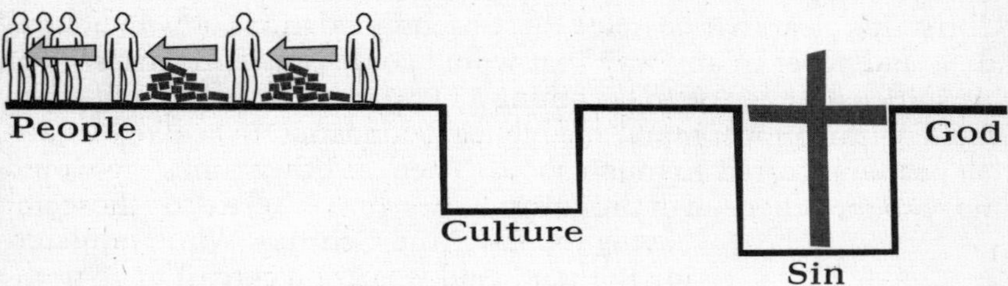

The culture chasm consists of the barriers that keep a secular person from hearing and understanding our message. These include things like language, dress, musical tastes, personal motivators, cultural norms, habits, beliefs, degrees of spiritual interest, styles of learning, and traditions (both secular and religious)—and the list could go on.

I'm not talking here about the explicitly sinful aspects of a culture. I'm not using "culture" as a synonym for "the world," which is the term often used in the New Testament (especially in 1 John 2:15–17 and James 4:4) to describe the evil, anti-Christian values and systems of our present age. These things are all part of the larger sin chasm on the right side of the diagram. Rather, I'm talking about the more generic, spiritually neutral aspects of living in any society. While these may be in some sense neutral, they certainly are important and have a huge effect on what people think and understand as well as on how they hear the gospel.

These are the kinds of things Paul was talking about in 1 Corinthians 9:19–23, when he wrote,

> Though I am free and belong to no man, I make myself a slave to everyone, to win as many as possible. To the Jews I became like a Jew, to win the Jews. To those under the law I became like one under the law (though I myself am not under the law), so as to win those under the law. To those not having the law I became like one not having the law (though I am not free from God's law but am under Christ's law), so as to win those not having the law. To the weak I became weak, to win the weak. *I have become all things to all men so that by all possible means I might save some. I do all this for the sake of the gospel, that I may share in its blessings.* (emphasis added)

Paul was more than willing to accommodate himself to various cultural norms wherever and whenever he could—"by all possible means"—if it would help the people in that culture come to know Christ. It's clear that he made these accommodations only in neutral areas and never in any way that would compromise his message or his spiritual integrity. In becoming a "Jew to the Jews," he did all he could, within proper moral and biblical boundaries, to be like the Jewish people he cared so much about. Then, at other times, he would move to the other end of the cultural spectrum to relate to "those not having the law," the Gentiles. While ministering to them, Paul was again careful to do nothing that would be spiritually out-of-bounds. He was driven to stretch in this way by the love of Christ and by a passion for reaching lost people wherever they might be found.

Being culturally relevant is a biblical mandate that we ignore only to the peril of the church and the people God has called us to reach.

But Paul didn't stop in this passage with his own situation. Rather, he focused his example back on us, his readers: "Do you not know that in a race all the runners run, but only one gets the prize? *Run in such a way as to get the prize*" (1 Corinthians 9:24, emphasis added). It seems clear that running "in such a way as to get the prize" corresponds to "[becoming] all things to all men so that by all possible means I might save some." It also seems clear that getting the prize corresponds to his earlier phrase, to "save some" (verse 22).

Paul is telling us that it is not his private mission or personal bent to communicate relevantly within the various cultural groups in order to spread the gospel. No, *he's challenging you and me to follow his example.* We must take appropriate risks to reach as many people in as many settings as possible, including those who are very different from ourselves. In short, being culturally relevant is a biblical mandate that we ignore only to the peril of the church and the people God has called us to reach.

It's also clear that Paul didn't—and neither should we—try to reach out to every person and every group in the same way. There is not merely *a* culture but *multiple* cultures, often overlapping each other. We, like Paul, need to adapt to each person and each setting so that we can effectively reach into that person's world, speak his or her language, illustrate the true gospel, and, by the power of the Holy Spirit, lead that person to Christ.

Figure 2.9 illustrates this by showing progressive embankments from the right to the left, filling in the cultural chasm. These represent our efforts to bridge the cultural chasm. Our efforts must be ongoing, for they are never perfect or complete. This is a lifelong commitment for every follower of Christ.

Figure 2.9

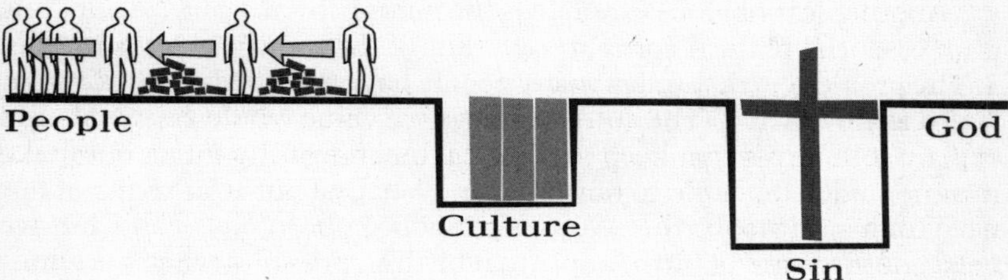

Without trying to present a comprehensive list, I will illustrate this point with a few examples of things we can do to pave over much of the cultural chasm. These examples will come out of the context in which I personally work to reach non-Christians. As you read, keep in mind something Bill Hybels often says about reaching people in our varied cultures: "We must each crack the cultural code where we live."

Language

It is fascinating that at the very beginning of the rapid missionary expansion of the church—on the Day of Pentecost told about in Acts 2—God saw to it that each group of people in the crowd had the opportunity to hear the gospel message in their native language. It is easy to get caught up in the miraculous nature of this and to miss its practical implications. What God did that day supernaturally, we need to do in our day with careful thought and, in many cases, hard work.

It is in this area of language that, perhaps more than anywhere else, the missions principle of contextualization becomes critical. In effect, each Christian and each church need to strive to do what a good Bible translation committee does: Put biblical truths into language that will be understood by the listener within the context of his or her own culture. This will require, at times, replacing biblical terms with more readily understood words that will help the listener better grasp what the biblical term was meant to convey.

Here's an example. We probably would not announce to someone that he or she needs to be "washed in the blood of the Lamb"—at least not without further explanation! We wouldn't do this, even though it's a biblical phrase and, properly understood, one of our most precious truths. Rather, we'd explain what Jesus' death meant, that his shed blood pays the penalty we owe for our sins, and that we each need to receive his payment for ourselves.

Another less-obvious example is the phrase "born again." Again, this is an essential biblical concept, right out of the mouth of Jesus in John 3. The problem is that today many people have a distorted view of what "born again" means. The cultural relevance value would say we should explain it in terms that keep the biblical meaning fully intact but make it more understandable to our listener. Usually I put it in terms of our need for a spiritual birth. "We've already been born physically, but we need another kind of birth, a spiritual birth that results when we admit our sins, receive Christ's forgiveness, and let him begin to lead our life."

I also tend to talk in terms of receiving Jesus as "Forgiver and Leader" rather than "Savior and Lord." This is an attempt to convey the biblical concepts while avoiding misleading connotations in some people's minds of medieval "lords" who were rulers over castles. I also avoid the word *Master,* which for some people might evoke images of slavery and oppressive taskmasters.

You may not like the way I translate some of these concepts. That's okay. But it is your responsibility to figure out how you will "become all things" and translate these terms for your own friends. Just be sure your language is true to the meaning of Scripture while being clear to the person you are seeking to reach.

Let me caution you not to hide behind the well-intentioned idea that "I don't need to do any of this—I'll just say it the way the *Bible* says it." That really won't work unless you're willing to learn to speak Hebrew and Greek and then teach it to all of your friends! The Bible you use *already* attempts to put the original biblical words and concepts into the common language of the day. That's true regardless of which translation or paraphrase you use, from the King James Version to the *New International Version* or the *New Living Translation.*

The question is whether the particular version you use communicates clearly to the people you are trying to reach. If it does, quote it directly. If not, then do your part to convey the biblical truths in terms your friends can understand. Again, part of following Paul's example of "becoming all things to all people" is becoming conscious of how you are being heard and doing your best to make Christ's message clear to every person to whom you speak.

CLOTHES

Is it really important what you wear? God looks at what's in our heart, right? Maybe so—but everyone else looks at what's on the outside!

Now, I certainly don't think this means we need to be at the leading edge of every fashion trend. But we should try to dress in a way that minimizes unnecessary cultural barriers. Hudson Taylor had the courage to dress in the traditional clothing of the Chinese people he was trying to reach. He was misunderstood by many of his fellow missionaries but accepted by many more of the Chinese men and women. Sometimes you just have to choose which group you are going to fit in with—and which ones you won't.

We need to pray for wisdom on this, but, in general, if you're trying to reach the business community, you'd be wise to wear business attire, like Bill Hybels at Willow Creek does. If you're trying to reach students on a university campus, you'd be wise to dress down a bit, like InterVarsity's Cliffe Knechtle does. If you're reaching out to a relaxed culture in Southern California, you're probably wise to wear informal, short-sleeve shirts and deck shoes (minus the socks) like Rick Warren at Saddleback does.

MUSIC

It is amazing that something designed to bring us together in worship can so often divide us. My primary comment on music is this: Figure out who it is for and what you hope to accomplish with it, and then choose it accordingly. When it comes to music at outreach events or services, don't let your personal tastes be the primary deciding factor. Get to know the people you want to reach. Find out *their* tastes in music. Ride with them in their car and see what they listen to. Then "become all things" by trying to find appropriate music that will speak truth using sounds that are familiar to them.

This can become particularly challenging in transitional situations in which a church is trying to move toward greater sensitivity to spiritual seekers. After choosing and using the right music for the people you're trying to reach, you may have a well-meaning, sincere church member come up to you and say, "I want you to know that music didn't minister to me!" You have to be ready to look that dear brother or sister in the eye and say gently but firmly, "I'm sorry, but that music wasn't *intended* to minister to you. It was designed to communicate to your friends [or children or grandchildren] who have not yet discovered the love and truth of Christ. I'm sure you want us to help you reach them, don't you?" Their answer will help you understand the degree to which our first value, "People matter to God," has taken root in their heart.

To give just one example of the results of a church trying to be culturally relevant with music, one of my closest friends came to Christ at our church after first being invited by his wife to "come and hear the music." He, being a spiritual cynic at the time, responded with amazement. "You've got to be kidding! You want me to come to that place so I can listen to *church music?*"

"I really think you're going to like it," his wife gently responded. "Why don't you just give it a chance?"

"Because I hate organ music!" he shot back.

"But they don't *have* an organ!" she replied. "I know it's hard for you to believe, but the music at this church is a lot like what you enjoy on the radio every day."

His resolve softening a bit, he finally decided that one visit couldn't damage him too badly. So he attended a service with his wife. And guess what? He enjoyed the music! But much more important than that, he heard the biblical message, both in the music and in the spoken word. This launched him on a two-year search that ended with his trusting and following Christ. Today this man, Lee Strobel, is in full-time ministry and is a writer whom God is using to communicate the gospel to thousands of spiritual seekers who have questions just like he once had.

Lee and his wife, Leslie, along with their two children who are now both very involved in similar kinds of ministry, celebrate the fact that a church had the energy and courage to crack the cultural code by presenting music—and biblical teaching—that brought truth into their world.

Personal Motivators

In our church's setting, we have mostly been reaching baby boomers, and now, increasingly, baby busters. One of the things that has been clear since the beginning is that in our neighborhoods we had better not pin our outreach efforts to a "get ready now so you can go to heaven when you die" approach. "Die?" these people think to themselves, "Maybe by the time I get close to that stage they'll have a *cure!*"

Instead, we have put less emphasis on the afterlife and more on *this* life. We genuinely believe that being a follower of Christ is the only way to die, but it's also the best way to live! Not that the Christian life is easy—often it is even harder than the alternatives—but the wisdom, guidance, power, and presence of God are available to help us with relational difficulties, work problems, family stresses, ethical dilemmas, and the like. We try to convey in practical ways what Jesus was saying when he told his disciples, "I tell you the truth, no one who has left home or wife or brothers or parents or children for the sake of the kingdom of God will fail to receive many times as much in this age and, in the age to come, eternal life" (Luke 18:29–30).

What aspect of the gospel message and Christian life would best relate to those you are trying to reach in your community? How does that information help you determine what your emphasis and approach should be? Don't deny or try to cover up the difficulties in following Christ. God's Word teaches that we have to take up our cross daily and follow him. But don't forget to spell out the benefits too.

Cultural Points of Reference

Much of the culture in biblical times was agrarian. Planting, watering, and harvesting, as well as raising and shepherding animals, were part of everyday life. Where I live, it's the opposite. Soon after moving to the Chicago area, I met a college-age girl who had never even seen a real cow!

How about your area? What kinds of illustrations, examples, and stories could you best use in both your personal and church-wide outreach efforts? Notice that Jesus, who was a carpenter and the son of a carpenter, stretched beyond his most natural context and related to his listeners by talking about planting and reaping. Similarly, you might need to stretch yourself by talking about investing, or manufacturing, or mining, or fishing, or—you fill in the blank. But whatever you say, be sure your words and illustrations fit your friend's cultural point of reference.

Habits

When would people in your community consider going to church if they were inclined to go? In our area, Sunday morning is still the time when most people would be willing to visit a church, so we designed our outreach for Sunday mornings. If the same is true where you minister, maybe you could start a few seeker-oriented Sunday school classes or a second, simultaneous service in another room or location.

Or perhaps non-Christians in your area would be open to coming on a Friday or Saturday night. What could you design around those times? The key is to *work with* these neutral aspects of culture, not to waste time and energy trying to change them.

Degrees of Spiritual and Relational Openness

How receptive are the people you are seeking to reach? It is important to identify their level of openness and then try to work as much as possible within their comfort zones. Jesus, for example, challenged Nicodemus about his need to be born again, but he did not chide him for coming to talk under the cover of night.

Similarly, many churches, ours included, have found that in reaching a skeptical audience, it is best to give them a bit of distance by letting them be anonymous and not forcing newcomers to stand up or otherwise identify themselves. We often reassure those who are thinking about visiting that they "won't be asked to sing anything, sign anything, say anything, or give anything." This takes the pressure off and lets them know they can advance at their own pace. We then do all we can to keep that pace healthy and moving in the right direction.

By contrast, some churches have found, especially in the southern part of the United States, that if they keep the anonymity factor too high, it starts to feel cold and unfriendly. So what works in Chicago in this regard is out of place a few hundred miles away where there's a natural expectation of southern hospitality.

We are also learning that the younger generations, especially Gen-X, want more relational connection when they attend a service. Dieter Zander says that one of the primary questions they have in their mind when they show up is, "Do you really want me to be here?" For people with this mind-set, we're learning to lower the anonymity factor a bit while we work harder to make people feel welcomed and accepted.

Adjusting to be "all things to all people" is an ongoing effort. But when it helps us reach more and more people, it's certainly worth it!

Styles of Learning

The founders of our church realized early on that they were trying to communicate biblical truth to biblically illiterate people who were accustomed to learning by ways other than reading or listening to people speak. This was the first generation to be baby-sat and tutored by the television. Consequently, our audience has become much more visual in its learning style. And the influence of television and movies on the younger generations is only increasing.

This is an example of where we as Christians can bemoan the cultural reality and try to reform society first by weaning people from all their media influences. Or we can work with people where they are, responsibly using up-to-date approaches to communicating the age-old gospel message.

This is what our church has tried to do. We have found creative ways to teach visually, using tools such as drama, video, and multimedia to raise spiritual interest and present biblical truths.[8] These methods do not replace biblical preaching but instead supplement it in ways that are powerful and effective for a TV generation. Much like the parables of Jesus, these approaches capture the imagination, bring the teaching alive, and make the lessons more personal.

Do the people you're reaching learn in similar ways? What kinds of creative ideas or tools could you utilize to supplement your communication efforts?

Traditions, Both Secular and Religious

Do many of the people where you live have religious heritages you can reference without compromising biblical teachings? Are there holidays or traditions that provide rich opportunities for building bridges and doing outreach events? One of our church's outreach events, for example, was a Jewish Seder that had an emphasis on knowing the Messiah, and a number of the Jewish people in our area were willing to attend.

Other examples might include highlighting the spiritual side of Patrick's life on Saint Patrick's Day, or the biblical theme of justice on Martin Luther King Day, or the real life of a Christian named Saint Nicholas on Christmas, or the significance of Ash Wednesday and Lent, or even the emphasis on finding spiritual wisdom among Native Americans—wisdom that can be truly found in the Bible and in a relationship with Christ.

Rather than viewing other cultures and traditions as enemies, missionary Don Richardson, in his book *Eternity in Their Hearts,*[9] shows how we can find stories that come out of those traditions—what he calls "redemptive analogies"—and present them in ways that illustrate biblical teachings. Obviously, we must take care to be clear about what we are actually teaching versus tacit endorsements that we don't want to make. But applied properly, this can be another example of "becoming all things" in order to reach people.

Before we go on to our final value, I want to tell you a story that drives home the critical importance of what we've been discussing. I was teaching these values and presenting our picture of the ever-widening secular landscape in a church on the West Coast when a woman came up to talk to me during a break.

"You know," she said, "you've been discussing these ideas as if they only related to non-Christians living out there somewhere. But they apply in here too." Then, pointing at the cultural chasm I'd drawn, she said with emotion rising in her voice, "That's where my husband and I lost our kids. We raised them in the church, and they know all about the Bible. But because they couldn't relate to much of what they experienced in the church, they've left, and I don't know if we'll ever be able to bring them back."

I couldn't stop thinking about that later. The same thing had been true of me and some of my friends growing up. We believed the right things, knew the Bible stories, and could quote a lot of verses. We even had our eras of spiritual fervency. But we had a hard time relating to the culture of the church. It didn't seem very relevant to our daily experiences—to the real world where we spent most of our time. The music was from a different era, much of the language was foreign, the questions being discussed were often not the ones we were asking, and many of the leaders were not highly conversant with our world.

I must own responsibility for my own sin and actions—and I do. But I often wonder whether I might have been able to avoid much of my prodigal era if the church had been better able to relate its timeless truths in a timely way to my generation. The woman who talked to me in the church that day certainly felt this would have made a difference for her children.

In the church in which I serve now, we have a solid commitment to cracking the cultural code for each upcoming generation and to relevantly communicating the message—full strength—to each group that comes up through the ranks. This is why we have ministries not only for children and students, but we also have a dedicated Gen-X ministry working overtime to reach and teach those from the baby-buster generation. The importance of every church learning to overcome the barriers and relate to the younger generations became exceedingly clear when the Barna Group shared statistics recently that "a majority of people who accept Christ as their Savior do so before the age of 18—nearly two out of three believers."[10]

Once we understand there is a cultural chasm that separates us from the people we hope to reach (whether they are outsiders or our own children), the question becomes simple: *Who's going to move?* Are we going to force people to take the leap in our direction, or will we follow the example of Jesus and Paul by stretching out across the cultural chasm in order to get up close to people and help them move toward Christ? As Chuck Colson put it in his talk "Kingdoms in Conflict: The Gospel in Context" at the 1994 North American Conference for Itinerant Evangelists, "This is what we Christians have to do today: go everywhere, anywhere, to boldly proclaim the truth of Christ. We must do it lovingly, understanding the culture but never backing away from any opportunity. We do this, and God will use it."[11]

VALUE #7: PEOPLE NEED TIME

Secular men and women who are way over on the left side of our chart don't generally come to Christ in one fell swoop. They don't hear one good sermon, read one solid Christian book, have one strategic spiritual conversation, or go to one knockout seeker event, and then decide on the spot to repent of their sins and turn over their lives to God. Saul-to-Paul Damascus Road conversions are the exception, not the rule. When they happen, we call them miracles—and celebrate.

Most of the people we are trying to reach need more time. Think about this, by way of comparison: Paul, hostile as he was toward Christianity, was committed to God. He had no question about the Father being the eternal, all-powerful, miracle-working Creator of the universe. Nor did he have any doubts about the authority of Scripture. He was convinced that it made complete sense to give himself fully to following God and seeking to please him in his everyday life.

Paul did not have a secular mind-set. Nor did he have the barriers that so many people have today. In fact, he was confident that God would someday send a Messiah to the Jewish people. Once he was convinced that *Jesus* was this Messiah, he quickly trusted in him and dedicated the rest of his life to reaching others with the message about the Christ.

Today, however, many people doubt the existence of God or, if they believe he exists, lack confidence in his power and wisdom. They wonder how much he really had to do with "creation" and whether he really cares about what happens here on planet earth. They don't know what to think of the Bible. To them, it's merely one of many "inspired" but error-prone religious books. And they certainly don't want to sign up for a life of service to God or any other form of what they would consider to be religious fanaticism.

People with these kinds of beliefs need extra time to think about spiritual truth claims. They need some space as they put the puzzle pieces together to see if the rational side of Christian teachings makes sense and as they weigh the costs and benefits of actually following Christ. In short, we must allow people to move ahead at their own pace. To be sure, we should encourage and sometimes challenge them to keep up the pace and to continue taking steps forward. And we certainly don't want to do anything that will slow down their progress! But I've learned the hard way that pressing people to take steps for which they're not yet ready will backfire. In some cases it can even short-circuit the whole process.

Time spent in prayer talking and listening to God—and an outpouring of wisdom from the Holy Spirit—is what's needed to help us find the right balance between patience and persistence.

PROCESS-ORIENTED EVANGELISM

Inherent in all of this is the fact that for most people today the movement toward Christ will be a *process*. Contrast this to what I said previously about earlier forms of evangelism, which were largely designed to be an *event* that reminded semireligious people of what they already knew and then challenged them to commit to it right there on the spot. Rather, the process approach deepens the trust and understanding of secular people over time and, along the way, urges them to put their faith in Christ.

I'll illustrate this with one more addition to our drawing. Notice the timescale I've added across the left side of the secular landscape in Figure 2.10. This denotes that we have to let people take steps at their own pace, and each step is a vital part of their coming to Christ. It's a process that leads to the point of stepping across the line of faith and trusting fully in him.

Figure 2.10

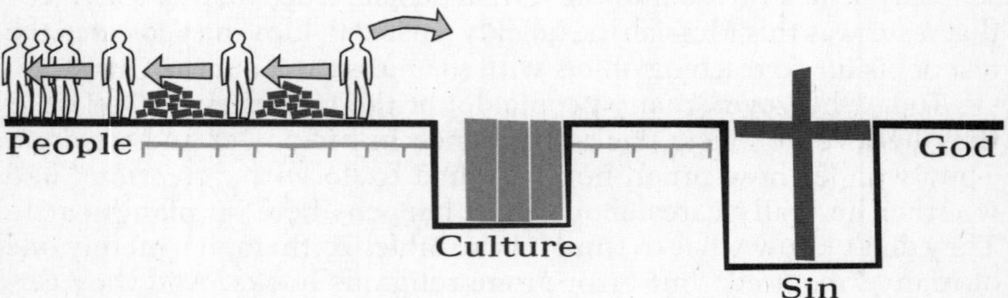

This, I believe, is an accurate portrayal of what we're up against in reaching people for Christ in today's world. They live way off to one side, separated by relational distance, secular thinking and values, multiple questions and objections to the Christian faith, the cultural chasm, and the sin chasm, which represents their moral failure and spiritual hopelessness. Then, way over on the other side live the Christians, many of whom are focused on their own needs, problems, and issues, but who are positioned—if they're willing to move—to reach a lost and dying world with the ever-relevant message of the cross of Christ.

A CHALLENGING TASK

I hope this picture proves helpful to you in understanding our task—but I know it also shows graphically just how daunting this task is. How can we take these values—(1) people matter to God, (2) they're lost, (3) they need Christ, (4) they need answers, (5) they long for community, (6) they need relevant communication, and (7) they require time—and put them into a plan that will help us meet our objectives?

In chapter 3 we will explore a biblical, church-tested strategy for involving every Christian in reaching men, women, and children who are far from God. I'm confident that this approach, combined with prayer and the power of the Holy Spirit, will help us build increasingly contagious churches and reach more and more people for Christ.

To Consider and Discuss

In this chapter we've talked about seven essential evangelistic values for building a contagious church. They are listed below. Consider how strong you think each of these values is in you as well as in your church or ministry. Next, list one or two constructive steps you can take to deepen the values you think are the weakest. The goal is not to induce guilt or point a finger at anyone but rather to produce focused thinking and creative solutions that will help you and your church become more ready to reach lost people for Christ.

1. *People matter to God*

   Present strength of this value:

   Steps to deepen this value:

2. *People are spiritually lost*

   Present strength of this value:

   Steps to deepen this value:

3. *People need Christ*

   Present strength of this value:

Steps to deepen this value:

4. *People need answers*

   Present strength of this value:

   Steps to deepen this value:

5. *People need community*

   Present strength of this value:

   Steps to deepen this value:

6. *People need cultural relevance*

   Present strength of this value:

   Steps to deepen this value:

7. *People need time*

   Present strength of this value:

   Steps to deepen this value:

3
A STRATEGY FOR REACHING SECULAR PEOPLE

HOW ARE WE GOING TO ACCOMPLISH OUR MISSION?

One overseas church championed many of the values we discussed in chapter 2. It was a great church with godly leadership, vibrant worship, solid biblical teaching, strong discipleship programs, and an authentic passion for reaching lost people. In fact, during the summer months as many as forty percent of its members spent time in various forms of direct evangelism. And, in spite of being a ministry of just a few hundred members, they had a full-time evangelist working tirelessly for them, and each year they would bring in several American seminary students to assist them in their outreach efforts.

One summer my wife, Heidi, and I had the privilege of serving with one of those groups. It was exciting to be part of a committed church that made it such a high priority to reach lost people. We were inspired by their zeal and emboldened by their efforts to courageously meet people in the neighborhoods and lead them to Christ.

There was only one problem: few people were coming to faith. In fact, the summer we were there, I know of only one person who clearly made a commitment to Christ through our weeks of outreach efforts. What about the hundreds of other people we talked to in their homes and on the streets? What happened to them? We hope some of them took to heart what they heard. We hope, but we don't know.

Why weren't our efforts more fruitful? The answer to that question probably has many facets. Certainly, doing any kind of evangelism in that large, post-Christian city was a huge challenge, since many of its residents were skeptical and even cynical toward Christians and the church. But I'm convinced there was more to the problem. There was a fundamental breakdown between the church's admirable evangelistic intentions and the way those intentions were expressed in their outreach efforts. In other words, the church's evangelistic mission did not get translated into an effective strategy that took into account the culture of the people they were trying to reach.

THE NEED FOR AN EFFECTIVE PLAN

What was the strategy? We would go out in groups of two or three, each taking a section of a neighborhood around the church, and we'd knock on doors. We didn't know these people, we weren't invited by them, and they had not visited the church. We were there simply to try to meet them and, in short order, to engage them in a spiritual conversation and share the gospel message with them. If they were ready to respond, we were prepared to lead them in a prayer of repentance and commitment to Christ. One way or another, whether they were willing to talk with us or not, we would always try to point them in the direction of the church and invite them to the Sunday morning worship services.

The response? Usually a polite "thank you . . ." quickly followed by "but no thank you" and a closed door. In most cases it soon became clear that they were not interested in visiting the church the following Sunday—or ever.

Then one day things were different. Heidi and I knocked on the door of one of the more upscale homes in the district, and a friendly young woman answered. She was very open to talking and appeared to have plenty of time. It turned out she was a nanny at this home, and she had already finished her chores. So we spent some time getting to know her and then ventured into a discussion about her spiritual background and her understanding of God. We tried to help her understand the gospel, but it was all brand-new to her. It seemed it would be a long journey before she would be ready to trust Christ. We ended our visit by inviting her to attend the church with us the following weekend. To our delight she accepted.

The next Sunday morning we went to the service with her. I remember thinking that, on the one hand, we had done exactly what we had been asked to do. We were right on target with the church's strategy. On the other hand, I had a nagging doubt about whether this was really the most strategic thing to do. This would be a fairly traditional worship service, designed for Christians. How would she relate to it? Would she be drawn in, or turned off?

It was hard to read her reaction to the exuberant hymn and chorus singing, the announcements, or the offering. But then the pastor got up and preached his sermon. Much to our surprise, it was on the question of whether Christians can be demon-possessed! He really got into it, reading the biblical texts on demonic activity, telling frightening real-life stories, and arguing for his answer to this obscure question. To this day I can't remember which side of the debate he landed on. All I remember is thinking, "I wonder what in the world *she's* thinking! What should Heidi and I say to her after the service ends? There's got to be a better approach to reaching people than this!"

When it was finally over, our friend was polite. She didn't criticize the service or the church. But it became clear that she wasn't willing to come back. She quickly lost interest in talking with us about spiritual matters and, before we knew it, we lost all contact with her.

I pray that something we said or something she saw in us or in some of the authentic believers in that church sparked an interest in her that will grow. But I can't help wondering how things might have turned out had there been a more appropriate evangelistic strategy in place—one that would honor biblical teachings while at the same time helping the church connect with people in a secular, post-Christian culture.

LEARNING THE HARD WAY

Here's what I've learned: We can be filled with love for lost people and can have a lot of good intentions. We can also have the most powerful mission statement in the world. We can be very clear on what we're trying to do and make certain that all of our members know our church exists to fulfill the Great Commission in our own little corner of the world. But unless this mission and these values and good intentions get translated into a sound step-by-step strategy specifically geared to reaching the people in the subculture we're working in, we probably won't make a very big impact.

This challenge reminds me of the time years ago when in the middle of November I wanted to find my friends who were out hunting and camping somewhere in the North Dakota badlands. I had every intention of locating them, and I gave it my best effort. (I'd just made my commitment to Christ the week before, and I wanted to be with them that weekend so I could tell them about it.)

I threw a few essentials into a backpack and persuaded a friend to fly me in a rented prop-plane to a landing strip near the edge of the badlands. From there I hitchhiked to the main entrance of the wilderness area where they were supposed to be camping. Then I walked down a dirt road for several miles, late into the night. Not finding them, I ended up camping next to a patch of trees, alone and in subfreezing temperatures.

Unless this mission get translated into a sound step-by-step strategy specifically geared to reaching the people in the subculture we're working in, we probably won't make a very big impact.

The next morning a gruff old rancher came out with his loaded six-shooter to scare me off his land. Through a carefully worded apology—and a quick prayer—I managed to befriend him and actually ended up in his home for a hot breakfast! Later he drove me deeper into the badlands to the area where I thought my friends might have their camp. Not finding them, he finally dropped me off to look for them on my own, and we said good-bye. Soon another hunter gave me a ride, and we searched several other sites where hunters were lodging.

After a two-day adventure, during which I met some wonderful people and saw some spectacular sights, I finally had to concede that I was looking for a needle in a haystack. Realizing I would not find my friends, I managed to catch a long ride back home.

Give me an A for effort but an F for execution. I had not done a very good job of translating my desire to find my friends into a thought-out strategy that would help me reach my goal. I later found out I had been right across a small stream in the area where they were camping, but even at that short distance I had failed to recognize their tent and equipment.

Similarly, the leaders of that overseas church deserved an A—or even an A+—for their strong commitment to reaching unchurched people for Christ. They were willing to pull out all the stops and give themselves fully to the work of evangelism. But they had not placed this commitment into an appropriate step-by-step plan that would take them where they wanted to go.

SHARPENING THE STRATEGY

What might that kind of plan, or strategy, look like? Is there an example we can look at that will give us a starting point for developing our own approach?

Yes! Over the next several pages I present part of a message given by Bill Hybels to the core believers at Willow Creek Community Church, in which he spells out the church's seven-step strategy. We'll look only at the first three steps, since these are the ones that focus on evangelism. I include this message for two reasons: First, it has vital elements that are transferable into virtually any setting (although it contains a few details that are distinctive to Willow Creek's own context); second, it is presented in a compelling way that I hope will motivate you personally and model for you how you or other leaders in your church can cast vision and clarify strategy for your own congregation. I'll break in at several points to add comments and to expand on our drawing from chapter 2.

People in churches ask, "What's the target we're shooting for? What is the mission? And if we know what the mission is, how are we proceeding toward it? Do we know if we're succeeding or failing? Why are we fasting and praying? Why are we giving considerable sums of money? Why are we breaking our backs in service?"

As leaders of this church, we have worked very hard to keep in the forefront of all of our minds the fact that this church has a mission. Simply put, that mission is to reach nonchurched people, to lead them to Christ, and to grow them up to be fully devoted followers—difference makers in their worlds and in the church.

You say, "Well, what is our strategy? How are we going to accomplish that mission?" That's what we're going to talk about tonight. We have a seven-step strategy. Many of you have heard it, but you need a refresher course on it. For others, this is brand-new.

In our seven-step strategy, we always start by looking out our windows and seeing those houses with their lights on over in the subdivision. We know that in those houses, right next door to us, are some families that get up every Sunday morning, have a cup of coffee, and read the *Chicago Tribune.* But they don't go to church, and they don't know Christ, and they probably aren't even in a relationship with a Christian they respect.

If you believe what the Bible says about the afterlife, you know they're headed for hell, and there seems to be no way of connecting with them. It's like they're in a little world of their own. Churches are functioning all over the place, and yet these people are sitting alone in their family rooms on Sunday mornings. How are they ever going to be reached? How is it going to happen? How are they going to come to Christ?

When we were first working on our strategy, we kept asking, "What are we going to do? These lost people matter to God. They're right in our driving radius. How are we going to reach them?"

Right off the bat, we said we're not going to put our eggs in the basket of Christian television. We're not going to pretend that vast numbers of nonchurched people are sitting on Sunday mornings clicking through Christian television and saying, "Oh, there's a good program," and then falling on their knees in front of their TVs.

Now, that happens sometimes. It just doesn't seem to happen *en masse,* and statistics bear that out. *Christians* tend to be the ones who watch Christian television. Just a fraction of the nonchurched world ever turns to Christian television. I believe the same thing is true with most of Christian radio.

We decided we wouldn't put our eggs in the basket of passing out pamphlets, putting on bumper stickers, doing telephone campaigns, or even advertising. Other churches pursue these avenues, and that's fine. It's just not us. The line item in our budget for advertising is, incidentally, infinitesimal compared to the overall budget. We just don't put much stock in that approach.

STEP 1: BUILD RELATIONSHIPS

From day one, we've said we're going to follow the example of Jesus and lots of others in the pages of the Bible, and we're going to challenge believers in this church to build relationships with nonchurched people. On a regular basis, we've got to leave the huddle of close Christian fellowship, take some risks, and get to know some nonchurched people. This will mean reaching out in the neighborhood, inviting neighbors over for dinner, golfing with people who are outside of the family, spending lunch hours at work with people who don't know Christ. We've got to build relational bridges over to these people. When we do, their defense mechanisms will relax a little bit, and matters of the heart can be discussed.

I don't know about you, but when strangers approach me, my walls go up. I say, "What's your angle? What do you want? What are you trying to sell me?" But when a friend wants to talk to me about something that's important, my walls go down, and I say, "Talk to me." I'm open to it, because I know and trust them.

When we look through the pages of Scripture, we see the example of Jesus. He notices a seeker named Zacchaeus sitting in a tree, and they arrange a dinner get-together. It's in the context of relationship, after Jesus has dinner with Zacchaeus and establishes rapport with him, that he brings transformational truth his way, and life change happens.

We've put almost all of our eggs in the basket of you people caring enough about nonchurched, hell-bound, lost people that you'll establish a bridge of relationship with them. If we as a congregation are not building bridges to the people in that family room in the neighborhood right near here, odds are, friends, they'll wind up in hell. There's just a resistance, there's just a defense mechanism that keeps them from responding to other kinds of input.

If we succeed in our strategy, if all of us would live with what I call a seeker-consciousness—in other words, if all of us throughout the course of our day were saying, "Lord, talk to me. Lead me to somebody. Help me just make a little inroad with someone I can establish a friendship with"—there's no telling how God would use us.

I've talked to you before about frequenting the same restaurants, going to the same gas stations, developing a kind of consistency in your daily patterns so that you can eventually put names with faces. Why? Because in the context of a trusting relationship, someday you'll probably have an opportunity to share Christ.

I'm going to go so far tonight as to ask you this: Do you have three nonchurched people in your life with whom you're trying to establish rapport right now? When was the last time you built a fresh relationship with a nonchurched person?

I was on a retreat with some of the other leaders of this church earlier this week, and it was so exciting for me to talk to one of our most recent additions. He's new in the community, yet he could tell me the names of men and women he's building relationships with in the hopes that someday he can share Christ with them. That's seeker-consciousness.

That's the first step—all of us committing, as a whole congregation, to build relational inroads with people who need to be reached, just like Jesus did.

Before we continue on to the next point in Bill's message, I'd like to push the pause button and comment on the first step of this strategy.

As I've had the privilege of teaching and doing evangelism all over the world, I've observed a consistent human dynamic in every culture I've been to: *Friends listen to friends.* People are growing increasingly suspicious of strangers, sales pitches, and institutional authorities. But when they need help or advice, they turn to someone they know and trust—someone they believe has their best interests at heart.

I'll bet that's true where you live too. If so, then you should do all you can to get up close to as many people as possible and extend the love and truth of Christ to them in ways they can understand. There is a temptation in Christendom to look toward grand-scale programs to reach huge masses of people with the gospel. Certainly, large events have their place, but the foundational place to begin is with relationships. In fact, the premiere issue of *The Barna Report* presented statistics showing that more than three times as many people came to faith through the personal witness of a friend than through hearing gospel preaching in a church. And the ratio went up to almost ten times as many reached by friends as by evangelistic events or crusades alone.[1]

I've observed a consistent human dynamic in every culture I've been to: Friends listen to friends.

It is vital that we help all the people in our churches build authentic, no-strings-attached friendships with the people around them. This strategy doesn't have the level of pizzazz that most big events offer, but the truth is that those events don't usually work right unless they are positioned as supplements to the individual efforts of ordinary Christians like you and me.

In addition, it's at the relational level where we learn enough about nonbelievers to know how to design an outreach event that will effectively speak to them. Having non-Christian friends prevents us from theorizing wildly about what might reach some generic, nondescript seeker out there somewhere. Instead, we begin to think about what would or would not work in terms of communicating to our own friends. In effect, relational evangelism helps us become realistic when it comes to event evangelism.

Also, applying the values we discussed in chapter 2, it is at a friendship level that we can best find out what spiritual questions people are asking and then learn to give them relevant, biblical answers. It is here that we can extend community to them at its most personal level. In fact, our relationship with them may be the first real taste they've ever had of what true community in the body of Christ can be like. As they watch our lives up close, they will begin to see how natural the Christian faith can be across the various arenas of life. Also, in genuine friendships we can allow others the time they need to process the information they're learning and to "count the cost" of following Christ.

Let's look again at the drawing from chapter 2 but add another element (Figure 3.1). The addition to the picture is a contagious Christian who is willing to take the risk of moving from his or her comfortable position on the right side of the chart all the way over to the left side in order to befriend someone who doesn't yet know Christ. It's an uncomfortable move and one that can be a bit dangerous, but it's the one Christ modeled for us and then commanded us to take for the sake of lost people.

Figure 3.1

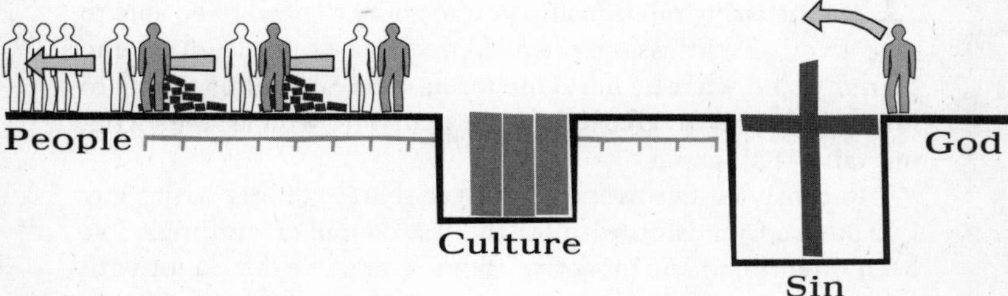

I mentioned earlier that during the entire summer Heidi and I worked with the church overseas, I remember only one clear-cut example of a person coming to faith in Christ. His name was Tony. It's interesting to note that we met him through his sister who attended the church. It was through eating a meal together with Tony in her home that we became friends with him. This led to conversations about the gospel and, several weeks later, he committed his life to Christ. We spent eight weeks trying to talk to strangers, but in this one brief friendship, God worked—and the man experienced salvation! If there is a better place to start today than by building relationships, I don't know where it is.

Let's not leave this discussion in the theoretical realm. Take a moment right now to write down the first names of three people in your life you hope to reach with the love and truth of Christ.

1. ____________________
2. ____________________
3. ____________________

In the *Becoming a Contagious Christian* training course,[2] we call this your "Impact List." I encourage you now, as we do in the course, to begin to pray daily for these people. Ask God to help you deepen your relationship with them and to work through your conversations with them to draw them to himself.

Now let's continue with the message given by Bill Hybels to see what comes next.

STEP 2: SHARE A VERBAL WITNESS

The second step in our strategy says that in the context of that trusting relationship you're going to need to be able to give a verbal witness—a crisp, compelling explanation of who Christ is and what he has done for us. The Scriptures tell us to always be ready to give a defense to anyone who asks us what our faith is all about.

Recently I drove over to Michigan to have dinner with a guy I've built a friendship with for the last couple of summers. I've been intentional and proactive about it, and I've done a lot with him recreationally and socially. I've also been praying for him.

He's driven 180 miles two times to come to church here. He doesn't know Christ. His family doesn't go to church. He didn't go when he was growing up either. He's full of vitality and life—a great guy who's heading for a Christless eternity. I love the guy.

When you build these kinds of relationships, I don't know if God just serendipitously hooks you up or what, but your hearts get knit together. And you find yourself getting increasingly concerned about the person.

So I'm sitting with my friend in a little restaurant in Michigan. All of a sudden he says to me, "Bill, I've known you for a couple of years. I know you're religious. I've been to your church a couple of times, but I still don't get it. What is Christianity?" In the words of that song we love around here, he was saying, "Would you show me the way?"

I once again articulated the essence of the gospel message to him. I said, "It's not by works of righteousness we do. It's not trying to get on a religious treadmill and pumping out a bunch of performances to appease a God you know you violated. Salvation is a gift. Christ paid for it on the cross."

I explained that whole thing to him. But I knew he didn't get it. He strained. He tried to understand it. He asked a couple of questions. But after a while I could tell it had been enough for that evening. I said, "These are really important issues; let's talk about it more soon."

I could barely sleep that night. I said, "I believe I just did one of the most important things a human being can do: I tried to do a little soul surgery on someone whose destiny is hanging in the balance."

My question to you is, "Do you know how to explain the gospel in a crisp, compelling way? When you're building relationships and the Holy Spirit opens up the door and someone says, 'Show me the way,' can you show them?"

That's why we keep offering the *Becoming a Contagious Christian* seminar on a repeated basis. I think all of us ought to cycle through that course at least once every two years. We ought to go back, get our blades sharpened, get our senses refocused, and get our hearts beating fast again about being ambassadors for Christ. Friends, if you'll do that, you'll learn how to build relationships, and you'll learn how to give a crisp, compelling verbal witness.

Do you know how the kingdom of God advances in the world? One life at a time. It's one hand reaching out to another hand. It's through people like you and people like me.

Can we count you in on being prepared to give a defense for your faith, maybe going through that seminar sometime soon, sharpening your skills so that you get the first two steps of our strategy under your belt and you're ready to go?

Let's pause again. What Bill is describing flies directly in the face of a very popular approach to evangelism—the approach that tells believers, "We don't really have to *say* anything—we can simply live out our faith and the people around us will see it, be drawn to it, and eventually embrace it."

Contra that philosophy, we're saying, don't count on it! There's a half-truth there, to be sure—people *do* need to see Christ in our lives and be drawn to what they see in us. That's the prerequisite to becoming a contagious Christian. But we're fooling ourselves if we think they'll figure it out on their own or come to us and ask us to explain it to them. *We* have to go to *them*. We have to be willing to take risks and initiate spiritual conversations. We have to articulate the message of salvation in ways non-Christians can understand. Figure 3.2 signals this by showing the Christian speaking to his or her friend, putting spiritual truths into everyday language. Notice too that this conversation continues as the Christian walks with the friend to the right, progressively closer to the cross of Christ.

Figure 3.2

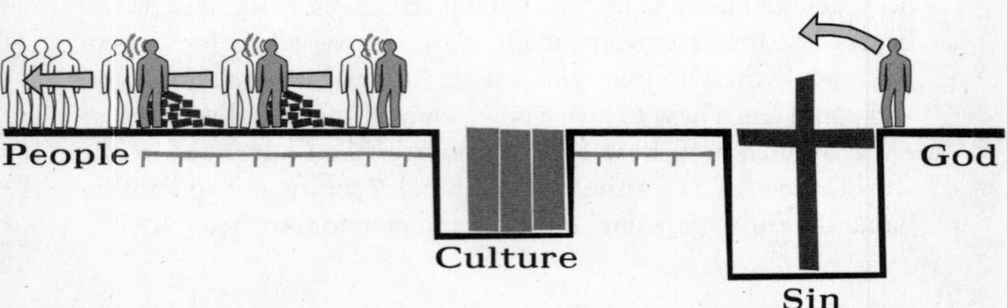

As leaders it is imperative that we take action to prepare all the people in our churches to build relationships and to articulate the truths of the gospel. The problem is that most of us severely overestimate our natural ability to communicate Christ clearly and effectively.

I am reminded of a huge wake-up call I had in one of my first college courses. I came to class the day of our first major exam convinced that I knew the information thoroughly enough to do well on the test. But I didn't know the material as well as I thought I did. In reality, I came prepared merely to *recognize* the right answers on the kind of multiple-choice examination I'd grown accustomed to in high school. You can imagine my shock when the test papers were handed out and every question was either fill-in-the-blank or essay. There was no easy menu of answers to choose from! I had convinced myself I was ready for something I wasn't. And my test grade reflected that fact—it was a D-, one mere tick away from being an F.

I decided that day I was going to start preparing in ways that would not depend on easy examinations, luck, or obvious clues. I began to develop study habits that included plenty of repetition and practice. I would continue the study process until I not only *thought* I could say the answers but to the point where I was actually *saying* the answers out loud, word for word. This new approach revolutionized my college experience—and my grades with it! I hadn't suddenly acquired a higher IQ; I'd simply put to work a process for getting ready so that on test day I could come through with the answers.

Studying for those tests was trivial compared to the importance of learning to effectively communicate the gospel. We have to do everything we can to help ourselves and the people in our churches become "prepared to give an answer to everyone who asks you to give the reason for the hope that you have" (1 Peter 3:15). We'll talk more about how to do that in chapter 7.

Let's go back to Bill's message for the third step of the evangelistic strategy. This section will include details that may differ from the approach of your own ministry. Read it carefully, though, because I'm convinced that the principle of using outreach events—regardless of what you call them, how often you do them, or what they look like—is relevant to every church.

STEP 3: INVITE FRIENDS TO OUTREACH EVENTS

The third step relates to our weekend service, which we've designed especially for spiritual seekers. The Scriptures say, "How, then, can they call on the one they have not believed in? And how can they believe in the one of whom they have not heard? And how can they hear without someone preaching to them?" (Romans 10:14). They've got to hear. Somebody's got to do the preaching.

As staff and leaders, here's what we're trying to do on the weekends: We're trying to say to all of you, "Look, let's do team evangelism. You don't have to lead your friends to Christ all by yourself. If some of you can, go ahead and do so! But most of us can't. We need a little help."

So we enter into this trust-filled relationship. We say to you, "Here's our guarantee again for this next ministry year. We're going to do everything in our power every seven days to serve up to you and your invited guests the most prayer-filled, practical, creative, compelling, Christ-centered, relevant weekend services that we possibly can. We will give 110 percent fifty-two times as you're building relationships and leading people into dialogue about Christianity."

You can say to your friends, "I know you're thinking about this a little bit. Can I encourage you to come with me to a service at our church this weekend? You won't have to sign anything, say anything, sing anything, or give anything. It's going to be creative. It's going to be relevant. It's going to be practical. It's going to be biblical." Friends, as we do evangelism together like that, I've got to believe that God smiles.

I saw it work recently in another relationship with a friend I've been inviting to this church and trying to lead to Christ for six years. He's having some trouble in his life these days and said to me recently, "You've been telling me about Christianity and your church for a long time. Maybe I'll show up for a service."

Well, for the last six weekends at 9 A.M. on Sunday, he's been right down in this section over here. And do you know what? I think he's just weeks away from trusting Christ!

So, I've seen again for myself how wonderful it is to have a powerful tool like our weekend service to invite friends to. It's a high-impact supplement to your personal evangelistic efforts.

Here's what I want to ask you: Can we count you in to pray about who you can invite to the weekend services this year, and to utilize these services in the strongest way possible?

What if we all had a prayer goal that we would each try to invite one seeker a month to the weekend services? If you would wholeheartedly commit to that, I think you'd pray differently. I think you'd be on your knees more. I think you'd walk through your world differently. I think when you came and saw that other people had friends on their elbows, you'd be rooting more intently for what God is doing in our weekend services. The excitement level for your participation in the work of God here at this church would go up.

So can we count you in to do steps one, two, and three? If you'll take that challenge of bringing one person a month, you just watch what God does. I mean, you watch what he does in our weekend services this year. We'll be baptizing hundreds and hundreds of people if you'll do that. If those of us who are putting on the services do our part and you do yours, incredible things are going to happen.[3]

When we think back to our discussion of the secular landscape (chapter 2) and to all the challenges we face in bringing people to Christ today, we can see how difficult it is for most Christians to handle alone. It's challenging even for church leaders! But when we follow a strategy that combines individual efforts with well-executed outreach events, we'll see powerful results. We see this synergy at Willow Creek, and it seems to be operative wherever evangelism is strongest today, whether in local churches or in parachurch ministries.

For example, Billy Graham crusades work best when churches teach and practice the principles presented in their "Operation Andrew" training, which emphasizes relationships and personal communication of the gospel to friends. The North American Ministries director for the Billy Graham Evangelistic Association, Sterling Huston, wrote in his book *Crusade Evangelism and the Local Church* that "effective evangelism is built on relationships.... One person who has found new life, meaning, and forgiveness through an encounter with Jesus Christ is motivated by love to bring another to experience that same relationship with the Savior.... This is what must happen in all evangelism methods, from person to person [to] city-wide Crusades."[4] The Billy Graham crusade team knows there must be a marriage between relational evangelism and high-quality outreach events in order to have a maximum impact.

The same strategy is employed in evangelist Luis Palau's citywide campaigns. Before Luis comes to town, his teams spend months in churches teaching people to build relational bridges to people around them and to articulate their testimony and a gospel illustration. They also coach them on how to effectively invite their friends to the live event.

InterVarsity Christian Fellowship has found that strategically combining personal evangelism with outreach events has a powerful effect in reaching students. In fact, they call the universities where they're trying this approach "contagious campuses"!

In John 4 we see Jesus using this combination. The woman at the well, having talked to Jesus, ran up to her town in Samaria and declared to her friends that she had met the Messiah. She explained to them how he'd had supernatural insights into her life and had told her of everything she had done. It's not surprising that this kind of testimony—especially from someone with a colorful background like hers—had a huge impact. In fact, verse 39 tells us that many people from that town believed because of her words.

The townspeople also accepted the woman's invitation to come and hear Jesus for themselves. They went to the well and listened to what he had to say. The combination of their friendship with this woman (step 1: relationship), her verbal witness (step 2), and this experience of a larger "outreach event" (step 3: hearing Jesus talk to the whole group down by the well) resulted in even more of them coming to faith. John 4:42 reports that the people later told the woman, "We no longer believe just because of what you said; now we have heard for ourselves, and we know that this man really is the Savior of the world."

Now, obviously, Jesus talking to a group of people by a well is a bit different from Billy Graham or Luis Palau speaking to an arena packed with people. It is also different from a seeker-oriented service or event that includes contemporary music, multimedia presentations, and drama performances. But that's the point—outreach events don't all need to look alike in order to be effective. They just need to strategically utilize a group gathering to communicate biblical truth in the language of the people who are there listening; they need to be public expressions of our working together to "become all things to all people . . . for the sake of the gospel" (1 Corinthians 9:22 NRSV).

And "becoming all things" in your town will probably look different than it does for us in our town. That's fine as long as all of us are careful to never compromise biblical truth or standards and all of us are working with the pure goal to "by all possible means . . . save some" (1 Corinthians 9:22).

"Becoming all things" in your town will probably look different than it does for us in our town. That's fine as long as all of us are careful to never compromise biblical truth.

So what might an effective outreach event look like where you minister? That's a great question—one I can't answer. Remember, "we must each crack the cultural code where we live." However, in chapters 10–15 we will give many examples of various approaches churches are trying, all built around six biblical styles of evangelism. In these chapters you'll find ideas you can use as is or adapt to fit your own outreach needs.

Figure 3.3 shows what our drawing looks like when we add the third step of the strategy. Notice that as a supplement to the efforts of its individual members the church itself gets involved in the effort by moving to the left and into the fray. This church is not waiting passively for a few seekers to come its way. Rather, it's moving their direction in an effort to "go into all the world and preach the good news" (Mark 16:15). It's working to bridge the cultural chasm and follow Jesus in the effort to "seek and to save what was lost" (Luke 19:10). It's

Figure 3.3

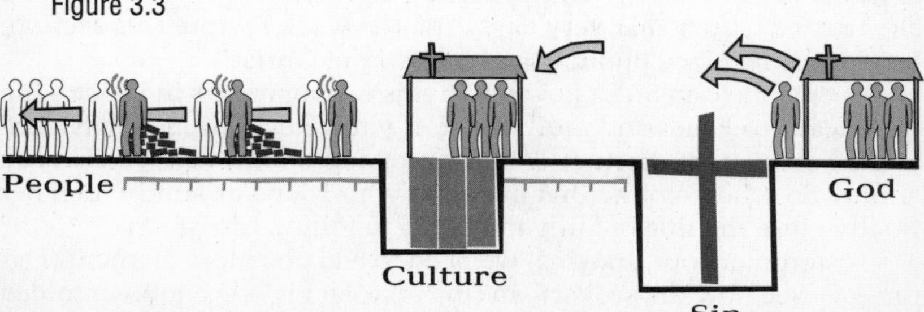

doing team evangelism. Note too that this church has intentionally left room for another person to join the fellowship.

The strategy we have discussed in this chapter is more than theoretical. I have seen the Holy Spirit work through it countless times to lead people to Christ, sometimes through my own efforts and many more times through the efforts of others in our church and through Christians in other churches.

This approach was especially precious to me when God used it to reach my own sister-in-law. Todd and Jackie moved into our area near Chicago several years ago. Jackie had a religious background and believed in God, but God wasn't a vital part of her life. Naturally, Heidi and I already had a relationship with Jackie through our family connection, but it was casual and surface-level. We were excited to now have the opportunity to spend more time with both Jackie and Todd. In the course of being together, spiritual topics would come up from time to time, especially with Jackie. We'd try to respond to her questions, explain what Christ has done in our own lives, and point her toward the truths of Scripture.

We also invited Jackie and Todd to join us for our church's weekend services, and they often attended with us. Sometimes the services would address questions Heidi or I had talked with Jackie about earlier. Other times they would raise new issues that we would discuss later. God worked in Jackie powerfully during the services. Sometimes during a drama, a song, or the message, she would be deeply moved by what she was hearing—even to the point of tears. We'd try to talk to her about what was going on inside, but she'd often feel embarrassed or confused, and she'd just close up.

The pattern continued for months. During this time the Holy Spirit was clearly at work in Jackie, using our relationships, our words, and the services she was attending. Finally, after almost a year of this process, Jackie came to us one Sunday after church. With great joy she told us that during the service she had finally understood the message of salvation. The light of the gospel had broken through, and she trusted Christ that very day. (And the week I wrote this section, Jackie was baptized publicly as a follower of Christ!)

Do you have any idea how much this turn of events in Jackie's life has meant to Heidi and me? You do if you've ever been deeply concerned about the spiritual condition of someone you love. There's simply no other joy like that of seeing your friend or family member finally cross the line of faith and begin to follow Christ.

To complete our drawing, we need to add one more element (Figure 3.4). See how the seeker—in this case, Jackie—becomes enfolded into the church fellowship even before receiving Christ? But notice also that she has to keep moving toward him and finally make the decision to step across the bridge of the cross and receive his forgiveness and leadership for her life.

Figure 3.4

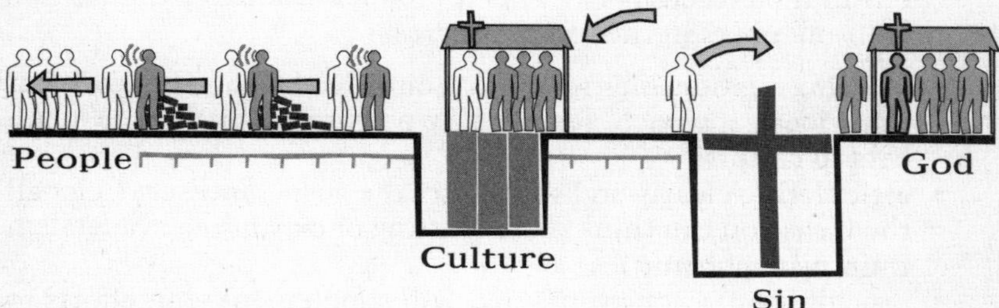

Now Jackie is an integrated member of the church. She's no longer a seeker, but a daughter of God and a sister in Christ. For her the adventure of Christianity has only begun!

I hope that reading about how God worked in Jackie's life will revitalize your hope for those in your own life who have not yet crossed the line of faith. I also hope it illustrates the power of combining individual efforts with team efforts and motivates you to adopt an approach similar to the three-part strategy presented in this chapter. I'm convinced this kind of step-by-step plan is critical to building a contagious church.

While it's tempting to stay at the objective level of discussing mission statements, values, and strategies, what prevents us from forming contagious churches goes much deeper. Jesus warned that the real root of what we observe on the surface of our lives is our *heart* (Matthew 15:18). Its condition shows through in whatever we say and do.

Truth be told, evangelism often fails to happen because in our innermost being we don't really care much about people who are outside of God's family. We see them as a nuisance, a bad influence, or even as the enemy. We need to let God change our minds and warm our hearts toward those he loves so much. In the next chapter we will look at some practical ways we can cooperate with God to make that happen.

To Consider and Discuss

1. Have you thought through your own church's evangelistic strategy? Like the overseas church in the beginning of this chapter,

you probably have a strategy that's being employed, whether it's written down or not. But a good question to ask is whether this strategy is proving effective in fulfilling your church's evangelistic mission. Is it helping you lead unchurched friends, step-by-step, to the point of trusting and following Christ?

Whether or not your strategy matches the order of the one laid out in the preceding pages, is it producing activity that assists your members in the following areas?

- building relationships with those outside of God's family? What other ideas/approaches might help prepare and encourage members to do this?
- articulating clearly and succinctly the gospel message? List all the ideas you can think of for starting or expanding evangelism training opportunities.
- providing outreach events that will supplement your efforts to reach their friends and family members?

2. Discuss ways to maximize any upcoming opportunities (these may already have been designed for outreach, or they may be events that could be repositioned that way).

3. What other ideas do you have for outreach events that you think would fit the people you hope to reach?

4. What other elements are important to your evangelistic strategy?

5. Can you list your present or updated strategy steps here? If not, I highly recommend working with the other leaders to hammer them out, looking to the elements in this chapter for ideas and encouragement.

PART 2
A CONTAGIOUS CHANGE PROCESS

In part 1 we looked at a broad picture of a contagious church. We saw that it is a church that is clear about what it is trying to accomplish—a church that has evangelism at the core of its mission. It is permeated by the beliefs and values needed to support this mission in the context of the culture within which it is working. And, this kind of church puts its mission and values into action through a practical, step-by-step strategy that helps it reach and enfold increasing numbers of lost people. The picture is clear. Now the stage is set for us to move toward actually *building* a contagious church.

But there's a problem. How do we get all the members to play their parts? For that matter, how do we get ourselves to play our own parts? How can we reverse the drift of most churches and ministries—as well as most Christians and church leaders—toward becoming inwardly focused? Short of a strong intervention, this reversal doesn't seem likely to happen.

So how can we intervene? What can we do to fight the gravitational pull toward self-centeredness and help our churches start looking more and more like the picture we've drawn? That's what this next section is all about. In the next six chapters I'll introduce the 6-Stage Process for bringing our churches back to the kind of biblical mission, values, and strategy we've been exploring.

Don't succumb to the temptation to jump immediately into launching outreach ministries and events (stage 6). We'll get there, but we can't start there. Change must begin in the leaders themselves; as *we* change our *church* will change. We have to start with the heart.

4

STAGE 1: OWNING AND MODELING EVANGELISTIC VALUES

I was making a routine visit to an ordinary discount store. You know the drill. You are surrounded by a lot of people, but you're on your own, fending for yourself. You search for what you need, buy it, and you're out of the store before anyone even notices you were there. This was my usual experience.

This day, however, was different. I'd barely gotten into the door of this newly built store when a woman greeted me and offered me a shopping cart.

That's interesting, I thought. *I've never been welcomed like that before.*

A little while later as I was perusing the aisles, another employee walked up and asked me if I needed help finding anything. In a state of mild disbelief, I politely said, "No thanks, I'm just looking." After the person left, I came to my senses and realized that I really did need some help finding a few things, but I'd been too surprised to say what they were!

The real shocker came when I finally got to the checkout counter. The woman at the cash register rang up my items and, after processing my credit card and seeing my name on it, looked me in the eye and said, "Thank you for shopping with us today, Mr. Mittelberg."

By this point I thought I'd entered the twilight zone! In all my years of dealing with discount stores, about the most I'd ever received from employees was passive indifference. I had never encountered such friendliness, helpfulness, or courtesy! I walked out of the store in complete amazement. "What makes this place so different?" I wondered.

Whenever I've told this story in an area where one of these stores exists, my listeners have guessed the name of the business before I've revealed it. Perhaps you have too. It was Wal-Mart. The fact that so many people around the country know what company I'm describing only amplifies my question. What makes this entire chain of stores so different? Why, with rare exception, do people all over the country who go into a Wal-Mart experience the same thing—a corporate climate of customer service?

As I pondered this question that day, I was tempted to reach for simple solutions. For instance, perhaps it was the result of some powerful employee training program where they instill a sense of respect for customers and teach employees to listen well and to work cheerfully to solve customers' problems. I was tempted to think this was the answer, but I knew it must go deeper. It wasn't long after that initial visit that I began to hear more about the company's founder, Sam Walton. A peek into his beliefs and values helped me begin to understand what made this store so special.

Sam Walton was clear about his mission. He embodied the values that I saw manifested in his store that day. I later read in his autobiography, *Sam Walton, Made in America,* what Walton himself said about this: "Everything we've done since we started Wal-Mart has been devoted to this idea that the customer is our boss. . . . The customer always comes ahead of everything else."[1]

You and I want to build churches that value outsiders. We looked in chapter 1 at our central mission—to fulfill the Great Commission or, as we put it at the church I'm a part of, "to reach irreligious people and turn them into fully devoted followers of Christ."

In chapter 2 we examined some foundational values: (1) people matter to God, (2) people are lost without Christ, (3) people need the gospel message, (4) people need answers to their questions, (5) people need real community, (6) people need cultural relevance, and (7) people need time to process the gospel message.

In chapter 3 we explored a strategy that has proven successful in many churches and ministries around the world: (1) we need to build relationships with non-Christians, (2) we need to verbally communicate what Christ has done for us, and (3) we need to offer at least periodic, high-quality outreach events or seeker services that present biblical truth in clear and relevant ways.

STARTING WITH THE HEART

How can a discussion about Sam Walton and Wal-Mart assist us in these all-important efforts? By helping us understand that the shape of an organization will simply be a magnified version of the shape of its leaders. The mission of an organization is an extension of the mission of the leaders. The values that permeate the culture of an organization are the values that flow out of the people who run it. So if you want to reshape the priorities of the organization, you're going to have to reshape the priorities of the men and women who guide it.

Likewise, truly contagious churches don't grow out of programs, initiatives, conferences, curricula, or big ideas to "take this town for Christ." Ultimately, they must grow out of the beliefs and values—the very *hearts*—of the people who lead them. That is why stage 1 in the 6-Stage Process says that we must "own and model evangelistic values."

George Barna, in his award-winning book *Evangelism That Works,* observed the following:

> In our work with secular organizations, the leader shapes the heart and passion of the corporate entity. In our work with non-profit organizations, we have found the same principle to be operative. When it comes to the focus of the organization, the people who serve there tend to take on many of the core personality traits of the leader toward fulfilling the mandate of the organization. If this is true, and most churches seem to lack fervor and focus for evangelism, is it reasonable to conclude that it may be because of the lack of zeal most pastors have for identifying, befriending, loving and evangelizing non-Christian people?[2]

Wal-Mart is a customer-focused store precisely because its founder was a customer-focused leader. Your church will be an outsider-oriented ministry only if you and those around you are outsider-oriented leaders. It's as simple as that—and as difficult, because the hardest person in the world for any of us to change is the person we each refer to as "me."

Your church will be an outsider-oriented ministry only if you and those around you are outsider-oriented leaders.

Paul says in Ephesians 5:1, "Be imitators of God, therefore, as dearly loved children." He goes on to talk about loving people the way Christ did when he gave himself as a sacrifice on our behalf. In effect, Paul is saying, "Lost people matter to God; make certain they matter to you too!" Our caring for others must go deeper than mere outward activity, such as occasionally trumping up the courage to talk about God to the people around us. It really is a *heart* issue. As Jesus said in Matthew 12:34: "Out of the overflow of the heart the mouth speaks." I've discovered this to be true in my own life. When I'm walking close to Christ and my heart is right with him, opportunities come that I never would have expected.

A Heart Overflowing

Not too long ago I wanted to telephone a friend of mine named Bill Craig. You may have heard of him. Dr. William Lane Craig is an author, lecturer, and one of the most powerful defenders of the faith alive today. In fact, a few years ago our church hosted a widely publicized debate between Bill and an atheist on the subject, "Atheism vs. Christianity: Where Does the Evidence Point?" My problem was that Bill had recently moved to a different city—and I didn't have his new phone number. So I called directory assistance and asked for the listing for William Craig; I wrote it down and then dialed it.

A cheerful voice said, "Hello!"

"Hello, I'm calling for Bill Craig," I said.

"This *is* Bill Craig," the man assured me.

"It sure doesn't sound like Bill Craig to me," I kidded. "I'm looking for the *real* Bill Craig."

"Well, which Bill Craig did you have in mind?" he inquired.

"I'm looking for William L. Craig," I answered.

"Well, this isn't William *L.* Craig; this is William *Z.* Craig," he said with enthusiasm.

Normally I would have acknowledged that I had a wrong number and left the poor guy alone. But not this day! I was walking close to Christ and feeling the joy and exuberance that go along with that. So I took a redemptive risk and let the more adventurous side of my personality come out.

"That sure is unfortunate," I replied.

"Why's that?" he asked.

"Because you're just one initial away from being a world-famous speaker and defender of the Christian faith!" I lightheartedly quipped.

"Well, you certainly do have the wrong Bill Craig," the man assured me. "No one's ever mistaken me for a *religious* person!"

"Why not?" I asked. "Don't you believe in God?"

"Well, yes—in my own way, I guess ..." he said, and off our discussion ran! I was as surprised by this conversation as the stranger a thousand miles away was!

We talked for a few minutes about spiritual matters, and I challenged him to read some of the books and materials written by his "namesake—the other, more famous Bill Craig!" Before we got off the phone, he even gave me his address, so I wrote him a letter and mailed him a tape of the debate and some other Christian materials. All this emanated from my dialing a wrong phone number!

That is the kind of evangelistic adventure that flows out of walking close to Christ and staying open to the split-second opportunities he brings our way. If I had not had a Holy Spirit boldness and a heartfelt concern for lost people that day, the conversation never would have taken place.

Unfortunately, I can also illustrate the flip side of the equation out of my personal life. When I'm spiritually disconnected and preoccupied with my own concerns and desires, even much more overt opportunities just seem to pass me by.

A Heart Not Flowing

I was on an out-of-town trip and had some time on my hands, so I decided to stop at a shopping mall to find a place to get a haircut. I remember feeling spiritually off that day. I didn't feel very close to God and, looking back, I know I wasn't motivated to speak to anybody about matters of faith.

The "problem" was that the woman assigned to cut my hair was very friendly and outgoing. She asked me questions about where I was from, why I was in town, and so forth. These were potentially easy entrées into a spiritual conversation, but I'm embarrassed to admit I sidestepped them. I was immersed in my own world and preoccupied with my own concerns, and I failed to seize the chance to tell her about my ministry or my relationship with Christ. I missed a great opportunity to tell her that she is loved by God and that she can know and follow him. She was receptive; I was distracted.

I hate knowing that I let such an open opportunity pass me by, and I tremble at the possibility that God had appointed me as his representative to help her in her spiritual journey. (And I'm waiting for the chance to get back to that town for another haircut—whether I need one or not!) But just as it is true that "out of the overflow of the heart the mouth speaks," so also with the lack of the overflow of the heart, the mouth doesn't speak!

Contagious Christianity Begins with You and Me

The key, especially for leaders, is to do everything we can to keep our hearts warm toward God and toward people, and then to

The congregation needs to see that we genuinely live out our evangelistic mission, values, and strategy. If we want to build contagious churches, we as leaders must first become contagious Christians.

consistently express our hearts in ways that model this value of evangelism for the rest of the people in the church. The congregation needs to see that we genuinely live out our evangelistic mission, values, and strategy. If we want to build contagious churches, we as leaders must first become contagious Christians. There is no dodging the truth in the saying, "Speed of the leader, speed of the team." The biblical corollary comes from Jesus in Luke 6:40: "A student is not above his teacher, but everyone who is fully trained will be like his teacher." As leaders of would-be evangelistic churches, we need to be able to say with Paul, "Follow my example, as I follow the example of Christ" (1 Corinthians 11:1).

How important is this owning and modeling of evangelistic values by church leaders? *It's everything.* Unless you first catch God's concern for those outside his family, you may as well ignore the rest of the ideas in this book. Why? Because without a heart that beats fast for lost people, you won't have the foundation or spiritual resources needed to sustain evangelistic programs and ministries.

But if we grow bigger and bigger hearts for those who don't know Christ, and if we increasingly model his bold example of being a "friend of sinners," then those around us will take their cues from us. They too will begin to take strategic relational risks for the sake of the gospel.

LIVING A LIFE WORTH IMITATING

The preeminent question is, *how,* on a practical level, can we gain God's heart toward spiritual outsiders? Well, I'll share a few of my own ideas, but I also wanted to tap into the wisdom and experience of the wider community of outreach experts around the country; I wrote to many of them and asked what they do to keep their own hearts warm toward lost people. Their responses follow in the next several pages. Combined, I list fourteen things we can do to raise our evangelism temperature and keep it high.

1. Admit That Evangelistic Values Have Slipped

The first step to change is admitting there is a problem. Sure, we can all quote John 3:16 and talk glowingly about outreach-oriented mission statements or inspiring evangelistic stories from the past, but if your passion for reaching people isn't burning as brightly as it should, the best thing you can do is simply admit it.

This is what I had to do after my visit to the hair salon. I felt a low-grade guilt that I could either push down or listen and respond to. Why resist the Holy Spirit's whispers? We're always better off to acknowledge reality, let God put his finger on the problem, and deal with it accordingly. Many of us feel guilty when it comes to evangelism. When this guilt is from God, who "disciplines those he loves" (Hebrews 12:6), it is a gift from him designed to get us back on track. But we're not supposed to wallow in the guilt. Rather, we need to let it move us toward repentance and godly action.

Today you may have cared about lost people. Tomorrow there's no guarantee. We need to keep confessing our failures, keep "forgetting what is behind and straining toward what is ahead" (Philippians 3:13), and keep striving to do better. We must thank God for his grace in our lives and keep trying to spread more of it into the lives of others.

The most natural thing to do after admitting to yourself that the value of evangelism has slipped is to talk to God about it. The battle to raise this value to its proper place is won first in the private arena through heart-to-heart interaction with him in prayer. I like to use the time-honored *A-C-T-S* outline. Below is an example of this prayer formula applied to evangelism. You may want to use it as a guide for your own prayer.

A–Adoration

> *Father, thank you for being a merciful and grace-filled God. I worship you for your goodness toward me and for your patience toward my friends and family members who don't yet know you. Your Word says that you are slow to anger and that you don't want any of these people to perish but to come to know you. What a great and loving God you are! How gracious and forgiving! I'm glad you are my Lord and that I have the privilege of being your child.*

C–Confession

> *Lord, I'm sorry I so often fail to love lost people the way you do. You moved heaven and earth to reach them, you gave up everything when Jesus died on the cross, and yet I often resist taking even small steps to reach the people I know and care about. Even today, Lord, I saw an opportunity to speak,*

but I kept quiet. I'm really sorry. You are not willing that anyone would perish, but too often I think I am! Forgive me and change this attitude in me. Wash me of my sins of self-centeredness and fearfulness. Help me to know that as I've confessed these things, you've been faithful to forgive and to cleanse me.

T–Thanksgiving

Thank you that the payment Jesus made on the cross extends to me today. I'm so glad to be in your family, to know I'm forgiven, and to have the privilege of serving you. Thank you for putting purpose in my life and for entrusting me with opportunities to make a difference in the lives of people around me. Thank you that your love and grace are examples for me as I try to express my faith this day.

S–Supplication

Father, help me catch your passion and love for those around me. Help me remember that every person I lock eyes with today matters deeply to you. May they matter to me too in ways that move me to action. Help me realize that if they don't yet know you, they're lost and in desperate need of the good news of Christ. Lord, prepare me and give me boldness so I'll be able to explain the gospel and give good answers to their questions. Help me to be a genuine friend who will attract them to you and your church. Give me wisdom so I'll know how direct to be and when to back off, so that I can help them keep taking steps toward you.

Please, Father, use me! Make me skillful in your hands today as I try to spread your love and truth. Help me to abide in Christ and to bear much fruit. Thank you for this unspeakable privilege.

In Jesus' name I pray, Amen.

2. Stay Spiritually Authentic

Living a Christ-honoring, genuine Christian life is a prerequisite to having and expressing God's heart toward lost people. You have to be convinced, through fresh, ongoing experiences with Christ, that following him is the best way to live. You must have an unwavering conviction that all of your friends need what you have found in him—

then you will be motivated to tell them about his love.

Living a Christ-honoring, genuine Christian life is a prerequisite to having and expressing God's heart toward lost people. You have to be convinced that following him is the best way to live.

In *Becoming a Contagious Christian* we spent a lot of time talking about developing a contagious Christian character, especially in the areas of authenticity, compassion, and sacrifice. We also talked about the importance of the age-old spiritual disciplines, like prayer, Bible study, solitude, and fasting. These are the nuts and bolts of gaining the heart of God and of developing the spiritual potency needed in order to truly impact those around you.

Peter Grant, pastor of Cumberland Community Church in Atlanta, Georgia, wrote, "For me there's probably nothing more motivating for evangelism than time spent in God's presence. Out of that comes a compelling desire to share the Good News, not only of salvation past, but of salvation present and future as well."

Bob and Gretchen Passantino, who have faithfully reached out to skeptics for nearly three decades personally and through their ministry called Answers In Action (see Church and Ministry List in the back of the book), said this:

> Our first priority is not to raise the impact of evangelism in our ministry. Our first priority is to learn to discern and follow God's will in our lives individually, as a couple, and as a family.
>
> We don't believe that any ministry will fulfill God's plan if its members have not already consecrated their lives, marriages, and families to God through learning, discipline, experience, prayer, and accountability. It is very tempting to lose one's personal responsibility to God, spouse, and children in the complexity of a noble public calling. But how can we call others to Christian obedience if we are not personally obedient?

Notice the same progression in Psalm 51, starting with personal purity and commitment. First, King David repents of his sins:

> Hide your face from my sins
> and blot out all my iniquity.
>
> Create in me a pure heart, O God,
> and renew a steadfast spirit within me.
> Do not cast me from your presence

or take your Holy Spirit from me.
Restore to me the joy of your salvation
and grant me a willing spirit, to sustain me.

PSALM 51:9–12

Then, after addressing his own walk with God, David's natural next thought is to proclaim God's grace to others who don't know him:

Then I will teach transgressors your ways,
and sinners will turn back to you.

PSALM 51:13

Similarly, John 15:5 tells us that if we'll abide in Christ and let him abide in us, we'll bear much fruit.

3. Genuinely Worship God

"Supremely, I believe that the real incentive for witnessing comes from the worship of God," said Robert Coleman, author of *The Master Plan of Evangelism,*[3] in his response to my question. Coleman is a man who has modeled God's heart for lost people for over half a century. "It is the adoring love of Christ" he went on to observe, "that compels us to declare the glory of his grace. Of course, this love is not of ourselves; it is the fruit of the Holy Spirit. No one had to motivate the 120 Spirit-filled disciples in the Upper Room to go out and proclaim the wonderful works of God. Evangelism is the overflow of authentic Pentecost."

Time spent worshiping God, both in private and in public services, has a way of aligning our desires to his—which includes gaining more of his heart for lost people.

4. Spend Time Daily with God in Prayer

Not surprisingly, most Christian leaders responded that what keeps their hearts warm toward lost people is prayer. "I hang out with God every day," noted Becky Pippert, author of the classic book, *Out of the Saltshaker & into the World.*[4] "How can we engage in intimate dialogue with God and not become aware of his heart? The apostle Paul tells us that simply by gazing into the face of Christ we become transformed into his likeness (2 Corinthians 3:18). That means that the more time we spend in God's presence, the more . . . we have something to say and give to others."

Jon Gauger, an evangelism enthusiast at Moody Radio in Chicago, wrote, "I use printed-out prayers I've written on behalf of unsaved friends. This keeps me praying and doing some of the work even when my passion seems to have ebbed."

Lon Allison, director of the Billy Graham Center in Wheaton, Illinois, told me, "My prayer list for lost people has over forty names on it. As I bring them regularly before Christ, he increases my sense of urgency and compassion for them." He added that he regularly updates and adds to the list, and that this is a practice he has utilized for nearly a decade. What an encouraging model for the rest of us, to pray not only because of what God will do in the lives of our friends but also as a way to keep our hearts evangelistically in tune.

Joe Aldrich, longtime evangelism activist and author of the groundbreaking book, *Lifestyle Evangelism,*[5] wrote this to me:

> I find myself praying regularly for strangers on the street, as I did just this morning. I saw a young gal in her early twenties but who looked like she was twice that age. Obviously, she's had a rough time and needed the Lord. I couldn't stop the car, but I pleaded with the Lord to send someone across her path that could lead her to a living faith.
>
> I guess part of the reason I keep going is because the Lord has given me eyes for these kind of people and a burden to pray for them. I have had dry spells in my "efforts in evangelism." On several occasions I have prayed that the Lord would bring a prepared heart across my path, and sometimes within twenty-four hours that is exactly what happened. That is always a joy and confirmation!

Both Aldrich and Gauger also mentioned the benefits of *prayer walking.* They're not talking about doing anything that draws attention, but just quietly walking around their neighborhood with a focus on interceding for the people who live there. This results not only in God's response to these prayers but also in expanded vision and passion for reaching the people who live around us.

Jim Cymbala, pastor of the Brooklyn Tabernacle and author of the powerful book *Fresh Wind, Fresh Fire,* closes his book with this challenge:

> What is it really that stops us from becoming mighty warriors in the Lord? God has not changed. He is still superior to anything the enemy can throw against us.
>
> No personal or church situation is too hopeless for the all-sufficient power of the Holy Spirit. God will be no more eager to act tomorrow than he is right now. He is waiting for us to take his promises seriously and go boldly to the throne of grace. He wants us to meet the enemy at the very point of

> attack, standing against him in the name of Christ. When we do so, God will back us up with all the resources of heaven.[6]

What a great reminder of the importance and the power of focused prayer!

5. FOLLOW GOD'S PROMPTINGS

Another vital aspect of prayer is listening to God's voice and staying attuned to his leading. Chuck Colson wrote to me,

> I have disciplined myself to listen to the Holy Spirit. For example, I was giving the closing lecture at the C. S. Lewis Conference in Oxbridge recently, and in the prayer time ahead of my speech, one of my colleagues prayed for those who might be there from the Cambridge campus who were spiritually adrift or searching or seeking. Halfway through my talk when I was describing the influence of Lewis on my life, I stopped and said, "I'd like to share the same message with you that Lewis shared with me." We had a prayer of invitation in the middle of the closing address at the Oxbridge Conference! But that's only because I felt the prompting of the Spirit.

Lee Strobel relayed a similar experience that happened at a more personal level. He was meeting people after he had spoken at one of the seeker services at Willow Creek. A man poured out his heart to Lee about issues he was facing and told him how much he needed God's help. Lee said his natural inclination was to simply encourage the man and offer to pray for him. But Lee was dialed in to the voice of the Spirit, who prompted him instead to challenge the man concerning what was keeping him from trusting Christ. Before their time together was over, the man prayed with Lee to receive Jesus as his Forgiver and Leader.

Who knows what doors of opportunity God will take us through if we will just keep listening to his voice. God is actively reaching out to lost people. We just need to respond to his promptings and seize the opportunities he gives us. When we do, he'll use us to touch the hearts of others—and he'll also work in us, expanding our own hearts.

6. STAY IN GOD'S WORD

Bill Hybels, in his vision talk at the beginning of the *Becoming a Contagious Christian* training course video, tells how he was influenced early in his ministry by Jesus' words in Luke 15—where Jesus, in response to the hard-heartedness of the religious leaders, tells three stories in rapid-fire succession that illustrate how much lost people matter to the Father. Many others have been moved as they have studied and reflected on these lessons of the lost coin, the lost sheep, and the lost son—and the heart of God that is revealed through them.

I find myself motivated when I reread John 4 and see how Jesus interacted with the woman at the well. He took interest in someone society had labeled a nobody. He winsomely used her curiosity in order to raise spiritual topics of conversation. He forthrightly told her who he was. Then he allowed her time to go get her friends and bring them back to the well.

What impresses me most in this passage is that after spending time with this social outcast, Jesus summed up his experience by telling the disciples in verses 32 and 34, "I have food to eat that you know nothing about. . . . My food . . . is to do the will of him who sent me and to finish his work." In effect, he was saying, "I don't care who this person is or where she stands on the social ladder. I just had a chance to alter the eternity of a human being who matters more to my Father than any of you can imagine—*and I eat that up!*"

The reason Jesus' words affect me so much is that I've experienced what it feels like to be so caught up in the exhilaration of sharing Christ with another person that I really don't care about eating or sleeping or any other trivial physical matters. On the other hand, I've known all too often what it's like to be consumed by daily concerns and distractions and to lose focus on my primary purpose. So when I read Jesus saying, "My food is to do the will of him who sent me," my spirit says, "Yes! That's what *I* want to live like a lot more of the time. I want to feed on the satisfaction that comes from communicating the gospel to those around me." It raises the value of evangelism in me and warms my heart toward people and toward God.

Perhaps other passages besides Luke 15 and John 4 will impact you in similar ways: maybe John 3, Jesus' encounter with Nicodemus; Luke 19, the story of Jesus and Zacchaeus; Luke 16, the rich man and Lazarus; Acts 1 and 2, Peter and the spread of the gospel in Jerusalem; Acts 8, Philip and the Ethiopian; or Acts 26, Paul boldly taking a stand for the gospel and evangelizing some of the very people who put him on trial for his faith!

The list of Bible references goes on and on. A friend of mine who is a relatively new Christian commented to me recently that he is amazed at how much of the Bible is about reaching lost people. "It almost seems like every other verse is on this theme," he said. You may want to read through the New Testament and use a highlighter to mark all of the evangelistically oriented passages. But then go back to those that especially made your heart beat fast. Meditate on them, write them out, post them where you'll see them. Memorize some of them, and let God's vision fill your heart.

The Bible won't influence our lives much unless we get regular and frequent exposure to its contents. Yet, what pollster George Gallup Jr. and Jim Castelli once observed is still true today: "Americans revere the Bible—but, by and large, they don't read it."[7]

Let's change this trend, at least in our own lives. Let's stay in God's Word and watch how we'll gain God's mind and heart—especially toward those who don't yet know him.

7. Respond to the Truths of the Bible

Jim Petersen, author of the book *Evangelism as a Lifestyle* and the video training curriculum *Living Proof*,[8] wrote me this:

> What helps keep my heart for evangelism and the Great Commission? It's the gospel itself. It overwhelms me. The great truths of the gospel eclipse all else:
>
> - That the infinite God entered time and space and lived among us as one of us.
> - That he became the Lamb of God and died the way he did.
> - That he walked out of his tomb—destroying death forever.
> - That his Holy Spirit now lives in me, making his life mine!

On the more sobering side of the equation, Dr. D. James Kennedy, pastor of Coral Ridge Presbyterian Church in Fort Lauderdale, Florida, and author of the powerful program *Evangelism Explosion*,[9] said that one of the things that keeps his commitment to evangelism high is "the realization of the incredible blessings of heaven and the indescribable loss of hell."

Dr. James Martin, pastor of Mt. Olivet Baptist Church in Portland, Oregon, adds that he stays challenged by the fact that "the Bible says every individual must someday stand before the Lord in judgment."

And evangelist Luis Palau said in his book *Say Yes: How to Renew Your Spiritual Passion* that if we want to cultivate a heart of compassion for people, we must "believe absolutely what the Bible says about the eternal condition of the lost. Let the Lord's words about the hopelessness and agony of the lost sink in. He speaks of hell as a place of weeping, wailing, and gnashing of teeth."[10]

How can we be reminded of these truths and not be moved with concern and compassion—and the resolve to take decisive action?

In *Singing with the Angels,* Robert Coleman reports that when the infamous criminal Charles Peace was on his way to the scaffold, a prison chaplain offered him "the consolations of religion." He responded by turning to the chaplain and asking, "Do you believe it? Do you believe it?" Then, with obvious bitterness, he cried, "If I believed that, I would crawl across England on broken glass on my hands and knees to tell men it was true."

Coleman adds, "Indeed, if we really believe that Christ is God and that He died to save the world, then we cannot sit idly by while multitudes perish. Jesus is the only way whereby we can come to the Father. This message must be heard, else there is no hope for mankind."[11] Hell is real, and real people will spend eternity there. We can't allow ourselves to remain unmoved by this reality.

Before we move on, let me again address an important issue. A number of teachers and writers are having second thoughts these days about some of the hard teachings in the Bible, like the reality of hell, the narrowness of Jesus' claim to be the only way to the Father, and the absolute need for every person to hear and respond to the gospel. Their conclusions stem more from sentimental thinking than from thorough study of and humble submission to the message of the Bible. We must beware of teachers who "say what [our] itching ears want to hear" (2 Timothy 4:3)—even when they have evangelical credentials and teach in reputable churches, schools, or seminaries. Like Billy Graham did so many years ago, we need to make the deliberate decision to stick to the simple, straightforward teachings of Christ and the apostles as recorded in Scripture. They've proven true for hundreds of years and in millions of lives, and they will keep our hearts, minds, and ministries on track.

8. Obey the Commands of Scripture

Peter Wagner, professor of Church Growth at Fuller Theological Seminary and author of numerous books on the church and the Christian life, gave a direct answer to my question of how he keeps his heart warm for evangelism: "The day I accepted Christ in 1950, I dedicated my life to fulfilling the Great Commission." He made a deliberate decision to obey God and dedicate his life to the cause of Christ, and this decision set the trajectory he's still on today.

Similarly, D. James Kennedy told me that a primary thing that has motivated him these last forty years is the continued realization that Christ, in his first and last commands (Mark 1:17 and Acts 1:8), charges us to witness. "This was the passion of our Savior," said Kennedy. "He came 'to seek and to save the lost.'"

Mike Silva, frequent evangelistic speaker at Promise Keeper events and Palau crusades, said, "Initially I shared Christ out of simple obedience, but now I've become passionately addicted to the rush and exhilaration of leading others safely across the great divide."

John Ortberg of Willow Creek once said in a sermon that "loving feelings follow loving actions." This statement reflects what these other leaders are saying. If we'll obey Christ and take action, then joy, passion, and excitement won't trail far behind.

Maybe there's some evangelistic activity God has been leading you into. As you move in obedience, your heart will also grow toward the people you're trying to reach.

9. Review What God Has Done in Your Life

James Martin told me, "Because I know what I was and what Christ has done for me, I want others to know God's love and to experience the freedom and peace I have in Christ even in the midst of a troubled world." Gary Habermas, professor of Apologetics at Liberty University in Lynchburg, Virginia, echoed, "Our motivation is to introduce others to the best possible news in the universe!"

Similarly, Chuck Colson said,

> What happened in Tom Phillips's driveway twenty-five years ago when I surrendered my life to Christ remains as vivid in my memory and consciousness today as it was at the time. I have never forgotten—and I don't want to forget—what happened that night. I realized for the first time in my life that I was a sinner, desperately in need of salvation and forgiveness. And that night it became clear to me that God was offering that to me—that Jesus Christ the Son of God actually went to the cross, died in my place, and took my sins upon himself, enabling me to be free.
>
> Now, if someone does that for you, how do you respond? G. K. Chesterton said that gratitude is the mother of all virtues. One should be overwhelmed with gratitude for what God has done for us, and this gratitude then inspires us to do our duty, to do whatever God calls us to do. And the simple fact is that Jesus calls us to share that good news.

Time and again I've seen that when we review God's merciful activity in our own lives, our passion grows for spreading his mercy to others. Spend a little time writing or verbally explaining the story of how God reached you, and you'll find yourself becoming more motivated to tell others of his love and salvation.

10. Keep Your Evangelistic Edge Sharp

Our evangelistic passion increases whenever we are exposed to evangelistic training. I've certainly found this to be true over the years as I've had the privilege of training thousands of participants through the *Becoming a Contagious Christian* evangelism course. Many church leaders who teach that course or use other training materials have told me the same thing: Those leading the course, as well as their students, all get fired up to reach more and more people for Christ.

Passion for reaching others also grows when you hear a powerful sermon. I recently listened to a tape of Bill Hybels giving a message called "One Life at a Time."[12] It made me want to heat up the evangelistic fire further in my own life. Many others have reported similar responses to a five-week series we recently taught at our church called "The Unexpected Adventure."[13] Another tape with this kind of effect on listeners is called "When We Move Out," by the Moody Broadcasting Network.[14]

The same kind of motivation results when you read a good evangelism book. Just try to read the classics by Paul Little, *How to Give Away Your Faith,* and Rebecca Manley Pippert, *Out of the Saltshaker & into the World,* or the more recent works by Lee Strobel, *Inside the Mind of Unchurched Harry and Mary,* and George Barna, *Evangelism That Works*—and not have your evangelistic temperature rise.

There are also quality Christian videos that will rekindle your fire for outreach. The *Jesus* film[15] makes you want to give more of your life to that which Jesus devoted his life—loving and reaching others. John Nyquist, professor of Evangelism at Trinity Evangelical Divinity School, in Deerfield, Illinois, also mentioned the powerful effects of videos like *The Harvest,*[16] distributed by Campus Crusade for Christ, and *"EE-TAOW!"*[17] (the Mouk tribe responds dramatically to the gospel), distributed by New Tribes Mission. One of the most powerful motivational tools at our church is a video of new believers being baptized in our pond, with heart-stirring worship music playing in the background.

Expose yourself to fresh doses of evangelistic training and ideas as often as possible to keep at your evangelistic best.

11. Spend Time with Other Contagious Christians

One of the most important ways I keep my evangelistic fervor is by spending time with others who nurture this value in their lives. This is especially true of the time I spend with my close friend Lee Strobel. He and I have worked together in ministry for more than a decade. Without question, one of our favorite things to do is to go out for lunch with no formal agenda and just let our minds and conversation run free with ideas of ways to reach people for Christ. (Many of the events and ministries I talk about in later chapters have come out of these chats.) As Hebrews 10:24 puts it, we "spur one another on toward love and good deeds."

I recently spent time with another friend who is also in full-time ministry. Being around guys like him and Lee makes me want to work harder to evangelize outsiders. And, apparently, that influence can go both ways. His e-mail message to me illustrates the effect leaders can have on one another when we spend time together dreaming about reaching a lost world:

> Thanks again, Mark, for the burst of encouragement you have provided me—especially personally. I simply cannot express the wonderful feeling of being with brothers of like mind with regard to lost people. This is especially so in light of the spiritual desert I've felt I have been traveling alone in for so long. It's nice to have the wind at your back once in a while!

Who could you get a "burst of encouragement" from? It might be someone in your church, a leader from another church in your area, or someone from across the country—but whoever it is, find ways to get and stay in touch with them. Invest in the relationship. Encourage one another. Pray together. Challenge one another, and watch God work!

Robert Coleman and John Nyquist both said that these kinds of relationships not only give them encouragement but also provide them with needed accountability. We're just naturally more on our toes when we know someone is going to ask us who we're praying for or what kinds of relational risks we're taking with non-Christians.

As church leaders, we can also have a contagious effect on those with whom we spend time. The result will be increasingly expanded evangelistic hearts and greater fruit bearing.

12. Learn from Contagious Christians with Whom You Can't Spend Time

I know you can't have lunch with Dwight L. Moody, but you can read books like *A Passion for Souls*[18] by Lyle Dorsett and experience a similar effect. I don't think it's even possible to read about the life of Moody and not have your own passion for souls charged up. The same is true when you read books about people like Salvation Army founder William Booth, John Wesley, Hudson Taylor, William Carey, and many others.

Most of us don't have personal access to someone like Billy Graham, but we can listen to his messages and read his autobiography, titled *Just As I Am*.[19] When we do, some of his contagious influence rubs off on us. Rick Warren can have a similar effect through *The*

Purpose-Driven® Church,[20] as well as Bill and Lynne Hybels through *Rediscovering Church.*[21]

Even at a distance, people like Bill Bright, D. James Kennedy, Chuck Colson, Luis Palau, E. V. Hill, Elisabeth Elliot, John Guest, Ravi Zacharias, and Greg Laurie can impact our attitudes and help us become more driven to reach the seekers who live all around us.

13. Get in the Game

Other than the emphasis on prayer, the most common response I received to my question on how we can keep our evangelistic embers burning brightly was to simply spend time with seekers. After decades of teaching others to do evangelism, D. James Kennedy said that he continues "the discipline of going out weekly with our *Evangelism Explosion* teams, which keeps the edge on your evangelistic sword."

Kerby Anderson of Probe Ministries said he is "strengthened by the e-mail messages we get through our Probe Web page [www.probe.org]. The angry people who often write us are truly lost. This nearly daily contact with the lost world in cyberspace keeps me motivated."

Wayne Coreiro, a pastor who is extremely busy with his rapidly growing ministry at New Hope Church in Honolulu, Hawaii, told me one of the main ways he keeps motivated is to "take time to be with people. I play on a city league soccer team every Tuesday evening, I belong to the Rotary Club, and I often speak to companies about leadership, excellence, and restructuring. This keeps me in contact with non-Christians weekly."

Bob and Gretchen Passantino said, "We think one of the big mistakes Christian leaders make is that they tell their listeners to witness to the unsaved, but they themselves spend all their time in a Christian cocoon and don't regularly do what they teach others to do. There are lots of ideas that sound good, but until you experience their practical application, you can't effectively equip others to do the same."

Gene Appel, pastor of the dynamic Central Christian Church in Las Vegas, Nevada, said, "Nothing keeps my embers for the lost 'hot' like sharing my faith. The more I get to interact with lost people the more fired up I become. The more distant I get, the colder my heart gets."

Face-to-face evangelism, without question, is what most motivates me too. I can listen to good teaching about outreach, read Scripture verses about the priority of evangelism, and hear statistics about how many new unchurched families are moving into the neighborhoods around the church, but nothing moves me like getting to know some of these families. Then they're no longer generic "non-Christians." They are people I care about, with real names and faces. And I'll do whatever I can to try to help them meet Christ. How can you not value lost people when they've become your close friends?

14. Stay in the Game

Everything I've said to this point about raising our evangelism temperature will require a sustained effort. That's because this value—evangelism—always seems to be slipping. About the time you think you have it for good, it starts to dissipate. No one is permanently motivated to reach others for Christ. This motivation is like water in a leaky bucket that needs constant mending.

I call this the "second law of spiritual dynamics." Think back to your physics class for a moment. You may remember that the second law of thermodynamics tells us that everything in the physical universe, left to itself, moves toward disorganization. This principle is evident all around us, from the crumbling of old buildings to the rust underneath your car to the disarray in your sock drawer. The fancy word for this is *entropy.* (By the way, if you have forgotten these terms, that's just another illustration of this very principle! Our own minds move toward disorganization and entropy, so we forget facts like these.)

The second law of spiritual dynamics warns us that all of us in the Christian community, left to ourselves, move toward spiritual self-centeredness.

Similarly, the second law of *spiritual* dynamics warns us that all of us in the Christian community, left to ourselves, move toward spiritual self-centeredness. The evangelism value we're trying to reinforce must constantly compete with this gravitational pull inward. Another term I use for this is *evangelistic entropy.* With frightening speed, the warmest, most outreach-oriented hearts turn into cold, inwardly focused hearts.

Overcoming the second law of spiritual dynamics is possible, but it takes unrelenting effort and cooperation with the work of the Holy Spirit in us. We must make the full effort, doing everything necessary to expand our hearts for lost people and to own and live out our evangelistic mission, values, and strategy in ways worthy of imitation by the rest of the people in our church.

MODELING THE VALUES

How about you? Are you so busy with "church work" that you don't have time to do the most important work of the church? Especially as Christian leaders, we have to discard unnecessary meetings, appointments, and the ever-present sense of busyness, and make certain we are getting up close to the people we want to reach.

If you teach a strategy like the one presented in chapter 3, make sure people see you living it out. Let them watch you build relationships with lost people. Tell them about your efforts to start spiritual conversations and convey biblical truths to your friends. Tell them when it goes well, and tell them when it doesn't. They'll learn equally from your successes and your failures and will be inspired by both. Let them know when someone you're reaching out to attends an outreach event you've sponsored. The people in your fellowship need to know that you are working as hard or harder than they are to reach friends.

A primary reason Willow Creek is an evangelistic church is because Bill Hybels consistently owns and models this value in visible ways. You may have read in the opening pages of the *Becoming a Contagious Christian* book about Bill's decision to participate in sailboat racing with a completely non-Christian crew. Recently Bill informed our congregation that the fourth person from his racing team circle made a commitment to Christ after one of our holiday outreach services. Then, during our summer baptism service we all watched Bill baptize Dave in our pond. This kind of experience obviously will keep Bill motivated, but it also inspires the rest of us.

ENJOYING THE ADVENTURE, DANGERS AND ALL

If you think about it, Bill's decision to put together a crew of non-Christians was a risky move. What about the bad influence they may have had on him? What about the negative impact they may have had on his reputation as a Christian leader?

I've found that no matter who you are, what role you have in the church, or what step God is leading you to take in evangelism, it will always feel risky. It might be a relationship to build, a conversation to start, a question to ask, a misconception to correct, a group to train, an event to innovate, or any number of other possibilities. Whatever it is, it's going to feel a bit threatening, and you're going to be tempted to put the action off or skip it entirely. Perhaps you've been avoiding it for some time already.

Both the Old and New Testaments say that "the righteous will live by faith" (Habakkuk 2:4; Romans 1:17). The Christian life involves living out our trust in and dependence on God. That was true in a grand way when we trusted God for salvation, but the text is saying much more than that. Notice Scripture does not say, "The righteous received eternal life by faith." Rather, it says we *live*—present tense—by faith.

Just what is faith? One way to view it is as "God-inspired risk taking": living with a simple trust in God's unseen promises and protection, obeying his unseen Spirit, building his unseen kingdom, looking forward to his as-of-yet unseen home in heaven. It is taking the risk of trusting him at his word and finding him to be completely trustworthy. A rough paraphrase of the verse might be, "The righteous will live lives marked by patterns of obedient, God-honoring risk taking." The question for you today is this: Are you living by that kind of biblical faith?

We must become *courageous* Christians if we're to become *contagious* ones. We must get on board with what Scripture and the Spirit are leading us to do.

We must become *courageous* Christians if we're to become *contagious* ones. We must get on board with what Scripture and the Spirit are leading us to do, even if it is new, even if it seems unorthodox, even if it might be misunderstood. We have to move ahead and set the pattern for the rest of the church. We need to lead the way and then, like the apostle Paul, say to the rest of the congregation, "Follow my example, as I follow the example of Christ" (1 Corinthians 11:1). We must show what it looks like to live out the value that lost people matter to the Father and to us. If we'll do that, soon these people will matter a whole lot more to the church too, and we'll be well on our way to creating and sustaining a genuine evangelistic culture. This is the kind of culture that will care for lost people in even greater ways than Wal-Mart cares for its customers.

Contagious churches grow out of the flaming hearts of contagious leaders. But as we'll see in chapter 5, you'll need to take intentional steps to transplant what's in your heart into the hearts of those around you.

DEVELOPING A RELENTLESS EVANGELISTIC SPIRIT

Before we conclude this chapter on owning and modeling evangelistic values, let me issue a challenge: Most of us need to do a lot more than merely turn up our own evangelistic thermostats a notch or two. We need to take more drastic measures. We need to get radical.

We often use phrases like, "We have to make outreach a *priority*," or "We have to develop evangelistic *urgency*." While these statements are true, they fall far short of conveying the level to which our commitment must rise. Try descriptions like "evangelistically obsessive-compulsive," or "bulldog-like tenacity," or "unstoppable evangelistic passion," and you get a lot closer. Picture a Smart Missile locked onto its target!

I know these ideas can be abused. Unbalanced Christians have given us all a bad name by pushing too hard, being manipulative, or becoming downright obnoxious. I understand that. But I'm not going to back off. Let me give a few examples of what I'm getting at.

I have a friend who took a week of vacation, drove alone from Chicago to Iowa to pick up a former college classmate, and then spent days driving with him all over the Midwest. Why? Because he wanted a lot of uninterrupted time to share with his friend the faith he'd found since they were together in college. Is that "balanced behavior"? I don't think so—no one has ever accused this friend of being balanced! It is certainly not *typical* Christian behavior. But on the last night of the trip, my friend's friend committed his life to Christ.

I know a woman who was so concerned about the salvation of her aging and ill father that she made special arrangements to have her already overscheduled pastor take a trip hundreds of miles away just so he could sit and talk with this man about Christ. She knew her pastor was effective in relational evangelism, and since she had not been able to break through to her dad, she decided to try to persuade her pastor to go. He did, and he helped her father move several steps closer to the cross. If this woman decides she needs Luis Palau or Josh McDowell to talk to her father, she'll find a way to get him there. Her radar is locked on.

I have another friend, Wende, who as a first-year Christian led her father, Bob, to Christ. Then the two of them began conspiring immediately to reach another family member, Uncle Lynn, who was aging and in poor health. They called him on the phone. They wrote to him. They sent him evangelistic books and tapes and *The Journey: A Bible for Seeking God and Understanding Life,*[22] designed for spiritual seekers—something Lynn had never admitted to being. Bob took several trips to the East Coast to try to talk to Lynn about his need for a relationship with Christ. They even arranged for a minister in Lynn's area to meet with him and encourage him to trust in Christ. The term *tenacious* seems tepid when I think of this father-daughter team. Recently Bob called to tell me he had taken yet another trip out East to visit Uncle Lynn—who committed his life to Christ! Then, just two weeks later, Lynn passed away. He is in heaven today to a large extent because Bob and Wende refused to give up, even at the risk of making him and other family members angry.

When I received Christ at the age of nineteen, I started telling my best friend and his girlfriend, Lisa, about what had happened in my life, and how they could know and follow Christ too. At the time, Lisa was more open than he was. So I went all out to reach her. I called her long-distance and shared my faith with her. I told her pretty much everything I knew about the Bible and Christianity—for three and a half hours straight!

When I got the phone bill, I concluded it would be more cost-efficient to just drive to where she lived and talk to her in person! So I invited my friend to ride with me five hundred miles from our town in North Dakota to her home in Billings, Montana—which gave me a thousand miles of drive time to challenge him with the gospel as well as the chance to talk to her face-to-face!

I was greatly disappointed on that trip when Lisa didn't become a Christian. A few months later we took another trip. Then I went on still another trip. On that third visit, after a long discussion, Lisa finally told me she had heard enough, that she was already religious, and that she was sure she was okay with God just the way she was. I tried the best I could to explain to her that there is a big difference between being religious and being in a relationship with Christ, and that I was fairly sure she didn't have that kind of a relationship.

Three weeks later she called to say that she finally understood what I had been trying to explain—because she had just given her life to Christ!

Can you see the pattern in these stories? As leaders and key influencers of churches, we have to do more than make incremental changes in our lives. We can't do minor tweaks of the dial and expect to have a contagious influence on the congregation we are seeking to change. We have to develop an unquenchable evangelistic spirit. We need to show by our words, demeanor, and actions that this is serious, serious business.

I close this chapter with the powerful words of Chuck Swindoll in his book *Come Before Winter and Share My Hope:*

> Extreme dilemmas are usually solved by radical adjustments. It used to be called "fighting fire with fire." Minor alterations won't do. If the situation is getting completely out of hand, a slight modification won't cut it. . . .
>
> Radical adjustments make waves, not friends. Heads sometimes roll and hearts often break. The uninvolved public seldom understands or agrees, especially at the outset. But the strange thing is that radical adjustments, more often than not,

make pretty good sense when reconsidered through the rearview mirror. After the fact, stone-throwing critics ultimately nod their approval . . . calling the decision "courageous" or even "visionary." . . .

Had Christ not taken a drastic step, sinners like us would've never survived the fall. We would never have been rescued. We would be permanently lost. The cross was God's incredible response to our extreme dilemma. Christ did something radical.

Now it's your turn.[23]

STAGE 1: KEY IDEA

Leaders must model contagious lives.

"Set an example for the believers in speech, in life, in love, in faith and in purity" (1 Timothy 4:12).

To Consider and Discuss

1. What pours gas on the evangelistic fire in your heart? What do you need to do to pour on a gallon or two today?
2. How much time are you investing in praying for those outside of God's family? How do you need to adjust your schedule to make more time for prayer? Why not take a few moments right now to pray for the people whose names you wrote down on page 72.
3. What is one area in which God has been prompting you to act or speak but you have been resisting?
4. What is one divine prompting you have responded to recently? How did God work through your efforts?
5. What practical steps do you need to take to immerse yourself in God's Word and let it ignite your heart for evangelism?
6. Consider making a commitment to tell someone at least weekly for the next month your story of how you came to faith.

5

STAGE 2: INSTILLING EVANGELISTIC VALUES IN THE PEOPLE AROUND US

I was having lunch with a couple of ministry leaders who wanted input on how they could raise the value of evangelism among their leadership peers. "We do a pretty good job of nurturing new believers and growing up those who are already followers of Christ," one said, "but we're weak in outreach. We want to help our ministry become effective at reaching people with the gospel. Where do you think we should start?" This was a great question—and a huge challenge.

These leaders already owned and modeled the values of evangelism in many of the ways we discussed in chapter 4. They did not lack a commitment or passion for reaching lost people. But the ministry they led was a different story. It was filled with warmhearted Christians who only knew what it was like to focus their ministry efforts on the already convinced.

In his book *The Purpose-Driven® Church*, Rick Warren tells of a survey done by Win Arn, a leading church consultant:

> He surveyed members of nearly a thousand churches asking the question, "Why does the church exist?" The results? Of the church members surveyed, 89 percent said, "The church's purpose is to take care of my family's and my needs." For many, the role of the pastor is simply to keep the sheep who are already in the "pen" happy and not lose too many of them.

> Only 11 percent said, "The purpose of the church is to win the world for Jesus Christ."[1]

Then the pastors of the same churches were asked why the church exists. Amazingly, the results were exactly the opposite. Of the pastors surveyed, ninety percent said the purpose of the church was to win the world, and ten percent said it was to care for the needs of the members. Is it any wonder we have conflict, confusion, and stagnation in many churches today?

In spite of the good intentions of their leaders, somewhere along the way most churches start turning inward. They begin investing more and more of their time, energy, and resources in plans that serve insiders almost exclusively. They don't think very much about how they can reach more people for Christ. They tend to focus on whether the pastor and the other leaders are doing all they should do in order to meet their needs and expectations.

When the mission of the church gets reduced to keeping the sheep in the pen happy, the mission is falling woefully short.

This trend is not entirely unreasonable; much of it is in line with the broader purposes of the church. But when the mission of the church gets reduced to keeping the sheep in the pen happy, the mission is falling woefully short. I'm sure the ninety-nine sheep in Jesus' parable believed they deserved the undivided attention and full protection of their shepherd. I can even imagine several of them complaining, "What's the big deal about finding one little lost sheep when there are so many of us right here who need a good meal and a warm place to sleep?"

Clearly in Jesus' mind it was—and still is—a big deal. Therefore, we have to try to overcome this tendency toward self-absorption.

ATTACK ON EVERY FRONT

My friends next asked me, "What do you think we should do to turn the tide and help our fellow leaders start to value this whole area of evangelism? What do you think it's going to take for our ministry to start reaching lost people again?"

"This may not be what you want to hear," I said, "but in my opinion, you're going to have to declare an all-out war! If you want to change values and create a real evangelistic culture, you're going to have to attack on every front—and do it relentlessly. You can't let up until your team is buying into a whole new set of priorities and living them out day to day."

Why was I so bold about this? Certainly not because I'm a person who enjoys warfare! I had three reasons: First, because *God has given his church nonnegotiable marching orders.* Jesus was clear about his own mission: He came "to seek and to save what was lost" (Luke 19:10). He later made it clear that, in similar fashion, he was sending us into the world to further this mission (John 17:18). Then, lest there be any confusion, he summarized our task one more time when he said in Matthew 28:19, "Therefore go and make disciples of all nations."

There is no ambiguity about our mission. We just need to keep it clear in our own hearts and minds and then get it into the hearts and minds of those around us. Pastor Gene Appel of Central Christian Church in Las Vegas, Nevada, put it to me like this: "When the church is absolutely clear on what the 'main thing' is, it makes you face it at every turn—in the way you pray, plan, prepare, preach, and give." This is true not just of the leaders but of everyone in the body who understands and supports the "main thing."

This brings me to the second reason I'm so emphatic about "declaring war": *I know from my own ministry of helping churches with evangelism how difficult it is to turn the ship around and get real ownership of the mission.* One of the greatest leadership challenges you'll ever face is trying to convince people to look beyond their own needs to the "main thing" of valuing and reaching those outside God's family.

One of the greatest leadership challenges you'll ever face is trying to convince people to look beyond their own needs to the "main thing" of valuing and reaching those outside God's family.

Third, *we really are in a war!* I know this is strong language that conjures up images of conflict, deadly weapons, and bloodshed. But it is the kind of battle we're actually fighting. Paul wrote in 2 Corinthians 10:3–5,

> For though we live in the world, we do not wage war as the world does. The weapons we fight with are not the weapons of the world. On the contrary, they have divine power to demolish strongholds. We demolish arguments and every pretension that sets itself up against the knowledge of God, and we take captive every thought to make it obedient to Christ.

And in Ephesians 6:12–13 he wrote,

> For our struggle is not against flesh and blood, but against the rulers, against the authorities, against the powers of this dark world and against the spiritual forces of evil in the heavenly realms. Therefore put on the full armor of God, so that when the day of evil comes, you may be able to stand your ground.

In our battle for the souls of men and women, we have an enemy who is giving it all he's got to try to sidetrack or stop us. It's going to take relentless effort and the power of the Holy Spirit if we're to prevail in our mission and mobilize our members to the cause.

OUR EXAMPLE FROM BUSINESS

In a very different context, think back to the example of Wal-Mart. Its founder Sam Walton personally modeled great customer service, and he also worked hard to instill this value into the people who worked for him. In his autobiography, *Sam Walton, Made in America,* we get a glimpse of his tenacious commitment to communicate this value. "For my whole career in retail, I have stuck by one guiding principle. It's a simple one, and I have repeated it over and over and over in this book until you're sick to death of it. But I'm going to say it again anyway: the secret of successful retailing is to give your customers what they want."[2] We must have that same kind of passion for instilling the biblical principle of giving people not necessarily what they want, but what they really need—the love and truth that are found only in Jesus Christ.

In a later section of the book, under the heading "Communicate, Communicate, Communicate," Walton adds emphatically, "The necessity for good communication in a big company like this is so vital it can't be overstated."[3] Do you remember the story of my first experience at a Wal-Mart? I was surprised by the level of service, including the attention of a friendly employee who walked over to see if I needed any help. Prior to the opening of this store, Walton had sat in front of a camera and broadcast a message by satellite link to Wal-Mart employees all over the country. He said to them,

> I want you to take a pledge with me. I want you to promise that whenever you come within ten feet of a customer, you will look him in the eye, greet him, and ask him if you can help him. Now I know some of you are just naturally shy, and maybe don't want to bother folks. But if you'll go along with me on this, it would, I'm sure, help you become a leader. It would help your personality develop, you would become more

> outgoing, and in time you might become manager of that store, you might become a department manager, you might become a district manager, or whatever you choose to be in the company. It will do wonders for you. I guarantee it. Now, I want you to raise your right hand—and remember what we say at Wal-Mart, that a promise we make is a promise we keep—and I want you to repeat after me: From this day forward, I solemnly promise and declare that every time a customer comes within ten feet of me, I will smile, look him in the eye, and greet him.[4]

Wow! You get the impression he was *serious,* don't you? It's no wonder he was able to build such a customer-oriented and successful organization.

THE CHALLENGE FOR US

Leaders who communicate a value as consistently and aggressively as Sam Walton did will reshape, over time, the culture of their entire organization. The same can be true for us in our efforts to instill evangelistic values in our church. We need to start, as we did in chapter 4, with stage 1 of our 6-Stage Process: "owning and modeling evangelistic values." There's an adage that says, "You can't give away what you don't already have." Applied here, it means the evangelism mission, values, and strategy we talked about in the first three chapters must take root first in our own hearts and lives.

Many well-meaning leaders stop there. They fail to spread this vision to the key influencers around them. They work in isolation, holding their dream of widespread evangelistic impact close to their chest. Or they forge ahead alone and try to plug in programs that worked successfully elsewhere. What they don't realize is that without broad ownership of outreach-oriented values, these efforts will almost certainly collapse. That's why we can't ignore stage 2 in the 6-Stage Process, which is "instilling the values in the people around us." This step is critical because, as Joe Aldrich wrote to me, "In my estimation, the number one challenge in churches is to get the leadership to not only model an outward focus, but to make it a matter of lifestyle in the congregation."

One of the most frequent questions I hear from church leaders is this: "We've reviewed your *Becoming a Contagious Christian* training program, and we think it looks pretty good. The only problem is, if we tried to run it in our church, we don't think anybody would come. Our people just aren't excited about getting involved in personal evangelism. What can we do to motivate them?"

Can you relate to this problem? In many settings evangelism is an "ought to" but not a "want to." People know they should be doing evangelism—or at least they know the church leaders think they should be doing evangelism—but the dreaded "E-word" evokes feelings of guilt, fear, and inadequacy. How can we overcome this obstacle? How can we help people get a new view of evangelism? What will it take to get them to see evangelism as a privilege and an adventure—one that can evoke feelings of "want to" or even "get to"?

How can we take this value and instill it in the hearts of those around us? Here are some ideas to help you get started. You may edit or add to the list as God leads.

INSTILLING EVANGELISTIC VALUES

Pray for It

Until the Holy Spirit is working through us and in the hearts of the people we're trying to reach, nothing of lasting value is going to happen. Therefore, we must pray and ask God to do his work. This needs to happen at several levels, the first being our own lives as leaders. It seems ingrained into some personalities that we should work hard and then pray only if we get stuck! But even Jesus, the very Son of God, prayed hard first—and then he worked. We need to follow his example.

Second, we need to equip everyone we lead to pray for the lost. In the *Becoming a Contagious Christian* evangelism course, we challenge every believer to keep an "impact list," which is simply a list of three names of people in their sphere of influence whom they want to see come to know Christ (like the one we started on page 72). The list helps us become intentional, and three seems to be a reasonable number of friends on whom we can actually focus. We teach them to pray regularly for the people on their lists and then to take steps to deepen those relationships and try to initiate spiritual conversations. This has proven to be a great way to get our people praying for and reaching out to their friends. I've recently been practicing what I call the "3-for-1 Prayer Plan," which entails praying for each of the three names on my list for at least one minute per day. It's simple but revolutionary, especially if you haven't been praying for lost people in the past.

Third, we should encourage outreach-related prayer times at the various team meetings, classes, and services that take place throughout the church. We occasionally do this in our church-wide worship services. We hand out cards on which people can write their friends' names. Then we ask them to pair up and take turns praying for their friends. This is a great way to raise evangelistic awareness and inspire commitment among the congregation's members. It also gets them involved all at once in taking a tangible step—praying—to reach people for Christ.

Another idea is to have a short prayer time at the end of your communion services. In addition to thanking God for the sacrifice of Christ on the cross, give members a moment to pray for one unchurched friend or family member they would like to have sitting next to them as a new brother or sister in Christ at a communion service in the near future. This will bring a whole new appreciation to the meaning of Christ's shed blood.

God promised, "If my people, who are called by my name, will humble themselves and pray and seek my face and turn from their wicked ways, then will I hear from heaven and will forgive their sin and will heal their land" (2 Chronicles 7:14). Is there any question that this kind of healing is needed? We *must* humble ourselves and pray.

Lead It

You and the leadership team of your church will need to make it clear that evangelism is central to what your ministry will be about. There is no room for debate on this issue. Why? Because our Leader has already prescribed what we're supposed to be about.

Jim Denison, pastor of Park Cities Baptist Church in Dallas, Texas, presented the centrality of evangelism to his church members in a compelling vision message I heard him give recently. He said:

> You know, we love to vote on things. We vote on everything! But not on this one thing—because this one is not up to us to decide. Jesus already told us what our mission is. When he said, "Go into all the world and make disciples," he didn't leave room for deliberation or debate. We just need to see his vision for the church, make that vision ours, and spend our energy finding ways to implement it as quickly and effectively as we possibly can.

You know the proverb, "Where there is no vision, the people perish" (Proverbs 29:18 KJV). People need to know where the church is going. They need to know that Christ's mission is your mission—and your top priority. So spell it out again and again. If you want people to become personally and sacrificially involved, you'd better convince them that your mission is biblical, Christ-honoring, essential, and urgent—and the lives and the futures of hundreds of people around them depend on it.

In his book *Doing Church as a Team,* Pastor Wayne Cordeiro said, "There's one thing worse than a church without vision. It's a church with many visions! In this kind of congregation, everyone is lobbying for their own personal agendas and the church ends up becoming a political body of individuals, each one pulling for his or her own viewpoint. With too many visions, a church will have the seeds of dissension at its very inception."[5] Then Wayne quoted Philippians 2:2 (NASB): "Make my joy complete by being of the same mind, maintaining the same love, united in spirit, intent on one purpose."

The pastor and leaders are responsible for making sure the church is aligned with the purpose Christ gave us: reaching people for him and helping them become fully devoted to him. Our people need to hear this over and over. They need to be reminded, refreshed, rechallenged, remotivated, and reinvigorated.

It's often said in corporate circles that the vision of any business must be restated every twenty-eight days or else workers lose sight of their purpose and revert to old, less productive patterns. What's true for industry, at least in this area, is true for us in the church. If we're to overcome the second law of spiritual dynamics—evangelistic entropy—it's going to take a constant lifting of people's vision in order to overcome the gravitational pull toward self-centeredness.

We all have roles to play in this effort, but the senior pastor in particular needs to lift the church's vision in small ways regularly and in big ways annually or semiannually. At our church we have an annual "Vision Night," where Bill Hybels teaches us again about our mission, values, and strategy, and then challenges every member to commit to doing his or her part in executing that plan. For many of us, it's one of the highlights of the year.

Tell the Truth about It

A vital part of leadership is honest and complete communication of the problem you're trying to overcome. If you've only had one genuine adult conversion through the ministry of your church in the last year, say so.

If thirty-six out of thirty-nine recent baptisms involved church transfers or children of church families, admit this to be the case. If you have a membership of 1,200, but only 400 people actively attend services each week, don't hide behind the 1,200 figure. If nine out of ten people who "make decisions" during altar calls are merely deciding to transfer membership from another church, don't pretend a revival is erupting. If only eighteen percent of the people in the neighborhoods around your church actually attend a church, let your members know about the problem. If the number has dropped three points since the previous poll, talk about it. If feedback from nonchurched visitors says that your church is unfriendly, or hard to relate to, or "stuck in the '50s," then make it a topic of constructive conversation.

In his must-read book, *Leading Change,* Harvard professor John Kotter says that the first step in bringing about change is to magnify the problem. "Establishing a sense of urgency," Kotter says, "is crucial to gaining needed cooperation. With complacency high, transformations usually go nowhere because few people are interested in working on the change problem." Later he adds, "People will find a thousand ingenious ways to withhold cooperation from a process that they sincerely think is unnecessary."[6]

The only thing worse than the pain of change is the pain of staying the same when change is what is really needed.

One of the most important ways we can convince people that change is necessary is by breaking the bad news of how far short we're falling in fulfilling our mission. This can come in the form of numbers or stories—preferably both. Bad news becomes the vehicle for good news if it causes action and growth. The only thing worse than the pain of change is the pain of staying the same when change is what is really needed.

Can you see why we started in stage 1 at the heart and values level? If lost people really matter to us, then we really have no choice but to move to stage 2 and try to spread these values and engage the church. We have to speak the truth, admit where we're missing the mark, and help people cultivate hearts that are willing to make the needed changes.

Teach It

Whether you are the pastor, a Sunday school teacher, a small group leader, or someone who speaks in one of the ministries of the church, you have a vital role. One of the most important ways you can raise the evangelism temperature in your church is through the straightforward teaching of these biblical values.

Teach regularly from some of the key passages we discussed earlier, like Luke 15, John 4, and Acts 1 and 2. Remember that the evangelism value, more than any other, is the one that needs to be lifted up over and over. Keep on teaching and reinforcing it by showing the actions of various leaders in the Bible, especially Jesus, the Leader *par excellence.* You may also want to present an evangelism series on a regular basis. This is one of the most effective ways to help people in your church see that personal evangelistic activity should be normative. It will help them develop what we sometimes call at Willow Creek "a redemptive want-to." Some of the series we've taught over the years include "Adventures in Personal Evangelism," "Becoming Brighter Light and Stronger Salt," and "The Unexpected Adventure."

During some of your messages or lessons, focus on your church's mission and show how it flows out of the teaching of Scripture. Also, help your listeners understand that what you're teaching is rooted in the original mission that drove the founders of your church—and probably of your entire denomination. Help them see that any changes needed are not really about something new as much as about something very old—the clear mandate of Scripture and the strong vision of your own spiritual ancestors.

Another area to speak about is the list of seven values we discussed in chapter 2, starting with the heart of God and how much lost people matter to him. You might want to highlight these values by drawing the picture I presented in that chapter on a chalkboard or on a transparency for projecting on a screen. In addition, teach frequently about your church's outreach strategy, along the lines of the three-part approach presented in chapter 3.

You can also help your people see that evangelism should flow naturally out of each individual's God-given personality. This can be explained through the six styles of evangelism,[7] which we'll look at in later chapters. It is freeing for Christians to realize they can be used by God to impact people's eternities while still being themselves.

From time to time you may also need to address the issue of separatism. Some people may have grown up in settings where leaders took Bible verses out of context to make it appear that we are to avoid being around non-Christians—that they're the enemy to be avoided at all costs. If any trace of this attitude or belief exists in your congregation, you need to go after it with passion. I wrote about this problem in the *Becoming a Contagious Christian Leader's Guide:*

> First, God does warn us to use caution, because the dangers are real. Jesus said, "I am sending you out as sheep among wolves" (Matthew 10:16a). That is a dangerous place for sheep to be, but notice that *he* is sending us out there. That is why we need to be "as shrewd as snakes and as innocent as doves" (Matthew 10:16b). He tells us later to go into the whole world on his behalf and promises that he will be with us to the very end (Matthew 28:20).
>
> Second, a closer look at the verses that talk about being separate reveals that they are referring primarily to separation from the *sins* of people, not the people themselves. Jesus prayed that we would be "in the world, but not of the world" (John 17:15). Jesus himself was accused of being a "friend of

sinners" (Luke 7:34), and, rather than denying it, he accepted the label and modeled it. We should likewise be friends with people in the world, without being a friend to or in any way compromising with the evil in the world.

Finally, in any relationship with nonbelievers, we must be certain that we remain the dominant spiritual influence. Whenever that ceases to be the case, then the other person becomes to us the kind of bad, corrupting influence that the Bible warns about (1 Corinthians 15:33). It is then necessary to pull back, at least for a while, and do whatever is necessary to reestablish our spiritual strength and stability. In this way we can stay on the offense rather than the defense.[8]

When it comes to instilling the value of evangelism, don't underestimate the importance of clear, passionate biblical teaching—you can't build a contagious church without it. And remember, the congregation must hear much of this teaching from the senior pastor. The people need to know that this value is championed at the highest levels of leadership. It is not the hobbyhorse of a few fanatics. It is not a side issue entrusted to one or two specialized ministries. It is mainstream to the entire church and church mission.

ILLUSTRATE IT

We can't rely purely on messages or lessons focused on evangelism to raise the evangelism value. Why? Because we have to cycle through a variety of topics and Scripture passages to serve a balanced teaching diet to the church. Nevertheless, this value needs to be lifted constantly.

So what can teachers do? You can continually elevate the value of evangelism through illustrations, even when you're teaching about something completely different. I heard Pastor Jim Denison present a message about the Holy Spirit, but he didn't just talk about the guidance, gifts, and nature of the Holy Spirit. He also emphasized the *influence* of the Holy Spirit, seen throughout the book of Acts as people who were filled with the Spirit testified boldly about Jesus Christ. Denison's listeners learned about the third person of the Trinity generally, but they were especially made aware of the Holy Spirit's desire to help us tell others about Jesus.

I remember a time when Bill Hybels was preaching about how we can discern God's will for our lives. One of his key illustrations was about a recent experience he'd had in which the Spirit led him to share God's love with someone who was sitting alone outside a store.

The main subject of his message was *guidance,* but a key value being reinforced was *evangelism.*

Keep this value in front of the people to whom you speak, no matter what your primary topic is at the moment.

Study and Discuss It

Another thing we can do is give members opportunities to study and talk about evangelism in small group settings. Doing so will help them process and digest evangelistic values. Studying key outreach-oriented Bible passages will be helpful, as will reading books like *Inside the Mind of Unchurched Harry and Mary, How to Give Away Your Faith, Out of the Saltshaker & into the World,* and *Becoming a Contagious Christian.* Small group study is especially effective when done in concert with teaching and vision casting from the pulpit and evangelism training made available in seminars or classes. Remember, we're declaring war—and attacking from every side!

Disciple It

A principle that has been drilled into leaders at our church for a long time is that life change happens best in small groups. As Bill Hybels puts it, "Most people don't really take our challenges to grow or change seriously until they hear them from across a dining room table."

If we are serious about instilling the value of evangelism into the people around us, we have to be involved in the direct discipling of others. Occasionally that may include direct wake-up calls to people who are refusing to let God's heart for lost people affect them. But more often it will be gentle reminders about this value and respectful questions about people's progress with those they are trying to reach.

I'm not suggesting heavy-handed, controlling kinds of discipleship. I'm talking about personal communication with a few key people who say they want to become more like Christ. I'm also talking about two-way accountability, where your colleagues have the freedom to ask you the same questions you're asking them. Another important aspect is actually partnering with these people by getting to know some of their friends and trying to help them communicate their faith to these friends. Jesus modeled this by sharing his life directly with his disciples for three years. Paul stated the principle in 2 Timothy 2:2: "The things you have heard me say in the presence of many witnesses entrust to reliable men who will also be qualified to teach others."

Who are some people you know who would be receptive to a deeper relationship as well as to consistent encouragement and partnership in the area of evangelism?

Inspire It

In his book *The Diffusion of Innovations,* Dr. Everett Rogers has shown that innovative leaders are willing to travel outside their normal circle to get new ideas and fresh inspiration.[9] Doing so expands their world, stretches their thinking, and lifts their vision, giving them a fresh perspective on their situation.

At one of the first Church Leadership Conferences at Willow Creek my vision for evangelism was radically and rapidly raised. I've seen the same thing happen in thousands of leaders over the years at our various conferences and training events and now especially each fall at our annual Contagious Evangelism Conference. God just seems to work in hearts and in teams at events like this.

Where could you go and where might you send other leaders and key influencers in your church to become inspired toward greater evangelistic vision and action? Willow Creek's conferences and regional training events are available to you,[10] as are a variety of events sponsored by other churches and organizations. The dividends for making moderate investments in training can be huge.

Personalize It

Most people are not moved by statistics or strategic initiatives alone; they need to see the issue on a personal level. Help members to see how evangelizing will affect the people they care about most. They may not be interested in a new evangelism emphasis until they start thinking about their son, daughter, or grandchild who has lost all interest in the church and in spiritual matters. Or perhaps they are concerned about a parent, friend, coworker, or neighbor. In any case, when a loved one's life and eternity are at stake, levels of personal interest and motivation climb sharply.

Following is a letter from a woman who had been happy with her church experience and initially didn't want the church to change. Notice what moved her to express openness to fresh approaches:

> I would like to add my vote for having a regular contemporary worship service in our church. My husband and I have four kids who would greatly benefit from this type of service. Three of them will not attend a traditional service but have said they would attend a service that had "cool music." I have also talked with other people and invited them to church, but they think the traditional service is "too stiff and boring." I believe that if we are going to reach out to all of our community and the lost, we *have* to offer something more appealing to them, yet

with the true gospel message. Please help this type of service happen at our church.

As I stated earlier, we need to create urgency for change. One of the best ways to do this is to remind people that reaching their own children, relatives, and friends will very likely require some new approaches.

Fund It

Churches often make the mistake of raising the rhetoric about outreach without budgeting the resources needed to back up the talk. George Barna reports in *Evangelism That Works* that "the average annual budget allocated by the typical church for all of its local evangelistic endeavors amounts to only about 2 percent of the gross annual revenues received by the church."[11] If we are going to build a contagious church, we need to invest well beyond that paltry level. Money is needed at every stage, from planning meetings and retreats, to attending evangelism conferences and workshops, to training costs, to team-building events, to personnel expenses for setting up and overseeing evangelistic work, to sponsoring quality outreach events. Although evangelism can be expensive, the money spent is truly an investment in the souls of men, women, and children, and it will lead to the future health and vitality of the church.

Where can you find enough money? First, *expand this part of your regular budget and make the needs known.* If there is no section of the budget for evangelism or local missions, add one. Second, *ask key donors in your church to help you reach more lost people.* Wise kingdom investors are usually more than willing to give to evangelism, because they know it will bring lasting returns to people's eternities and to the church.

A major step toward growing our hearts for people is opening our wallets for evangelism. Jesus said in Matthew 6:20–21: "Store up for yourselves treasures in heaven, where moth and rust do not destroy, and where thieves do not break in and steal. *For where your treasure is, there your heart will be also*" (emphasis added).

Schedule It

Just as we should invest our money in things that really matter, so too with our time. Remember what I quoted my friend saying earlier—that if this value really takes root, it will show up in your checkbook *and in your calendar.* That is true on a personal level as well as on a church-wide level. Making time for evangelism will mean scheduling rooms and time slots for outreach-oriented prayer times, training seminars, strategy sessions, team meetings, outreach events, and perhaps seeker services. It might also mean going on multiple-day trips to observe effective churches and ministries or to attend vision-lifting conferences and workshops.

Be warned about two things. First, conflict will occur when outreach needs compete with established programs designed for the nurture of believers. The Catch-22 is that you need these training and outreach events, in part, to help build believers' hearts for evangelism. But what if there isn't enough heart there yet to make room for the events? My advice, which is distilled from some insightful teaching by Gene Appel in a message called "Your Church's Next Step" at one of our Church Leadership Conferences, is to stretch as much as you can now, but don't push too far too fast. As people see the fruits of these efforts and feel the exhilaration of watching God work in the lives of their friends, support will grow and other things will start to move out of the way.[12]

A second warning: In scheduling outreach training and events, don't wait until you feel completely prepared or until you've caught up on your other goals. It will never happen! Renowned motivational speaker and author Les Brown says that in fulfilling our goals the secret is to "make your move before you are ready." It's like the challenge, "Leap and the net will appear!" I suppose this advice could be abused, but my experience tells me that when it comes to evangelism, it's usually right.

Measure It

We need to measure our evangelistic effectiveness so we'll know where we're making progress and where we need to put more effort. As the saying goes, "If you can't measure it, you can't manage it." Some opportunities for measuring are counting conversions, baptisms of new believers, attendance at outreach events, people in seeker small groups, people in training courses, and members involved with your evangelism team. You may want to track some or all of these factors.

As you're instilling values in the people around you, beware of the wrong benchmarks. The ultimate question is not whether your church is larger than it used to be or that it's even the biggest in town. We sometimes have attendees come up to us at Willow Creek and say things like, "We already have 17,000 people attending—isn't that enough?" Our standard response is, "No, not as long as there are still lost people within our reach!"

We have to aim high—Jesus says to go into *all* the world. And we need to track progress so we know when to reexamine our strategy or increase our efforts, as well as when to celebrate success.

REINFORCE IT

One of the most important but neglected ways to fight against evangelistic entropy is to reinforce the good things that are happening by affirming the people who are in the middle of the action. We need to make heroes out of ordinary Christians who have had a contagious influence.

George Barna notes with surprise in *Evangelism That Works* that even among the most outreach-oriented churches, there is a tendency to "recognize the evangelized but essentially ignore the evangelizers."[13] Obviously we need to be careful how we give recognition. We don't want to start giving out merit badges to those who have led the most people to Christ. But it's amazing how far a word of thanks from a leader will go. This gratitude can be communicated through a note, a phone call, or perhaps a mention at an appropriate place and time during a ministry meeting or public worship service.

One of the most important but neglected ways to fight against evangelistic entropy is to reinforce the good things that are happening.

One of the things we have begun to do at our church is encourage friends and family to accompany new believers when they're being baptized. Often this results in having the person who was the primary influence in leading a new believer to Christ stand in front of the church with that person during the baptism and then during the ensuing celebration. This gives honor to the evangelizer while reinforcing evangelistic values in all who watch.

I saw a little different twist on this at Spreydon Baptist Church in Christchurch, New Zealand, during a high school ministry baptism service. Friends of the person being baptized were allowed to get up and say a word or two to encourage him or her. This was meaningful to the one being baptized, and it gave the evangelizers the opportunity to participate directly in the event that represented the culmination of their efforts.

Those doing evangelism often feel like they're out there all alone, cut off from the centralized activity and warm fellowship of the church. It's vital that we affirm them and, in front of the entire congregation, underscore the importance of what they're doing.

CELEBRATE IT

Nothing fires up an individual Christian or a church more than seeing the tangible results of evangelism in the form of new believers! We need to find appropriate ways of telling stories about how they came to

Christ or, without setting them up as role models or teachers, letting them tell their own stories. This can be accomplished in person or through various forms of media, including audio, video, or newsletters.

One of the reasons to turn up the heat in evangelism is so we can reach a lot of people as quickly as possible. The vibrant presence of new believers will generate excitement in a church, benefiting both seekers and believers. Tom Youngblood, vice president of U.S. Field Ministries at International Bible Society, described to me the effect on Christians: "Lead a seeker to Christ and you will experience spiritual growth on steroids!"

Once we get through the initial inertia, evangelistic activity can begin to build on its own success. Tell the stories, profile the testimonies, celebrate the changed lives, and expand on what God is doing in your midst.

RESULTS OF INSTILLING EVANGELISTIC VALUES

When we "declare war" and apply the preceding steps to lift up evangelistic values, three things tend to happen.

Most People Accept the Values

Renewing your commitment to evangelism will deepen the value in the majority of the people in the church. When you insist on emphasizing a biblical value like evangelism, and when listeners are committed to the life-changing truth of the Bible and are led by the Spirit, they generally respond with great enthusiasm. Over time the evangelistic temperature rises in each person and in the church collectively.

A Few People Resist the Values

Invariably, when you draw a line in the sand, a few people will refuse to accept it. Some just need a bit of time. Change is hard for everybody, but for some people it is downright painful. We must be patient and empathetic and realize that people will often say negative, reactionary things out of a fear of the unknown. Later some of them will be won over and wish they hadn't said what they did. A few of them may even become your strongest advocates, and they'll thank you for standing firm on what the Scriptures say about the church and its mission.

But not all of them! For a variety of reasons, some people will be unable to go along with you and the other leaders in your efforts to reach lost people. They may like the broad concept but not the methodology or the ministry style. In the long run, these people may be happier if they find another church that better fits them.

And some people won't even like the broad concept! I hate to say it as much as I hate to see it, but there are some people who profess to be Christians yet who don't care one whit about people outside God's family. They are typically self-centered people who think the church revolves around them and exists solely to meet their needs, and everyone else can go to hell—*literally.* These people need to be confronted directly for their sinful attitudes and called to repentance. The hope is that they will turn around and begin to develop a love for lost people. If this happens, everybody wins. But if they refuse, you must hold firmly to God's guidance and the priorities of his Word for your church.

Be advised, though, that if those who resist your evangelistic values leave, they'll likely do so with a very different perception of reality than you and the other leaders in your church have. Some will be very vocal about what they describe as your overbearing leadership, your unbiblical ideas, your watering down of the gospel, or—fill in the blank. Some of what they say will shock you. Listen to their complaints calmly, but don't give an immediate response. Search your heart to see if there's any grain of truth in what they're saying, and, if so, address it humbly. Then do your best to gently but firmly confront any errors or misrepresentations in what they are saying—and after that move on. Be patient, but don't get sidetracked. You have to keep your focus on the ministry God has given you.

New People Will Be Attracted Who Carry the Values

On the brighter side, an exciting phenomenon occurs when you lift up a vision and commitment to evangelism: New people who already *have* the value will be attracted to your church! Contagious Christians are looking for a church that is serious about reaching lost people, and when they find one, they are excited to join and advance the cause.

A number of years ago, right after I'd first started attending Willow Creek, I heard rumors that Marie Little had been visiting our services. Marie is the widow of Paul Little, who wrote such books as *Know What You Believe* and *Know Why You Believe,* as well as the wonderful classic volume on personal evangelism *How to Give Away Your Faith.* The rumors turned out to be true, and I soon met with and befriended Marie. She later told me that when she first started coming to our church, friends from her previous church were surprised that she would pick what seemed to be such a youthful, raucous place. I'll never forget what she told them: "All I know is that people are getting *saved* over at Willow Creek—*and I've got to be where the action is!"* For more than a decade now, Marie Little has been one of our key volunteers and one of our brightest examples of those who love lost people, as she has helped lead numerous people to Christ and discipled even more.

The point is not that we should try to recruit people from other churches—we didn't recruit Marie. What I'm saying is this: When a church turns up the heat on evangelism and says with its words and its actions, "We're going to burn brightly with evangelistic intensity," it won't be able to keep away evangelistically impassioned Christians from the surrounding community. They'll simply insist on being where the action is.

Why can't that be your church?

It can if you'll first own and model evangelistic values, and then with God's help do all you can to instill those values in everybody around you. We need to do these things not only until there are a few more warm hearts for lost people, but until there is a strong and growing evangelistic culture. You'll know you have developed that kind of culture when caring for lost people becomes the normal way of life, when increasing numbers of people are coming to faith, and when the mind-set of both the leaders and the members is to do whatever it takes to reach more and more people for Christ.

STAGE 2: KEY IDEA

Create a contagious culture.

"Hold to the standard of sound teaching that you have heard from me, in the faith and love that are in Christ Jesus. . . . and what you have heard from me through many witnesses entrust to faithful people who will be able to teach others as well"
(2 Timothy 1:13; 2:2 NRSV).

To Consider and Discuss

1. What are clear signs that a church has declared war when it comes to reaching lost people?
2. What will a church look like if its leaders refuse to declare war in this vital area?
3. If you have a leadership role, how can you get into the action by teaching or influencing your church?

4. How can you invest more time and energy in praying for lost people?
5. Would you commit to implementing the "3-for-1 Prayer Plan" (see page 117) this week? For whom will you pray?
6. Take time to examine your checkbook and calendar. How are you doing in terms of investing in evangelism?
7. When you consider your church's calendar and budgets, how do you think it is doing in terms of prioritizing evangelism?
8. What one or two scheduling or budgeting changes would you suggest to help your church raise its evangelistic effectiveness?

6
STAGE 3: EMPOWERING AN EVANGELISTIC POINT PERSON

I was feeling good. I had just poured out my heart for a day and a half to a gathering of friendly and responsive senior pastors at an East Coast conference. They seemed to have hearts for lost people and appeared to connect well with the approaches I shared. I had encouraged them to keep their passion levels high for the Lord and for lost people, and I had talked about the importance of instilling this value in the people around them, especially in their fellow leaders. I had presented practical ideas for training all the members of their churches in relational evangelism and for doing team evangelism in the form of innovative outreach ministries and events.

If you're a speaker, you know that some days you're on, and some days you're not. This was an *on* day! When the sessions were over, I got plenty of encouragement and positive feedback, and I felt confident the conference would rejuvenate evangelism in many churches.

What happened next burst my bubble.

A RUDE AWAKENING

The pastor who had arranged for me to speak at the conference mentioned that he'd have to drop me off at the airport a few minutes early. He said he needed to do a hospital visit before going back to his office for final preparations on the sermon for the next morning.

"Oh," I said, "is somebody in your church sick?"

He smiled. "Someone in our church is *always* sick," he said. "We have an aging congregation, so I'm constantly making trips to the hospital."

"And," I said, hoping for more of a good-news answer, "how many other people are on the ministry team that visits people in the hospital?"

"Just me," he said. "I've tried to involve other people, but our members really want—and expect—an appearance from the pastor. So I'm doing visitations almost daily. On top of that, there are all the funerals I have to do—about thirty funerals last year alone!"

"Thirty funerals—all by yourself?" I asked with amazement, starting to feel a bit uneasy. "So you must not do all of the teaching on Sunday mornings, right? Do you have a team of teachers who preach on a rotating basis?"

He looked surprised. "I'm the *pastor,*" he said patiently. "I do all of the preaching, not just every Sunday morning but also every Sunday night and every Wednesday night. I'm up front teaching three times a week."

"My goodness!" I exclaimed. "How in the world do you keep up with preparing and delivering three messages a week, a funeral every other week, and a hospital visitation almost every day? You don't do the weddings too, do you?"

At this point he gave me a look that said, "You just don't get it, do you?"

"Yes, I do the weddings, as well as the premarital counseling—not to mention pastoral counseling later if there are problems," he said. "And to tell you the truth, it's really tough keeping up with my ministry and trying to be a good husband and father in my own family too."

All these pastors left with great intentions, and their spirits were saying "yes" to seeing growing numbers of lost men and women coming to Christ through their churches. But they simply can't do it all.

"I'm seeing that," I said, my mind reeling. *And,* I thought to myself, *there's not a chance in the world he'll be able to find the time or energy to employ the ideas he heard me teach at the conference today. All these pastors left with great intentions, and their spirits were saying "yes" to seeing growing numbers of lost men and women coming to Christ through their churches. But they simply can't do it all.*

LESSONS LEARNED

That day marked me. It left me with three distinct impressions. The first was a deepened respect for the many faithful pastors who deserve honor for the incredible effort they put into their ministries day after day, week after week, year after year. The next time we're ready to criticize something the pastor did or did not do, we need to pause and extend some grace. We need to honor those who so steadfastly serve us. As Paul says in 1 Timothy 5:17, "The elders who direct the affairs of the church well are worthy of double honor, especially those whose work is preaching and teaching."

My second impression, however, was that the church as a whole needs to get back to a more biblical way of doing ministry. We claim to believe in "the priesthood of all believers." Many churches even put it in print with statements like, "We have one pastor but many ministers," implying that every member is actually serving in a ministry position.

This *sounds* good, but look around. Is it true? Often the reality is that there is one person who is both pastor and minister, and then there are many helpers. These helpers are assigned to limited and often menial roles, while the pastor is dying while trying to keep up with all of the real ministry functions. This approach will nearly (and in some cases, perhaps, *actually*) kill the pastor, and it will limit the quality and quantity of the ministry happening in and around the church. It will also squelch the spiritual passion and potential of the people in the church. Romans 12:3–6 says,

> For by the grace given me I say to every one of you: Do not think of yourself more highly than you ought, but rather think of yourself with sober judgment, in accordance with the measure of faith God has given you. Just as each of us has one body with many members, and these members do not all have the same function, so in Christ we who are many form one body, and each member belongs to all the others. We have different gifts, according to the grace given us.

It's time to start letting all the members express themselves and their gifts in meaningful ways.

But, as you know, change is not easy. It requires the teaching—and gradual acceptance—of a whole new set of expectations. For example, people need to understand that when they're in the hospital, they will be visited by those in their closest circle of fellowship, and then, additionally, by a volunteer member from the church's pastoral care team. This person should have the gifts, passion, training, and energy to make the visit. Possessing these qualities, combined with sheer availability, means he or she can generally minister more effectively than the pastor could have.

Who wins in this equation? Everybody!

The hurting people win because they are ministered to by people who can focus on serving them. The ministering people win because they experience the joy, fulfillment, and affirmation that come with serving according to their gifts. The pastor wins because he can concentrate on his primary roles. And, consequently, the whole church wins because all members can now be better led and taught.

Remember how the early church followed this pattern in Acts 6:2–5?

> The Twelve gathered all the disciples together and said, "It would not be right for us to neglect the ministry of the word of God in order to wait on tables. Brothers, choose seven men from among you who are known to be full of the Spirit and wisdom. We will turn this responsibility over to them and will give our attention to prayer and the ministry of the word." This proposal pleased the whole group.

And what were the results of this decision? This is what Acts 6:7 says:

> The word of God spread. The number of disciples in Jerusalem increased rapidly, and a large number of priests became obedient to the faith.

In short, this biblical approach to dividing the labor frees up pastors—like the one sitting across from me that day—to better own and model evangelistic values and then instill them in the people in their church.

We need to select and empower a leader who will partner with the pastor in championing the evangelism cause.

I realize I've opened a huge subject here, but it's a vitally important one if we're to build contagious—or, for that matter, healthy—churches. For further reading, I recommend *What You Do Best in the Body of Christ* by Bruce Bugbee[1] and *The New Reformation: Returning the Ministry to the People of God* by Greg Ogden.[2] More than that, I urge you to use a program such as the *Network* training curriculum, developed by Bruce Bugbee, Don Cousins, and Bill Hybels.[3] It is an eight-hour course that will, if taught repeatedly over time, help all your members discover their God-given spiritual gifts, ministry passion, and personal ministry styles so that they can be placed in appropriate ministry positions.

This leads to the third thing that struck me that day: Most of the big ideas about making a church evangelistically effective are never going to materialize if we are relying on senior pastors to do all of the work. Instead, *we need to select and empower a leader who will partner with the pastor in championing the evangelism cause* and then lead the way in implementing a strategic outreach plan.

THE MISSING PERSON

In keeping with our "declare war" motif, let's look at what Robert McNamara, the United States secretary of defense (who served in the administrations of presidents Kennedy and Johnson), said in his recent book *In Retrospect* about a leadership mistake made by the U.S. government during the Vietnam War.

> No senior person in Washington dealt *solely* with Vietnam.... We should have established a full-time team at the highest level—what Churchill called a War Cabinet—focused on Vietnam and nothing else.... It should have met weekly with the president at prescribed times for long, uninterrupted discussions.... The meetings should have been characterized by the openness and candor of the Executive Committee deliberations during the Cuban Missile Crisis—which contributed to the avoidance of a catastrophe.[4]

Did you catch that? No single individual was in charge of figuring out what the United States should do during the Vietnam conflict. What a shocking revelation!

Bill Hybels applied this illustration at a Leadership Summit conference:

> Some of us do the same thing. We say we need a thrust in the area of evangelism. So we talk about it, we identify it, but we never assign it to a person. We never say, "Look—we're going to ask you to put this as the front-burner item on your job description. We need you to lead us up that hill. Here's the path, here are some mile markers. We're going to meet back regularly to see that you're making progress."
>
> Friends, if you don't do that, you're going to be in trouble. You won't make the progress you want to make.
>
> If pastors are going to juggle multiple challenges, the challenges must be identified and prioritized. Then someone has to carry the ball. Someone has to be thinking full-time, either on a lay-level or a paid-staff basis, about just that one chal-

> lenge. This person needs to be pulling in teams around himself or herself in order to make progress.
>
> We have to manage the progress of those people. We have to evaluate the rate, and the process, and the strategies, and the achievements of these thrusts that we're trying to make. Are things moving quickly enough? Are they moving too slowly? Are the problems being solved appropriately? Do we need more resources or more expertise? It has to be managed to the point of effectiveness.

Using a different metaphor, my friend Karl Singer, a leader in the financial services industry for many years, put it to me like this: "Any business that wants to succeed over the long haul must do two things really well: Give great service to its present customers, and constantly acquire new customers." Then, with characteristic frankness, Karl looked me in the eye and asked, "So why is it that most churches—churches that *say* they want to prevail for generations to come—don't have *anyone* in charge of acquiring new business? If they're serious about surviving in the future, they're going to have to find and equip the missing person whose job it will be to reach people outside the church."

STRATEGIC MINISTRY REQUIRES STRATEGIC LEADERSHIP

Can you imagine a church without a head of children's ministry? *Somebody* has to be responsible for the care and teaching of the children. What about students? It is almost inconceivable that a church would try to function without a youth minister. And adult education? If church leaders take seriously Jesus' mandate to teach people to obey everything he has commanded us (see Matthew 28:20), they must put someone in charge of adult education. Just go down the list: music directors, worship leaders, choir directors, Sunday school superintendents, camp directors. Whenever a ministry is deemed important, somebody is put in charge of it. That person may be a paid staff member or a volunteer, but if the ministry matters, you'll be able to find a name on it!

Yet in most churches you'll find no name when it comes to evangelism. Or there may be several names but no one really responsible. Or there may be one name, but outreach is just one of eight "priorities" on that person's job description—and in reality it generally falls to number seven or eight. Or the senior pastor may be in charge of evangelism. As I've shown earlier, the pastor must be involved, especially at the broader leadership and vision level, but the pastor will never find the time to start and manage everything needed to make a church truly contagious.

That's why stage 3 of our 6-Stage Process says we must "empower an evangelistic point person." We need to find a leader who has the right mix of gifts, experience, and abilities. He or she must be given the freedom to focus. Call the role Director of Evangelism, Pastor of Evangelism, Associate Pastor of Outreach, or whatever creative title you come up with, but every church ought to appoint and empower someone to fill this vital role.

When possible the evangelistic point person should be a paid staff member so that he or she can spend sufficient time each day furthering the cause. If the church cannot afford to pay a point person (as will often be the case, at least initially), then find the best volunteer leader you possibly can. Challenge that person to give the position everything they've got. As seekers are reached and the support base of the church grows, the position might naturally expand into a staff role.

You might be thinking, *This must be a "big church" concept; at our level, we could never think of having someone focus just on evangelism.*

Well, big churches do need an evangelistic point person, but so do smaller churches—perhaps even more so. Often in smaller churches much of the work is done by one person, the pastor, and there is very little division of labor. Intentional evangelism, therefore, with all of its challenges and demands, typically gets relegated to a later time. "We're already too busy just keeping up with meeting the needs of our small congregation," the logic goes. "I can't imagine how hard it would be if we started getting a bunch of new people to join us!"

This situation never improves much on its own. Five or ten years later, the pastor is *still* trying to keep up with meeting the needs of the members. The key is to start implementing division of labor now—regardless of your church's size—and to view new people not so much as people the church will need to serve but as potential members who will soon serve and support the church. This mind-set, combined with taking the real step of empowering the right person to take the evangelistic lead, can begin to revolutionize your church and its potential for future growth and impact.

THE MISSING PERSON PROFILE

Identifying the right leader may not be easy. What does he or she look like? Although it's hard to paint a comprehensive picture, let me list some important attributes under the broad headings of *character, competency,* and *chemistry.* You won't find all of these to the same degree in any one person, but I'd proceed with great caution if any are weak or missing.

Character

- unquestioned integrity and reputation
- authentic walk with Christ
- heart for lost people
- passion for the truth of Scripture
- courageous and persevering

Competency

- proven leadership skills
- projects a vision for limitless kingdom growth
- track record of impacting seekers for Christ
- strong desire to equip others for evangelistic impact
- able to articulate and defend Christian doctrine
- creative strategist, organizer, and communicator
- able to promote ideas and rally support

Chemistry

- strong affinity with the senior pastor
- relates well to a broad range of personality types
- works with teams and can accomplish goals through groups
- approachable, open to the ideas and evangelistic styles of others
- has an enthusiastic lifing influence with the church

FINDING THE MISSING PERSON

Where do we find this missing person?

Apply the first two stages in our 6-Stage Process: (1) Own and model evangelism values and (2) instill those values in others. As you do, qualified candidates within the congregation will surface, or you may attract new candidates to your church. Keep holding the banner high, and make it clear that *this is a church that will be known for its evangelistic passion.* Often a leader will just show up. But if not, you'll have to look for one. Start within your own congregation, but don't assume that the person in your church who is "known for doing evangelism" is the right person. You need a leader and a people-person who relates well to a broad range of personality types. Sometimes strong evangelists are admired for their zeal but avoided for their approach. They might be regarded as a bit fanatical, and when they talk about evangelism, others discount what they say because, after all, "That's just ___________________, and he/she is *always* talking about that stuff."

Another danger is that the current leader may be locked into one particular approach to evangelism and tend to project it onto everybody in the church. This will attract a few people who happen to fit that approach, but it will repel everyone else. A vital part of enrolling *all* the believers in the church is a strong belief that there are *many* valid ways to do evangelism. This principle must be taught wholeheartedly and then applied consistently throughout the outreach ministries and evangelistic events (I'll develop this theme later in the book).

Someone who presently leads the visitation team may or may not be able to make the leap to embrace and espouse a variety of legitimate options. If he or she can, this person may be the right evangelistic point leader for your church. If not, this person may still be a key player leading a certain niche of evangelism under the direction of the new point leader.

Don't assume that the point person needs to be a flamboyant extrovert who is always the life of the party, or be a particular age, or look like an evangelist (whatever that means!). Beware too of assuming the leader has to be someone with a formal degree in biblical studies or evangelism. That can be a definite asset—I'm all for theological training—but it doesn't have to be a prerequisite. And in some cases it can bring with it the limiting viewpoint of "the way things should be done according to such and such a book or Professor So-and-So." Sometimes the most creative and effective leaders are those who take up the challenge but who "really don't have the background for it." This may be just the person to put into active duty, who will then be given additional training, formal or informal, along the way.

Carrying this thought a bit further, avoid thinking that the point person has to be someone with many years of experience in evangelism—which will severely limit your slate of candidates and diminish the value of on-the-job training. One of the most effective people I know in local church evangelism was recruited straight out of the marketplace by the same church God had used to reach him just a few years earlier. Look for sharp leaders throughout your ministries who have a concern for lost people and an affinity with people on both sides of the spiritual fence. Set a higher goal for character than for breadth of evangelistic experience. It's always easier to develop skills than it is to build character.

If necessary, look outside your church for an evangelism point person. A local or denominational Bible college or seminary can be a good resource, as long as the selection is based more on the criteria we have been discussing than on formal degrees alone. Sometimes by networking with other church leaders you'll find that they have someone in their ranks who fits the description but who, for any number of reasons, they have been unable to fully utilize. For the sake of kingdom gain, ask them if you can "borrow" that leader with the awareness that their church gets to have the first-round draft choice the next time around.

You might even come into contact with someone who has been beating his or her head against the wall trying to create evangelistic action in another church but has found that wall unmovable. You'll probably discover that both the person and that church's leaders are frustrated about it. Perhaps everyone would win if this evangelistic pioneer had an opportunity to put his or her energy into a different church that really wants to try some new things to reach lost people—yours!

One other place to look is in classified listings put out by ministries trying to help people find appropriate places of service. Intercristo has had such a service for years. The Willow Creek Association also has a publication for this purpose called *The Exchange,* which includes a section for people looking for positions as well as listings of available openings (see our Web site at www.willowcreek.com).

A couple of final thoughts about finding the right leader to head up the evangelism thrust in your church: First, *pray specifically and consistently.* Don Cousins used to remind me that in Matthew 4, before Jesus selected his disciples, he went into the desert to fast and pray. We should follow his example, because this is a critically important decision. Seek God's guidance and protection as you select a leader. Second, *set your sights high.* People may come across your path about whom you'll think, *"if only . . . ,"* but you'll be tempted not to pursue them because you think they wouldn't be interested. Don't say no for them before they have a chance to say yes! Let them catch a glimpse of the vision and gain an understanding of the importance of the role you have in mind. Then they can prayerfully decide if they're interested in signing up for the most exciting adventure of their life!

I've seen highly successful people in the marketplace begin to see how God can use them and, in the words of the Stephen Curtis Chapman song, they "abandon it all for the sake of the call." I know one businessman who left his role as a corporate executive, accepted a ninety percent pay cut, and got involved in full-time ministry. Not only that—he now gives more money to the ministry than he actually makes working there! (But don't ask me for his name and number—I can't give it to you!)

Don't limit God. And don't shrink back from challenging the person you think is right for this role. He or she is going to be in charge of "new business," which represents the future of the church and the eternal destiny of everyone you'll reach. What could possibly be more important than this?

THE EVANGELISTIC POINT PERSON'S JOB DESCRIPTION

The point person's role is to champion the six-stage contagious process, especially stages 4 through 6. In the case of the first three stages, his or her efforts should supplement those of the pastor and other senior leaders. Here's a look at how this should work, along with a preview of the last three steps, which constitute this person's primary job description.

THE POINT PERSON'S *SUPPLEMENTARY* ROLE

Stage 1: Own and Model the Values

In addition to the senior pastor and other highly visible leaders, people will naturally look to the evangelism point person to be an example of someone who cares deeply about lost people and takes practical steps to reach them. This should provide extra motivation for the person in this role. Every time the point person takes a risk in a relationship or conversation with a non-Christian, he or she has the opportunity to impact that person's eternity and to encourage and influence Christians who are watching.

Don't limit God. And don't shrink back from challenging the person you think is right for this role.

Like the rest of us, the point person needs to have some space for inevitable evangelistic ups and downs. As long as the overall desire and effort to reach others is there, the people in the congregation can learn from and be motivated by the leader's example—which includes the ongoing fight against personal evangelistic entropy and the battle to overcome discouragement when outreach efforts don't go as planned.

Stage 2: Instill the Values in Others

The evangelistic point leader should take a strong role in partnership with the senior pastor in raising evangelism values in the church. They can declare war together! A synergy will form when the general and this first lieutenant, along with other officers and troops, put their best efforts into taking back lost ground and expanding the boundaries of the kingdom. They can inspire and encourage one another, hold one another accountable, and pray for one another.

Ecclesiastes 4:9–10 says,

> Two are better than one,
> because they have a good return for their work:
> If one falls down,
> his friend can help him up.
> But pity the man who falls
> and has no one to help him up!

Stage 3: Empower Additional Evangelistic Leaders

Originally this stage was titled "Empowering an Evangelistic Point Leader." But now that we've found our key point leader, it is part of his or her job to find and equip other leaders, as well as teams of people, who can come alongside and help carry out the evangelism plan. The roles these people fill will become evident as we move through the next three stages. The volume of work it takes to build the evangelism thrust needed to help a church become truly contagious is way beyond the efforts of one person.

We need to elevate our expectations of what will be required. This is a real war, and wars are costly. They require leadership, troops, creativity, planning, and courage. They demand our best efforts—especially this war, because we've already been losing on many fronts! In the power of the Holy Spirit, we need to mount a massive counterattack to weaken the enemy, take back lost ground, and reclaim the captives—the church *must* prevail!

While the point leader may assist the pastor and the other leaders on the first three stages, the last three are the responsibility of the point leader alone. These are the "how-tos" of helping the church bring into reality the three-step evangelism strategy outlined in chapter 3. Remember, this strategy says: (1) Believers need to build authentic relationships with nonbelievers; (2) in the context of these relationships, they need to share a verbal witness about Christ; (3) they need to bring these friends to appropriate outreach events that will help lead them to Christ.

The Point Person's Primary Role

How are we going to make this evangelistic strategy work throughout the church? By continuing our 6-Stage Process. Stages 4 through 6 make up the primary day-to-day activities—a three-part job description—of the point person.

Stage 4: Liberate and Equip Every Believer

People don't develop skills just by hearing about something or by watching other people model those skills. They learn by practicing these skills themselves. The problem is that most people in churches don't want to try evangelism for themselves. They're afraid of it and feel unprepared. We need to get every believer into a confidence-building, ability-enhancing, hands-on training experience that will literally change the way they view and do evangelism. The first thing this training time needs to accomplish is to convince others that evangelizing is something they can do in natural ways—in other words, that *evangelism can look like them.*

One of the first and most important jobs of the point person is to implement and continually repeat this kind of training. This is a job that never ends, because additional people keep needing to be trained, and those who have been trained need to keep coming back for refreshers. The point person should teach some of these courses personally but should also identify and train others who can teach at a variety of times and locations. We'll look at the training component in detail in chapter 7.

Stage 5: Develop a Diversified Evangelism Team

One of the advantages of offering ongoing training is that it gives the point leader and his or her team endless opportunities to recruit people with gifts or passion for evangelism. These are the people to approach and encourage to attend occasional evangelism rallies. You don't want to pull them out of their other ministries; you want their salty influence to stay dispersed throughout the church. But you do need to get them together once in a while to charge up their evangelistic batteries and to alert them to upcoming outreach opportunities. This also provides an occasion to reinforce them in their various outreach styles and point them to customized training and events.

When the point leader gets this group of enthusiasts together, evangelism really starts becoming fun! In chapter 8 we'll look in-depth at how to build and lead a diversified evangelism team.

Stage 6: Innovate High-Impact Outreach Events and Ministries

Once the point leader has developed a broad-based evangelism team, he or she now has the human resource pool out of which to develop a wide and diverse range of outreach ministries and events. These are the people who will help the leader dream and scheme about what else can be done to reach lost people. Once an idea is agreed on, they will be fired up and ready to help make it happen. These are people who want to be where the action is!

When you've laid the groundwork with stages 1 through 5 and have begun to expand with stage 6, look out! The sky is the limit when it comes to the varieties of evangelistic activities—and degree of evangelistic impact—that can result.

The person who fills the point leader role is in for incredible rewards and unparalleled exhilaration. One church's point leader told me recently, "There's an awful lot going on all at once, and I'm a bit tired, but this is a dream job! There's nothing else in the world I'd rather be doing than what I'm doing right now!"

MAKING THE POINT PERSON POSITION WORK

Evangelism Requires Resources

As I hinted earlier, church-wide outreach efforts have price tags on them! A point leader ideally should be a full- or part-time staff member; but even if this person is a volunteer, you still need to provide training, perhaps in the form of courses taken locally or by correspondence. You may send your point leader to evangelism and leadership conferences to expand his or her vision or to workshops to deepen skills and multiply contacts with like-minded leaders. You'll also want your point person to have access to outreach-oriented books and tapes. And he or she will need a budget for phone calls, office expenses, and meetings and meals with leaders, team members, and spiritual seekers.

Then when you start training the whole church and building the church-wide evangelism team, you'll incur more expenses. Some of those can be recouped by charging participants nominal fees for meals and materials. But if you try to run your training and various outreach events on a strict break-even basis, you're going to strangle creativity and restrict opportunity.

Going back to Karl Singer's illustration, why wouldn't we be willing to invest in the part of our organization that is in charge of "new business"? If you have to skimp somewhere, Singer would tell you, skimp somewhere else, but not in the area that can breathe new life into every segment of the organization—not to mention bring new life to the people you'll reach!

You may be wondering how much the evangelism budget will need to be expanded. Looking at the studies, it may well have to be substantial (though not necessarily all at once). As we saw earlier, George Barna found that the average church spends less than two percent of total revenues on local evangelism. No wonder the war effort isn't going very well! If we want to make headway in building contagious churches, we're going to have to get a lot more serious.

In comparison, Barna indicates that "among the *leading* evangelistic churches, we found that it was more common to spend 10 percent to 20 percent of the annual budget for that purpose. . . . In general, the churches that are most serious about evangelism seem to put their money where their mission is."[5]

Barna cautions, however, against the mentality that money alone produces results. But he asserts, "For a ministry that has creative thinkers, passionate evangelists, strong leaders, and wise strategists, providing a significant budget for evangelism can multiply the other gifts and abilities residing within the church many times over."[6]

Before leaving this topic, I want to address the issue of churches investing large amounts in foreign missions yet almost completely neglecting the lost people in their own community. Why does this happen? Is it because it is easier to write a check than to get involved personally? Is it a spiritual way of saying, "I'll let someone else do the work of evangelism for me"? Do we think that people on the other side of the ocean matter more to God than the people who live next door?

Please don't misunderstand. I'm an enthusiastic and active supporter of foreign missions. I realize that evangelism is absolutely essential in other countries too. In many cases these ministries reach people who've never had the chance to hear the gospel. In addition, people live in incredibly poor areas where such things as food, water, medicine, and shelter—as well as books, schools, teachers, and training—are needed. We in Western societies who have been blessed with so much should give consistently and sacrificially to lighten these burdens and to reach people for Christ in distant places.

But we also have a responsibility to address the spiritual needs of those near us. In fact, some would say it is a priority, based on Acts 1:8. Jesus said, "You will be my witnesses in Jerusalem, and in all Judea and Samaria, and to the ends of the earth." I don't want to argue that this command should be carried out in a sequential manner, with the mandate to completely reach our "Jerusalem," or local area, before we move outward. But neither do I want to argue that any part of it is optional! We have no business deciding to reach our Judea or Samaria *instead* of our Jerusalem. Yet this is often done, and our own children and grandchildren pay the price.

I heard about a large adult Sunday school class in a vibrant evangelical church where the teacher became especially vulnerable one Sunday morning. With tears in his eyes he admitted that his own children had long since refused to attend their church because they couldn't relate to it. According to my friends who were there, many other class members came up to this man afterward and told him that the same was true of their own kids. Clearly, they wanted to change things and to figure out ways to invest in more relevant communications. Yet their church's budget from the previous ministry year showed that they had spent less than one percent on local evangelism. Thankfully, this church's leadership has recognized the problem, and they are taking comprehensive steps to turn things around and raise the priority of relating to and reaching their own community while continuing to support overseas missions.

Consider whether in your church enough is being invested in ministries that can reach your own children as well as your friends and neighbors who don't know Christ. In a broad sense, the strong warning of 1 Timothy 5:8 applies here: "If anyone does not provide for his relatives, and especially for his immediate family, he has denied the faith and is worse than an unbeliever."

What can be done to increase funding for local evangelism? As with everything else related to evangelism, it starts with the heart. As we lift up this value and then put it into action along the lines of our discussion in this book, people will give the necessary financial resources. The goal is to raise the overall support and investment level for evangelism without harming other important causes. Also, you may have people in your congregation who, if you went to them personally and presented your plan, would joyfully write a check to help make it happen—especially when they consider the potential effects on their own loved ones!

You may also need to reallocate some of the funds that have been going elsewhere. Raising the value of evangelism will often put it higher on the priority scale than other ministry areas, and this should be reflected by levels of financial investment. But don't forget it's just that—an *investment* in lost people and in your church's future. As it brings returns in the form of newly redeemed people, the base of investors will grow, and even more ministry will become possible.

The Point Person Must Be Empowered

With the deep-seated resistance to evangelism we find so often, it is vital that the pastor and other senior leaders do all they can to *empower* the person who is leading the evangelism cause. This can be done initially, and then reinforced repeatedly, in vision talks that clarify the church's mission and lift up evangelistic values. That's a natural place for the senior leader to explain the strategic importance of the point person's role as well as to publicly pray for this leader and his or her work. It would be wise to also actively include the point person in the vision service, letting him or her teach or say a few words about the plans being developed in the area of evangelism.

Empowering also comes through giving the point person a strong position and title, such as Associate Pastor of Evangelism or Director of Evangelism. It's also vitally important to provide for regular interaction with the other leaders. This can be accomplished, in part, by adding the evangelism point person to the leadership team and inviting him or her to the appropriate elder, deacon, or board meetings, depending on your church's structure.

The point person must have a measure of authority with other ministry leaders in the church. If your point person becomes just another leader in one of many departments in the church, then you've already positioned him or her to lose the battle. Evangelism is the razor's edge of what your church claims to be all about, so be sure to treat it that way!

George Barna writes, "A degree of freedom must exist and a measure of control must be granted to the people who are putting themselves on the firing lines. One of the marks of effective leadership is the ability to identify qualified people, to prepare them for action and to release them to do what they do best with not just verbal blessings but with the mandate to do what is necessary to get the job done."[7] This mandate needs to include a position that has some clout among the other leaders in the church.

Another key to empowerment is to free up the point leader to focus on evangelism. When your church is healthy and not feeling an immediate need for new members, the urgency of evangelism can quickly wane. Evangelistic entropy can occur when the point person is pulled into other projects that seem more urgent at the time. Getting involved in other projects may be the exception at first, but it can quickly become the norm. We must resist this, and let this person do what he or she is called by God to do; we must also be careful not to load up their job description with activities like weddings, funerals, unnecessary meetings, and broad teaching responsibilities. In particular, beware of making the point person director of "Evangelism *and Discipleship*." Giving your point person responsibility for the full gamut of activity included in both the front and back halves of the Great Commission is a great way to overwhelm him or her!

The Point Person Must Be Accountable

Because the role of the evangelism point person is so expansive and multifaceted, the point person can easily get sidetracked—not necessarily doing bad things, just lower-priority things. Accountability needs to be built in to make sure this person is focusing on the agreed-upon goals. These, as we'll discuss in a later chapter, need to be measurable and evaluated against the objectives.

One of the easiest places for the point leader to get off the track is to begin responding personally to all of the cries for help in the evangelism arena. These can come from non-Christians themselves or, more often, from church members who want personalized help in reaching their friends and family. Certainly some of these should be dealt with directly by the point leader. He or she should never become isolated from that kind of up-close ministry. But, on the whole, point leaders should see themselves as facilitators whose role is to equip and enroll others in the front lines of ministry action—others who will have the background and abilities needed to respond to the various outreach opportunities.

I've met evangelism leaders who buoyantly tell me how many people they've personally led to Christ in the past year. The number is always impressive. And my reaction is invariably twofold. First, I'm thankful that God is using them to reach so many. But, second, I wonder how much more fruitful their long-term effect might be if instead of handling all of these situations themselves, they were empowering other Christians and leading them into opportunities in which they could get a taste of the excitement of bringing someone to Christ.

Sharing the responsibility with others would ignite and embolden every one of these Christians and make them that much more able to be used in evangelism again and again. Once believers have led one person to Christ, they believe so much more in the power of the gospel, the presence of the Spirit, and the potential of their evangelistic efforts. Soon they lead another person to Christ. And then another. And another.

Here's a different way of looking at what I've learned: 1 x 100 < 100 x 1. What this means is that one person leading a hundred others to faith is not nearly as powerful as that person helping one hundred others each lead one other person to faith. Why? Because in the second scenario, you not only end up with a hundred new believers, you also have a hundred fired-up evangelists who now know the exhilaration and feeling of fulfillment of leading someone else to Christ. As with any activity, they've gotten through the awkward beginning stages, and they're now gaining confidence and a sense of excitement in communicating their faith to others. They will, as a result, be much more likely to lead more and more people into God's family.

By acting primarily as a facilitator, the evangelistic point person is investing long term in the exponential effects of empowering ever-increasing numbers of Christians who will each reach many others. In short, the church will become contagious!

The Point Person Must Be Encouraged

The point person is a servant who leads the evangelism team into battle. Frustration, discouragement, and times of weariness are all periodic by-products of this arena of ministry, especially since spiritual battles are continually being waged. Thus, this brother or sister in Christ needs our prayers, our love, our support, our understanding, our encouragement, and our expressions of appreciation. Often just a little bit will go a long way.

With the kinds of investments we've discussed in this chapter, a well-chosen point leader will be able to lead your church into effective evangelism at many different levels—evangelism that goes against the odds and starts winning the war. Every church, whether large, small, or even in the initial planting stage, needs to identify and empower a point person. Then this leader can begin to train and empower all of the rest of the people in the church to reach their lost friends for Christ. We'll look at how this can happen in the next chapter.

STAGE 3: KEY IDEA

Empower a contagious leader.

"It was he who gave some . . . to be evangelists . . .
to prepare God's people for works of service, so that
the body of Christ may be built up"
(Ephesians 4:11–12).

To Consider and Discuss

1. How would it help your church to have a point person for evangelism in addition to the senior pastor?

2. How could your pastor and the point person work in concert with each other?
3. If you don't yet have somebody in this role, who are two or three people inside or outside your church who might make an effective evangelistic point person? Begin praying for wisdom as you seek the right leader for this vital area.
4. Why is it essential for the evangelistic point person to be freed up to recruit, train, and deploy more evangelists and leaders in this ministry?
5. What can your church do to maximize this leader's freedom and strength in order to make him or her more effective?

7

STAGE 4: LIBERATING AND EQUIPPING EVERY BELIEVER

We have a math problem.

Go into most churches and ask the pastor, "Who does the work of evangelism here?" You'll likely get the sincere reply, "Oh, the *sheep* make new sheep! Shepherds can't make sheep; my role is to equip the flock and send them out to do the work of evangelism."

This sounds like a good answer—until you discover how few people in most churches are being adequately equipped to communicate their faith to others. Of the churches that do train their people, most do so infrequently, teach just one approach, and have a relatively low number of members who actually participate. Is it any wonder the job isn't getting done?

What's worse, if you talk to church members, they will often give you a very different picture. With great exuberance they will say to you, "Evangelism? Oh, that's the *pastor's* job. The pastor is the one with the training and tools and whatever else it takes." They view it like one of those "extreme" sports programs where a skier stands on top of a huge mountain, smiles defiantly at the camera, and then pushes himself off the edge of what looks like a mile-high wall of sheer ice. But just before he launches into this death-defying feat, a warning flashes on the screen: THESE ARE PROFESSIONALS WITH SPECIAL EQUIPMENT AND TRAINING. DO NOT TRY THIS AT HOME!

In spite of hearing the occasional sermon that tells us we're all supposed to be active witnesses for Christ, most church members don't take the challenge personally. "Why should I jeopardize someone's eternity when there's somebody else much more qualified to help them?" they muse. "I'd better leave this one to the experts—either the pastor or the outreach director."

Sometimes this evangelistic finger-pointing becomes more creative. Someone will remember that, according to the people who study these matters, as many as ten percent of Christians have the spiritual gift of evangelism. "Of course," church members will say, "this is the job of those with the gift of evangelism. For whatever reason, God has made it easy for them and hard for the rest of us. We'll just support them in their efforts!"

So the pastor stands in the pulpit pointing at the congregation while the congregation sits in the sanctuary pointing back at the pastor. Or together they all look around with hopes of pointing at their comrades who have the gift of evangelism. But *where* are they? *Who* are they?

Imagine yourself or another leader standing in front of your church this Sunday morning and saying, "Okay, we know from the surveys that one in ten of you has the spiritual gift of evangelism. We'd just like to find out who you are. Could those of you with that gift—and you know who you are—please stand up?" What kind of a response do you think you'd get? Would anywhere near ten percent of the congregation be standing? Maybe five percent? Perhaps only two percent, or even less?

Let's be honest. In most churches, the actual number of people who would stand and say, "Evangelism is my area of giftedness" is extremely small. Of those few who would make that claim, many are undertrained and ill-prepared. And let's be even *more* honest: Some of them are offbeat characters you would not want representing your church and on whom you could never build an effective outreach effort.

Do you see why I say we have a math problem? We have billions of people in the world—and thousands in the areas right around your church—who don't know Christ. And most of our congregations have, at best, a handful of qualified, motivated, and equipped believers—with or without this spiritual gift—to do the actual reaching. It's no wonder that in so many corners the church is losing ground or merely maintaining the status quo. And it's no wonder Jesus so earnestly challenged his followers, "The harvest is plentiful, but the workers are few. Ask the Lord of the harvest, therefore, to send out workers into his harvest field" (Luke 10:2).

THE MATH PROBLEM HITS HOME

This situation is, for me, more than mere theory or casual observation. At one time I was a casualty of this math problem. For a season I lived on the wrong side of the redemptive ratios. In fact, I reached the point of actually writing off personal evangelism and deciding it wasn't for me!

Why? Well, it was the fallout of my summer of evangelism described in chapter 3. I had been on a team with an overseas church that was trying to share Christ with people in its neighborhoods. The problem was that we were using approaches that didn't fit my personality. I remember asking our team captain soon after we arrived what we were going to do the next day. He said with great enthusiasm, "We're going to knock on the doors of houses throughout the area and tell people about Jesus!"

I swallowed hard and then tried to spit out a positive response. "Oh, boy!" I said with less than complete enthusiasm. And then I spent the rest of the evening trying to gear myself up for what promised to be a challenging day.

The next evening, at the end of what was, in reality, a fairly challenging day, I asked what we were going to do the following day. "We're going to knock on the doors of strangers again!" he said exuberantly.

"Oh . . . boy," I muttered.

Day after day we went out trying to find people who were interested, taking every opportunity we could find, doing our best to faithfully communicate the good news of Christ to a culture that desperately needed it but didn't seem to want to hear it.

Some people are gifted and called to do door-to-door outreach. It fits their God-given evangelistic style, as we'll explore in chapter 10, and they see lasting results from their efforts. I honor them. I'm just not one of them. For me, this direct, hard-hitting approach felt unnatural. I was literally forcing myself, day after day, to do things that were not only difficult for me but that seemed to go against the grain of my God-given personality and temperament.

When the eight weeks were over, I'd done my time. I'd completed my tour of duty. I was ready to go into evangelistic retirement. "Let somebody else sign up for the next campaign," I said to myself. "Evangelism is clearly not for me. I'll find other ways to serve the church. I'll support it. I'll give to it. I'll pray for it. But don't ask me to go on any more outreach excursions. From here on out, I just want to be an *ordinary* Christian."

CHURCHES OF "ORDINARY" CHRISTIANS

How the term *ordinary* ever came to be associated with being uninvolved in evangelism I'll never know. However this link evolved, it certainly felt natural to me at the time. And, looking around, it seems to be natural to most Christians in most churches. Together we're going to have to help believers get a new view of "ordinary."

I suspect that the problem stems in large part to a misconception of what evangelism really is and what it can look like in your life. It's what I call the "problem of perceptions." Even though most Christians have never spent a summer with a church team knocking on doors and talking to strangers, they have similar pictures in their minds of the kinds of things they'd have to do if they really became outreach-oriented. They have determined in advance that these approaches don't fit them.

How the term *ordinary* ever came to be associated with being uninvolved in evangelism I'll never know.

In fact, I think most of us tend to have widely polarized stereotypes of what evangelism is—ones that are either very positive or very negative. We view it as an activity for superstar Christians who are outgoing, articulate, equipped, and effective. Or, at the other end of the spectrum, it's for pushy, manipulative, out-of-touch, and out-of-style individuals who cram the gospel down people's throats.

The result is that the "average" Christian concludes, "I know what evangelism is. It's an activity for someone who's extraordinary enough to do it really well—or who's just obnoxious enough to do it anyway!" But either way they're sure it's not for them, because they view themselves as neither extraordinary nor obnoxious! "Whatever evangelism is," they muse, "I'll leave it to somebody else who's better suited for that kind of activity."

If we're to ever solve the math problem, change the ratios, and enroll the Christian masses in the adventure of relational evangelism, we're going to have to adopt—and spread—a new view of what it can look like, a view that includes every believer.

What's interesting is that even though many Christians are repelled by the idea of being involved in evangelism, they really do want to make a difference with their lives. They want to be players on the field and not just spectators in the stands. They want to make investments that will bear fruit and have an impact on eternity. I think the Holy Spirit has inbred these desires in every believer. As Joe Stowell, president of Moody Bible Institute, once said in a leadership talk at our church, some people are "just waiting for permission to change—like stallions held back in the corral . . . just hoping, dreaming that someone [will] say sic 'em . . . 'go!'"

This brings us to stage 4 of the 6-Stage Process, "liberating and equipping every believer" for effective evangelism. We'll use the three components as the outline for the rest of this chapter, starting with the concept of "liberating."

<u>LIBERATING</u> AND EQUIPPING EVERY BELIEVER

How can we as leaders set people free from their menacing misconceptions about evangelism and help them see what it might look like in their own lives? We can do so in part through the three stages in the process I've been discussing.

- As we own and model evangelistic values, we're giving people a vivid new picture of how evangelism can be expressed in their particular context. This is a value that is "better caught than taught."
- But this value does need to be taught too! As we pray, lead, teach, illustrate, cast a vision, disciple, discuss, encourage, and challenge, church members will, over time, gain a fresh understanding of what we're talking about.
- Then, when we've selected and empowered an evangelistic point person, we'll have another leader who will, by his or her actions and attitudes, help liberate people from the problem of perceptions.

But there's another vital part of the evangelistic liberation process. I believe that the key idea to be taught, both by the senior pastor as well as by the point person, is that there are a variety of legitimate approaches to evangelism. In other words, you don't have to squeeze yourself into a specific personality mold in order to be used by God to reach others. In fact, you'll be much more effective if you work within your God-given personality.

This, to come back to my own story, was the concept that salvaged me from the evangelism sidelines. Months after "writing off" evangelism, I went to one of our church's midweek worship services. That night Bill Hybels was teaching a message titled "The Style of an Evangelist." I was tempted to tune him out as he began to speak, presuming that this topic was not relevant to me. But as he developed the theme, I began to get more and more interested in what he was saying.

The first thing he explained was that there is a diversity of approaches to evangelism right in the pages of the New Testament.

People didn't all do outreach the same way, and they didn't lay guilt trips on each other to do it the way they themselves did. Reflecting on my recent experiences of feeling out of place doing door-to-door evangelism, I was beginning to perk up already.

Bill said he was going to describe six evangelism styles he'd discovered as he perused the pages of Scripture. The first was the confrontational style, seen in Peter in Acts 2. Peter was very bold and direct and hard-hitting with the gospel. He just looked people in the eye and let 'em have it! I thought about how that was more or less what we had tried to do that summer and how it hadn't felt right for me.

Then Bill got to the second example: in Acts 17 Paul stood on Mars Hill in Athens and challenged the philosophers with the claims of Scripture. He presented truth to them logically and compellingly, and he even quoted some of their own Greek scholars to make his point. For some strange reason my heart was beating a bit faster! *Wow,* I found myself thinking. *What an exciting thing to stand in front of a bunch of skeptics and declare and defend the truth of the gospel! I love debating truth with people who aren't yet convinced.* At the time, I was getting my master's degree in Philosophy of Religion, but I hadn't fully linked in my mind my education with the word *evangelism.* I'd been plagued by the problem of perceptions!

What I realized that night was that my real motivation to study, to read books, and to talk to those with different points of view was to help people move past their intellectual roadblocks and get to the point where they could trust in Christ. I began to understand that I was made to do evangelism, but it needed to look different from the approaches I had tried to use that summer. I discovered a new, expanded view of what evangelism is, as well as what it could look like in my life—and in the lives of others.

The Holy Spirit used Bill's words to reorient my thinking and, in effect, to turn the key that unlocked the door to my involvement in the area of outreach. And, as a clear manifestation of God's sense of humor, I was hired just a year later to lead the evangelistic charge at that place, Willow Creek Community Church, a church rapidly becoming known for reaching unchurched people. Since that time, I've had the thrill of developing and deploying my own intellectual approach to evangelism. I love talking to and trying to convince skeptics and cynics, both on an individual level and in groups, whether small or large.

Through speaking as well as writing (including the *Becoming a Contagious Christian* book and evangelism training course), I've also had the privilege of helping many other believers discover and develop their own style of evangelism. I have never found a concept that better liberates people who have written off evangelism as something that's not for them. Whether it be the confrontational style of Peter in Acts 2, the intellectual style of Paul in Acts 17, the testimonial style of the blind man in John 9, the interpersonal style of Matthew in Luke 5:29, the invitational style of the woman at the well in John 4, the serving style of Dorcas in Acts 9, or some other biblical approach, all believers can express their faith in a natural way that will fit their unique personality.

We'll go into more detail on these six styles, and look at how we can maximize them for church-wide outreach, in chapters 10 through 15, but for now we simply want to affirm that God has built diversity into the body of Christ. We need to see it, teach it, live it, and celebrate it as we release believers to communicate Christ in ways that fit them. It takes all kinds of Christians to reach all kinds of non-Christians, and this concept of the six styles of evangelism gives us a strategic tool for liberating every believer.

LIBERATING AND EQUIPPING EVERY BELIEVER

The Critical Need for Evangelistic Training

Most churches and Christian leaders greatly overestimate the ability of their members to communicate their faith—at least in part because many of us leaders are the kind of learners who can hear an idea, reflect on it a bit, and then figure out how to put it into action in our own lives. We assume that if all we needed was to hear the basic idea, then that's all others are going to need too. But according to training experts, most people *don't* have the natural ability to make this kind of connection. The average person hears ideas, likes them, and forms good intentions to do something with them, but he or she is at a loss when it comes to knowing how to put those ideas into action. In between the idea and execution stages, they need an added "how-to" stage that is clear and specific and that gives them hands-on opportunities to give the new skill a try. This insight seems especially true in the area of evangelism, where many believers have low levels of confidence—which is why practical evangelism training for every member of the congregation is so important and is at the heart of stage 4.

Most churches and Christian leaders greatly overestimate the ability of their members to communicate their faith.

Some of the lines blur between the parts of the 6-Stage Process. We've already talked through the stages of owning the values, instilling them in others, empowering a point person, and now having him or her train all those who have begun to gain the personal "want-to." We've acted as if this were a linear process that moves from point *A* to point *B* to point *C* and so forth, but in reality there's a lot of overlap, and none of the stages is ever complete. We must continually wage war on every front if we're going to enjoy sustained victory.

Looking at this broader process, the fourth stage is interesting because, on the one hand, it needs to build on the instilled value of evangelism from the second stage. I mentioned earlier that many leaders have told me of the difficulties they've faced by trying to jump straight into training. They say, "We want to teach the course, but how do you get people to come to it?" or "We've tried to get something going, but almost nobody was interested." The lesson they've learned—and I'm relearning with them—is that we have to *start with the heart* and help our people love and care about lost people the way God does. We have to do the hard work of instilling the evangelism values so they become embedded in the very culture of the church. Then when we announce a training course, the members more readily see it as a tool to help them do what they already want to do. In this sense values precede new experiences.

On the other hand, John Kotter, an expert in organizational change, has found that the opposite is also true: New experiences often lead to the adoption of new values. In *Leading Change*, Kotter reveals that at one time he believed the conventional wisdom, which says, "the first step in a major transformation is to alter the norms and values. After the culture has been shifted, the rest of the change effort becomes more feasible and easier to put into effect." But Kotter no longer holds to this view, because "culture is not something you manipulate easily . . . [it] changes only after you have successfully altered people's actions, after the new behavior produces some group benefit for a period of time, and after people see the connection between the new actions and the performance improvement."[1]

Rather than getting into a "Which came first—the chicken or the egg?" debate, we can learn from and put into practice both sides of the equation:

- *Values.* We need to do all we can to lift up the value of evangelism and help people begin to grow hearts for lost people.
- *Training.* While continuing this effort, we need to build on the evangelism values that presently exist in order to move people as quickly as possible into training opportunities. These opportunities will provide them with new, exciting experiences in

sharing their faith, first within the confines of the group and then out among their friends.

- *Values.* These new experiences will, in turn, further raise their evangelistic values.
- *Training.* This heightened sense of evangelistic values will make them even more receptive to ongoing teaching, which will better prepare and motivate them for the next witnessing opportunity.

Can you see the synergistic upward spiral that happens when you combine the stages of our process, especially stage 2 (instilling the values) and stage 4 (training every believer)? Stage 2 should begin first, stage 4 should not trail far behind it, and both need to be ongoing as they continually feed off of each other.

Running an Effective Training Program

As a rule, training should be the foremost responsibility of the evangelistic point person. The leader needs to make it his or her goal to train *every* Christian in the church—one hundred percent—with no exemptions. This training needs to be strongly supported and promoted by the senior pastor, who should at least attend the first evangelism presentation. Ideally the point person should teach along with the pastor the first time through and then become the primary trainer. This will send a signal from the beginning that evangelism training is of utmost importance and has the full endorsement of the senior leader.

Southeast Christian Fellowship, a rapidly growing church in urban Washington, D.C., provides a great example of how the training process works. This church does constant evangelism training, using the *Becoming a Contagious Christian* curriculum. They teach one session per week for eight weeks, and then immediately start it all over again. Their goal is to train and retrain all of their people. The senior pastor, Rickey Bolden, supports and bolsters this program by frequently preaching sermons that heighten evangelism awareness and by giving repeated challenges to attend the course. But he doesn't stop there. Rickey tells the members to meet him at the training, because he teaches part of each course in partnership with the church's evangelistic point person, Mack Edwards. Rickey usually kicks off the first week and then comes back and leads session five. Mack carries the ball the rest of the time. Can you imagine what this does to create an outward focus in their church? Think about the impact an approach like this could have in your church!

How should the actual training be structured? I'll answer that by briefly detailing the thinking behind the *Becoming a Contagious*

Christian curriculum, which we designed specifically to fill this need. This is only one of several courses available, but it is the only one I know of that starts with a strong emphasis on overcoming misconceptions and that liberates believers by showing them how they can discover and deploy their own natural style. This helps the ninety-plus percent of the participants who are skeptical about evangelism to stay engaged long enough to catch the vision and start developing new skills.

As Figure 7.1 shows, this eight-hour course takes an A-to-Z approach, starting with the understanding and character of the individual Christian. From there it moves him or her all the way to the point of being able to pray with friends and lead them "across the line of faith" into salvation and a relationship with Christ.

Figure 7.1

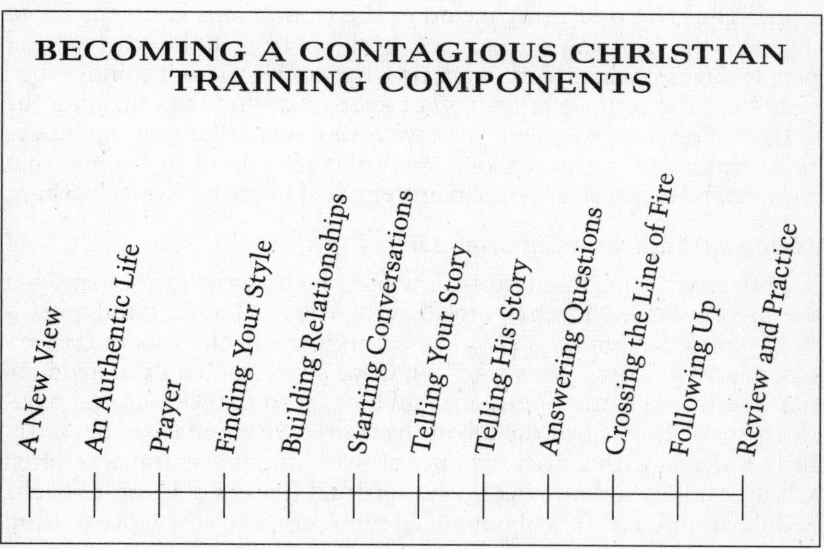

Before going into the specifics of the training components, let's recall what we are trying to accomplish. Our goal is to *equip every believer* in the church so he or she will be able to personally get involved in carrying out the three-step evangelistic strategy presented in chapter 3. By the end of the course, every participant should be ready, able, and motivated to do the following:

- build and deepen relationships with people outside the family of God

- raise spiritual topics and articulate the message of the gospel
- invite friends and acquaintances to outreach events that will help them move toward Christ (we'll go into more detail about these in chapter 9)

In addition to equipping people to execute this evangelistic strategy, we will also be naturally reinforcing the mission discussed in chapter 1 and the values presented in chapter 2. In many ways, the activity of training people brings together everything discussed so far—which is why this element is so vitally important.

KEY EVANGELISM TRAINING COMPONENTS

Getting a New View of Evangelism

The essential first step in getting the broader church body involved in evangelism is helping members see it in a new, more positive light. The first thing we do in the *Contagious* course is try to displace the limiting stereotypes, both positive and negative, that people have. We ask them to tell us what comes to their minds when they hear the terms *evangelism* or *evangelist.* You can imagine the variety of responses we get! Then we assure them that they don't have to fit themselves into personality molds that don't fit them—that they can be themselves while being engaged in trying to reach others.

Living an Authentic Christian Life

Effective evangelism must flow out of who we *are,* not just what we *say.* As Steve Macchia, president of Vision New England, puts it in his book *Becoming a Healthy Church,* evangelism is in its very essence "overflow." He says, "What we experience on the inside of our hearts and souls eventually bubbles up to the surface and overflows to others."[2] So at the top of the course we emphasize that faithfully walking with Christ not only pleases him, it also impacts, often without our even knowing it, the spiritual lives and destinies of the people around us. Talk about added motivation to stay close to him!

Praying for God's Intervention

Because nobody is going to be reached unless the Holy Spirit is at work in hearts and lives, we have course participants make an "impact list" by writing down the first names of three family members or friends they hope to help bring to faith. We teach them to pray specifically and continually for those people, asking God to draw them to himself. Then we take a few moments to pray together along these lines.

Finding Your Own Style

Using the six biblical styles mentioned earlier, we help participants see that God intentionally built diversity into the body of Christ. We assure them that we don't have to try to become something we're not. We each can develop an approach that fits us. We do this through teaching, discussion, and the use of a short questionnaire that helps them discover their most natural style of evangelism. Then, building on this new self-awareness, we focus on steps we can each take to further develop our own style.

This session is pivotal to all of the rest of the training. It frees members to flourish within their God-given designs. It exposes them to the styles of other church members around them and helps them to see how they can join with them to reach all of their friends for Christ. It also encourages them to stay involved in the rest of the course so we can train and equip them with relational evangelism skills.

The impact this teaching has on participants is like taking shackles off them. Many find an incredible sense of freedom and exhilaration as they contemplate the future and consider how *God might use them* to redirect the lives and eternities of the people they love the most.

Building and Deepening Relationships

Most Christians have very few non-Christian friends. In an often-quoted, eye-opening statistic, Joe Aldrich, president of Multnomah School of the Bible, tells us that within two years of becoming Christians, most of us lose contact with all of our non-Christian friends. We address this problem in the course by giving ideas for deepening relationships with the people participants already know, reigniting relationships with people they used to know, and beginning new relationships with people they'd like to know.

Don't take this area for granted. The battle will be won or lost right here, so this is where we need to fight the hardest. Even the godliest of Christians—in fact, *especially* the godliest of Christians—will need ongoing encouragement, examples, ideas, and inspiration—and sometimes a flat-out challenge.

Starting Spiritual Conversations

Some Christians break out of their safety zones and build relationships with unbelievers, but this is as far as they go. They become a friend to the other person but not a contagious carrier of the gospel of Christ.

Paul asked in Romans 10:14, "How can they believe in the one of whom they have not heard? And how can they hear without someone preaching to them?" I paraphrase it like this: "Your friends aren't going to *see* it unless you go to them and *say* it." And most Christians won't ever say it unless we teach them how to turn a conversation toward spiritual topics. Therefore, we teach a variety of practical approaches to raising spiritual topics. But we don't just talk about it. We also show it through true-to-life videos of drama vignettes that help participants to see how they can start spiritual conversations in their own everyday settings (the video is part of the published curriculum). Then we let them break into groups and practice it right there on the spot.

We also challenge participants to watch during the week for opportunities to make split-second decisions to raise spiritual topics of conversation. These are times when you know it would be easy to raise the topic, but you feel tempted to take the safe way out. I encourage each person, when he or she is in that situation, to follow this highly technical four-part set of instructions: "Take a deep breath, say a quick prayer, open your mouth, and let it rip!"

Simple as it sounds, this is where the real action begins!

Telling Your Story

Being able to articulate our own story is a weapon we all need in our evangelistic arsenal. The problem is that when most of us think of "giving our testimony," we think of presenting a memorized speech. And all too often we sound like that's what we're doing!

Because of this and other pitfalls, we've moved away from employing traditional memorized approaches. Instead, we look at Paul's testimony in Acts 26 and use six questions to flesh out our own stories, adopting the three-part outline that Paul followed: (1) what our life was like before Christ (we refer to it as our "B.C. life"), (2) how we met Christ, and (3) what our life is like since meeting Christ (our "A.D. life"). This sequence provides an easy-to-remember outline that you can use to tell your story in your own words.

Then, after letting participants think through how they can put their story into everyday language and after watching a sample testimony on video, we have them pair up and tell their stories to each other.

This role-playing opportunity is very important in doing training. In general, we are wise to involve as many of the senses as possible in the learning process. Most people don't learn as much from hearing or seeing as by doing. There is something clarifying about knowing you will put what you're learning into practice in just a few moments. Although role-playing may seem a bit intimidating, unless we throw people in feet first, they'll probably stop right here. They'll finish the training, and their participant's guide will end up as just another book on their shelf, never to be looked at again. We all need to be thrust into situations where we try something, learn from our mistakes, and then try again. That's how we become skillful at everything else in life, so why wouldn't it apply to evangelism as well?

The following is what I say to groups just prior to our first practice time:

> Recently I was on a trip, and I went by air. About the time we were at 38,000 feet, flying over a tall mountain range, I started thinking about something. *I sure am glad that this pilot learned how to fly first in a flight simulator,* I said to myself. If you've ever flown in an airplane, I'll bet you're glad too.
>
> Now, I imagine that pilots going through flight school get tired of sitting in the flight simulator. I'll bet they say, "This feels artificial. I want to get out in a real plane where I can hear the rush of the wind and feel the exhilaration that comes with actual acceleration and navigation."
>
> That's a natural inclination. But aren't you glad they made their mistakes in the simulator first? Aren't you happy they crashed into their full share of mountains there, where it was safe, before taking your life into their hands and flying you over the real mountain range? Crashing into mountains in a simulator is no big deal. It's probably kind of fun! And it helps prepare them to fly safely in the real airplane.
>
> Now, let me welcome you to flight simulation school! In a moment I'm going to have you pair up with one other person and let you test-fly your skills with him or her. Yes, it'll feel a bit artificial—simulators always do. But this is a great place to make a few mistakes and learn from them. Remember: we're among friends. And when we're done, we'll be that much more ready to talk to people outside of this place, which is the real reason we're here.

Giving that explanation ahead of time helps participants willingly join in, because they understand that this is not just something that the trainer invented to fill time and keep them busy. It really is an important step toward becoming competent communicators of the faith. The irony is that as hard as it is to motivate them to practice, it's usually even harder to get them to stop! Once they get into it, they realize how fun it is to remember and talk about God's activity in their lives. This motivates them all the more to tell others their story when they get outside the confines of the training group.

Telling His Story

The most important part of evangelism training is teaching people to convey the central message of the Christian faith. They must have the message down cold and be able to communicate it concisely and clearly.

We try to accomplish this in several ways. First, we teach the theology of the gospel. I resist racing into giving participants a simple tool or illustration until I feel they first have some depth of understanding to undergird the tool. In particular, I key in on the meaning and the significance of the substitutionary atonement of Jesus Christ. Trainees need to understand who Christ is and what he did for us on the cross. They need to know that he is not just some outside party who was unwillingly dragged into the situation. He is actually the God we've sinned against (the second person of the Trinity), who justly sentenced us for our sin and then willingly came and paid the penalty we owed in our place. As Romans 3:26 says, he did this "to demonstrate his justice at the present time, so as to be just and the one who justifies those who have faith in Jesus." And now he offers us this justification as a free gift of grace, available to everyone who will receive it. (The best description of this I've read is in J. Oliver Buswell's book, *A Systematic Theology of the Christian Religion,* in the chapter "The Doctrine of the Atonement.")[3]

We just have to put this gospel into the hands of all of our people, challenge them to take some risks, and let God show his power through it.

We teach the meaning of the cross first. Then, building on this essential foundation, we teach two illustrations that Christians can use anywhere and anytime to present the gospel clearly. They are "The Bridge" (a modified version of the illustration developed by the Navigators) and the "Do versus Done" illustrations. These, again, are taught by the leader, shown in real-life situations on video, and then practiced by the participants. This technique cements their understanding and increases their confidence level so that they're able to put these illustrations to work during the week.

I can't tell you how many times I've heard stories within a week's time of how trainees have presented one of the illustrations, God has used it, and a friend has already come to Christ. And on a broader scale, after our last Contagious Evangelism Conference at Willow Creek, in which we taught the participants a gospel illustration, one volunteer who had been at the conference used the illustration the following weekend with the second and third graders in her Sunday school class. Fifteen kids came to Christ on the spot!

The gospel truly is "the power of God for the salvation of everyone who believes" (Romans 1:16). We just have to put this gospel into the hands of all of our people, challenge them to take some risks, and let God show his power through it.

Addressing Questions and Objections

Scripture tells us to "always be prepared to give an answer to everyone who asks you to give the reason for the hope that you have" (1 Peter 3:15). That's why we include addressing questions and objections as part of the standard curriculum for every believer we train.

As our society becomes increasingly secular, being prepared to answer questions is becoming all the more important (as we discussed in chapter 2), so we expose participants to eight of the top questions non-Christians raise, along with some street-tested answers. These are presented through a set of video vignettes, as well as being printed in the participant's guide. After seeing answers presented, we have trainees choose the questions they think their friends are most likely to ask. We let them review the printed answers and then practice giving answers to the person next to them.

Leading across the Line of Faith

More than in any other part of the evangelistic process, Christians are tempted to bail out of the action and call in a "professional" when the time comes to lead others across the line of faith. But the thing is, their friend trusts *them*—not necessarily the pastor or church leader they might want to call in. More than that, this is the most exciting and fulfilling part, so why not experience and enjoy it? Thus, we need to equip every believer to lead their friends in a prayer of commitment.

This preparation involves more than just learning some practical how-tos; it also requires that we shore up trainees' faith and courage. I try to do this by telling stories of ordinary Christians who, in spite of waning confidence and wavering voice, were used by God to lead someone across the line of faith. Sometimes I tell these stories myself, but I prefer to let participants hear them directly from someone in the class. This has the highest impact, because everyone knows the person in their own group is not some professional evangelist to whom these kinds of things happen all the time.

In addition, we try to take some of the mystery and fear out of this final stage in the evangelistic process. Specifically, we explain to our trainees how they can lead their friends in a natural, conversational prayer in which they prompt their friends to ask Christ, in their own words, for his forgiveness and leadership. We follow this teaching with our most powerful video segment of the entire course and then have participants role-play actually praying with each other.

A few times I've been asked if I think it's really appropriate to have people practice a prayer. While for some this may feel like too sacred an area to practice, there's no other part of evangelism where the need is greater to help Christians get comfortable. Not practicing this part would be like letting the pilot in the flight simulator skip the act of landing!

Think about this: If it's one of *your* loved ones being helped by somebody in the church, I'll bet you'll want the helper to feel confident and prepared when it comes to leading your loved one in a prayer of commitment. Practicing in a safe training environment is the best way to help Christians get to that point.

Ensuring Follow-Up and Discipleship

The final part of the process is following up with those who have put their trust in Christ. We teach participants to help new believers form healthy relationships with other Christians in a biblically functioning church and to encourage them to establish regular patterns of prayer, Bible study, and worship that will enhance their spiritual growth.

I also challenge trainees to make sure the person gets into an individual relationship, small group, or class where immediate and ongoing discipling can take place. I tell them that they've helped bring a new spiritual child into the family, and that they must never commit the crime of abandoning this baby. Rather, they have two legitimate options: natural parenting and adoption. *Natural parenting* means they'll personally meet on a regular basis with the new believer to help him or her establish patterns of growth. *Adoption* means they'll arrange for someone else who may be more appropriate (due to gender, geography, or areas of common interest and affinity) to meet with the person and help him or her stay on track and grow spiritually.

Review and Practice

In a final session of the *Becoming a Contagious Christian* course, we take everything we've done, put it into sequence, review it, and give participants the chance to practice the main elements one more time. It's important to do this, since we have dispensed so much information and spread it out over a number of weeks. In effect, we're helping participants put all the puzzle pieces together and see the big picture. What's more, training experts have shown that practicing new skills a second time helps establish those skills exponentially.

The review video segment and role-play help build confidence and give participants a sense that this is something they really can do—because they've just done it!

LIBERATING AND EQUIPPING EVERY BELIEVER

Notice who this training is for: *every believer.* Everyone may reach out in his or her own style, but we need one hundred percent participation. Every Christian in the world—regardless of the spiritual gifts he or she may or may not have—is part of the church to which Jesus gave the Great Commission. We, as leaders, need to make sure that believers understand this, and then we must do everything in our power to equip them for it. This is the only way we are ever going to solve the math problem, fix the redemptive ratios, and build highly contagious churches.

What's involved in equipping every believer? Along with making this task a high value and priority in our churches, we need to make sure the evangelistic point person offers multiple and ongoing opportunities for training. And we also must communicate clearly and boldly that this training is for *everybody.*

FREQUENCY OF TRAINING OPPORTUNITIES

The biggest mistake I see churches making in the area of evangelism training is to view it as a one-shot deal or even as an annual event. With such sporadic efforts, the law of evangelistic entropy is sure to triumph. When that happens, everybody loses.

Sometimes leaders say to me enthusiastically, "We're making this the year of evangelism." I have mixed reactions to that statement. I'm often tempted to ask them, "And which year is going to be your year of worship? And then of Bible teaching?" I'm sure they'd give me a puzzled look and say something like, "Well, we do those things every week!" If so, they would be well on their way toward understanding my point.

We need one hundred percent participation. Every Christian in the world is part of the church to which Jesus gave the Great Commission.

Evangelism is the heartbeat of the mission Christ gave to the church, and we dare not relegate it to something we do in even, or odd, years, or toward the end of a ministry season because we're starting to feel guilty. Now, I know that when some leaders talk about a year of evangelism what they mean is that they're giving it special emphasis in order to try to establish it as a higher priority, not *just* this year, but from here on out. I'm all for that! But no matter what year it is or what aspect of the church's ministry we're presently trying to expand, evangelism must remain consistently central. This means we must devote disproportionate amounts of personnel, energy, and resources toward this task. That's the way wars are won, and no war is more important than this one.

So when it comes to training our people for personal outreach, we must have an ongoing program. Members need to see constant symbols of the leader's commitment to evangelism training. More than that, they need to know they have no excuse for not going through the training in the near future. If they can't go this month, they can go next month—or the time after that.

Since people will be interested in training at different times, we need to make it available at all times. In January they're busy, in March their heart isn't in it, in May they meant to attend but something big came up at work. But then comes July, and they're at a class reunion and have the chance to share Christ, but they don't feel prepared or confident. Now they want to know why they "have to wait until September just to get a little simple evangelism training." You may not be able to offer training every month, but try to offer it at least once a quarter. This would be almost impossible if the pastor tries to lead every session, but with an evangelistic point person in place, this is a relatively easy pace to maintain.

In the late 1980s, when we first developed the training that eventually grew into the *Becoming a Contagious Christian* evangelism course, we taught it at Willow Creek virtually every month—about ten times a year. We'd teach it over the course of four weeks (two one-hour sessions per night) and then start over. We'd say, "Come on Saturday mornings in April. If you can't make it then, we're offering it on Monday nights in May." Today, more than a decade later, our church enjoys a strong reputation for evangelism, and by God's grace, we're baptizing over a thousand people each year. So now we can let up and teach evangelism less often, right?

Wrong! We're actually turning up the heat even more, offering the training in additional settings, at multiple times, and with a greater number of people on the team teaching it. One of the most exciting things happening right now is that more and more of our ministries are taking ownership for evangelism training, and they're developing their own trainers who custom-fit it to their particular ministry.

The person from the sports ministry teaches it by using a lot of football, soccer, and tennis illustrations. The person from our Promiseland children's ministry tailors the illustrations to fit the workers who serve the children, and I could give you many other examples from places like the men's ministry, women's ministry, Gen-X ministry, student ministries, prison ministry, and international ministry. In addition, more and more small groups are using it, with the advantage of discussing evangelism at a very personal level and then encouraging one another and holding each other accountable to put it into action.

Stories will multiply. Courage will grow. Faith will expand. Leaders will emerge. Seekers will meet Christ, and the presence of new believers will motivate more believers to get into the action.

What gives this approach its synergistic power is that, while all of these ministries are customizing the course to fit their own situations, the basic curriculum is still the same. That means we are developing a common language throughout the congregation. So when someone says, "I'm the interpersonal style," others know what he or she means and can compare and contrast their own style—and then make plans to synergistically use the various styles together as "links in the chain."

As this kind of understanding grows and spreads throughout your church, powerful things will start to happen. Stories will multiply. Courage will grow. Faith will expand. Leaders will emerge. Seekers will meet Christ, and the presence of new believers will motivate more believers to get into the action where they can be used to reach still more.

Things get *contagious*—inside the church first, and then increasingly outside the walls of the church.

The Importance of Strong Promotion

When you're introducing the training—especially at the beginning—you have to follow the three-part rule: communicate, communicate, and communicate. Putting an invitation in the bulletin and having someone read it as part of the announcements at your weekly worship service is not enough. Evangelism training needs to be highlighted, explained, and promoted—especially by the senior pastor. In fact, at our church, Bill Hybels regularly challenges every member to go through the training at least once every two years!

Evangelism training needs to be a point of application in the annual vision talks, a call-to-action response at the end of sermons, a next step for people in membership classes, an opportunity for growth in the discipleship process. We also need to inform members through stories, testimonies, and features in the newsletter, on the bulletin board, and on the Web site.

At both the personal and the public levels, we need to invite, encourage, and compel people to attend training sessions. A number of individuals in our church who are now strong in evangelism would not have gone through the training had there not been a leader who looked them in the eye and challenged them to go.

And we must also let people know what we're inviting them to. Sometimes I make an announcement at our worship services, which goes something like this:

> For the four Monday nights in May we're going to be offering the *Becoming a Contagious Christian* course, which is a great opportunity to learn how to naturally and effectively communicate your faith to people you know.
>
> I'll tell you in a moment how to preregister, but first there's something I need to say to those of you who have already started to tune me out! Some of you have figured out that this is about personal evangelism, and you're convinced it's not for you. Well, if you were just thinking that, then you need to know that the course was designed *especially* for you! This is the evangelism course for nonevangelists!
>
> Just ask around! Many others who were initially put off by this area have come through this training and have changed their minds. They now know that impacting the lives of others is an unparalleled adventure.
>
> But don't take my word for it. Come find out for yourself. I'll guarantee that after the first session you're going to be fired up about reaching your friends for Christ. If you're not, I'll personally buy your book back from you!
>
> For more details, or to sign up, stop by immediately after the service and see us at the *Contagious Christian* booth.

This message can be reinforced with mailings, flyers, and posters, as well as by the leaders throughout the ministries of the church. You might also want to make it a standard expectation for church membership and certainly for serving in any kind of a leadership role. Attack from every angle!

A bulletin announcement might look something like this:

BECOME A DIFFERENCE MAKER!—God can use you to impact the spiritual lives of your friends and family. Join us on Monday nights in May for the *Becoming a Contagious Christian* seminar, where you'll learn to naturally and effectively communicate your faith to people you know. It's an adventure you won't want to miss any longer! Stop by the *Contagious Christian* booth after the service to find out more or to register.

Having a large number of attenders, especially at the first few presentations of the course, is important. People have enough doubts about evangelism without being subjected to the feelings that come with walking into a large room with only a few people in it. My advice is to get a sense for the number of people who will be there, and then book a room just barely big enough for that number. You want people to be seated fairly close to one another and to the trainer. This will help build intimacy and trust as well as foster excitement and enthusiasm.

Ten Tips for Training Events

Here are a few key suggestions concerning training events (some of these especially pertain to the *Becoming a Contagious Christian* course, but the principles are easily transferable):

1. Ask people who are planning to attend to sign up ahead of time (and make it easy for them to do so through multiple paths: booth, telephone, regular mail, Internet, and so forth). This will help you plan room size, refreshments, and the right number of participant's guides and any other handouts. Allow for a few walk-ins, and be sure to make them feel welcome.
2. Keep records of who attends in case you want to get back to them about other training or outreach opportunities.
3. Consider setting a course fee or "suggested donation" to help cover the cost of materials and refreshments. Most people don't mind investing a little in something they consider important. Just be sure to keep it at a reasonable level. We've generally recommended ten dollars per person, with the understanding that anyone who can't afford it can attend at no charge. Other churches charge five dollars. Some even offer it for free and subsidize the costs through their evangelism or local missions budget.
4. Book the best room you can get (in terms of quality), set it up in advance, and make sure it is as clean and organized as it possibly can be. This is one of the church's most strategic events, so treat it as such.

5. Depending on the size of the group and the room, you may need a sound system as well as lights focused on the trainer. If so, be sure to use a lapel microphone; use the best equipment you have available, and make sure it is tested and ready long before people arrive. Do the same with the video player and overhead or PowerPoint projector.
6. Pick the sharpest, friendliest, and most winsome volunteers you can find to greet people, distribute materials, and serve refreshments. Then make sure they go through the training themselves so they'll be able to talk enthusiastically about the course and the impact it has had on their own outreach efforts.
7. Play upbeat instrumental music as people arrive, with the volume a little higher than typical background music. You don't want it to be blaring, but you want it to be at a level that will help people relax and that will force them to chat with each other at higher than whispered tones. They need to see—and feel—that this will not be a formal church service but an exciting group of friendly people gathered to gain skills that will help them make a difference in their friends' lives.
8. Start and end on time. Even though the eight sessions can be done in about an hour each, I'd recommend allowing some extra time for questions and storytelling.
9. Make sure that you or whoever is facilitating the training is thoroughly familiar with the materials and prepared to lead. This will help you to not be too tied to the leader's guide or worried about when to switch screens on the overhead projector or when to put on a video vignette. Every time you teach the course you'll feel more relaxed and it will become more fun. Soon the biggest challenge will be to stay within the time frames, because you'll be gaining more and more stories and illustrations you'll want to tell.
10. Be sure to announce to the group, both verbally and by means of a printed flyer, when the next offering of training will be. Especially at the last session, you need to commission the freshly fired-up evangelists to go out and be your ambassadors in encouraging others in the church to come to the course. Remind them that when they first entered the room many of them were convinced evangelism training wasn't for them. Now they know otherwise and need to help their friends discover the same thing. These people will be your best promoters. Give them the dates and the flyers, and put them to work! Also let them know that as alumni they're always welcome to come back for a refresher whenever the course is taught.

PARTNERS IN TRAINING

As I've already observed, I encourage every church to appoint and empower a point person who will serve as the primary evangelism trainer and the quality control leader who will monitor all of the other outreach training going on throughout the ministries of the church. *Becoming a Contagious Christian* materials are published by Zondervan and are available through them and through the Willow Creek Association (see ordering information in the back of the book). They are designed to be easy to teach, even for someone without a background in evangelism or teaching.

In addition, the *Becoming a Contagious Christian LIVE Seminar* is a great way to jump-start your evangelism training. A small army of highly qualified trainers whom I've helped train, in partnership with International Bible Society (IBS) and Zondervan, are available to come to your church to teach a single-day presentation of the course. This can be a one-shot event (to be followed by your own team presenting future seminars using the published materials), or you can have a member of this team come back and offer the *Contagious LIVE Seminar* at regular intervals.

These trainers are available throughout the United States and in many other parts of the world. In fact, I was recently with a group of leaders in the mountains of Slovakia, in a former communist training center. Together with the team, we taught Contagious/IBS trainers from fifteen Eastern and Western European countries. We did this through translators in seven different languages simultaneously. What a privilege and a thrill that was, and how exciting to hear the stories of ongoing evangelistic impact in churches in those countries!

In all likelihood, there is an equipped and experienced trainer within reach of your church. For more information call 1-888-222-5795, or look on the Internet at www.gospelcom.net/ibs/cos. This is a great opportunity to enhance your church's evangelism training efforts.

I'm also excited that Willow Creek Resources and Zondervan have now published a youth edition of the *Becoming a Contagious Christian* course that includes new video and printed materials and is designed to train high school and junior high students to reach their friends for Christ.[4] In addition, InterVarsity Christian Fellowship has adopted the course, and their media department, 2100 Productions, has developed a university edition of the video that can be used in conjunction with the regular printed materials (you can obtain more information or order these products by calling the Willow Creek Association at 1-800-570-9812).

The Impact of Evangelistic Training

I could tell many stories about people and churches that have put evangelism training to work. Some are grand scale, like the church in Georgia that taught nearly a thousand people all at once through their Sunday school classes. Others are unexpected, like the church in Iowa, where a seminar participant who had been spiritually sitting on the fence decided to trust Christ and prayed right there in the middle of the class! Some are heartwarming, like the woman at our church who led both of her aging parents to faith, or the junior high boy who used his toy building blocks to show his grandmother the Bridge illustration and ended up leading her in a prayer of commitment. Others are humorous, like the woman who took a coworker to lunch the day after the session on how to explain the gospel. She told her friend what she'd learned, presented the plan of salvation, and ended up praying with her in the car as they drove back to work—while the friend was driving!

Do you see what's happening? It's the replacement of the old 1 x 100 approach to evangelism with the much more powerful 100 x 1. Instead of one "professional" trying to lead everybody to Christ, more and more ordinary Christians are getting in the game, and the impact is expanding exponentially. It's a reversing of the ratios—and it's the initial step toward solving the math problem we raised at the beginning of the chapter.

I conclude this chapter with a story that poignantly illustrates the power of training people to share Christ. The story is told in a letter from Todd, a church leader in Ontario, Canada, who had just returned home from our first Contagious Evangelism Conference at Willow Creek. After a brief introduction, he wrote this:

> Currently we are teaching the *Becoming a Contagious Christian* material on Sunday evenings. Keith, the newly appointed coordinator of our Strategic Evangelism Ministry, and I were teaching session 5 of the curriculum, the one about "Telling His Story," this past Sunday night. As you know, this is the session that presents the Bridge illustration.
>
> I laid out the theology portion, and then Keith taught through the drawing. As he explained each component, we had people reproduce the drawing on napkins he'd handed out in order to simulate a real-life scenario! Many children were there for the service, and they drew the picture too. At least one ten-year-old boy, Matthew, decided to accept Jesus after drawing the picture and discussing it with his father.

But I want to tell you about my own son, Joel, who is six years old and quite a little "intellectual." Up until this weekend he had no interest in talking to us about spiritual things. Perhaps he was a bit of a junior skeptic! But Sunday was different. In his class that morning, Keith had encouraged the children to pray to receive Christ, and we found out later that Joel had done so.

Then, Sunday evening during the service, Joel, like the other children present, drew the Bridge drawing. When my wife later asked him where he could be found on the drawing, he said, "I prayed with Pastor Keith this morning, and I think I'm over here with God." Needless to say, we were very excited! His hesitancy to talk about spiritual things was lifted, and we enjoyed a fantastic conversation in the van on the way home.

But then, as soon as we drove into the driveway, Joel jumped out and announced that he was going to show his napkin to Agnes, our next-door neighbor we've been trying to reach out to! He ran to her door and explained his Bridge drawing in detail!

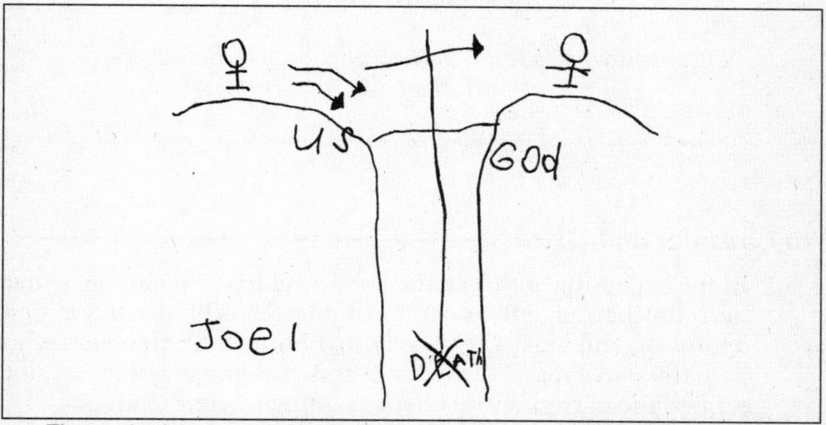

The work of Joel, an evangelistically liberated and equipped six-year-old.

Then he asked her, "Where are you on the drawing?" She placed herself one step onto the Bridge. He then proceeded to invite her to our church, and she accepted without hesitation.

This little boy accepted Christ in the morning, learned the Bridge illustration in the evening, and within a half hour of the service had used it to explain the gospel to an unchurched person! What an incredible answer to the prayers I've been praying since Joel came into the world six years ago.

If Joel, a six-year-old boy who had just met Christ, can be used in this way, then so can you and I! But that kind of action won't happen in most of our members' lives without an ongoing evangelism training program to equip and encourage them.

Building a contagious church that reaches into the unchurched community around it depends on that kind of training. The task is too huge to be done on the backs of a few pastors, church leaders, or evangelism enthusiasts. We need nothing less than a movement to unleash the whole body of Christ—*every* member of *every* church being trained and deployed to communicate his or her faith with confidence.

STAGE 4: KEY IDEA

Train every member—one hundred percent— to be contagious.

"Everyone who is fully trained will be like his teacher" (Luke 6:40).

To Consider and Discuss

1. In the beginning of this chapter you read that "of churches that do train their people, most do so infrequently, teach just one approach, and have a relatively low number of members who actually participate." How does this statement reflect (or not reflect) the current evangelistic training in your church?
2. What do you think would be the optimal frequency of training in your church's setting? What incremental steps could you take to get there?
3. When it comes to evangelism, what do you think an "ordinary" follower of Christ should look like?
4. What are some practical and creative ways you can promote evangelism training in your church?
5. If you've been through an evangelistic training program, how has it influenced your effectiveness as a witness for Jesus Christ? How might you be helped by a refresher course?

8
STAGE 5: DEVELOPING A DIVERSIFIED EVANGELISM TEAM

I had a problem. I knew that among the one hundred percent of church members we were trying to train to share their faith there was an elusive core of about ten percent we needed to find. These were the ones who were gifted and impassioned by God to take outreach much further in their own lives and in our church. They were the missing link to building and sustaining the kinds of outreach events and ministries that would truly turbocharge the church's efforts to reach lost people. We could not afford to ignore them.

But how could we find them? And once we had identified them, how could we best encourage them and then put them into action?

AVOIDING COMMON PITFALLS

I wanted to avoid two extremes into which churches fall. The first is to simply leave these gifted people alone. This approach says, "We know they're out there somewhere, God bless 'em! And we sure hope they're doing their job!" But Paul admonished Timothy to "fan into flame the gift of God, which is in you" (2 Timothy 1:6). We need to find these people and challenge them in the same way—particularly because they're faced with the obstacles of evangelistic entropy, the problem of perceptions, and the ongoing efforts of the evil one to keep them sidetracked on less important ventures.

I knew that somehow we had to call these people out of isolation and begin to develop and deploy them. But I also wanted to avoid the other extreme of keeping them together all of the time. This is a danger inherent in starting a traditional "evangelism team." Members can easily end up moving from being isolated *from* one another to being isolated along *with* one another. All of a sudden they're hanging out with other outreach types most of the time and are no longer participating in or influencing the rest of the ministries of the church.

As Becky Pippert reminded us years ago in her classic book *Out of the Saltshaker & into the World,* salt has to be spread out before it does any good. "Salty" people not only need to be spread throughout the neighborhoods, they also need to be spread throughout the church's ministries. Think about it. If we really want to build a contagious, outwardly focused church, are there any ministries that don't need at least a few evangelism "carriers" in their midst? I can't think of any!

We need these people among the greeters and ushers who have direct contact with seekers who come to visit our services. We need them with the children, the students, the singles, the couples, the men, and the women. We need them on the hospital and nursing home visitation teams, around the food pantry, in the homeless ministry, on the missions board as well as on the mission field, on the small group ministry or Sunday school teaching team, and certainly mixed in with the elder or deacon boards. We need their catalytic influence everywhere!

To build on Paul's "fan the flame" metaphor, every evangelist in the church (using that term broadly to include anyone with gifts or passion in the area of evangelism, regardless of which of the six evangelism styles he or she might have) is like a burning ember in a bonfire. If we leave those embers out on their own, isolated somewhere in the church, they will lose their intensity and grow cold. On the other hand, if we go to the other extreme and keep them together in one place, they'll burn bright and hot, but they'll have a negligible effect on the environment outside of their immediate circle. So we can't leave them alone, to be sure, but neither can we pull them completely away into an evangelism team that is completely separated from the other ministries.

See the problem? I spent weeks trying to find a workable solution to this conundrum that would allow us to meet with and build into the evangelists in the church yet keep them strategically spread throughout the ministries of the church. What I finally figured out with the help of a couple of our other leaders was that we needed to develop *a new kind of evangelism team.* It would be a centralized, cross-departmental, multistyled, easy-access, regular-but-not-too-frequent gathering of evangelism enthusiasts from all over the church.

In the terms of our 6-Stage Process, we needed to move into stage 5: "developing a diversified evangelism team."

THE SHAPE OF THIS MINISTRY

This new ministry provides a place where evangelists visit for inspiration and information but not a place where they set up permanent residence. Our goal is to bring them in, build them up, and send them back out. Thus, it is a *team* only in a loose sense. In reality it is a gathering of all of the ministries' evangelism leaders and teams, which is organized and led by the church's evangelism point leader. The evangelism team is *centralized* and *cross-departmental,* because evangelism is a value and activity that transcends any one ministry or group of people. We wanted to build a contagious *church,* not just a contagious department or two.

The evangelism team is *multistyled,* because we believe in a wide range of evangelistic approaches. We're convinced it takes all kinds of Christians to reach all kinds of non-Christians. So it is crucial that the team not be dominated by one style or one ministry emphasis that pushes everybody else to conform. Rather, it embraces and celebrates evangelistic diversity and then builds on it (in ways I describe in part 3).

Our team meetings at Willow Creek are *easy access* in the sense that we try to remove all unnecessary barriers to attendance (evangelism has enough barriers built into it already). This means picking a convenient time, choosing a central location, keeping the registration process simple, holding costs for food and any materials to a minimum (sometimes completely subsidizing these costs), and promising people that there are no other implied commitments that come with showing up.

Easy access also means assuring potential attendees that they don't need a lot of outreach experience or confidence in their evangelistic abilities to be part of the team. We avoid projecting the idea that this is an elite core of specialists. We tell people that if they have a passion in this area, or if they'd like to develop more passion for it, they ought to give one of these events a try.

Our team meetings are frequent enough to build some relationships and momentum but *not too frequent.* Too many meetings force people to choose between this ministry and the other areas in the church where they're already involved. At our church, therefore, we hold these gatherings only four to six times a year. The inner core of evangelists want more, and we give them other next-step opportunities. But this limited number of meetings enables the broader group of people from the other ministries to stay active with the team. Often when I'm inviting a new participant, this person will start to tell me that unfortunately he or she is already involved in another ministry. My standard reply is, "That's why we only have these meetings a few times a year—so you can do both!"

Another advantage to offering meetings less often is that it enables us to do better planning and invest in higher quality elements, whether guest speakers, special music, media presentations, or printed materials. This is essential in helping busy people stay motivated to participate on an ongoing basis.

We avoid meeting immediately before or after our weekend services, because these services are designed for seekers and we like to keep team members free to attend the services with friends. We work hard to send consistent signals to our people and not to ask them to attend outreach team meetings when what we really want is for them to be *doing* outreach. Instead, we've found that Saturday morning breakfast meetings work best for us. We schedule about two-and-a-half hours, which includes time for eating, talking at the tables, a short break, and then the main program.

GIVING THE MINISTRY A NAME

You may be wondering what we call this strategic gathering at Willow Creek. We didn't want to name it the "Evangelism Team" because of all of the stereotypes conjured up by such a name. After brainstorming and considering many different names, we finally decided to call it the "Frontline Team." If you're going to declare war, you need a team on the front lines of the battle. This name suggests that its participants are in the center of the action.

Since we started the Frontline Team in the early 1990s, other churches have recognized the need to begin similar ministries, and more and more are picking up the name as well. I welcome this trend and hope this book will help more churches, yours included, learn how to begin Frontline Teams for themselves. Bill Hybels talked with Lee Strobel and me about the need for this kind of a team in a taped interview for *Defining Moments,* Willow Creek's audio journal for church leaders. He said, in part,

> I think you've picked up on an idea here that has been almost completely undiscovered in the church for the last one hundred years—that is, the importance of identifying the people in the congregation with the spiritual gift of evangelism and then paying special attention to them. Put it on a comparative

basis. The church has for a long time identified the people who can teach things, and they have them teach the Sunday school, or the people who can lead the youth group or the Sunday services. They identify the people who can sing and let them sing. The same is true for those who can greet, and usher, and so on.

Now, if we say we're fundamentally concerned with bringing large numbers of people to faith in Jesus Christ—which is a primary mission of the church—then it's almost unthinkable that for the last one hundred years probably less than one percent of churches worldwide have even identified the people in their congregation who have the spiritual gift of evangelism—let alone create an environment of training and inspiration and prayer and motivation for that group, and then give them clear marching orders like you guys do. . . .

There's a lesson here for pastors of churches. Most pastors pray and dream about having an evangelistically alive congregation. Well, I believe this is one of the most practical ways to get that dream actualized. I think there ought to be a Frontline group or some other identified gathering of gifted evangelists in every local church all around the world. It needs to be consistent. It needs to be a catalyzing activity so that the evangelistic dreams of a church can become reality.[1]

COMPONENTS OF FRONTLINE MEETINGS

Following are some of the main elements we've found to be important in our Frontline Team meetings. Depending on the priorities of the particular meeting, these will vary in order and degree of emphasis. As you move into stage 5 and begin to plan these gatherings, you'll be able to determine what is appropriate each time based on prayer and a general consensus between your point person and the other leaders of the evangelism ministry.

Strategic Leadership

You're becoming a church with clear evangelistic vision. But apart from organizing a regular gathering—along the lines of a Frontline Team—when do you ever have the chance to speak to and lead the evangelistically gifted and impassioned core of your church? Apart from something like this, you're left, at best, with a shotgun approach that tries to envision, guide, and encourage the evangelists at the same time that the whole church is gathered. This provides the forum for strategic evagelistic leadership.

RELATIONAL CONNECTIONS

One constant in every meeting is the opportunity for these people to connect relationally with other like-minded outreach enthusiasts. I've often said that if all we did was get these people together in a room and turn them loose to talk to each other about their evangelistic efforts, we'd be serving an important need. It's the "logs in a bonfire" effect. The key is to schedule plenty of time for this. You'll be tempted to fill the entire time with teaching and activities. Don't do it, or you'll deprive people of what they need most—personal interaction and encouragement.

If all we did was get these people together in a room and turn them loose to talk to each other about their evangelistic efforts, we'd be serving an important need.

That's why having a meal together works so well. We start by letting people pick up food on their way in, sit at tables, and talk. We usually have some instrumental music playing in the background to help people relax and feel at home. Also, we often seed the conversations by giving people questions to discuss that relate to some aspect of evangelism we're going to address in the meeting.

MUTUAL SUPPORT

It's easy to underestimate how important this connecting time is for evangelists. A lot of them are confident, outgoing people who seem to thrive on challenge and individuality. But the truth is that evangelism can often be a very lonely endeavor. Discouragement and feelings of inadequacy can easily set in. This is why we need to facilitate discussions that help members realize that such feelings are common and that none of us is alone.

STIMULATING STORIES

The strongest tool for encouraging evangelists is the sharing of stories about how God is working among us. Since nothing has a more powerful effect, we make this the heart of most of our meetings, giving it more priority than even teaching or vision casting.

Today as I was writing this chapter I received an e-mail message from Jim, a member of our Frontline Team, telling me that at a Matthew party he recently sponsored, eight people made first-time commitments to Christ. (A Matthew party is what we call social events designed to mix believers with unbelievers in a safe social setting. We took the name from Jesus' disciple, Matthew, who held such an event in Luke 5:29.) A few days ago I received a note from another friend who had written out his testimony, explaining what had convinced him to become a Christian. He told me about a letter he had received from an atheist who just five days earlier had read his story and trusted in Christ. I was not directly involved with either of these situations, nor did I know any of the non-Christians who were reached, but this news greatly encouraged and motivated me.

We facilitate the sharing of stories like these in several different ways. Sometimes one of our Frontline leaders will encourage those who have an exciting story (or a difficult experience they've learned from) to tell the rest of the group. Usually we'll caution them with the "A-B-C-Ds" of group sharing, which I learned from my Willow Creek colleague and evangelism partner Garry Poole: A, be *audible;* B, be *brief;* C, be *Christ-centered;* and D, *don't preach.* Giving these directives ahead of time helps keep people focused. Opening up the floor has its risks, and occasionally one of us needs to step in and help the person speaking to get back on track. But some of the most inspiring and joy-filled stories have emerged in this way.

Another approach is to ask a team member ahead of time to be prepared to tell the group about how God has worked through him or her. Like the Matthew party story I mentioned, these stories find their way to someone in leadership, and then we decide to use them in the group. Many times one of us will informally interview the person with the story. That gives us the chance to clarify facts, correct any misunderstandings, interject a bit of humor, and occasionally drive home an important point. This format also tends to put the one telling the story at ease.

I remember interviewing a guy named Bob at one of the first meetings. Bob had taken some evangelistic risks in a conversation with a friend a couple of weeks earlier. In animated tones Bob told us how inadequate and nervous he felt going into the situation. In fact, he said his hands had been shaking so badly that he literally had to sit on them while he shared the gospel with his friend! Nevertheless, before the conversation was finished, he led his friend in a prayer of commitment to Christ!

As Bob told his story he could barely force himself to stay seated on the stool next to me. You can imagine the excitement this evoked in the evangelism enthusiasts who listened. They were all salivating and saying to themselves, "Man, I want more of that kind of action in my life! I could take the kinds of steps Bob took—my hands don't even shake as much as his did! Surely God can use me that way too."

They walked out at the end of the meeting more motivated and better prepared to take risks for the sake of the gospel.

Look for success stories you can highlight for your team. They will encourage and challenge the team as nothing else will. In addition, you can choose the best stories and use them in your worship services—either you can tell them, with permission, or the persons can tell them themselves. This will honor them for their service and further instill evangelism values throughout your church.

Teaching, Inspiration, and Skills Reinforcement

Teaching is another important component of the Frontline Team, although we don't view meetings as seminar classes or as duplications of the *Becoming a Contagious Christian* course. Rather, we remind members that if they haven't been through "basic training" yet, they ought to attend the course as soon as possible. We make them aware of the course dates and encourage them to repeat the course periodically as a refresher and to bring church friends who haven't yet gone through it.

Frontline meetings are, however, a great place to expose your core evangelists to teachers from inside and outside the church. We look for speakers who can encourage them in their efforts, inspire them to express their God-given evangelistic potential, and challenge them to make the most of every opportunity. Sometimes we also expand on the broad themes of the training course and give new ideas and examples that members can add to their evangelistic arsenals. For example, we'll teach a fresh illustration of the gospel message—or even review an old one—and have people pair up and practice it.

At one particular meeting we felt we needed to reinforce the importance of all of us being ready to help people make decisions for Christ. Many team members were doing pretty well at encouraging friends in their spiritual journeys but not at assisting these friends in actually putting their trust in Christ. So we designed a Frontline meeting around the theme of "Crossing the Line of Faith."

First, we talked about the soccer metaphor of "putting the ball in the net." Then I role-played with a friend named Dan, who had recently come to Christ. He was fresh enough in the faith that I knew he wouldn't use a lot of religious clichés. Our short "drama" seemed to go well, and later many in the group told us they found it helpful. We ended the meeting in prayer, asking God for opportunities and for boldness to apply what we'd learned.

Two days later I got a call from Jim, one of our key members, who told me that he'd already applied the lessons while heading out on a business trip over the weekend. He said, "Mark, normally I would have simply presented the gospel, encouraged the man to consider what I'd said, assured him that I'd be praying for him, and then dropped the subject. But after what I learned on Saturday morning, I decided to take a little risk and ask him if he would like to receive the forgiveness and leadership of Christ. Much to my surprise, he was ready! We prayed together right there on the plane, and today we have a new brother in Christ." When you see results like this, it's easy to stay motivated in planning quality Frontline events!

Below are a few other examples of topics you may want to address in your meetings, although in some cases you may not want to announce the topic until the team arrives. Build excitement around the team event itself, with its relationships and shots of encouragement, rather than around the specific topic or speaker.

- praying for lost people
- leading small groups for spiritual seekers
- designing creative Matthew parties
- building confidence in the reliability of the Bible
- answering your skeptic friend's toughest challenges
- pointing to the evidence for creation over evolution
- reaching your Jewish friend for Jesus
- understanding Muslim teachings
- mastering the gospel message
- exploring new arenas for redemptive relationships
- finding fresh ways to start spiritual conversations
- taking steps to develop your evangelistic style
- finding the courage to take spiritual risks

Depending on the size of your Frontline Team and the resources available, you may want to consider adding some programming elements to your meetings, such as special music, short movie clips, dramas, worship segments, or multimedia presentations. But only add what fits the theme, what can be done with excellence, and what will relate to the group. Never add elements just for the sake of having more elements. You'd be better off expanding the storytelling or teaching time.

Guest Speakers

Outside speakers can be an important asset—or a detriment. You have a limited number of opportunities to encourage this team, so choose meeting elements and teachers carefully. A guest speaker may be well known and powerful in other arenas but not necessarily fit your Frontline Team. Search for the right teachers, ones who understand and personally relate to the unique challenges of reaching others for Christ.

Where can you find speakers? Some may already be on the team or in the church. Others may be in different churches in your town or region. Perhaps you know a leader in your denomination who would fit the bill (but don't assume someone will fit just because that person has "Evangelism" in his or her title). Another possibility is a Christian professor at a college or seminary in the area. I've tried to keep my eyes open for opportunities to piggyback on other events happening in town. Perhaps an evangelistic teacher or writer is coming to speak for a conference or outreach event. Maybe he or she would enjoy spending an hour encouraging a team of budding evangelists. Remember, don't say no for the person without letting him or her have the chance to say yes! Also, especially when you're first starting out, don't overlook the option of using effective videotaped talks. These can be strong supplemental tools for teaching and inspiring the troops.

My rule for inviting guest speakers is that I must first personally hear them speak or have a recommendation from someone I trust who has heard them speak and who understands the team's needs. At an absolute minimum, I want to hear speakers on tape or see them on video. I once asked an out-of-town speaker I was considering inviting to send me a video of his teaching. "What is this, an audition?" he chided. "Well, yes, I guess it sort of is," I said, quickly adding, "so when can you me send a tape?" He sent a tape, we invited him to speak, he served us well, and we're good friends today!

Asking someone for a tape may feel a bit awkward, but it's far better to take a few relational risks up front than to end up sitting through an excruciating hour while the wrong person squanders your opportunity to build up the group. Also, after hearing a potential speaker elsewhere, you may be able to coach him or her to better fit your group's needs. This is what happened with the man who sent me the videotape, and doing so served him and us well.

Whatever you do in terms of teaching, keep the standard high and make sure it speaks directly to the needs of your team members.

Upcoming Opportunities

One of the most strategic aspects of having your key evangelists together in one room is the opportunity to highlight and explain upcoming evangelism training and outreach events. Your goals in doing this will vary. In some situations, you'll want the Frontliners to attend for their own development. At other times, you'll want them to have the inside track on an event so they'll know how to invite non-

Christians. In many cases, you'll actually be looking for them to get involved in making the event happen, from planning to promotion to execution. Frontline meetings provide a pool of prequalified candidates for a whole range of strategic initiatives you'll want to make happen. Frontline is your *team,* so let members have a share of the action. They'll thank you for giving them an important role to play.

Redemptive Resources

One of the things I enjoy most is introducing high-quality outreach tools to people who will use them. Almost all of the books and magazines in Christian bookstores are designed for Christians, but once in a while you come across a resource that was published with spiritual seekers in mind. When you find one, tell the team about it! Better yet, give them samples at your meeting (see "Fund It," page 125) and help them think through how they can use them. At our meetings we've done this with products like *Pursuit*[2] and *The Life@Work Journal,*[3] two evangelistic magazines that look and read like something you'd feel good about giving to a friend. We've also done this with *Sports Spectrum,*[4] which features stories about the lives of well-known Christian athletes.

We also highlight the gold mine of low-cost, high-grade Scripture tools from International Bible Society (IBS). They put out a vast array of specialized products to help reach such diverse groups as AIDS victims; the homeless; unwed mothers, pregnant women; prison inmates (as well as their families); the suffering or grieving; truck drivers; motorcycle riders; New Age proponents; and Native Americans. They also offer a variety of products for reaching children. (For a free IBS catalog, call them at 1-719-488-9200.)

Other valuable seeker-oriented resources include:

- *The Journey: A Bible for Seeking God and Understanding Life,* an NIV reference Bible designed specifically for spiritual seekers and new believers who are just getting to know the Bible[5]
- *The Case for Christ* by Lee Strobel[6]
- *The Case for Faith* by Lee Strobel[7]
- *The God You're Looking For* by Bill Hybels[8]
- *Leadership by the Book* by Ken Blanchard, Bill Hybels, and Phil Hodges[9]
- *A Search for the Spiritual: Exploring Real Christianity* by James Emery White[10]
- *More Than a Carpenter* by Josh McDowell[11]
- *The Reason Why* by Robert Laidlaw[12]

- *Tough Questions,* a curriculum for seeker small groups, by Garry Poole and Judson Poling[13]

We also frequently recommend the tapes of the messages given at Willow Creek's weekend seeker services. God has used these to lead untold numbers of people to Christ. Hundreds of these messages are available on cassette through the Willow Creek Association, and downloadable transcripts are available online at www.willowcreek.com.

These kinds of products are not just great tools for the team to have available to give to people after they've started talking to them; they are actually catalysts to help them start talking to people about spiritual matters in the first place. Recently, for example, I was on an airplane, and just as we were about to land, I struck up a conversation with a woman sitting next to me. As we talked, I remembered I had a copy of the *Journey* edition of the Gospel of John (distributed by IBS and Zondervan) in my briefcase. Just knowing I had it gave me the confidence to move this friendly little exchange in another direction by saying, "By the way, I have something here I think you might enjoy reading. I'd like to give it to you." She seemed to appreciate it, and it led us into a conversation about spiritual matters. I'm pretty sure this wouldn't have happened if I hadn't had that resource in my briefcase. The key is to help all of our Frontliners keep appropriate outreach tools in their briefcases, purses, backpacks, desk drawers, and glove compartments. It's a tangible way to help them "be prepared to give an answer to everyone who asks" (1 Peter 3:15).

You may know of other tools to introduce to your people, or perhaps your church produces some of its own. Frontline is a great place to promote the use of these strategic resources.

UNITED PRAYER

Earlier I talked about the impact list of three names that participants in the *Becoming a Contagious Christian* course write down and pray for. It's easy to let that list grow cold after the course is completed, so Frontline is a good place to remind people to pray for their lost friends. Members can pair up and together lift up at least one person on each of their lists.

At our church we've also started a Frontline Prayer Team. At every meeting we place at each table forms labeled "Frontline Prayer Requests." Team members use these to write down prayer requests for friends and family members they're trying to reach. The forms then go to the prayer team members, who bring each request before

God. Sometimes they also check back with the person who made the request and ask for an update. When appropriate (and with the permission of the persons involved), we share answers to prayer with the whole group and celebrate what God has done.

Prayer is usually just a segment of a broader meeting program, but occasionally it's good to make it the whole theme, with teaching on prayer, encouragement to keep praying using something like the "3-for-1 Prayer Plan" (praying for each of the three people on your impact list for at least one minute each day), and extended time for members to pray together for their non-Christian friends.

Healthy Accountability

A natural outflow of team interaction is an increased level of accountability. At times I have updated my impact list or increased my prayer activity for lost friends because I knew someone might ask me about it. While I wish I was always moved to action by loftier motivations, the end result is still what I want in my life.

Accountability may be increased by encouraging entire small groups to attend Frontline meetings together or by forming small groups out of the larger team. In these small groups relationships can be built that enable ongoing communication and provide encouragement and challenges to stay active in praying for and reaching out to those on our impact lists as well as to new people we encounter.

There is a fine line to walk, however, in this area of accountability. People often feel excessive guilt and inadequacy about evangelism, so we must be careful not to harshly challenge them or shame them. If we do, they'll just feel worse, and many will start avoiding us rather than moving toward increased prayer and activity to reach others. Direct challenge has its place, but it's best to stay mostly on the encouragement and gentle-reminder side of the equation.

Appreciation and Thanks

In his book *Evangelism That Works,* George Barna says he has seen a lot of churches that "paraded new converts before the congregation to encourage the entire body with the harvest the Lord had brought forth. . . ." But they did this "without mentioning that the converts' decision to embrace Christ had been facilitated through the diligent and obedient efforts of a particular person or group of people. The attention of the church body was trained exclusively upon the evangelized, ignoring the role and model of the evangelizers."[14]

Evangelism can be a difficult, isolated activity, and the people engaged in it need encouragement and affirmation, especially from the church's leaders.

Unfortunately, the people in the church who are most gifted by the Holy Spirit to fulfill the Great Commission are often the most neglected by the church. This is terribly counterproductive. Evangelism can be a difficult, isolated activity, and the people engaged in it need encouragement and affirmation, especially from the church's leaders. Frontline Team meetings are a great place to do this, and it helps you identify those you might also want to recognize and thank in front of the whole congregation.

Every battle has its heroes. There are men or women who run ahead of the pack, set an example, and by their words and actions call everyone else to give their best to the cause. In the spiritual battle for souls, we need to highlight and encourage all the heroes we can find and let their actions inspire us all.

A MEMORABLE WORD OF ENCOURAGEMENT

Our Frontline Team had had a banner year. Members had filled out Frontline Feedback forms, sharing many stories of how God used their efforts throughout the year. Many seekers had come to Christ through them.

Since it was early December and this would be the final meeting of the year, we decided to take a fresh approach to encouraging, thanking, and celebrating with the team. We arranged for eight of the people who had made commitments to Christ that year primarily through the efforts of Frontline members to join us for our breakfast meeting. These eight new Christians and I sat on stools in front of the group, and I briefly interviewed each of them about the events that had led to their putting their trust in Christ. In particular, they described what a Frontline member had said and done to reach them with the good news about Jesus. Then, at the end of each story, we asked that particular team member to stand up and be recognized for allowing God to work through him or her. A man who thanked his wife, a young boy who expressed gratitude to his mother, and several others who thanked their friends. In each case, the rest of the team responded with heartfelt affirmation and applause. They were celebrating with their teammates while at the same time making decisions that *they* would take similar risks next year to bring some of their own friends and family members to Christ.

As if that weren't enough, next came the highlight! We had asked Dr. Gilbert Bilezikian, the college professor who many years earlier had inspired Bill Hybels to start a church for unchurched people, to say a few words in response to what he'd seen that morning.

With great emotion and moist eyes, Dr. Bilezikian said in his endearing French accent,

> I really didn't know what I was walking into today. I've been ambushed. You people have been shredding me. I was sitting there in pieces, because, ultimately, this is what it's all about. This is it. The programs, the schedules, the meetings. *This is what it's all about.*
>
> You people have reminded me of one of the most intensely impactful days in my life. When I was a child, we lived in Paris. That was my home, but my father had a summer house in the countryside in the western part of France.
>
> One day when I was twelve years old, in Paris, I saw the German troops coming. It was Hitler's army. They stayed in France for four years.
>
> They were the enemy. The oppressors. The occupants.
>
> But then, on June 6, 1944, I turned the radio on, tuned to the BBC, which we were forbidden to do. And I heard that the Allied troops had debarked on the coastline not far from us in Normandy, and that the invasion had started.
>
> It was one of the greatest days of my life—just to hear the news. And I knew that it was real, because for two or three weeks we had heard the roar of battle in the distance. The bombs, the cannons, the constant noise, which became louder and louder as the battle approached.
>
> Then one day we heard the tanks roll in, and I went down into the little village. And for the first time in my life I saw Americans. They were American soldiers who were there to push back the enemy. *They were the front line of the invasion, and today you people reminded me of them. That's what you are doing—pushing back the gates of hell and making it count for eternity.*

Then he simply ended in prayer.

Everybody sat in stunned silence. God had visited us in a special way that day, inspiring and motivating all who were there. The interaction, the stories, and now the powerful words of this impassioned leader—this was Frontline at its best, and for those of us who were there, its impact will never be forgotten.

FINDING THE CHURCH'S EVANGELISTIC CORE

You may still be wondering, *Where do you find these people? As you said earlier, they don't just stand up and identify themselves!*

The "Bubble Up" Approach

We can and must find them. Stage 4 (training the one hundred percent) causes the ten percent to surface in ways the other stages don't. The first three stages—modeling evangelistic values, instilling evangelistic values, and empowering the point person—are the prerequisites that help make it possible to get these people into a training situation that can draw out their evangelism gift. And even after all of that, they'll often attend the course hesitantly. That's okay. If you can just get everyone to go through the training, they'll all benefit, they'll all find their natural style and gain skills in communicating their faith, and those with the gift will tend to bubble to the surface.

My friend Karl Singer came up with a great description of this. He said, "What you're essentially doing is throwing everybody into the water and teaching them all to swim. But then you're watching for those who really take to it—the natural swimmers—and putting them on your champion swimming team."

Karl was right. Every church has at least a few of these potential champions, but you have to look for them, recruit them, and develop them.

Utilizing the Training Course

As you teach the evangelism course, you'll see these potential champions start to come alive. They inch toward the edge of their chairs, listen intently, and jot down a lot of notes. During breaks and after sessions (and sometimes during sessions) they can't wait to talk to you, ask questions, and tell stories. They're the ones who, at the end of the final session, come up and ask why the course has to be so short. *These are the right people!*

In the *Becoming a Contagious Christian* book, we talked about a man named Fred who was coaxed by one of our church staff members to go through the course (read, "intentionality"). Fred's initial reaction was to scoff. "I'm no evangelist," he assured the staff member. But he ended up coming to the training, even if under duress. And over the next several weeks I could see him coming to life. In fact, he'd never let me get a break during the break times! Like putting a match to lighter fluid, this man was ignited. This was the beginning of an ongoing friendship with Fred, including many discussions on the phone and in person when he'd ask me (his "coach") for advice on various witnessing opportunities.

The Frontline Team was a natural next step for Fred, and in the years since that time he has led more people to Christ than we've been able to keep track of. But Fred never would have shown up if we had simply announced, "Everyone with the gift of evangelism please meet this Saturday morning." We had to go after him—and this has been true of many others who have become part of the team.

For Fred and many others through the years, the *Becoming a Contagious Christian* course has been the catalyst for discovering their evangelistic passion, getting on the Frontline Team, and launching into increasing levels of outreach service and effectiveness.

That's another important reason for repeating the training over and over. You'll not only be equipping more and more of your church body, but you'll also be producing an environment in which fresh groups of people with gifts and a passion for evangelism will bubble to the surface.

Looking with Purpose

When you notice these people, seize the moment. Pull them aside and tell them you can see their growing passion for evangelism and that you have a next-step opportunity for them at a place called Frontline (but don't scare them away with too much talk about the "E-word" or the spiritual gift of evangelism). Write down the date or give them a printed flyer for the next meeting. Assure them that they'll enjoy it because they'll be with others who share their passion for reaching friends for Christ. Be sure to get their name, address, phone number, and e-mail address, and add them to your evangelism database so you can send them information about future events and opportunities. Developing ways to communicate directly with these people is very important, for they are the key to the rest of the 6-Stage Process. You can't build a truly contagious church without these key contagious Christians. In order for them to have a disproportionate evangelistic impact, you must first make a disproportionate investment in them.

Also, keep spreading the net widely with every group that goes through the training course. Tell them about the Frontline Team and when you'll be meeting next. Introduce them to some members of the team and let these members talk about how they've benefited from their experience. Utilize Frontline members to run the administrative side of the training; they can build relationships with the trainees and tell them about the team throughout the course of the entire training process. Hand out attractive invitations with all of the necessary information.

Give people the opportunity, right there during the training, to register for the meeting and to fill out a card so their name can be added to the Frontline mailing list.

Seize Strategic Opportunities around Services

Recently we did a teaching series on evangelism during our midweek worship services. We do this frequently to push back on the church's gravitational pull toward inwardness and to motivate and equip our believers. But we also used it as a way to find more of the gifted evangelists in the church. In fact, one of the nights Bill Hybels taught about the spiritual gift of evangelism and some of the ways to determine if you might have it[15] (stages 1 and 2, modeling evangelistic values and instilling those values in others). Then, at the end of the services, he asked those who thought they might have this gift to go down to our chapel for a ten-minute meeting with Garry Poole, who now directs our church's evangelism ministry (stage 3, empowering the evangelistic point person).

What happened was incredible. Almost exactly one out of ten people at the services went to the chapel—the elusive ten percent! Very briefly, Garry challenged them to do three things:

1. If they hadn't already been through basic training, to go to the next offering of the Becoming a Contagious Christian evangelism course, which was starting in three weeks (stage 4, equipping every believer).
2. Be sure not to miss our next Frontline meeting, which was coming up in four weeks (stage 5, developing a diversified team).
3. Consider serving as a leader or an apprentice leader of a seeker small group, which would begin by their attendance at the seeker leader's training, which was starting in two weeks (an example of stage 6, innovating high-impact outreach ministries and events, which we'll explore in the next chapter).

This one evening of focus produced the desired result—namely, finding many new Frontline members and evangelism leaders.

Work in Partnership with the Church's Ministries

Another vital aspect of building this team is gaining the confidence and support of the directors of the various ministries throughout the church. They must see Frontline as their ally, not as their competitor.

For clarity, let's say your evangelism point person's name is Steve. Ideally, Steve needs to help the ministry directors find and appoint their own evangelistic leader (or two or three) from within their own context. These people will then be the primary contacts that Steve should work with, as well as the ministry directors themselves, to strategize ways their ministry can move toward fulfilling its part of the church's evangelistic mission.

These evangelism leaders from the various ministries should attend all of the Frontline meetings and constantly be encouraging the right people in their own circles to attend the meetings with them. (At our Frontline gatherings we have tables set up with signs for each of the church's ministries. Each ministry builds it into their own ministry plan to designate and send at least one representative to Frontline meetings.) Gradually, this will help them develop evangelistic teams within their own ministries, and all of those team members should, in turn, become active Frontliners.

These evangelism leaders should also see to it that their ministry's director is kept informed of all evangelistic activities. Further, they should ensure that appropriate verbal and written announcements are made within their ministry to help maximize all outreach-oriented opportunities. In effect, these leaders should mirror within their own ministries many of the activities that Steve is engaged in church-wide.

One more note on gaining the trust and cooperation of the various ministries. Steve must tell the ministry directors, and then prove by his actions, that he will not hurt their ministry by trying to take away their volunteers. On the contrary, he is trying to serve them by training, encouraging, and informing their people, making them more effective in their own particular ministry. He wants them on the Frontline Team so they'll be stronger in their service to their own ministry and therefore to the whole church.

That's not to say, of course, that people will never shift from primary service in that ministry to serving with other evangelistic ministries within the church. There will always be some movement and migration—which is natural and healthy. But this should not be Steve's intent, nor should it become the reputation of the Frontline Team. Further, that migration pattern should go both ways, with give-and-take from both the evangelism ministry and the other ministries, all for the goal of furthering the church and God's kingdom.

In addition, the directors of these ministries should know that Steve and his team are actively looking for ways to give broader exposure and support to their ministries' outreach initiatives at Frontline meetings. For example, if the women's ministry is sponsoring an evangelistic breakfast or the sports ministry is hosting an outreach-oriented 5k run, Steve shouldn't leave them to fend for themselves.

These are broad-based ministries for which evangelism is just one of many values, and these ministries need all the encouragement they can get. Their outreach events provide great opportunities for the Frontline Team to come alongside and, in a supportive role, help make their efforts a success.

So, for instance, Steve and his team need to go out of their way to get the details about the women's breakfast. Then they should talk it up at the Frontline meeting, hand out the flyers, encourage women in the group to attend with their friends, highlight opportunities for volunteers to get involved, and pray with the team for the event. Then, at the next Frontline meeting, they should let the women's ministry director or evangelistic leader report back on the event, sharing testimonies of how God used it to draw others to himself.

This kind of cooperation, repeated over and over, will gain the enthusiastic support of the ministries throughout the church. It will position Frontline as a ministry that not only does its own team building and outreach events but also serves and maximizes the evangelistic efforts of the ministries throughout the church. It'll soon become known that the members of this team want to be on the front lines of the ministry action wherever the battle is being fought.

Give Compelling Announcements

In your worship services, the evangelistic point person or another leader who is passionate about evangelism and involved with the Frontline Team should give a compelling, upbeat announcement to spur interest in this team. This person should explain what the ministry is and invite everyone interested in reaching his or her friends for Christ to attend. The announcer should use first-person language, saying "*We're* doing such and such. . . . *I* hope *I'll* see you there."

The senior pastor should also make announcements for the evangelism team on a regular basis. Thus, he or she needs to be kept up-to-date on what the ministry is doing and attend a meeting personally on occasion. In addition, the pastor should make Frontline attendance a point of application when preaching a sermon related to outreach. Attack from every side!

Don't forget to add a winsome printed announcement or insert to the bulletin. Avoid the typical yawn-inducing, "The evangelism team will be sponsoring a pancake breakfast next Saturday morning. If you are on this team or want to join it, go to the booth after the service. . . ."

Instead, try something like this:

GET IN ON THE ACTION!—If you have a passion for the adventure of reaching friends and family members for Christ, or if you'd like to catch some of that passion, join us next Saturday morning at the Frontline Team breakfast. We'll enjoy a meal, share some encouragement, hear some incredible stories of how God is using people from this church, and get the inside scoop on the upcoming Easter outreach event. For more details or to sign up, stop by the Frontline booth after the service or call the church before Thursday. Miss at your own risk!

Notice in the opening paragraph of this section I said to invite "everyone interested in reaching his or her friends for Christ." It's important to spread the net broadly. Tell listeners in no uncertain terms that your meetings are for anyone who wants to grow in the area of evangelism, and that they don't have to have a spiritual gift of evangelism to come to the event.

Those who attend are a self-selecting group with undoubtedly a high concentration of those who have the evangelism gift—but let them discover this for themselves! If you talk about it too early, it may prevent many of them from attending. In fact, I know some members who have come to our group for years and love it, but who still insist to me that they don't have the spiritual gift of evangelism. I just smile and let them talk. Their ongoing passion and steady involvement reveal the truth. Besides, what's really important is that they're trained, plugged in, growing, and taking risks for the sake of the gospel. Call it what you will—gift or no gift—God will use it!

SEND INVITATIONS TO THE ENTIRE CHURCH

When you're first launching a new initiative like the *Becoming a Contagious Christian* training course or the Frontline Team, a letter addressed to the entire congregation can go a long way toward creating support and involvement. Ideally the letter should be from both the pastor and the point person. It should be positive and optimistic but serious in tone. People need to get the signal that this is not just another class or program; this is part of a new way of life that gets the church back to its age-old biblical mission.

This message will, of course, fit right in with the broader teaching and vision casting that people are beginning to notice in the church's worship services, membership meetings, small group training, Sunday school classes, and everywhere else they turn. It's all part of a God-glorifying evangelistic conspiracy!

Connect with People in Spiritual Gifts Classes

I mentioned earlier the importance of every church training its members in the area of spiritual gifts. Courses like *Network: Understanding God's Design for You in the Church* help them discover who God has made them to be and what he has made them to do. About ten percent of them will find out they have the spiritual gift of evangelism. Go after them!

How? The point person or someone else from the evangelism ministry should go to the class when the gift of evangelism is the subject. As part of the teaching or right before a break, tell participants that if they have this gift, they're really blessed, because it's the most exciting one! (People with each spiritual gift think theirs is the best, so why can't we?) Then point them toward the evangelism course and the Frontline Team. To maximize the opportunity, hand out invitations and then stay to talk with anyone who wants to know more.

Hopefully, the ministry that teaches these classes also keeps track of who attends and what their spiritual gifts are. If so, you can send follow-up mailings or have a key volunteer call the people who listed evangelism as one of their top gifts.

Challenge Frontline Members to Expand the Team

One other easy-to-overlook place to build the Frontline Team is at the team meetings themselves. If people are having a great experience, they'll want to bring others. Ask them to do so, and provide invitations they can give to their friends to attend the next meeting. Tell them that they of all people—as evangelists—ought to be able to bring others. There is no more potent way to expand this team than through the enthusiastic encouragement of its active members, because they're contagious!

A WORD ABOUT SCALE

Although I'm writing out of my own large-church context, the Frontline Team concept is in no way limited to any particular church size. Let's say, for example, you're in a congregation of eighty people. You cast the vision, model and instill the values, empower a leader, and begin to train the people. Eight members go through the first *Becoming a Contagious Christian* course, and all eight of them move up a few notches in terms of evangelistic motivation and skills. But one person in particular gets really fired up and wants to take it further. Believe it or not, you already have the makings of a Frontline Team!

The two of you start to meet occasionally for breakfast, where you tell stories, share ideas, encourage each other, and pray together. One of the things you pray for is more team members.

The next month, you teach the course again. Word has gotten out about the training, and nine people from the congregation attend. At the end of the last session when you talk about the Frontline Team (which, you assure the group, "still has room for a few more members"), two people show interest. Now there are four of you.

Then the first one leads a friend to Christ. Being the evangelism zealot that he is, he tells this new convert that a normal part of the Christian life, along with prayer and Bible study, is going to the Frontline meetings. Now you have five!

As the participation and activity levels of this team go up, so does the contagion factor of the entire church.

One loses interest, but two more join. Your team is really starting to get contagious! After a while, other people start hearing about this group, and they want to get in on the action. Tell them you *might* let them in if they can prove they're really serious about it. Some of them insist, so you allow them to join—and now there's a contagious movement afoot!

You might even want to consider pooling resources with other churches in town and do some combined Frontline events together. It's a great way to build momentum and to start seeing a broader impact on your entire region.

Whatever number your team starts with, that's okay. It doesn't take very many to "spur one another on toward love and good deeds" (Hebrews 10:24). But always keep your recruitment engines running. As the participation and activity levels of this team go up, so does the contagion factor of the entire church.

A CLASSIC FRONTLINE TEAM MESSAGE

I end this chapter with the text of a message given by Bill Hybels, a guest speaker at one of our Frontline meetings. I hope you'll benefit both from the content of the teaching and from the modeling of how to communicate to this group of outreach specialists.

I've had the opportunity to speak in different environments where certain spiritual gifts are the reason for people being together, and I've noticed that dynamics change according to the gift. Like when I'm called to speak to small group leaders who primarily have the spiritual gift of shepherding. In those groups it's usually kind of quiet, with lots of hugging going on and deep community and those kinds of things.

And sometimes I speak where people with mercy gifts are together, like the caring groups. And that's a Kleenex-fest! Everybody's sobbing over each other's circumstances and showing great empathy.

And then I lead the Leadership Summit each summer, and that's people with the gift of leadership. They walk around saying, "Kick butt, Bill; just kick butt! Come on, raise the bar, raise the bar!"

Last weekend I spoke at the Promiseland children's ministry conference and everyone was singing and doing hand motions like little kids. I couldn't get out of there quickly enough!

But when I've had the opportunity to be together with people with the spiritual gift of evangelism, I've felt an enormous kinship. As you may know, I believe my top spiritual gift is leadership, and my next one is evangelism—not stadium evangelism, but personal evangelism. And then probably my third gift would be teaching.

When I'm interacting with people who have other gifts, I often feel like a fish out of the water. I really do think that those of us with gifts of evangelism are wired a little differently. We see the world a little differently. We see people differently. We see the gospel differently. We see the whole landscape through a different set of lenses.

Let me tell you some of those differences I've seen in my own life. First, I *like* lost people. I can't believe how often I run into Christians who tell me, "I don't like my job because there's all these non-Christians around." Or, "I don't like my neighborhood because these people swear and cuss and drink."

They're telling me, in so many words, that they don't like lost folks. And they're expecting me to show sympathy! They want me to say, "Oh, there, there, you should just pull out of the world."

Instead, I say, "That's the funniest thing. I *love* lost people."

I mean, I like being with them, and being around them with their habits and their morals and values. They don't bother me. I think they're quite consistent! They're acting right out of their value base. And I'm acting out of mine.

I've bailed friends out of jail. I've picked them up when they were too drunk to go to their car, and I've put them in the back of mine and driven them home. And I've helped them out of domestic arguments and terrible situations of one kind or another. I never do so with a sense of begrudging or drudgery—it doesn't feel like a burden to me.

I think if you have the spiritual gift of evangelism, one of the first things you notice about your own spirit is this overwhelming love and appreciation for lost folks. You see them for what they are—people made in the image of God who, in most cases, we would be just like had we not stumbled across amazing grace.

Can you identify with that? Is that how most of you feel? I think it is.

Here's another one. I like being part of a person's entire journey toward faith. I think the perception of evangelists is that we only like leading people across the finish line. That's not true with me. I mean, it's great when it happens. But I love every inning of the game. I like the pregame. I like the whole run.

To me, it's just as thrilling to see a hard-core, nonchurched, unsaved person take those first few steps of softening up. I consider that to be great progress. I don't get discouraged if it takes quite a long time for people to show signs of softening. I celebrate every little mile marker of the process and get enormous energy out of the fact that we're making progress.

When I first started my sailing program with all these nonchurched guys on my crew, and Tommy first started showing real spiritual interest, another guy on the crew who was a close friend of Tommy came to me. We'd only raced together for a few months at that time. But he pulled me off to the side and stuck his finger in my chest and, to paraphrase him mildly, said,

"I want you to stop messing with Tommy's mind. I don't like this spiritual talk. You're bending his mind around. You've got him talking about stuff he has no business talking about!"

That's where I started with this guy! Well, I talked with him on the phone yesterday. Now it's six years later. He's not a Christian yet, but he's in a seeker-oriented church in his area. He's in a seeker Bible study. He's coming this Good Friday to our services. He's going to drive all the way over here from Michigan.

We joke together because I have pictures of baptisms on the wall in my office. And now whenever he's in my office he points and says, "That's the spot reserved for my picture, right?" And I say, "Yep, we're saving that place right there."

He's not a Christian yet, but every single step of that journey has been filled with joy for me. I think God has given those of us with this gift a loving kind of patience to watch the Spirit work, to be a part of his activity, and to celebrate and enjoy every part of the journey. *[Let me interrupt here to say I'm happy to report that a little more than a year after Bill made these comments, his friend put his trust in Christ at our Christmas Eve service. Bill recently baptized him in the pond by our church.]*

After a service some months ago, I had a whole family stop down to talk to me. It was a mom, a dad, and a couple of little kids. The guy just stuck his hand out and said, "Hi, we're the such-and-such family, and we're all seekers."

I wasn't aware that they're supposed to know that terminology! But I asked, "So how is it that you started this whole seeking process?"

He answered, "Our neighbors invited us to the church, and we really enjoyed it, so now we come every week."

Since the guy was so open, I decided to press this a little bit. I said, "Well, do you think you're going to become Christians soon?"

And the guy said, "Wow, I don't know about that! We have a lot of questions still. But we're getting a lot of them answered week by week, and this has really been a great experience for us."

So I said, "Well, would you mind if I'd say a prayer for you and your family?" And the guy replied, "Well, no. We've never been prayed on before."

"I'm not going to pray *on* you," I assured him, "I'm going to pray *for* you!" So I huddled them up and said something like this: "God, I pray that this family's journey toward faith will be filled with moments of joyful discovery and with lights going on as they begin to see the goodness and the greatness of the Father. And I pray it will all lead to that day when we'll celebrate right here the coming to faith in Jesus Christ of every person in this family. Amen."

As soon as I was finished, the guy shook my hand and said, "That was a very good prayer." Apparently he'd heard some bad ones in his day!

That prayer came right out of my spirit, and it expressed my desire to be a part of walking people all the way through their hang-ups and problems to the point where they can make a responsible, solid faith commitment. And I think that's how God wired all of us up—to enjoy the process.

Another thing is when people don't respond, even for a long period of time, I rarely get discouraged. Just to be in the game is enough for me. Jesus said, "If you'll abide in me and my words in you, I will bear fruit through you." I don't live with the ultimate responsibility of whether or not someone winds up in heaven. That's their responsibility. That's the work of the Holy Spirit. My responsibility is to be energetically involved. My responsibility is to be there to try to catalyze the process, to be a friend, to answer questions, and to coach and to urge them along.

Two weeks ago I was on the phone with a man I've been trying to lead to Christ for twenty years. The guy is here at the service every weekend he's in town. He's an area business owner who's been a real friend to this church and has helped us in ways you could not imagine. But he's still the most profane man I know, and I haven't felt like my efforts have been making much of a dent at all.

But about six weeks ago he had life-threatening surgery. The night before he went in he called me and asked if I'd pray. I said, "I'll pray for you right now. I'll pray for your body, but I'm going to pray for your soul too, because you might not come out the other side of this thing. There's something a lot more important at stake here than whether or not you survive this surgery."

He said, "Bill, you can pray for anything you'd like!"

That phone prayer was the most progress I could discern in twenty years. But that doesn't bother me. I don't care if his time line is another ten years. Every time I can be with him to try to say a word for Christ, it's okay with me.

I think all of us who have the gift of evangelism see the world and the kingdom that way. We want to continue at whatever rate the Spirit is doing his work.

And when one of our friends comes to faith, there is no better feeling in life. I can say that, and I think every evangelist can say that. There is no other feeling like being there when someone passes from death to life, from darkness into the family of God. You know, I've been a part of a lot of things that people think must be really exciting, but nothing holds a candle to the transformation of the human heart by the divine activity of God.

One final thing that I think all of us with evangelism gifts share in common is the utter conviction of Romans 1:16: "I am not ashamed of the gospel of Christ, because it is the power of God for the salvation of everyone who believes." The older I get the more aware I am of all the things in the world that are fuzzy and gray, hard to figure out and unsure. The older I get the more convinced I am there is only one power on this planet that can transform a human life. That's the saving message of the gospel of Jesus Christ. Every year I get more of an understanding of why the apostle Paul would say, "I will not shrink back from declaring to you the whole counsel of God." Or those other rally cries where Paul would say, call me a fool, call me whatever you want, but I am going to proclaim Christ and preach Christ and share Christ and point people to Christ. That's the core of who I am.

And I think you would all share that too, wouldn't you? This core belief that we have the message. As those having the gift of evangelism, we of all people have been entrusted with the gospel. And we of all people have to be sure of its power and be committed to its proclamation.

So here's my final set of challenges to you, because I know evangelists love challenges. It's like giving Michael Jordan the ball with thirty seconds left and saying we need a three-pointer!

I want to remind you of some basics. You've heard them before. I just want to say them to you again and ask you to live them.

The Bible is really clear. We cannot win the spiritual battle in the power of the flesh. So live every day in vital union with Jesus Christ. I don't care how strong your gift is. I don't care how wonderful and engaging your personality is. I don't care how much you know about apologetics or how many verses you can quote. Unless you have the power of God at work in your life, unless you live in a yielded, surrendered condition, unless you have what Jesus called salt with savor, unless you are spilling over with that unboundaried work of God in your life, you're not going to have the spiritual impact he wants you to have.

That's what's going to help you see people for who they are. That's what's going to help you live with urgency. And you don't really believe in the power of the gospel unless you walk with God. You don't live with the realities of heaven and hell unless you walk deeply with God. So you folks, above and beyond everything else, must manage your lives in such a way that you live consistently in vital union with Christ.

Second, you have to have proximity to lost people. What good is it if you're aflame with the power of God in your life, and if you have the gift of evangelism, but you're not regularly interacting with unchurched folks? For some of us that means we need to be more intentional about getting into circles that include nonchurched people.

I've learned that after you're a Christian for a while, you gradually extract yourself from most of the circles that have lost people in them. It's the way the Christian life tends to work. It's because you're coming to services more. Then you're in a small group. Then you're serving. Pretty soon you just have no proximity with lost folks.

The breakthrough in my whole evangelistic effectiveness came when I started that sailing program with eight lost guys on my crew and saw what God could do through my life when I got in the middle of a bunch of non-Christians. So, friends, you've got to really turn up the thermostat on this one if that's not the way your life is going.

Then, obviously, we of all people need to have a crystal clear understanding of how to present the gospel when those moments of opportunity open up. We have to know the Bridge illustration, the Do versus Done, and other ways we can present the gospel. We ought to be the most prepared people on the planet when that window opens. So please, friends, I don't know how many times you've been through the *Contagious* course. I don't know how often you sharpen your skills. But sharpen them often. Because if *you* folks don't have these tools at your disposal when the time comes, everybody loses.

And then the final challenge is that as people with the gift of evangelism, more than anybody else in Christendom, we have to be the ones who "make the ask." We have to be the ones who say, "So what would prevent you from bowing your head and receiving Christ right now? What would stand in the way?"

You don't know how different that makes you. I could take you to some of the greatest leaders in Christendom. They walk with Christ. They can articulate the gospel. But you know what? They don't have that last five percent of faith to ask the question, "What would prevent you from receiving Christ right now?" God gives gifted evangelists this courage. But if we don't ask this question, probably no one else will.

I was driving home from Michigan this past week listening to tapes of messages I missed recently when I was teaching overseas. I put in Lee Strobel's message called "If Jesus Lived in My House." It's the first one in *The Unexpected Adventure* series.[16]

I got to the point where he was talking about taking the risks associated with being an evangelist, and I had to tell him later, "Lee, every time I looked down I was going ninety miles an hour! The more inflamed you got, the faster I drove." I just couldn't contain my enthusiasm and my energy. It's a wonder I didn't end up in jail over that tape!

But I really do think that we're supposed to do exactly that—not go out and speed!—but figure out ways to encourage and stimulate each other to go out and use these gifts.

Now, friends, I would like to sort of commission you in prayer. Let's just get on our knees for a moment so we can pray with an appropriate sense of commitment:

> God, right now, on our knees, we want first of all to bow in deep gratitude for your having saved us. We all

remember who we used to be. We all remember the lives we used to live and the kind of junk we came out of. The kind of stuff that the cross paid for. So we thank you for it.

And then, God, thank you for giving us the gift of evangelism. That central gift of being carriers of the gospel, proclaimers of the message of transformation. Of all the people on the planet, of all the people in Christendom, of all the people at this church, you have deposited this gift in us, because you felt we'd be faithful. You were counting on us to develop this gift and use it to the zenith of its potential.

So, God, on our knees right now we pledge to you that we will be faithful carriers of your message. And that we really will live in vital union with you. We will pray for people. We will get in proximity with those who need to be touched. We will declare the gospel when the opportunity is right. We will make the bold ask of what is keeping people from receiving Christ. And we will celebrate with great joy the conversion and baptism of everyone who comes to faith as a result of our efforts.

Now, Lord, we think of how you must look at this world. And we think of the time Jesus looked over the city of Jerusalem and wept. We think of the heartbreak that must happen every time you look at the darkness in this world. But then we also think of you looking down at us, carriers of the gospel message, and the joy it must give you to know that there are some who are willing to take this gift seriously and use it for your glory. I pray that you would delight in what you see in this moment, evangelists on our knees pleading with you to use us more. Pleading with you to sweep over us and give us the boldness and an understanding of the gravity of the situation. God, may we be fruitful and faithful evangelists.

We commit to you all of the opportunities coming up soon. And, God, we pray that we would seize these opportunities for people's salvation and for your glory.

And everybody agreed and said, Amen.

STAGE 5: KEY IDEA

Gather and encourage contagious champions—the ten percent.

"Since, then, we know what it is to fear the Lord, we try to persuade men. . . . For Christ's love compels us, because we are convinced that one died for all" (2 Corinthians 5:11, 14).

To Consider and Discuss

1. Who are two or three church members you can ask to be part of a new Frontline Team? What is it about their lives that makes you see them as candidates?
2. How can you begin to gather these people informally and see if the evangelistic temperature begins to heat up?
3. Where are some of the broader arenas and opportunities you can use to begin to promote and invite others into this new team?
4. Who are some of the people inside or outside your church you could draw on as resources to help you teach and inspire your team as you form it?
5. List two or three topics you think would be helpful to discuss with the evangelism enthusiasts in your church.

9

STAGE 6: INNOVATING HIGH-IMPACT OUTREACH MINISTRIES AND EVENTS

"Hi, Mark. Do you remember me?"

I wanted to say yes. I strained my memory in an effort to say yes. I opened my mouth hoping to get out a "yes." But I couldn't honestly say yes.

"Umm, you're going to have to help me out a bit," I said to the young woman standing in front of me by our church's pond, her hair dripping wet.

"We met briefly about four years ago when you and your wife were looking for an apartment in Streamwood," she informed me. "I worked for the real estate company that was showing the apartments. But you never came back. . . ."

"I'm sorry, we ended up in another area," I said, still reaching back into the dusty fringes of my memory.

"That's okay," she said. "You did what you were sent to do!"

"I did?" I said, feeling a mix of relief and curiosity.

"You sure did. Don't you remember that you started telling me about this church? You told me it was a great place to meet new friends and to learn about the Bible."

"It's starting to come back to me. . . ."

"You also gave me one of those little business card–sized invitations to the church. Remember, it had a map on it," she said.

"Of course—I try to carry them with me all the time," I replied, silently deepening my resolve to maintain that habit.

"Well, God used that conversation and another one with someone else from the church to get me to visit this place. After I was here for a while, I understood the message, asked Jesus to forgive my sins, and today I was baptized! When I saw you out here during the baptism service, I decided to come over and update you on what happened. Thanks for letting God use you!"

"You're more than welcome," I said enthusiastically, though half dazed, as I gave her a hug and congratulated her further. "That's really amazing!"

THE POWER OF A COMBINED EFFORT

This young woman's experience was yet another example of the synergy that can develop between individual evangelistic efforts—in this case, very limited efforts—and church-wide outreach events. I have seen many of these kinds of examples over the years, some in my own personal circle and many more in the lives of friends.

I told the story earlier about my sister-in-law, Jackie, to whom my wife and I reached out for several years. God used the combination of our efforts and our church's seeker services to lead her to the point where she was ready to trust in Christ. Today we have the thrill of watching her begin to have a contagious influence on the lives of others.

I have another set of friends, a couple named Tom and Lynn, who, along with Tom's sisters, Vicki and Cari, spent years trying to help Tom's parents understand the gospel. They kept up their attempts for years, including numerous conversations and multiple invitations to our church's outreach services. But it wasn't until one service in particular, when evangelist Luis Palau was speaking, that Tom's parents finally were ready. On that very night they both—a couple in their mid-sixties—crossed the line of faith and made Christ their Forgiver and Leader. About a year later I had the thrill of celebrating with them by the pond at their baptisms.

I recently riddled my own father, Orland Mittelberg, with questions about how he became a Christian. True to form, it was the pairing of the personal witness of his chief petty officer in the navy, a man named Bill Abraham, with a larger "outreach event" in Memphis, Tennessee, in the mid-1940s. That event was a revival meeting hosted by Youth for Christ, at which the great evangelist Charles E. Fuller spoke. My dad attended the meeting at the urging of Bill, as well as his own mother, Effa, who was praying daily for his salvation. He sat way up in the balcony "in order to stay at a safe distance." But when the invitation was given at the end of the night, he raised his hand, and Fuller pointed up at him and said, "I see your hand up there in the balcony, sailor boy. God bless you!" Before my father fully knew what was happening, he was standing down in front, praying with a counselor. His life—as well as the life of his family—has never been the same since!

Are you beginning to see why I describe this combination of individual evangelism efforts and larger outreach events as a synergistic one-two punch? The impact can be incredible! That's why in chapter 3 when I talked about the three-step strategy for evangelism, I discussed the relational side first in steps 1 (build a relationship) and 2 (share a verbal witness) but then also emphasized the team side in step 3 (bring the friend to an appropriate outreach event).

It's hard to do evangelism alone, without the supplemental team efforts of a broader church or ministry. It's getting increasingly difficult as our culture becomes more and more secular.

As we saw, the power of this pairing of personal and team efforts has been proven time and again, as far back as the Samaritan woman at the well in John 4 and all the way through to today at Graham and Palau crusades and at the evangelistic church services hosted by places like Willow Creek and Saddleback and many others.

THE DOWNSIDE OF MAKING MEMBERS WORK ALONE

Now let me state the flip side. It's hard to do evangelism alone, without the supplemental team efforts of a broader church or ministry. In fact, it's getting increasingly difficult as our culture becomes more and more secular. Let's take another look at our chart from chapter 2 (see Figure 9.1), and we'll quickly get reacclimated to the challenges facing anyone who dares to go it alone.

Figure 9.1

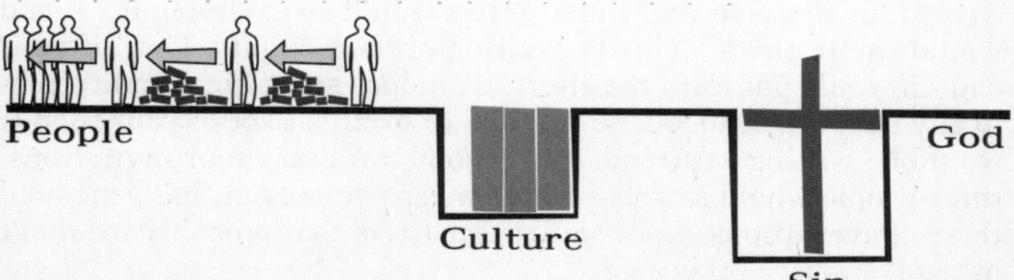

Looking at Figure 9.1, you begin to realize how great the separation is between the non-Christian, who is way over on the left side of the chart, and the desired destination, over on the right. Not only is there a great distance, there are also barriers and chasms between them representing all kinds of confusion, misinformation, competing ideologies, and the lures of sin—all of which tend to keep people far from God and moving in the wrong direction.

It's against that backdrop that many churches send out their people to fight the battle all alone. "You can do it," they say in effect. "If God is for you . . . *then why do you need our help?*" So they send their unprepared sheep out among the wolves and hope for the best.

As a result, these sincere Christians, full of fear and trembling, wander around the landscape without the encouragement and leadership of stages 1 through 3. They also lack the equipping we talked about in stage 4, the camaraderie and support we explored in stage 5, and certainly the group efforts we'll now look at under stage 6: "innovating high-impact outreach ministries and events."

The result? In far too many cases, the wolves are having the sheep for lunch.

We have to start preparing them better, reinforcing their efforts with a team, and strategically partnering with them by developing supplemental outreach ministries and events. We must work together to do what none of us can or should do alone.

THE IMPACT OF TEAM EVANGELISM

The larger, united outreach events of stage 6 can actually become engines that drive the values and skills we've been trying to build into our people. It was, for example, the fact that our church had a weekly outreach service that made it easy for my wife and me to talk to the woman at the apartment complex. The repeated event became the occasion for a natural invitation—and topic of conversation.

George Barna observes in his book *Marketing the Church* that one out of four adults in the United States would go to church if a friend would invite them.[1] This is exciting on two counts. First, if your church would put forth the effort to produce some high-quality, biblically relevant evangelistic services or events, a lot of your friends would be willing to attend. But, second, for every four invitations, three people would say no—which means your event has generated three conversations about spiritual matters that probably wouldn't have taken place otherwise.

We tell participants in the *Becoming a Contagious Christian* course that if they invite their friend to an event and they're turned down, that's okay—just turn it into an opportunity to talk. Say something like, "I'm sorry you won't be able to attend our Christmas Eve service with us. I'm curious, though, how does your family observe the holiday? What does that day mean to you?"

Whatever the event is—from a Christmas service to a contemporary Christian music concert—it can be the catalyst for hundreds of conversations all throughout your community, as well as being used by God to bear fruit in and of itself.

But the natural question is, how can we put together these special events? And with whom? Who would have the time, energy, and creativity to develop and promote such programs? The answer lies in the link between stages 5 and 6. Let me illustrate.

A MINISTRY CASE IN POINT

Several years back, some of us at our church began to think about starting evangelistic small groups. At the time we had a fairly strong small group ministry at our church, but the groups were mostly for discipling believers and not for outreach. We were intrigued by the idea that we could start groups primarily for spiritual seekers.

Right around that same time we interviewed a young pastor from Indianapolis named Garry Poole, who said he wanted to shift his focus to his primary gift and passion, which was evangelism. So we talked about this idea of building what we called seeker small groups. Garry was instantly excited about the idea and told us of similar groups he'd started while in college. Before long, Garry was on our team with the primary charge of starting these new, outreach-focused small groups. But immediately upon joining us, Garry faced the question I raised earlier: Where should he start, and with whom?

"The Usual Suspects"

In most church situations you'd have to start pretty much from scratch in order to build a seeker small group ministry. You might have a few people already teaching small groups who could "move over" and try to lead evangelistic groups. But this typically doesn't work very well, because it was their shepherding gifts that got them into their role in the first place—and people with shepherding gifts don't ordinarily have evangelism gifts as well.

You could also try recruiting from an existing evangelistic visitation team, but often the people in this ministry lack the patience and the interpersonal approach needed to sustain long-term friendships, meet weekly, and gently move people along in their journey to faith. If that were their approach, they probably wouldn't fit a traditional visitation team very well.

Where else could you look? In most church settings there aren't a lot of other options. You could make general announcements, but you'd very likely get a low response. And those who might respond would, in many cases, lack the necessary skills and training. So your chances of succeeding would be very limited.

The New Scenario

But what if you were in a church that had been instilling the value of evangelism into its members for a long time? A place where hearts were getting bigger for lost people? A setting where every attendee was being systematically trained for relational evangelism, and where those with gifts or a passion for outreach were being pulled together on a team that met on a regular basis? And what if those names and phone numbers were readily accessible in the church-wide database? That would be a different picture entirely!

This is the scenario into which Garry walked. The stage had already been set. His ministry was poised to win.

A Team in Waiting

Stepping back for a moment, remember that evangelism types are *action people.* You dare not get them trained and joined together on a team, and then fail to give them something significant to do. These men and women will be chomping at the bit, and if you don't give them a meaningful place to expend all of that spiritual energy, they may become downright dangerous! One way or another, they'll create some action!

Evangelism types are *action people.* If you don't give them a meaningful place to expend all of that spiritual energy, they may become downright dangerous!

This is a pretty good picture of what was evolving in our situation. We had this wonderful thing called the Frontline Team but limited opportunities in terms of specific ministry roles. This is one of the difficult aspects of emphasizing personal evangelism—it's so *personal!* It's not easy to build *group* efforts around it.

Our troops were trained and looking for some fresh battlefronts. No kidding, one member used to call me and say, "Give me something to do, Mark. I want some action. I'm ready to get bloodied for God!"

Whoa! It was certainly time to offer some well-thought-through opportunities.

Can you see what was shaping up? Supply and demand were both growing rapidly. The *supply* was a team ready to do something; the *demand* was an outreach-oriented small group ministry that desperately needed leaders. We just had to get the two sides together—which was a primary purpose of the Frontline Team in the first place.

The Natural Next Step

So at our next Frontline meeting, I introduced our newest staff member, Garry Poole, and together Garry and I cast the vision for this new seeker small group ministry.

I explained how we wanted to serve what we called "unsponsored seekers"—visitors to our services who were not yet in a relationship with anyone in the church. I described how these new groups would provide a place for these people to get to know a couple of knowledgeable Christians, develop trust, ask questions, and move forward spiritually to the point of trusting Christ. Then, after we had enfolded many of them, we planned to broaden the circle and reach into our neighborhoods and workplaces to attract people into these groups who hadn't yet visited the church.

Garry then portrayed the incredible potential in this approach by telling stories of how he had built these seeker groups in college dorms and, over time, had seen several of his friends—including some highly unlikely candidates—come into God's family. Then he gave specifics on how we planned to train many of those in Frontline and help them attract seekers into the groups they would be starting.

The team was inspired and ready for a call to action. We didn't have to persuade our audience that day that evangelism was important or that God could use them to be difference makers in the lives of others. That groundwork had long been laid. These people were ready to build on that foundation and make things happen.

Toward the end of the meeting, we invited all those interested in being part of this new ministry to sign up for the seeker small group training. About a third of the people who were there signed up to take the next step. In the days that followed, Garry interviewed these people, selected the ones he felt were right for the role, and began training them. Within a matter of a few weeks, he had thirty newly trained leaders.

Again, it's the *process* that's of importance here, not our particular numbers. We may have drawn thirty qualified candidates out of a large pool of Frontliners; in your situation it might be four out of a pool of sixteen. But four qualified leaders who already own the values and who have been through the basic evangelism training is a pretty good start.

This is how our seeker small group ministry was jump-started—and it hasn't slowed down since. Over the years since its beginning, hundreds have come to faith through the efforts of its faithful leaders. In fact, the great majority of people who stay in their groups end up trusting Christ, usually within about a year. Many other churches are now starting the same kind of ministries as well. Also, Garry, together with our Willow Creek colleague Judson Poling, has put his basic approach into a unique small group curriculum called *Tough Questions*, designed for groups of seekers as well as for Christians who are wrestling with their beliefs.[2]

Outreach ministries flow naturally out of a robust, broad-based evangelism team like the one I described in stage 5. In your church this might include things like a visitation team, a visitor callback ministry, a new kind of seeker Sunday school class, or a seeker small group ministry like the one I've been discussing here. The possibilities are virtually endless.

In addition to supporting these larger ministries, the Frontline Team should also sponsor a variety of high-quality outreach events to which your people can bring their friends. Some of these will be church-wide, like a major evangelistic concert or drama presentation. Others will be ministry-specific, like the women's ministry's outreach breakfast or the sports ministry's 5k run I mentioned earlier. Still more will be niche-specific, such as events targeted to narrower age or special interest groups, like an event for junior high students or a seminar designed to reach Jewish people.

This broad array of outreach ministries and events makes up the thrust of stage 6.

THE FRONTLINE MINISTRY STRUCTURE: A TEAM OF TEAMS

The Frontline Team is the overarching ministry that can help inspire, shape, empower, and execute these outreach activities throughout the church. This will include those activities directly under the evangelism ministry's own control, as well as those it helps with in cooperation with the other ministries of the church. Earlier I described this team as being cross-departmental. Figure 9.2 shows what the structure looks like.

Figure 9.2

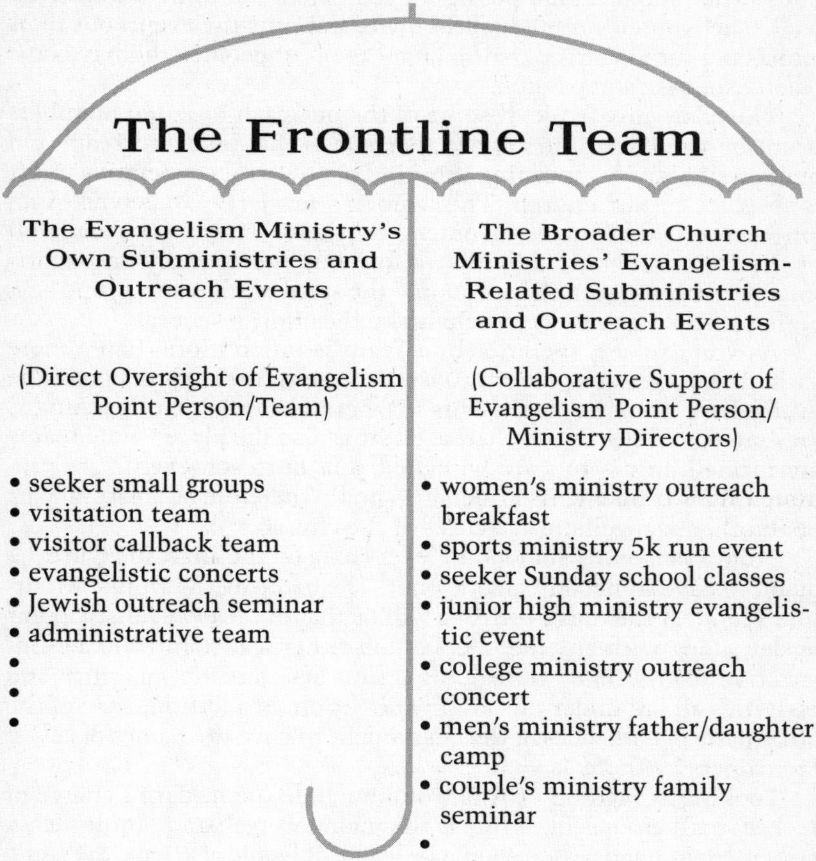

The Frontline Team

The Evangelism Ministry's Own Subministries and Outreach Events

(Direct Oversight of Evangelism Point Person/Team)

- seeker small groups
- visitation team
- visitor callback team
- evangelistic concerts
- Jewish outreach seminar
- administrative team
-
-
-

The Broader Church Ministries' Evangelism-Related Subministries and Outreach Events

(Collaborative Support of Evangelism Point Person/ Ministry Directors)

- women's ministry outreach breakfast
- sports ministry 5k run event
- seeker Sunday school classes
- junior high ministry evangelistic event
- college ministry outreach concert
- men's ministry father/daughter camp
- couple's ministry family seminar
-

The Frontline Team functions best as an umbrella ministry with two kinds of teams and activities under it. The first, shown on the left side, is the evangelism department's own specialized subministries and events. This would include things like the seeker small group ministry, any outreach-oriented visitation teams, and many others of the kind we'll look at in the next six chapters. The second category, on the right side, includes all of the other ministries of the church and their activities as they relate to evangelism.

So when the women's ministry is sponsoring an outreach breakfast, this activity becomes of vital interest to the Frontline Team. The evangelism point leader or team is not in charge of it; rather, it supplies ideas, support, and possibly even personnel to help pull it off well. The women's ministry still owns and runs the event, but their efforts are turbocharged by the larger team of people who have outreach expertise and passion.

This plan only works if some of the outreach-oriented members from the women's ministry are also part of the Frontline Team. On one recent Saturday morning this kind of powerful cooperative effort took place in our church. The women's ministry conceived of an outreach-oriented businesswomen's breakfast. They did virtually all of the organizing and administration, but the evangelism department/Frontline Team helped supply the speaker, the emcee, and several of its own members to help make the effort a success.

As you can see, the Frontline Team is much more than a mere gathering of evangelism enthusiasts. It's the central expression of the evangelism ministry itself. This is where vision is cast, teaching is presented, and stories are shared; but it is also the place where teams are formed, ministries are launched, and outreach events are promoted. This team and its leadership should therefore be a natural part of all other evangelistic activities of the church.

From a personnel standpoint, every area on the chart in Figure 9.2 ought to have somebody's name on it. The name by the words "Frontline Team" at the top of the page will be that of the evangelistic point leader, along with any members of his or her leadership and administrative teams. The strategic direction of Frontline meetings and activities all fall under this group's direction. In addition, each of the other parts of both sides of the chart ought to have the names of active Frontliners by them as well.

Looking at Figure 9.2, this would include the leader in charge of seeker small groups (or, if this is the main evangelism point leader, a primary right-hand person should be listed). It would also have the name of the person in charge of evangelism for women's ministries, including an activity such as their outreach breakfast. In addition, it should include names of the key leaders of all the other ministries and events that will eventually be listed on the left and right sides of the chart.

This collective group consists of the most important people for the evangelism point person to spend time with, learn from, and either lead (if on the left side—the evangelism department's own ministries) or collaborate with (if on the right side—other ministries with an outreach emphasis). It is out of this broader group of outreach-oriented leaders that he or she can naturally form a core evangelism leadership team to partner with in all that the role entails, from evangelism training, to the Frontline Team, to outreach ministries and activities.

TEN PRINCIPLES FOR HIGH-IMPACT OUTREACH MINISTRIES AND EVENTS

Without trying to slice the definitions too thin between outreach ministries and outreach events (they often overlap), let's look at ten general principles for planning and executing these kinds of activities for maximum impact. Then, in the next section of the book, we'll explore a number of specific outreach ideas built around the six styles of evangelism.

1. Define Your Purpose and Goals

The first question to ask is, "What are we trying to do?" Too often we assume that we know when in reality we don't. The purpose must be clear to both the leaders and the team.

Bill Hybels tells the story of three men who decided to put their resources together to start a new restaurant. The vision seemed clear enough until they got to the point of interior design:

> "We'll need lots of oriental fans and dragons on the walls," said the first man, "We can't have a Chinese restaurant without them!"
>
> "What are you talking about?" shot back the second man. "This isn't going to be a Chinese restaurant! It's going to be Italian—the only good kind of eating establishment!"
>
> "Reckon you're both wrong," said the third man. "What we're building is a Texas barbecue, with lots of cowboy boots and saddles and pictures of horses all over the walls—and country-and-western music playing too!"

See the problem? We often wait too long to put on the table what we—and each of the other members of the team—think we ought to be trying to accomplish.

When it comes to outreach, the principle is the same: We need to talk about what we want to accomplish until we reach clarity and consensus. Is this an early, primer event that we hope will get people started on a spiritual quest? (Some people would call this "pre-evangelistic"; I don't prefer that term because I see all outreach events as part of the actual evangelism process.) Or is it a middle-range event, designed to help seekers progress in their spiritual journeys? Or, finally, is it a net-drawing event, designed to help people make the decision to cross the line of faith and commit their lives to Christ?

These three purposes, though all legitimate aspects of evangelism, are about as different from each other as are Chinese, Italian, and Texas-barbecue restaurants! One way to understand this is to look again at the secular landscape drawing (Figure 9.3). This time we'll add a continuum along the top, helping us see that different ministries and events can be designed to help people at different stages of their spiritual journeys. This is the "Evangelistic Intensity Scale," and it ranges from low- to mid- to high-intensity.

Figure 9.3

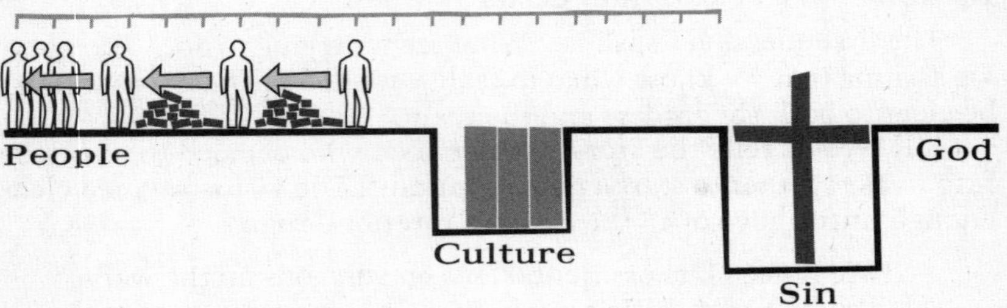

On the left side, the events are lower in intensity. This might mean they present less teaching content and spiritual challenge, and lean more toward relationships and areas of common interest. For example, we once held a sports breakfast at our church with a guest speaker who was known throughout the Chicago area for his work as a sports broadcaster on a prominent radio station. He is also a committed believer, and he did a great job of talking about Chicago sports while weaving in brief portions of his testimony along with stories about Christian athletes.

We held the event in a seminar room at our church. Our goal was simply to get visitors and seekers on the church campus; relate to them in an interest area we have in common; have fun together with contests, giveaways, and humor; and in the process provide non-threatening exposure to a group of real Christians.

We were thrilled later that day when a woman came up and said, "I'd never been able to get my husband to visit the church before. But as soon as he heard you were hosting a breakfast with his favorite sports commentator, he told me he wanted to attend. Well, he was here, and he loved it! And afterward he told me he's ready to come to the church service this Sunday."

Mission accomplished!

In that case, it was a low-intensity mission. More frequently we do events in the mid-intensity range. One example would be a Jewish outreach event where we invited Stan Telchin, author of the powerful autobiographical book *Betrayed!*[3] as our guest speaker for a Sunday night seminar. I titled the event and the talk "A Skeptic's Surprise," and we respectfully invited any Jewish person or other interested person to come and hear what this Jewish man had discovered when he looked into the life of Jesus. Hundreds attended.

While the presentation was passionate and intense, the appeal was gentle. We simply challenged listeners to seriously consider and investigate what they'd heard. We also assured them that our church was a place that welcomed people from all different racial and religious backgrounds, and that it would be a safe place for them to investigate the claims of Jesus.

Don, a man in his late fifties, called and took me up on the offer to talk further. We began to meet and discuss his questions—of which he had many! About a year later Don trusted Jesus as his Messiah. Now, several years later, he is finishing up course work at Trinity Evangelical Divinity School and is planning to go into full-time ministry.

Moving to the right end of the spectrum, we also do numerous high-intensity outreach events, usually at our weekend seeker services (which I described in chapter 3). The messages at these services cover a gamut of biblical topics, with the gospel constantly woven in. But also in regular "target" services, the focus of the entire service is to illustrate the gospel message. The goal is to strip away the confusion about its meaning and the excuses that often hold people back—and to challenge them to trust Christ as their Forgiver and Leader. Often we give attendees the opportunity to pray and receive him right then and there.

Countless people have come to faith in Christ over the years by means of these services. In chapter 16, "Communicating the Gospel without Compromise," I present the text of a message from one of these services that would sit quite high on the Evangelistic Intensity Scale.

I've illustrated these examples all across the scale because each one is critically needed. No one phase is more important than any other—every part has a vital role (in keeping with what we said about the process approach to evangelism in chapter 2). In fact, what is lacking in many evangelical churches is the low- to mid-intensity outreach ministries and events. Unless we get people into the process at the front end, we won't have any qualified candidates later when we attempt to "draw the net."

It's also important, once the broad purpose on the continuum is determined, to go a step further and articulate what your specific goals are for an event. What would success look like? Do you hope to expose a certain number of new people to the church? Are you aiming to help a particular number of seekers take a next step in their spiritual journeys? Would you like to launch a predetermined number of evangelistic Bible studies or seeker small groups? Is your aim to see a certain number of individuals put their trust in Christ before they go home? It is hard to hit a target you can't see and difficult to evaluate your efforts and improve the next time around when you have no agreed-upon mark you're shooting for.

2. Know Your Target

When I say, "Know your target," I mean two things. First, *know who your target is.* Who is it exactly you are trying to reach? Children, singles, marrieds, empty nesters, retirees? A certain section of the community, residents in an apartment complex, students at a particular university, an international or ethnic group, the coffee klatch at the local café? Once you know your target, you'll be able to begin shaping your approach to reach them.

In his book *The Purpose-Driven® Church,* Rick Warren says, "The Bible determines our message, but our target determines when, where, and how we communicate it." He also illustrates the fact that Jesus specifically targeted his message in order "to be effective, not to be exclusive."[4]

Second, once you know what group of people you are trying to reach, *get to know a few of them!* Find out what makes them tick. What are their questions? What interests them? What do they wrestle with? Get to know their heritage. Learn their language—find out what words and concepts connect with them and which ones make their eyes glaze over. Then speak to them in their own language. Design ministries and events that relate well to them.

For example, when I brought Stan Telchin to Chicago to do the outreach for Jewish people, he helped me understand that a term I tend to use quite frequently will unnecessarily alienate many Jewish people. The term? *Christ.* Stan taught me that the reason this is a problem word is because cruel people have sometimes called Jewish people "Christ-haters," or worse yet, "Christ-killers." So, he explained, you can spend the rest of your life trying to correct their misconceptions of who "Christ" really is, or you can sidestep the problem by referring to him as "Jesus." Stan recommended the latter route.

What a valuable lesson! It's one I try to apply whenever I talk to a Jewish person or group. And it's a good example of the kind of learning we need to gain in order to lovingly relate to the people we hope to reach—the kind of attitude Hudson Taylor modeled so well in his efforts to bring the gospel to the people in China.

Know your target. Become "all things to all" (1 Corinthians 9:22) so that the ministries and events you design will hit the mark.

3. Communicate Your Purpose and Your Target

Once you've determined your evangelistic purpose and your target group, it's crucial to communicate this information to the rest of the team and throughout the church family, especially to guest speakers who will be involved in the event.

At Willow Creek we almost had a disaster due to a lack of clarity in communication when we did the sports breakfast I mentioned earlier. Several days before the event, Lee Strobel and I decided to go to the radio studio and meet with the sports broadcaster we had invited to speak. We merely wanted to touch base and make certain everything was on track for the Saturday event. But in the course of talking together, this man casually mentioned that he was planning to make a strong appeal at the end of his talk and invite people to come forward and receive Christ.

Were we ever glad we were having that conversation! We assured him that our goal, like his, was to help people reach the point where they would respond to the gospel and embrace Christ. But we also explained that we didn't see this single event as the place to try to do all of this. Rather, we saw it as one link in the chain—an early one—that would lead naturally to further steps, including attendance at our weekend services. He immediately understood and supported our goals and, like us, was glad we'd talked before the event. And, as I explained earlier, his message at the breakfast turned out to be a home run in terms of fulfilling our hopes.

You can never go too far in making certain your entire team understands and supports your goals and purposes for every outreach event and ministry.

4. Innovate Outside the Box

Years ago, my friends and I tried to rent the main auditorium at our local college for an outreach concert. But the room, we discovered, was under construction and unavailable. So we rented the front steps and lawn of the building instead and had an outdoor concert that probably had a greater impact than if we'd used the auditorium inside.

When I helped bring a Christian expert on the cults, Kurt Van Gordon, to our town to speak about the unbiblical teachings of The Way International group, I was disappointed that none of the people I was befriending in that group expressed a willingness to come hear him. So after Kurt's seminar was over, I drove him to the house where the cult's leaders lived. They didn't look very excited to see us, but they let us in anyway, and we ended up talking with and challenging them about their aberrant teachings for over an hour. In this and a variety of other ways my friends and I resisted their influence in our community, and within months their whole team packed up and left town.

When we first decided to host a debate between a Christian and an atheist, the idea was nearly shut down. I had been told by some well-meaning believers that you should never do this kind of an event inside a church because of the damage it could do to the church's reputation. I thought and prayed about it for a long time, and I finally decided to set aside convention and do the event in our main auditorium. By God's grace, it turned out to be one of the most powerful events in the history of our church.

When we invited Phillip Johnson, renowned law professor at the University of California, Berkeley, to do a seminar on *Darwin on Trial,* we knew it would be a challenge to get the right people to come hear about the topic at a church, so we decided to target the teachers in the community. In partnership with InterVarsity Press, we gave each of our church's high school ministry student leaders copies of the *Darwin on Trial* book[5] to give to their teachers along with personalized invitations to the event. Then we mailed a letter to every science teacher in the communities surrounding our church, inviting them to come to the seminar and to enjoy reserved VIP seating. We also assured them there would be a question-and-answer time during which they could raise the first questions. Finally, we told the media that we had invited all the area science teachers and warned them that this could become a controversial gathering. Well, that got them excited, and they ran advance articles on it.

The result? An event that might have attracted a small group turned out to draw a huge crowd of about 4,300 people—and the evidence for a divine Creator was communicated to multitudes of people, many of whom wouldn't normally enter the doors of a church.

Right now I'm in discussions with a church on the West Coast that I've challenged to try to borrow or rent an aircraft carrier so we can host a different kind of evangelistic men's retreat. I don't know if the idea will "float," but if they can get the ship, I think the men will grab their friends and show up in droves. Who could turn down the chance to get away and ride on a real carrier while talking about things that really matter?

These are just a few examples from my own experience that prove you don't have to stay within the confines of convention when planning outreach events. Instead, get your creative types together and ask, "How could we do this in a fresh, interesting, and exciting way? What could we try that nobody else is trying? What kind of innovation might capture the attention of the community and turn out to be a coup for the kingdom?"

An event may be risky, but if it's biblical, ethical, and seems to the group to be a wise and God-honoring approach, why not try it? Whoever would have thought of having a bunch of Christ-followers stand up in the middle of Jerusalem, the city in which Jesus had been crucified just a few weeks earlier, and have them talk about him to the people gathered there? And then to cap it off with Peter telling them they'd crucified their Messiah and were in big trouble with God? What kind of a strategy was that?

Unconventional? Controversial? On the edge? Oh, yes, all of that—and a lot like God.

5. Design the Event to Fulfill the Purpose and Hit the Target

The room was warm. The large-print hymnals were easy to reach. We sang familiar, encouraging songs with words like "Happy day, happy day, when Jesus washed my sins away! He taught me how to watch and pray and live rejoicing ev'ry day. . . ."[6] The sanctuary was clean and tidy. The lighting was bright and the sound clear and fairly loud, making it easy to hear everything that was said. The minister wore a robe and spoke slowly and deliberately. The message was right out of the biblical text, straightforward yet simple. Before the service ended, we recited the Apostles' Creed and the Lord's Prayer. Then we sang "What a Friend We Have in Jesus" and heard the benediction—and the service was over.

It was one of the most relevant events I'd ever attended.

Why? Because it was the chapel service at the nursing home of my grandmother, Effa Mittelberg, and most of those attending were men and women in their nineties who had grown up in traditional churches. Whether or not they all knew Christ in a personal way, they knew this was what church was supposed to look, sound, and feel like. The message of the gospel was clearly evident in the words of the minister and of the music, and the method of presenting it was right on target. To have tried anything remotely contemporary would have been irrelevant and even offensive.

Two weeks later I walked into a crowded gymnasium. I was handed a bag of popcorn on the way in, along with a program that said, "Axis at the Movies." The atmosphere was dark, noisy, energetic, and filled with edgy music pouring through a high-powered sound system. Soon the stage lights came on and the music kicked in at an even higher decibel level for the portion of the service labeled in the program "Band Jam." In fast-moving sequence, youthful men and women stood up front and greeted us, led us in a few upbeat worship songs, performed a true-to-life drama, and showed clips from the recent movie *The X-Files*. Then a casually dressed teacher got up and presented an honest, hard-hitting message about how we can all search for truth—and find it—in the Bible and ultimately in Christ himself.

It was one of the most relevant events I'd ever attended.

Why? Because this was a ministry designed to reach people in their twenties—Gen-Xers—who grew up with these kinds of media and communication styles, and who needed to hear biblical teaching in language they could understand.

Relevancy is a relative concept. Different audiences, different events. Both well designed for the people they were intended to reach and for the intensity level of evangelism they were trying to execute. The message didn't change, but the methods certainly did.

This is the basic missionary principle of contextualization that we discussed in chapter 2. As Willow Creek puts it in our list of core values, "We believe that the church should be culturally relevant while remaining doctrinally pure." It'll take hard work and a lot of adjustments along the way, but make certain whatever events you promote fit the people and the purpose for which you're creating them.

6. Do Only What You Can Do with Excellence

Another one of our church's core values is, "Excellence honors God and inspires people." This value applies nowhere more than in the outreach arena.

I can't tell you how many conversations I've had with church leaders who've said, "We're getting really serious about reaching our city for Christ, so we're going to start offering high-impact outreach services every Saturday night—beginning next month."

Something inside me flinches. "Umm, I'm curious: Have you ever put together a service like what you're talking about—one that afterward your team felt great about? If so, have you ever tried doing two or three in a row, with only six days in between to get ready for the next one?"

In many cases these church leaders had never even tried one, or if they had, they weren't very happy with it. And now they're going to do fifty-two of them each year. My advice is to slow down. Plan a single outreach event. Or, at the most, start with a series of two or three. Brainstorm it thoroughly. Plan it well. Prepare to the hilt. Invest in it with prayer, resources, personnel, creativity, and energy. Muster all the excellence you can to make it as good as it can be. To do so is all a part of fulfilling Colossians 4:5, "Be wise in the way you act toward outsiders; make the most of every opportunity."

If you want to do outreach that will command attention and respect, start with fewer events and do them well. Deliver at a level that makes those who attend without bringing their friends regret it for weeks.

While we need to avoid taking this idea of excellence too far and getting paralyzed by perfectionism, we live in a culture where, in spite of all its moral blunders, technical excellence is assumed. Video has gone to high-definition, audio has gone to digital perfection, communication has gone to the cellular and cyber revolutions. In every arena of life, whether business, leisure, or entertainment, people are used to things being done well.

So if you want to do outreach that will command attention and respect, start with fewer events and do them well. Make them so good that the people who miss them will hear about it and kick themselves for not being there. Deliver at a level that makes those who attend without bringing their friends regret it for weeks. Communicate with such clarity and quality that people demand more. Then gradually expand the number and varieties of events while simultaneously growing and deepening the team and the support base.

7. Integrate Your Efforts with Other Events and Opportunities

Don't think of your outreach events in isolation. View them as important threads in the overall fabric of your church. Discuss with your planning team some basic questions: How does this effort fit into the church's overarching mission and goals? How could we adjust the timing or positioning of the event to help it create more ministry synergy? What will precede it that we could build on? What will follow our event that it could feed into?

For example, we conceived of the *Darwin on Trial* event as part of a larger plan. A series of Sunday sermons had been scheduled called "Christianity: Fact or Fiction?" and we knew that the final week would focus on the evidence for a divine Creator. So to expand the impact of that series, we scheduled the Phillip Johnson event for the Sunday night of that final week.

We were pretty confident that the momentum of the sermon series combined with the natural questions people have about human origins would make this a high-interest event. But we didn't want it to end there. In the process approach to evangelism, every effort and event need to move people in the right direction *and* show them their next link in the chain. This is a vital principle: *Always give seekers next steps.*

In the "Darwin" event the next steps included: (1) the opportunity to ask questions of Phillip Johnson and others during the program and immediately afterward; (2) a place to write down questions and then to receive a follow-up call from a member of our team during the week; (3) strong urging from the platform to take questions to a small group designed especially for that purpose, with sign-ups available this same night; and (4) encouragement to attend the new weekend message series beginning the following Sunday.

This latter one was important, because we knew there were a lot of people there that night who had come with friends for this special event but who had not yet attended a service. So we worked to help them understand that this is a church where people with doubts and questions are welcomed—and more than that, where the services are actually designed with them in mind. In everything we did and said, our goal was to not only serve them that night but to draw them back so we could serve them all the way to the point of salvation, and then have them join the team and serve others.

Another example of integrating your efforts is developing an overall outreach plan around your Christmas and Easter services. These are peak visitor attendance times, yet I've found that many churches fail to think strategically about what happens immediately after these holidays. Carloads of visiting friends and family members sit through the holiday service, which they probably enjoy and learn from. But then they may hear an uninspiring announcement for the following Sunday: "Next week we're going to continue our seventeen-part series on the Minor Prophets," the announcer says, "as Pastor Bob teaches us about the disobedience of God's people and the awful punishment that followed." This titillation is then completed with the words, "We hope you'll join us at 9:00 or 11:00 A.M." The average visitor appreciates the warning. The weekend at the cabin is sounding better than ever!

How much more effective could it be to start a series the following week that would be interesting and relevant to your visiting friends. It may actually *be* a study on the Minor Prophets, presented in a way that shows their connection to everyday life. It might include a title like, "Learning from the Mistakes of Others," or "Developing a Real-World Faith." Announce it in a winsome way and put an attractive invitation into visitors' hands that gives them the topic, the service times, and the location with directions (since they may have gotten a ride with their relatives and don't know how to get back to the church).

Granted, they won't all come back. Many will wait for the next holiday or special event before returning. But what if five out of fifty visitors come back? And what if you do the same thing at the next holiday services and some of these forty-five people along with a few new guests start seeing that your church is a place to learn about things that really matter? That next time around you might retain eight more. Now you have some momentum!

The earlier you can introduce this integrated thinking into your event planning, the better you'll be able to shape what you do for maximum synergy and impact.

8. Promote Your Events with Precision and Power

First, *promote your events with precision.* Watch out that you don't fall into what is known in business circles as a "bait and switch," a term that comes from an unethical sales tactic in which, for example, a low-end home appliance is promoted at a rock-bottom price even though that appliance is not even available. The goal is to lure customers in the door and then "sell them up" to more expensive—and more profitable—appliances.

The same thing happens all too often in Christian circles. We say, "Come to a sports breakfast," but in reality we're inviting guests to a thinly disguised evangelistic rally. Perceptive seekers leave angry. *Fool me once, shame on you,* they think, *fool me twice, shame on me.* Many of them will never come back.

Promotion must be done with integrity. If an event is advertised as a sports breakfast, then spend the vast majority of the time talking about sports. Weave in a moderate amount of spiritual content, but measure it carefully. If you want to make it a more evangelistically intense event, then communicate in a way that doesn't hide your intentions or mislead your audience. You don't have to put on the posters, "An event designed to convert you to Christ!" but a gentle tip-off will do, like, "Hear the inside scoop on the exciting career of [a well-known Christian athlete], and learn from his intriguing, behind-the-scenes spiritual journey." It's much better to have fewer people attend who know at least in general what they're coming to than to have a lot of people in attendance who will walk away feeling duped.

One more thought on precision in communication: Beware of promoting events as something new when they're really the same old thing with mere face-lifts. I remember Lee Strobel calling me at home one Sunday afternoon in exasperation. "I just came from a church that advertised itself as being relevant and geared to people who don't go to church," he said. "But boy, did they ever miss the target!" This was a rare tone for Lee, who is normally buoyant and upbeat, but he was outraged. Why? Because he had come to Christ largely through church services that really were relevant and designed for outsiders. He couldn't help imagining how this place might have derailed his own spiritual journey. He was simply putting himself in the shoes of any seekers who believed this church's advertisements and attended its services.

Lee described this experience in his book *Inside the Mind of Unchurched Harry and Mary:*

> The service started with someone asking the congregation to sing along with a chorus for which no lyrics were provided. Regular attenders, of course, knew the words, but I felt awkward. Other hymns, accompanied by an organ, dated from 1869, 1871, and 1874, with such lyrics as, "Heav'nly portals loud with hosannas ring." The microphones were tinny and the sound tended to cut in and out, prompting a vocalist at one point to pause with an embarrassed smile in the middle of a song.
>
> During the announcement time, a pastor directed newcomers to fill out a card "so we can put you on our mailing list." He also jokingly but with an air of desperation offered a $100 bounty if members of the church's board would attend a meeting that afternoon so they would finally have a quorum. He added with frustration, "We need to approve the painting of the church, which should have been done last year, and the painting of the house I live in, which should have been painted last year, too."
>
> The sermon, part of a series called "Issues in Christian Discipleship" ... talked about denying oneself to follow Christ, but there wasn't much explanation of what that meant on a practical, day-to-day level. He did say the Christian life has its benefits, although he didn't elaborate on what they were. At the conclusion, he offered only two steps for people to take: Either turn over your life to Christ, or commit yourself to deeper discipleship.[7]

Maybe we can get away with these kinds of things among believers. *Maybe.* But these tactics will never fly with most unchurched visitors who are checking out Christianity. We'll leave them confounded and confused—and then they'll leave us.

Don't promote relevancy until you're ready to deliver it. Be precise and honest in what you promise. Otherwise, it may be your only chance.

Concerning *promoting with power,* no matter how well planned and excellent your event is going to be, it can't have a maximum impact if it's not filled with the right people. You have to put as much energy into getting the word out as you do in putting the event together.

Recently there has been controversy in some circles about marketing and ministry. We should read and heed many of the warnings. Never substitute promotion for prayer. Don't try to put technology in the place of personal relationships. Don't let the mode of communication reduce the strength or soften the sting of the biblical message. Don't ever think that with the right slogan or ad campaign you'll be able to market the gospel or sell Jesus to the masses. This mentality cheapens our message and alienates our listeners.

On the other hand, don't throw up your hands in frustration and say, "Then I guess we'll just keep doing ministry the old way." If you have a sign in front of your church or a listing in the Yellow Pages, you're already in the promotion business. The question is how to do so in ways that honor Christ and fulfill your God-ordained purposes. If you're serious about maximizing your outreach events—if you agree that it would be better to have three hundred unbelievers in the room hearing the gospel than thirty—then you'd better put creativity, energy, and resources into getting the word out.

Finally, if you are in general agreement with our three-step evangelistic strategy spelled out in chapter 3, then do the bulk of your promotion in sync with the first step (building relationships with lost people) rather than apart from it. The way we do this at our church is by investing more resources in high-quality printed invitations than in any kind of advertising. In fact, we do almost no newspaper or radio advertising.

We do, however, design and print on a regular basis nice-looking, carefully worded pieces that we give to our members to use as tools to invite their friends. This kind of "advertising" has much more impact than the impersonal kind, because with this printed invitation comes the endorsement and encouragement of a trusted friend, not to mention the offer of a free ride and a nice brunch before the event or delicious pizza afterward!

In addition, we make small, high-quality business card–sized invitations available that list the name, address, and phone number of the church, the service times, and a map to help people get there. I like its straightforward approach and lack of gimmickry—just the basic information my friends and neighbors need in order to find their way to the weekend services. These cards are always available at our lobby information booth to all attendees—including visiting non-Christians—to use as tools for inviting their friends. It was one of these cards that I had given to the woman I mentioned at the beginning of the chapter.

Gather your team around a table to brainstorm creative, effective, and honest ways to get the word out to as many people as possible. This will multiply the effect of all of your outreach efforts.

9. Permeate the Entire Process with Prayer

It's hard to know where to place prayer in a list like this. It could almost be listed as a parallel point to every other idea, as well as to every stage in the 6-Stage Process. But regardless of where it is or isn't mentioned, please realize how important it is to every part and at every stage. *Prayer really does need to permeate the whole process.*

Individually and as a team, you should pray during the idea-generation phase, asking God to give you insights into where he is already at work, so you can align your efforts with his. Ask for his wisdom and guidance so that you know where to put your limited energies and resources in order to have a maximum impact.

In the planning and promotion phase, ask God for guidance on how to best get the word out, and then pray for his blessing on those efforts. Pray that every channel of communication will be used effectively to attract more and more people.

At the actual ministry event, ask God to draw the right people in and give them open hearts to hear and embrace his message. Ask him to protect every aspect of the meeting and to use everything that happens to change lives and build the kingdom.

When your ministry event is over, thank God for the work he has accomplished, and ask him to continue what he has begun to do in the lives of those who were there. Also, ask him what to do next.

To illustrate, when I was considering holding the debate on "Atheism vs. Christianity," I remember seeking God for wisdom and guidance as diligently as I've ever sought him. I knew that if we did this event, it would draw a lot of attention as well as close scrutiny. It would be a high-potential and high-risk venture. The last thing I wanted to do was to pull the trigger presumptuously and line it all up, and then inform God that I was counting on him as if he were somehow obligated to come through for us. The image kept coming to my mind of Satan tempting Jesus to throw himself down from the temple and trust God to protect him on the way down. Jesus answered him in verse 12 of Luke 4, "Do not put the Lord your God to the test."

I was so concerned that I delayed the decision to host the event for about two weeks. During this time I prayed alone and with informed friends, and I sought counsel from a number of older and wiser Christians. After getting a lot of green lights, I finally said yes and put the plan into motion, but with a deep sense of dependency on God. For the weeks that followed, right up to the event itself, the team and I prayed fervently for God's protection and blessing on the event.

During the debate, members of the prayer team sat alone in a room, watching by video monitor, asking God to let his truth prevail, to draw seekers to himself, and to build up the confidence of the believers who were there. By divine coincidence, the only video room left after the crowd overflowed into all of the other rooms was one directly below the stage in our main auditorium, where the debate was taking place. As Lee Strobel now describes it, "We had a secret weapon under that stage that the atheist never knew about!"

The potential in outreach events is huge—but only if we are led by God and empowered through submissive, persistent prayer.

"So, *did* God come through?" you ask? Yes, he did, in amazing ways. He protected and anointed every aspect of what happened that night—other than the words of the man defending atheism! In a later chapter I'll share the details of what happened.

The potential in outreach events is huge—but only if we are led by God and empowered through submissive, persistent prayer.

10. Measure and Evaluate Results, and Improve Next Time

Don't consider your outreach event complete until you have talked about it with your team to see what can be learned from the experience and what can be done better next time. This takes humility, gentleness, and a high level of trust among team members. They need to know that the purpose of evaluation is not to judge anybody or make anyone feel bad. In fact, much of what will happen will be celebration over the good things that occurred, along with a lot of laughter over funny things that happened along the way. But in looking back, priceless lessons can be drawn out and applied in order to help make the next event even more effective. If you don't evaluate, you will keep making the same mistakes over and over, and you will severely limit your ability to maximize your team efforts in the future.

Ministry teams never reach the point where they have learned all the lessons and gotten beyond the need for evaluation. In my church, after a quarter century of doing multiple evangelistic services every weekend, fifty-two times a year, along with many other special outreach events, our programming team continues to meet every Tuesday morning to reflect on and celebrate—as well as to laugh about and learn from—what happened the previous Saturday and Sunday. They keep learning valuable lessons and getting better at what they do, making them more and more effective at designing events that speak to the unchurched people we're trying to reach.

Our senior pastor, Bill Hybels, who has been teaching at these kinds of ministry events for about three decades, still gets written feedback from a couple of our leaders every Saturday night after the first of our four weekend seeker services so he can make adjustments at the other three. All of our teachers do! Sometimes the feedback contains nothing but encouragement. Other times it includes cautions about things that may be misunderstood or that may unnecessarily offend certain segments of the audience, suggestions for better clarity, additional ideas that ought to be brought out, or any number of other possibilities. If we really believe in the importance of excellence, we all have to remain active learners who are willing to receive constructive criticism from others.

More than just evaluating the programming or teaching elements, we need to measure actual results in terms of the number of people affected, and then compare these results to our original purposes for the event. Was this a low-intensity event designed with the hope of exposing one hundred new people to the ministry of the church? If that was the goal, then make sure you count how many showed up and compare the numbers. If eighty-four actually came, how does the team feel about this? Was the expectation of one hundred too high—or was it about right but communication, promotion, or prayer was lacking? What can be done better next time?

Or was this a more focused, mid-intensity event designed to attract spiritual seekers and get them signed up for seeker small groups? If so, how many seekers were there, and how many took the step toward joining a group? Was it what you hoped for? What can you celebrate? What can you learn from and then improve on at the next event?

If it was a high-intensity event, how many came to Christ? We know the Holy Spirit must do his work and draw people to the point of commitment, but did you do everything you could to produce the right environment for him to work? Did you pray for and seek after—and then follow—his guidance in the planning and execution of the event? Did you design it in a way that would help people relax and open up to the message? Did you clearly communicate the gospel? Did you, and the other members of your church, do everything in your power to make sure the people who needed to hear the message were there to hear it? Do you feel confident that the team took seriously the command in Colossians 4:5 to "be wise in the way you act toward outsiders; make the most of every opportunity"? Regardless of our specific purpose, we need to measure the actual results, compare them to our stated desires or goals, and then determine how we can do better next time.

A final thought on evaluation: Beware of what I call "the great evangelical rationalization." This is what comes out of someone's mouth when he or she is trying to make the team feel better about an unsuccessful outreach attempt. Everybody knows the event didn't go well, and it certainly didn't live up to the expectations you had for it. But rather than just admitting there were problems and resolving to make changes next time around, someone comes out with, "Well, at least one person came to Christ, and that makes it all worth it! This was hard work and it cost a lot of money—but it was all worth it for that one soul!"

The last line of the great evangelical rationalization is the zinger: "It was all worth it for that one soul." Who wants to argue with that? Who wants to weigh the value of this life that has just been affected for all eternity and then blurt out that the event was really a misfire anyway? It's pretty hard to draw this conclusion at that point. But if the goal was to lead a large number of people to Christ, then it must be drawn.

This rationalization has stopped countless evaluation sessions dead in their tracks. The problem is that it's a true statement, but it answers the wrong question. The soul of a person is of immeasurable worth, to be sure, but the question is not how much a soul is worth. The question ought to be, what could we have done to have reached as many people for Christ as possible? And what could we do next time that might reach five or fifty people—or even five hundred—instead of just one? Or, if it was a low- or mid-intensity event, what could have been done to expose more people to the church? or what might have better helped more seekers to take the next step in their spiritual journeys? These are the kinds of questions that will yield appropriate discussions and, eventually, greater results.

The next time someone in the group starts to kill the evaluation time with an eloquent rendition of the great evangelical rationalization, look him in the eye and say, "Yes, that's a good point. Before we get too caught up in figuring out how we can improve next time, let's acknowledge what God did this time and thank him for it and celebrate it. Someone came to Christ whose soul is of immeasurable worth! But then, after praying and thanking God, I think we should explore some ideas for what we can do next time that might help us reach a lot more of this person's friends for Christ too." It'll take some courage, but you have to make sure the team learns from the past and applies those lessons in the future. And then watch God work!

FIGURING OUT WHERE TO BEGIN

I hope you're seeing the potential of applying these six stages. When you have

- strong models of leaders doing personal outreach,
- more and more warm hearts toward lost people,
- an impassioned and empowered point leader working in tandem with the pastor,
- a trained and growing body of contagious Christians throughout the church,
- a team of fired-up and gifted evangelists placed strategically throughout the ministries,
- and a plan for starting effective outreach ministries and events,

then watch out, things are going to get exciting!

You now have the framework and personnel in place to unleash a plethora of outreach activities—and given the critical needs in the culture we're trying to reach, there is no better time to put it all into action than right now. But the question remains: "What kinds of outreach ministries and events should we initiate?"

Several clues can help you answer that question. First, what are the needs of the people you'd like to reach? What kinds of ministries and events would they relate to and be willing to attend?

Second, prayerfully seek to find God's direction for where you should expend your efforts. Survey the needs and opportunities you see, and ask him to guide you in whether to focus on one of those or to seek new ones. Pray that he'll give you and your team a passion for building ministries and doing outreach exactly where he wants you to work.

UNLEASHING THE TEAM ACCORDING TO EVANGELISM STYLES

Another important clue to our criteria list is to look at what would best fit your personal style of evangelism. (For more information on the styles, which include the confrontational, intellectual, testimonial, interpersonal, invitational, and service approaches, see chapter 7 and all of part 3 in this book, as well as session 2 of the *Becoming a Contagious Christian* evangelism course and chapter 9 of the *Becoming a Contagious Christian* book.)

When you explore your own natural outreach inclinations, you'll find they almost always flow along the lines of your evangelism style. So, rather than resisting your God-given design, consider where it might match up with the range of needs you've seen in your community. If God has molded you into *who* you are today, and if he has led you to be *where* you are today, then he has likely placed you right next to ministry opportunities that are crying out for what *you* can offer.

Once I discovered my own style of evangelism, I immediately began to see needs around me that I was uniquely made to meet. Since I have the intellectual style, these needs were naturally of an intellectual nature. That's why if you look back over the pages of this book you'll see that I'm sharing so many stories about people with questions and about seminars and debates designed to help people address their doubts. Even the book's opening story was about a man with serious objections. I can't help myself! It's who God made me to be, and he has provided me with opportunities to express this approach, answer people's questions, and in this way lead them to the cross of Christ. When I have the chance to work within this design, I'm naturally motivated and energized. I get excitement, satisfaction, and joy out of expressing my intellectual style of evangelism. And when I get around others who have this same style, the conversations flow, the ideas fly, the arguments abound, and we just have a ball!

Now, I fully understand that five out of six readers are scratching their heads right now. You're thinking, *You have a ball talking about that stuff? Really? What's wrong with you?* Well, apparently you have a different evangelism style. You have one of the other five—or maybe a new one we haven't discovered yet. But if I were talking about your particular approach right now, your heart would be pumping fast too.

What can we learn from this? That finding our own style of evangelism has value way beyond stage 4, where we help everybody in the church learn to communicate their faith in ways that fit them. It goes beyond stage 5 as well, where we can help everyone on the Frontline Team develop and grow within their natural style. It also has powerful implications for stage 6, where we can build entire outreach ministries and events around these six styles. When we do this, we're going to have a lot of high-octane ministry going on, because we'll be giving people permission, tools, and platforms to do what they were made by God to do.

Recently at Willow Creek we had everybody at a Frontline Team meeting retake the styles questionnaire from session 2 of the *Contagious* course just to confirm what their dominant style is. Then we had them move to designated parts of the room where they could interact with others who share their style. This gave them the chance to find their similarities and then to compare and contrast these similarities to the traits of the people in the other groups. It also helped them identify which team members, by virtue of their different styles, might make good partners for them in reaching out to non-Christians in their own communities. For example, interpersonal style evangelists realized they could team up with intellectual-style members to reach their friends or neighbors who are asking tough questions.

After a time of interacting within these six groups and letting them grapple with some questions we'd given them to discuss, each group's spokesperson shared his or her group's answers with the whole team. We had fun with the first one: "Why is your style the most important one?" The second question was, "How is your style sometimes misunderstood?" And the third was, "Where do you think your style can work most effectively?"

After each group gave their responses, Garry Poole and I had the chance to encourage and challenge the people with that particular style and to give them ideas for growing in their approach. This also gave us the opportunity to highlight ministries and events throughout the church where we needed their specific contributions.

At the end we asked team members to turn in a card listing their name and top evangelism style so we could enter it into our church database. Whenever we need people to serve in a particular outreach initiative, we can now pinpoint and talk to the people who would best fit it. And since there really is a fit, they *want* to know about the opportunity as much as we want to find people to help.

Corinth Reformed Church, in Byron Center, Michigan, took this a step further and structured their entire evangelism team around the styles of evangelism. Kevin Harney, the church's senior pastor, describes what they've done:

> Over the last several years we have repeatedly offered, and continue to offer, the *Becoming a Contagious Christian* course, with the goal of equipping all of our church members. As we've done this, we've helped each of them discover their primary evangelism style. We've also pulled together all of those who have a heart for being part of our evangelism ministry and started the Frontline Team.
>
> Next, we identified a lead person for each of the styles of evangelism. Each of these men and women work under the leadership of our evangelism point person. With great intentionality, they gather others who have the same style and forge a team of people who are ready to go out and do evangelism

the way God wired them up to do so. They lift up the value of that style, plan events, and strategize ways to have maximum kingdom impact using their particular approach.

We've found that when you gather a group of people around each of the styles of evangelism and ask them to dream, strategize, and pray, unbelievable energy and enthusiasm is generated. They want to get up out of their chairs, leave the room, and take action—right now!

We feel we're at the beginning of the learning curve on this, but we've discovered that by developing our team intentionally around the varied styles of evangelism, we're growing increasingly focused in how we can plan outreach events that will reach our community and world for Christ.

It's exciting to know that the six styles of evangelism provide us with six powerful conduits through which high-impact ministry can flow. What might the resulting ministries and events look like? This is the subject of part 3, where we'll examine what a variety of churches are doing to maximize their evangelistic potential by means of each of the six styles.

STAGE 6: KEY IDEA

Create contagious ministries and events.

"Be wise in the way you act toward outsiders; make the most of every opportunity" (Colossians 4:5).

To Consider and Discuss

1. Which parts of the Evangelistic Intensity Scale do you and your church need to concentrate on and expand most: low-, mid-, or high-intensity events?
2. List a few specific ideas of new events or ministries that would help fill that gap.
3. What are some ideas for forming clear communications and alliances between your evangelism leadership (or the Frontline

Team, if you've already begun one) and all of the other ministries in your church?

4. Choose a specific church-wide outreach opportunity and discuss how you might apply the ten principles discussed in this chapter.
5. Which of the ten principles tends to get overlooked by your team? What can you do to make sure this "missing link" is addressed in the future?
6. What can you do to increase the practice of prayer in every stage of the 6-Stage Process?

PART 3
CONTAGIOUS DIVERSITY

We've unpacked the 6-Stage Process for building a contagious church and have seen how evangelistic values must start in the hearts of the leaders and then spread to the rest of the congregation. We've looked at the necessity of strong leadership, both from the pastor and an evangelistic point person. We've seen how we can train all of the Christians in the church and, out of this training, start a diverse evangelism team. We saw how, with this diverse group, we can initiate a variety of outreach ministries and events.

Now we're set to explore the wide range of activities that can spring out of stage 6. This is not the end of the process, though—it's the springboard for an explosion of high-impact evangelistic activity.

And, without question, this explosion is needed! In his book *The Everyday Commission*, Dann Spader reports that in his study of a hundred ministries that claimed to be committed to fulfilling the Great Commission, "eighty-seven of the one hundred had all of their programs targeted to helping believers grow."[1] This is further evidence of the evangelistic entropy we've talked about. Don't let this tendency be true of your church! Help your people get into the action of doing what is so central to the heart of God and to the mission, values, and strategy of your church: *reaching lost people with the gospel of Christ.*

To help you carry out this mission, I'll present in the following chapters a wealth of ideas from outreach-minded churches with whom I've interacted. These ideas will flow out of the six styles of evangelism discussed earlier, expressed at a church-wide level. We'll discuss one style per chapter. Some examples actually spotlight two or more styles, but I've placed them where they seem to fit best.

You'll undoubtedly feel great affinity for some ideas and very little for others. Just remember that it really does take all kinds of Christians to reach all kinds of non-Christians. Embrace and empower a broad range of approaches that will deploy the full spectrum of believers in your church, and make it your aim to relate to the full spectrum of people in your community.

10

MAXIMIZING OUTREACH AROUND THE CONFRONTATIONAL STYLE

"I speak as one transformed by Jesus Christ, the living God. He is the Way, the Truth, and the Life. He has lived in me for twenty years. His presence is the sole explanation for whatever is praiseworthy in my work....

"That is more than a statement about myself. It is a claim to truth. It is a claim that may contradict your own....

"The God of Abraham, Isaac, and Jacob reigns. His plan and purpose rob the future of its fears. By the cross he offers hope, by the resurrection he assures his triumph. This cannot be resisted or delayed. Mankind's only choice is to recognize him now or in the moment of ultimate judgment. Our only decision is to welcome his rule or to fear it...."

I sat in stunned silence as God spoke so powerfully through this prophet for our time. It wasn't only his message that produced these feelings of awe—it was the setting. Seated on the platform behind him were prominent leaders from many different religious groups. Just prior to this forceful message, a Buddhist priest came to the podium and offered a chant, and then after the message a Muslim leader got up and said a prayer.

But cutting through the cloud of confusion, Charles Colson, in his 1993 Templeton Address, stood and delivered what I believe was one of the most effective presentations of the gospel given in this generation.

My friends and I felt like witnesses to a modern-day rendition of the apostle Peter, who stood before the religious-but-lost mass of people in Jerusalem just weeks after Jesus had been crucified there.

Acts 2 describes how Peter boldly challenged the people with the fact that God had sent Jesus, their Messiah, but they had put him to death. Then Peter straightforwardly declared in verse 32 that "God has raised this Jesus to life," and he extended to them God's forgiveness and grace if they would simply "repent and be baptized, every one of you, in the name of Jesus Christ for the forgiveness of your sins" (verse 38).

The confrontational style of evangelism is hard-hitting, direct, to the point, and it challenges everybody in its path to get off the fence and follow Christ.

In like fashion, Colson presented the truth in his characteristic no-holds-barred, no-punches-pulled style. This is a powerful and public example of the confrontational style of evangelism. It is hard-hitting, direct, to the point, and it challenges everybody in its path to get off the fence and follow Christ. (And it had *impact:* I know a young Mormon man, Rob, who had been brought there by some of my friends. He took the challenge, got off the fence, and trusted in the true Christ of the Bible that very night.)

A CHALLENGE FOR LIFE

You already know from my story of the summer of ministry with the overseas church that the confrontational style is not my personal style. But it is one I thank God for!

When I was nineteen, I was living on the wild side. I'd grown up in a Christian home, had godly parents, and had attended Bible-teaching churches all my life. But for years, including all the way through high school, I'd been mostly ignoring what I knew to be true. I was living for what was supposed to be "a good time," doing my best to keep my conscience at bay.

I was selling stereo equipment in the most prominent music store in our town. It was an exciting place to be and played right into my desire to be in the middle of the action. The irony is that while I was seriously partying with some of my coworkers, I continued to attend church services and even visited a Bible study with a few Christians I'd met. I was living a double life, doing my best to keep the two worlds from colliding.

One day there was a collision.

Terry, a guy I'd known in school, came into the electronics store that day. After discussing some audio equipment, he changed the subject abruptly: "By the way, Mark, I heard something the other day that really surprised me. I heard that last Monday night you went to a Bible study in somebody's home."

"Yeah, so. . . ?" I replied cautiously.

"Does that mean you're a Christian?" he asked.

"Sure I'm a Christian," I said a bit nervously. "What about it?"

"Well," Terry replied with a puzzled look, "I don't see how you can call yourself a Christian and yet have a reputation for doing so many things Christians don't do"—and then he started listing those things.

"Well," I explained matter-of-factly, "I'm a *cool* Christian!"

Without batting an eye, Terry shot back, "Yeah? There's a word for that—*hypocrite!*"

It won't surprise you that this "cool" Christian's initial response was, at best, lukewarm. Terry made me angry, but he made me think—because I knew he was right! After a few days my anger turned to reflection and then to repentance. The next week I went back to that same Bible study and afterward made a commitment to follow Christ for the rest of my life.

I hate to think of where I'd be today if it hadn't been for the confrontational style of evangelism. And there are a lot of other Mark Mittelbergs out there who need someone to get in their face with the truth too. Sometimes the manner of a confrontational evangelist will be hard-hitting and direct, like Terry's was. Other times it will be gentler, yet with a directness that cuts through the red tape and evokes serious reflection and decision making in the other person.

PUTTING THE CONFRONTATIONAL STYLE INTO ACTION

The question for us is, how can we deploy this evangelism approach in our churches? What are some ministries and outreach events that can unleash this high-impact style?

An Evangelistic Explosion

One of the best-known evangelism programs in the world, *Evangelism Explosion,* developed by Dr. D. James Kennedy, is built on this direct form of outreach. The same is true of the Southern Baptist curriculum *Continuing Witness Training.* These high-quality visitation programs are being used throughout the United States and all over the world. And while they certainly utilize people with some of the other styles of evangelism, they're best built on the bold, direct, and confident characteristics of those with the confrontational style.

And how God has used these church-based programs! Countless non-Christians over the last few decades have been confronted with the famous "diagnostic question" that asks, "Suppose you were to die today and stand before God and he were to say to you, 'Why should I let you into my heaven?' What would you say?"

People in these ministries help others discover the biblical answer, stop relying on their good deeds and religious accomplishments, and embrace Jesus as their Lord and Savior.

A Synergistic Combination

Some churches take an all-or-nothing approach, using a singular outreach program. They pick a particular way to reach people and put all their eggs into this basket, as if everyone will be reached the same way. Some even throw out everything they've used previously just to try something new. Not so with First Baptist Church of Smyrna, Tennessee.[2] Eddie Mosley, their education pastor, responded to some questions about their evangelistic approach:

Q: Tell us a little about First Baptist Church and your outreach efforts.

A: We are a congregation whose members are, on average, thirty-two years old, married, and have two children. That, combined with our active outreach program, means our community is very busy every night of the week. Our *Evangelism Explosion* teams do visitation on Thursday nights, and our pastoral staff does visits on whatever nights of the week they have opportunity. In addition, we've introduced the *Becoming a Contagious Christian* training to our congregation and feel it fits naturally with who we are as a body of believers.

Q: *Evangelism Explosion* is used effectively by many churches all around the world. How have you seen *EE* work for your congregation?

A: We've found that about ten percent of our church members feel called to go through the *EE* training. They gain very extensive training. They learn key Bible verses, helpful illustrations, and a clear method by which they can communicate the gospel and lead people through a commitment process. When it comes to training people to present the gospel and to "close the deal," we have found *EE* very helpful and effective.

Q: What additional value have you found in using the *Becoming a Contagious Christian* training course?

A: Our staff teaches the *Contagious* course on a church-wide level. We have received great reports each time we've taught it. It helps our people finally come to a comfort level with telling their friends about Jesus and their church experience. The key is the six styles of evangelism. Before taking this class most people feel guilty for not participating in the visitation night—knocking on doors and sharing Christ more boldly. After the *Contagious Christian* training they are so pleased to know that different people can share Christ in dramatically different ways. We've discovered that this training breaks down the undue fear some believers have when it comes to evangelism.

Q: How are you seeing these two training programs work side by side?

A: Each one benefits the other. The *Contagious Christian* training helps the broad membership of the church understand that they can give witness to their faith. They have a particular style that is God-given. They can be part of reaching out in a way that feels right to them. At the same time, when we discover that someone has a strong confrontational style or a desire for additional training, we point that person toward the *Evangelism Explosion* program. We don't see these two tools as conflicting with each other at all. They are parallel tracks heading our church in the same direction.

Q: And the results?

A: We are seeing many adults come to Christ and are rejoicing as we host weekly baptisms. These new believers, in turn, have many nonchurched friends. These friends are often open to attending gatherings where they can connect with believers. And so the cycle continues.

I heard about a similar situation at New Hope Baptist Church in Fayetteville, Georgia. They offered the *Becoming a Contagious Christian* training course simultaneously in all of their Sunday school classes—a total of 953 people all at once. When I asked the evangelism pastor what effect this effort was having on the church, he told me wonderful stories of people making commitments to Christ and of Christians becoming motivated to reach their friends. Then he added a very encouraging comment: "We had long since shut down our *Continuing Witness Training* team. But running *Contagious* has forced us to restart that too!"

Why? I believe there were two reasons: First, the value of evangelism had been lifted up all over the church, so people were more ready to jump at opportunities to express it. Second, the members with the more direct, hard-hitting personalities had realized that God made them this way, and that he wanted to utilize their personalities to build his kingdom. The first place they thought of getting involved was with the visitation team.

What an exciting example of what needs to happen in many other churches—a multipronged effort (as in, "Attack on every front!"). I'm not saying every church necessarily needs a particular visitation program, but we do need to develop and deploy all kinds of Christians to reach all kinds of non-Christians. We must stop thinking either/or and instead begin thinking both/and.

Variations on Visitations

Another direct-style evangelism program that has sprung up in recent years is *FAITH,* which stands for the *F*orgiveness of sin, which is *A*vailable to all. Without forgiveness it is *I*mpossible to gain eternal life. Unless one will *T*urn from her/his sin, he or she will never see *H*eaven. This program takes the general approach of *Continuing Witness Training* but applies it within an adult Sunday school framework.[3] The beauty of this is that it adds a more relational dimension to this approach, and the Sunday school class provides a natural place for members to invite the people they're reaching.

In addition to these formal evangelism programs, churches utilize the confrontational style in a number of other ways as they visit homes. Tabernacle Church of Norfolk, Virginia, for example, has a team of more than a dozen church members who knock on doors of low-income residents who live in apartments near their church. When people seem open, they try to strike up a spiritual conversation, present the gospel, and begin to establish a relationship. This team has seen as many as fifty people make first-time commitments within a single year. One woman greeted them at the door by saying, "I have waited so long for you to come!" and she soon put her trust in Christ. A seventy-eight-year-old gentleman said, "You know, I have always gone to church, but I never realized that I was supposed to know Jesus." With tears in his eyes he prayed as he received salvation and met Jesus personally.

First Presbyterian Church in Baton Rouge, Louisiana, uses a three-pronged approach. The team begins by contacting first-time visitors to the church. This contact is followed by an in-home visit. The third part of the strategy adds the interpersonal style to the mix, as friendships are formed.

At South Hills Community Church in Highlands Ranch, Colorado, two-person visitation teams call on church visitors. These teams interview them, using what they call the F.O.R.M. approach, a simple four-part outline:

F— Family (Tell us about your family background.)
O— Occupation (Tell us about your vocational life, inside or outside the home.)
R— Religious Background (Tell us about your journey of faith.)
M—My Testimony (As team members sense receptivity, they share their testimony and the gospel message.)

A Mugging Ministry

At Corinth Reformed Church, in Byron Center, Michigan, all guests are "mugged" within a week of attending. Thankfully, it's an activity related to outreach, not fund-raising! Pastor Kevin Harney explains how this ministry impacts visitors:

> When a new person or family visits us, they are invited to fill out a visitor card. They're assured we won't put them on a mailing list but are told right up front that we want to make two contacts with them. First, we'll send a letter answering questions about the church and including information about any specific ministries they're interested in. Second, we want to drop by and give them a gift as a thank-you for visiting. People seem to respect this direct approach, and many fill out cards.
>
> Within a week one of our ten trained calling teams drops by their home on an evening or during the weekend to bring them a coffee mug filled with candy, a refrigerator magnet, a pen, and a pencil. These serve as reminders because they're imprinted with our church's name, phone number, and e-mail address.
>
> This is not a get-your-foot-in-the-door approach with a forced gospel presentation. Rather, team members seek to discern the heart of those they visit, answer their spiritual questions, and tell them more about the church. Also, they're trained in presenting the Bridge illustration, so if the person is spiritually receptive, the gospel can be communicated in a clear and understandable way.
>
> We've visited hundreds of homes and have never heard about anyone who was offended or upset. Rather, many people who have made commitments to Christ and joined the church have commented how much it meant to have someone take the time to come to their home and bring them a gift. Person after person has thanked us for honoring them by stepping into their world and caring for them.

Sometimes God surprises us. One afternoon one of our teams went out to visit but couldn't find the house. They asked a young man for directions. When he inquired about what they were doing, they explained that they were out mugging church visitors. After he understood what they meant(!), he asked some questions about the church. They invited him to attend, and the next Sunday he showed up. What seemed at first to be a detour turned out to be a divine appointment.

The Direct Touch

When Willow Creek was beginning its ministry in the early 1970s the leaders did a survey among the homes in the neighborhood. Their question was simple: "Do you regularly attend a local church?" If the answer was yes, the team would encourage them to continue doing so, and they'd move on. But if the answer was no, they would ask the person why. "Is it a problem with believing in God, or is it something else?" they'd ask. In addition to providing valuable glimpses into the minds of unchurched people, the conversations created curiosity. Many of these people were willing to give their name and telephone number so they could be informed about church services or events that would address their issues.

Whether your church is new or old, this kind of direct interaction is a great way to stay in touch with people's attitudes and questions, as well as to invite them to upcoming outreach events. And it gives you a strategic place to deploy the confrontational style of evangelism.

Reaching Crowds

The confrontational approach is used on a wide scale by evangelists like Billy Graham, Franklin Graham, Luis Palau, Greg Laurie, John Guest, and Mike Silva. It's also used on a more intimate level by up-close communicators like InterVarsity's Cliffe Knechtle, who mixes it with the intellectual style.

One of the ways churches can support these wide-scale efforts is to recruit members who possess this evangelism style and add them to community-wide teams, especially as counselors to talk and pray with people who respond to invitations at the end of an event. Our church did this during Luis Palau's crusade in Chicago and during an outreach event with Josh McDowell and the music group Petra.

Some churches view these citywide events as threats that might take their leaders away. In my experience, they've actually served to strengthen and reinforce these people in their current roles. These are opportunities to give our people frontline exposure, and the people who come to Christ will be more likely to visit your church if the person who prayed with them is one of your members. In addition, for follow-up purposes, many large-event ministries will share with the involved churches the names and addresses of the people who responded. Thus, these are great opportunities to participate in what God is doing to reach people through these ministries, to give your people valuable evangelism experience, and to add freshly redeemed members to your church body.

Reaching Crowds at Home

It used to be that when the crusade was over and the evangelist went home, the outreach jets would cool and everyone would wait five or ten years until the next big event. But not anymore. Increasingly churches are providing high-quality seeker services or outreach-oriented worship services that furnish opportunities to express the confrontational style both in and around the events.

While it would be unwise when trying to reach a secular audience to be highly confrontational in every service, there's certainly a place for doing so on a regular basis, as Bill Hybels does at Willow Creek's seeker services. One weekend I remember him saying, "When one of the huge tanker ships comes into a harbor, it makes every other boat move either to the left or to the right. Jesus does the same thing. His teaching forces every one of us to make the choice, sooner or later, to turn his way or the opposite way. Today I want to help you know that you've moved in the right direction and are on his side." In a similar fashion, you can utilize those with the confrontational approach in an up-front role in your church services, classes, and seminars.

The worship leaders at Victory Point Ministries in Holland, Michigan, do this periodically. They gear up for a specific Sunday morning service where they plan the music and the rest of the service elements to culminate in a simple and clear gospel presentation. At the end of the message people are invited to stand up, come forward, and give their life to Christ. They don't see a response every time, but at one recent service twenty-five people made commitments.

The leaders of Northeast Christian Church in Louisville, Kentucky, sometimes design their seeker service to be confrontational, yet carried out with "gentleness and respect." After encouraging nonbelievers at one particular service to consider the claims of Christ, the pastor issued a challenge. But rather than having people raise their hand, stand up, or walk the aisle, he invited them to indicate their interest on a card and to turn it in after the service. There was a clear call to action, but people were free to respond with a measure of privacy.

For each person who turned in a card, the church provided a packet that included the following:

- the book *More than a Carpenter* by Josh McDowell
- a contemporary version of the "Four Spiritual Laws" booklet
- a copy of the New Testament in a modern version
- information about how to know Jesus and about the church

Then they set up appointments with those who had requested this packet. In these meetings they walked through the person's questions and tried to help him or her understand the message of salvation. They did all of this to challenge people with the truth—while giving them space to study on their own and discover answers for themselves.

At Mountain Top Community Church in Birmingham, Alabama, the leaders of the middle school and high school ministries have discovered that the confrontational approach can be effective in reaching young people in their community too. They don't do this every week, but they have "Target Nights" when they give a hard-hitting, no-compromise gospel presentation and call for a response. Their youth ministry team has seen great results using this approach.

OTHER CONFRONTATIONAL-STYLE MINISTRIES AND EVENTS

Back to Basics

Eastview Christian Church in Bloomington, Illinois, has a monthly dinner where people are invited to learn the "Basics," which is also the name of this event. Every month an invitation is extended to all their visitors to come to a dinner hosted by the preaching pastor. Once there, they enjoy a good meal, learn about Eastview Church, and hear the pastor give a straightforward presentation of the gospel. Each month between twenty and eighty people attend this two-hour event. One exciting aspect is that those with the service style of evangelism can also get involved by helping prepare and serve the food. Consequently, they're able to share the joy of watching as people hear and respond to the gospel. This is a great partnership of evangelistic styles.

Advancing on a Retreat

At CrossWinds Church in Dublin, California, men's retreats are used to boldly present the gospel. Speakers are selected for their ability to clearly articulate the message of Christ. The remote setting away from the everyday distractions of life helps make this ministry effective, as do the relationships the guests have with the men who invite them.

A Strategic Student Thing

The youth ministry team at Park Cities Baptist Church in Dallas, Texas, has utilized an event they call "The Thing-a-ma-jig." This is an overnight "lock-in" to which they invite their friends and then take them to places all over the Dallas area. They go skating, bowling, and go-cart riding, and then they stop for pizza. During the night the gospel is presented through media, music, and message, followed by a clear invitation and a call for response.

In Dramatic Fashion

First Assembly of God in Des Moines, Iowa, First Assembly in Kenosha, Wisconsin, and many other churches have used the radically confrontational drama "Heaven's Gates and Hell's Flames." This graphic presentation of what awaits us in the afterlife as a result of our decisions about Christ in life is followed by a challenge to receive him. While this may not fit the persona of every church, many ministries have seen numerous people come to faith through this means. In fact, several years ago a group of churches banded together in Modesto, California, to present this drama in multiple performances—and as many as 33,000 people put their trust in Christ.

A Faithful Partner to Churches

One ministry that has served as a role model for many years in unashamedly confronting people with truth is Campus Crusade for Christ. Their seemingly ubiquitous presence has carried with it everywhere the simple, straightforward presentation of the "Four Spiritual Laws," which has helped innumerable students and adults come to an understanding of the gospel and brought them into a relationship with Christ. I think we'll all celebrate in eternity this ministry's ability to embolden so many hard-hitting evangelists—on their own teams and in churches everywhere—to lovingly challenge lost people with the message of the cross.

CREATING ACTION THROUGHOUT YOUR CHURCH

In many cases, the best way to utilize the confrontational style is by dispersing those who have it throughout the ministries of the church. We need to keep these folks in people-contact positions but not necessarily with too many others like them. These are the kind of workers who can stand alone. So use them in key greeter roles, as ushers in visible positions, and as part of the team that interacts with people after services. Have them stand near the pastor after services to follow up with guests, so there can be strategic handoffs. Use them to talk to visitors who indicate an interest in Christianity during the service, and add them to your telephone teams during outreach events. Mix these people in everywhere, but make certain they understand their most important role—to bring truth to bear and to call for a decision as God's Spirit leads them.

Finally, link these impact players with others. Realize that they are the ones who often create action in the first place and then later bring it to a conclusion. But in between a lot of other evangelistic ministry must take place, so these people will typically need assistance from those who possess the other evangelism styles.

A CASE IN POINT

My friend Karl Singer and I went into a frozen yogurt shop. Karl, who is confrontational style with a capital *C,* noticed that the man working behind the counter was of Middle Eastern heritage. Before I'd had the chance to figure out what the flavor of the day was, Karl had asked the guy whether he was a Muslim or a Christian. And before I had a chance to be surprised by Karl's bluntness, the man replied, "I don't know. I guess to be honest with you, I'm somewhere in the middle right now trying to figure out what to believe."

This approach, more than any other, is able to create action. Let's not be afraid of it, or hold these people down.

Wow! After picking my jaw up off the floor, I kicked myself into gear to begin applying my intellectual approach. I began to talk with him about Jesus' claim to be the unique Son of God who died and rose on our behalf, and I told him about the overwhelming evidence that supports those claims. A few days later we went back to talk with him further and gave him some things to read to help him work through his questions and better understand the gospel.

Karl's direct hit started the action, but it also called into play my intellectual style, Barbara's (Karl's wife) interpersonal style, and some of their other friends' testimonial, invitational, and service styles. In fact, over time Karl and Barbara became friends with this man and his wife. They spent time getting to know them and invited them to their church.

Through a series of events, with a group of Christians who combined outreach efforts and prayed up a storm, a miracle finally happened. Almost a year after the original encounter, this man, his wife, and their six-year-old daughter all committed their lives to Christ—together! By God's grace, three more people were adopted into his family that day.

THE IMPORTANCE OF THE CONFRONTATIONAL STYLE

Although God used a team of people with a variety of styles, the initial conversation never would have started without Karl and his confrontational style. This approach, more than any other, is able to create *action.* Let's not be afraid of it, or hold these people down. Rather, let's encourage and coach them on how to challenge people appropriately with the eternal truth of the gospel.

To Consider and Discuss

1. What present activities in your church could be turbocharged with a few strategically placed confrontational-style evangelists?
2. What new initiatives could be started to give those who use the confrontational style additional opportunities?
3. Can you think of specific people in your congregation who would flourish in using the confrontational approach? What kinds of encouragement and training will they need to become more effective?
4. The confrontational style is generally the most high-octane of the evangelism approaches. Depending on how it's used, it can do great good or major harm. Do you see situations or ministries in your church where this style needs tempering or redirection?

11 MAXIMIZING OUTREACH AROUND THE INTELLECTUAL STYLE

"The question before us tonight is, when you weigh the evidence for atheism against the evidence for Christianity, which way, on balance, does the evidence point?

"In support of a Christian answer to that question, I'm going to defend two basic contentions in tonight's debate. Number one: There's *no* good evidence that atheism is true. And number two: There *is* good evidence that Christianity is true.

"Let's look, then, at my first contention. The claim that God does not exist is just as much a claim to know something as is the claim that God does exist. Therefore, if my opponent is going to maintain that the evidence points toward atheism, he's got to do more than just say there's no good evidence for God's existence. He must present evidence against God's existence.

"He's therefore simply mistaken when he says in the *Tribune* that atheism makes no claims, and so it has nothing to defend. Atheistic philosophers have tried for centuries to disprove the existence of God. But no one's been able to come up with a convincing argument. So, rather than attack straw men at this point, I'll just wait to hear a response to the following question: What is the evidence that atheism is true?

"First let's go on to my second contention. There is good evidence that Christianity is true, and here I'd like to present five lines of evidence that render the Christian faith highly probable in contrast to atheism. . . ."

After months of prayer, planning, and promotion, what had become known as the "Great Debate" was finally happening. Anticipation for this event had been so high that in the area two miles around the church the roads were almost completely gridlocked (the *Chicago Tribune* had run four advance articles). When we opened the doors to the auditorium a full hour ahead of the start time, the seats filled up in just seven minutes—all 4,554 of them! From there we directed people into video overflow rooms until we were able to accommodate a total of 7,778 attendees. In addition, thousands more around the country were listening via Moody Broadcasting Network's live satellite transmission on over a hundred radio stations. Moody even dispatched two on-site commentators to give the radio audience a blow-by-blow account of what was happening!

Dr. William Lane Craig began the debate with the challenging words I quoted above. In spite of the room being filled wall to wall with people, you could hear a pin drop—the audience was that fascinated by the arguments and the outcome.

This event was reminiscent of Acts 17, where Paul utilized his intellectual style of evangelism to challenge the thinkers of Athens with the gospel of Jesus Christ. What a thrill it was to watch Bill Craig, like the apostle Paul, "demolish arguments and every pretension that sets itself up against the knowledge of God, and . . . take captive every thought to make it obedient to Christ" (2 Corinthians 10:5).

At the end, when we took a vote to see which side the listeners thought had presented the stronger case, ninety-seven percent of the group said the case for God was stronger. Of those who marked on the ballot that they were not Christians, a whopping eighty-two percent still said the case for Christianity had prevailed. Of that group, forty-seven individuals said that by the time the evening was over, they had become believers in Christ!

THE NEED FOR THE INTELLECTUAL STYLE

There's a rumor spreading in Christian circles that people in our postmodern world no longer care about truth. Therefore, some would say, the intellectual style of evangelism is out of vogue and not needed at the present time. I couldn't disagree more.

Many people today have become increasingly relativistic, thinking there are many "truths" but being highly skeptical of anything claiming to be "Truth." Among the younger generations, people tend to be more experiential in their approach to deciding what to believe. They don't generally lead off with questions about scientific evidence or empirical verification. They're often more pragmatic and search out what seems to be working in the lives of their friends and others they respect.

But give these people some time, and earn their trust. Once the layers are peeled back, many of the classic questions will begin to surface—along with a few new ones. The issues are often the same, but the people raising them usually have far less knowledge about God and the Bible than those of past generations.

We won't reach people in a culture like ours by backing down and agreeing to stop talking about why we believe what we believe. While we can and should add other approaches to our evangelistic arsenal, we have to keep explaining the rational basis for our faith and helping people see we're building on a foundation of facts like no other religion has.

Further, we must help people see that even the claim that "there is no such thing as truth" is itself a claim to know truth about the subject of truth—and is therefore self-contradictory and invalid. We need to help them understand that, whether they like the "T-word" or not, *whatever is, is*—and our personal beliefs about what *is* have no effect on it one way or the other. If the liquid really is deadly poison, my believing it's just water won't save me when I drink it. A person's disbelief in the reality of large trucks won't save him when he crosses the highway in front of one. And one's ideas about God have no bearing whatsoever on whether he exists or on what he's really like.

Whatever is, is. Our job as humans is to find out what *is,* and adjust our lives to it. And our role as intellectual-style evangelists is to help people understand *what really is* in the spiritual realm. We need to help unbelievers understand why they can have confidence in God and can therefore experience forgiveness and new life through him.

We won't reach people in a culture like ours by backing down and agreeing to stop talking about why we believe what we believe.

Now more than ever we need to "be prepared to give an answer to everyone who asks." More than that, we need to find and equip those in our congregations who are naturally wired by God for this kind of outreach, people who think like Paul, Bill Craig, Josh McDowell, Ravi Zacharias—and maybe you!

Since my evangelism style is the intellectual style, leading and speaking at an event like the debate was exhilarating for me. What's really exciting is that such events don't merely give the main teacher a chance to use this style; rather, they create intellectual action all over the place. Before the debate, evangelistic thinkers were involved in doing research and participating in interviews. We also had teams on hand to answer questions after the debate was over and to follow up with calls to those who had written questions on their ballots. Today when we do similar events, we also have leaders ready to start question-oriented seeker small groups with those who are willing to go on to the next step in order to pursue answers.

PUTTING THE INTELLECTUAL STYLE TO WORK

Your church can do many kinds of activities to raise and address questions seekers ask and to put into action more and more of your members who have the intellectual style.

UTILIZING WEEKENDS

One of the easiest places to overlook with respect to engaging and addressing people who have questions is at your regular church services. Services designed for newcomers can be especially valuable times for addressing questions. At Willow Creek we plan answers-oriented services on a regular basis, and we inform our people ahead of time so they will make a special effort to invite their friends. Such a series usually lasts four or five weeks and covers the issues people in our surrounding neighborhoods are concerned about, as opposed to the in-house concerns that Christians often debate. Our series titles have included, "Faith Has Its Reasons," "Believing the Unbelievable," "Alternatives to Christianity," "Christianity: Fact or Fiction?" and "What Would You Ask God?"

We don't offer these series in isolation. We use them as springboards into after-service question-and-answer sessions, an Investigating Christianity class, and our seeker small groups—many of which study the issues further by using the *Tough Questions* curriculum.[1] Our verbal and printed announcements are very intentional in trying to move seekers to take these next steps in their spiritual journeys. Together these efforts help numerous people come to Christ, and they provide outlets for service for Christians with the intellectual style of evangelism.

Many other churches are having success using similar approaches on weekends. The leaders at Windsor Crossing Community Church in Chesterfield, Missouri, for example, offered a series called "The Frequently Asked Questions of Christianity." It included these topics: "Is the Bible Trustworthy?" "Did Jesus Really Rise from the Dead?" "What about Evolution?" and "Is Jesus the Only Way?"

The leaders at Scottsdale Family Church in Scottsdale, Arizona, know that more than half of their Sunday morning attendees have no church background at all, yet a majority are well-educated professionals. Therefore, they regularly present messages that address the questions these people are asking.

Chesapeake Church in Huntingtown, Maryland, has developed an apologetics ministry called "Impact." They create monthly handouts that correspond to the series being taught in their worship services. To encourage the use of these handouts, they've designed them to fit into binders people can keep for reference. What's more, they have begun a ministry that studies a variety of apologetics-oriented topics to sharpen their skills for reaching people, and this group also contributes ideas for the Impact handout.

Strategic Classes and Seminars

This broad approach can be adapted to a classroom and seminar level and offered much more frequently. For example, for a couple years I led a forty-five-minute class every week prior to one of our regular services. We called it the Foundations class because it was designed to present and defend the foundational truths of the Christian faith. Generally I'd teach for half the time and then open the floor to questions about the subject I'd just taught. We would announce the topics the preceding week at the class and at our church services. We'd try to address the natural questions and curiosity many seekers have and state the titles in terms of questions they might ask. Examples include: "Isn't the Bible Full of Contradictions?" "Isn't Jesus Just One of the Ways to God?" "What's All This 'Born Again' Business?" "Is God Three or One?" "Reincarnation: Do We Get a Second Chance?" "You Don't Take the Bible *Literally,* Do You?" and "What's So Good about Good Friday?" One week following the news of a major U.S. earthquake, I taught a session called "Does God Cause Earthquakes?"

The Firing Line

Occasionally we've even opened up entire classes to questions anyone wanted to ask related to the Christian faith. Usually we do this with two or three of us up front to share the responsibility of giving answers. We refer to this as a "firing line." The name alone seems to inspire curiosity! We've done this not only in smaller classroom and seminar settings but also in front of thousands at our weekend and midweek services.

Those of us who have the intellectual style of evangelism love this format, and so do spiritual seekers! Many of them had been told in the past to keep their questions to themselves, or that they just needed to have more faith and they wouldn't have all these questions. Can you imagine their delight when they discover a church that actually encourages them to talk about their issues?

When you make public announcements inviting everyone who has questions and objections—and their friends who might have tougher ones—to meet in the sanctuary on a Saturday or Sunday night, you'll attract all kinds of people. Some will come for answers. Others will attend to sharpen their ability to give answers. Still more will show up for the spectacle, hoping to see an exciting intellectual shoot-out.

This latter sentiment, quite honestly, is what brought many of the people to our debate. But it didn't keep God from working in their lives. A woman named Maggie came just to see the Christians get trounced! When this failed to happen, she became curious and began attending our weekend services, and later joined a seeker small group. Finally, after she spent months of searching, one of our Frontline Team members who has the intellectual style met with her several times and ended up leading her in a prayer of commitment to Christ. And it all started because we took the risk to offer this kind of event.

Another time I was challenged directly during the Q & A time at one of our Foundations classes by a visitor who was a professional astrologer. Word got out, and the next week attendance at the class increased by thirty percent!

Most likely someone in your church or community has the expertise and the sensitivity to answer questions in this kind of setting. The ministry of such a person can go a long way to help seekers and to unleash the intellectual style of evangelism within your fellowship.

LESSONS LEARNED

Often, however, the best apologists are not the best preachers or public speakers—perhaps because they have a different set of spiritual gifts or because they spend so much more time acquiring information than learning how to communicate it effectively. Whatever the reason, it's worth our effort to compensate and help them get their great knowledge out where it will help a lot of people. In many cases, this is not best achieved by putting them in the pulpit.

I once heard a powerful apologist preach from the Gospel of John at a Sunday morning church service. He spent the first twenty minutes (I timed him!) proving to his listeners that John really wrote John. As I looked around, it seemed pretty clear that not one person in this small, family-oriented evangelical church had ever even heard that John might *not* have written John. Needless to say, many of them had mentally checked out by the time this brilliant scholar finally got to the main part of his message.

But put this man on a stool and let him respond to questions and tell stories of his real-life encounters with spiritual skeptics, and he'll electrify your audience. Better yet, put him in front of the group along with someone else who understands what he's saying and, as necessary, can restate his answers in ways ordinary folks can understand. Then you'll have a truly winning combination.

EXAMPLES OF EXPANDING ON THE INTELLECTUAL STYLE

Discoveries Made Here

Kensington Community Church in Troy, Michigan, has developed a class for newcomers called "Discovery 1," which is offered monthly on a Friday night and Saturday morning. It includes a talk that highlights the gospel and underscores other core Christian beliefs and then provides a time for questions from the class. The leaders even invite skeptics to "take their best shot." Seekers are always present, and they never fail to ask good questions. At the end of the discussion, class leaders also make available a number of relevant books and articles for further study.

Better Than a 2 x 4

Unfortunately, evangelists sometimes make seekers feel like they're being hit over the head with a 2 x 4. How much better to teach and encourage them using 3 x 5s! At Mosaic Church in Los Angeles, California, a weekly outreach event is held in a downtown nightclub once owned by the rock musician Prince. Attendees are regularly encouraged to write their questions about God on 3 x 5 cards. Then the message time is used to present answers. These events are appropriately known as "3 x 5 Nights."

Hot Topic Zone (HTZ)

Paul Trainor, the evangelism director at Central Christian Church in Las Vegas, Nevada, explains an intellectually based outreach ministry they've recently started:

> The Hot Topic Zone (HTZ) is a place we've developed inside our church's courtyard. The courtyard is a place where people naturally congregate for food and interaction. So why

not include an area where questions of Christianity, life, religion, and values can be openly discussed? We staff this area with trained HTZ consultants who are available around weekend service times to help answer questions people have in these areas. In addition, people are encouraged to write out questions and drop them at any number of outlets (including the information desk, in the offering plate, or right at the HTZ). We then publish a one-page "answer of the week," addressing a question someone asked. This is available at the Zone or can be read in specialty menus at some of the tables spread throughout the courtyard, which also describe the HTZ and invite people to come and interact with our consultants. It's a mini-forum on a weekly basis!

As an example of what we might place in the specialty menus, we recently spoke to this issue:

> "Which God?" Many people say they believe in God, yet there are widely conflicting ideas about what God is like. Christians say God is infinite, personal, and triune. Jews, Muslims and Jehovah's Witnesses deny the Trinity. Mormons accept a plurality of gods. New Agers say each of us needs to discover the god within. So which god is the real God? How do you know? How should we describe God? What is he like? Can I know him in a meaningful way? Have you ever wondered about any of these questions? If you have, please stop by our Hot Topic Zone for more information. Or just stop by and ask us whatever question is on your mind.

Through the ministry of HTZ, stumbling-block questions are answered in a forum of respect, and seeker groups are beginning to be formed. Believers are also welcome to ask questions, and the process lends to their growth and helps them become prepared to answer the questions their friends are asking them.

A Guided Journey

Evergreen Baptist Church in Rosemead, California, takes a fresh approach. Pastor Ken Fong describes it like this:

> We've initiated a 10-week program called Quest. It's a sort of Socratic, postmodern evangelism course for skeptics and churched people who are wrestling with doubts and need a

safe place to ask questions. It's not an apologetics course or an attempt to give people all the answers; rather, it's about pointing people toward the truth. Quest students take part in small groups, personal journaling, and the reading of thought-provoking Christian articles and viewing excerpts from movies like *Contact, Shadowlands, The Shawshank Redemption, Matrix, Les Miserables,* and *The Joy Luck Club.* These produce conversation around our weekly themes.

STUDENT SKEPTICS FORUM

The members of Hudson Community Chapel in Hudson, Ohio, have developed what they call a "Skeptics Forum" designed to reach students. The forum deals creatively with pressing issues on the minds of young people. For example, after some students asked about the difference between Islam and Christianity, leaders invited a Muslim student to talk about his religion to the group. Then they explored the differences in a safe, open environment and respectfully presented reasons for trusting in Christ. They hope to develop a similar ministry with the adults in the church.

FRIEND TO FRIEND

Wooddale Church of Eden Prairie, Minnesota, has partnered with Faith Studies International to reach postmodern suburbanites with the gospel. Using a strategy called "Friend to Friend," Wooddale equips hundreds of believers each year to invite people they know to outreach events. One such event that always draws a crowd is The Faith Study seminar, in which evidence for the Christian faith is presented and people are invited in a nonthreatening way to make a commitment to Christ. Of those invited by a friend, more than sixty percent put their trust in Christ at the study. The Faith Study seminar is followed up with a Bible study guide called *The Owner's Manual,* which gives new believers a solid start in a life of discipleship.

CHRISTIANITY 101

The leaders at Christ Presbyterian Church in Edina, Minnesota, have developed a six-week Christianity 101 small group course. In it they address the core things people need to know in order to become followers of Christ and grow in their faith. Attendees are also asked to bring their questions. The church offers this class five times a year.

The Ultimate Quest

The Quest for God: Seeking Truth with Mind and Heart is a six-week course at Crossroads Community Church in Cincinnati, Ohio, designed for postmodern spiritual seekers. It does not assume they have any background in, or predisposition toward, Christianity. It does assume participants will evaluate Christianity in relation to other world religions and philosophies. Therefore, it builds a cumulative case by using familiar contemporary examples (including illustrations related to Mr. Spock, James Dean, and Elvis!) and by contrasting Christianity with its alternatives.

The Quest curriculum starts with the questions, "What is belief?" and "What does it take to believe in a religion?" The course builds from there, exploring the basis for belief in: (1) God's existence; (2) God's nature compared to human nature; (3) the accuracy of the Bible; (4) the significance of Jesus' life and ministry; and (5) the Christian religion in relation to other religions and philosophies.

The developer and leader of this ministry, Chuck Proudfit, really understands the quest for God. He was educated at Harvard and was active in the Unity church before he came to know Christ at Crossroads. There's a waiting list for the course, and the participants rate it very highly. More important, Quest has played an integral role in leading a number of seekers to Christ.

Harnessing the Potential of Books

Crossroads Community Church also harnesses the intellectual style of evangelism by means of their Crossroads Book Club. The club helps people delve deeper into Christianity through reading and discussing books about various aspects of the faith. It also offers a free-flowing format for participants, both Christian and non-Christian, to share their views about the particular book the group is reading. It does not require a long-term commitment, so there's no pressure to come every month.

Paul Caron, the founder of this ministry who also became a Christ-follower at Crossroads, explains:

> We made the conscious decision to read many different types of books—from conservative to liberal, from classic to modern, from theological to evidentiary, from biographical to fictional. For example, we've read:
>
> - C. S. Lewis, *Mere Christianity*
> - Patrick Glynn, *God: The Evidence*
> - Frank Morison, *Who Moved the Stone?*

- Corrie ten Boom, *The Hiding Place*
- Charles Colson, *Born Again*
- Cardinal Joseph Bernadin, *The Gift of Peace*
- Peter Gomes, *The Good Book*
- Joseph Girzone, *Joshua*
- Philip Yancey, *The Jesus I Never Knew*
- C. S. Lewis, *The Problem of Pain*
- Lee Strobel, *The Case for Christ*
- Rodney Stark, *The Rise of Early Christianity*
- Jimmy Carter, *Living Faith*
- Charles Sheldon, *In His Steps*
- Philip Yancey, *What's So Amazing About Grace?*

This ministry has proven to be an effective outreach tool in a number of respects. First, it sends a positive signal to seekers. One couple told me that when they heard the Book Club announcement at the first service they attended, they decided that Crossroads was the type of church they wanted to be associated with because it encouraged an open "academic" approach to Christianity. That couple has participated several times, and they've now become committed Christians and active members of the church.

Second, the Book Club has an influence even on folks who've never attended but who use our selections as a "reading list." One seeker told me he read *Mere Christianity* after seeing it in our flyer—and he said it changed his life.

Third, it allows me to bring my faith into the workplace. I am a law school professor, and I've convinced several of my colleagues to join us on occasion. I don't know if I would have been able to discuss my faith with these people any other way.

The Written Word

South Hills Community Church in Highlands Ranch, Colorado, uses its newsletter as an outreach tool. Each issue has an apologetics corner that gives seekers at the church a place to find answers to some of their most challenging questions.

The Wisest Word

Woodmen Valley Chapel in Colorado Springs, Colorado, utilizes something called the "Wisdom Project." It was developed by International Bible Society (IBS) in connection with a number of evangelistic churches. IBS published excerpts from the book of Ecclesiastes in a New Age–looking booklet called *Discovering Ancient Wisdom.* It was sold in secular bookstores and advertised extensively. The church did a sermon series on the book of Ecclesiastes and encouraged its people to spread God's Word using this creative tool.

"That's a Good Question!"

"Where did evil come from?" "Why do innocent people suffer?" "How could a loving God send people to hell?" "What difference does Jesus make today?" "Is there really a heaven?" These are some of the issues raised by various men and women in a series of television commercials aired by First Assembly of God in Des Moines, Iowa. A pastor from the church appears in each of the advertisements, restates the problem, and then ends by saying, "That's a Good Question!" Without directly saying it, the message is made clear that this is a church where doubters are welcome to come and where answers are offered.

Innovating on the Internet

For seekers who aren't yet ready to venture into a church, a group of volunteers at Windsor Crossing Community Church in Chesterfield, Missouri, developed a chat room for them to discuss questions about Christianity. Inquirers can stay in the privacy of their own home and interact with people from Windsor through this Internet service. Trained church members respond to the questions, and the pastors are occasionally invited to step in to field some of the "tough ones." One of the people who developed this ministry was an atheist just eighteen months previously. He received Christ, was baptized, and is now reaching others online.

DEVELOPING THE INTELLECTUAL STYLE

A Team of Defenders

We've talked a lot about ideas for unleashing the intellectual style of evangelism, but we haven't looked yet at what we can do to find and prepare people who have this style to fulfill their vital role. As with each of the styles, the best way I know to identify people who feel most comfortable with the intellectual approach is through the "Evangelism Styles Questionnaire," as well as through the "Being Yourself" session of the *Becoming a Contagious Christian* course. Then they'll also begin to be trained, at least in an introductory fashion, through the final session of the course, titled "Objection!"

But further training is needed. That's why we developed our Defenders ministry, which is an apologetically intense subministry within the broader Frontline Team ministry. We designed it to equip Christians to give seekers answers, reasons, and evidence, along with a clear gospel message, in the effort to lead them to Christ. We do this training for anyone who is interested, but we especially challenge those who have identified this as their style to be part of this ministry.

Defenders trains its members in monthly classes, as well as through small group interaction and support. We've also taken this group on field trips to places related to our current teaching topics. These have included visits to a mosque, a Buddhist temple, a Hindu temple, the Bahai' temple, and a Jewish synagogue. (We also tried to take the group to visit a local Mormon church, but when we called ahead, they declined to host us, saying they didn't think we were really open to the truths of Mormonism. And we hadn't even mentioned our ministry was called "Defenders"!)

We don't go on these visits to disrupt, but rather to politely observe for ourselves what these groups say and do. This on-the-scene exposure is very important, because it lets our people feel the challenge of meeting and talking to those who hold opposing beliefs. Nothing works better to motivate them to study! In addition, it helps them see that these are real humans, with deeply held convictions, who need our respect and love before they'll listen to our reasons and arguments. Simply reading about their beliefs in a book might cause us to scoff; meeting them face-to-face moves us to compassion.

Out of this larger Defenders group, we hand-select those who are spiritually mature and apologetically adept, and we ask them to serve as "consultants" for the rest of the church. We challenge them to keep growing in their breadth of knowledge about the full gamut of topics, including cults, world religions, and secular belief systems that challenge our faith. But we also ask them to "go deep" in one or two areas of specialization. So, for example, we have people on the team who have become experts in dealing with the teachings of the Jehovah's Witnesses, others who know a lot about Islam and how to share Christ with a Muslim, and still others who focus on scientific issues and how to defend the belief that the universe was created by God.

Then, when we need expertise or in-depth research in a particular area, we can go to the individual Defenders who know that area well. We also call on them to help when a member of our congregation is facing difficult situations related to their area, such as challenges from a skeptical college professor, visits from Mormon missionaries, or difficulties with a son or daughter who has become involved in New Age thinking or Eastern meditation.

As a busy church leader, it's wonderful to have a team to call on when these issues arise. "Evolution? Oh, you need to talk to Brad! Let me give you his telephone number and e-mail address." "Mithraism and its relationship to early Christian teachings? We have a team member named Julie who has been studying that. Can I have her give you a call?" "The Jehovah's Witnesses are coming back to your house tomorrow? Guy and Leigh would love to be there to help you talk with them, or at least help you get ready. Here's a pager number. . . ."

As a busy church leader, it's wonderful to have a team to call on when these issues arise.

This approach serves everyone well. Church staff and volunteer leaders are freed up to keep leading, training, and deploying more people; team members find incredibly meaningful service as they apply their hard-learned answers to real-life situations; and seekers get a level of expertise and service they never could have received from the small inner circle of leaders who are already working overtime trying to build a highly contagious church!

Sound Reasoning

Central Christian Church in Las Vegas, Nevada, has developed a ministry called "Sound Reasoning at Central," which is committed to developing intellectual-style believers to help accomplish Central's mission to "connect the unconnected to Christ and together to grow in full devotion to him." The ministry's fivefold purpose is:

1. communicating and teaching the Christian worldview
2. providing intelligent reasons for believing the Christian faith
3. providing a platform for the life of the mind through ongoing meetings, seminars, and special events
4. providing resources to the Central family for use in evangelism and discipleship
5. providing community for people with a passion for or interest in Christian apologetics

These purposes are accomplished through the following:

- *Group meetings*—held weekly for community building and for training Christians to understand what and why they believe.
- *Periodic seminars and special lectures*—drawing from some of the best Christian apologists and teachers in the United States, these strategic training sessions further equip Christians.
- *Study teams*—engage in research in a specific area of Christian thought to serve as a referral team for the Central family.

- *Sound Reasoning Perspectives*—brief written responses to questions or issues Christians face, designed to be a beginning resource and to point to additional recommended materials.

THE CROSSROADS PROJECT

Xenos Christian Fellowship in Columbus, Ohio, is one of the most apologetics-oriented churches I've ever encountered. Much of their intellectual-style evangelism activity is focused around what they call "The Crossroads Project," which provides educational and intellectual resources for Christians, ministries, and churches. This is offered through conferences as well as on their Web sites at www.crossrds.org and www.xenos.org. This effort involves a team of scholars and researchers who seek to provide critical and biblical analysis to contemporary secular thought.

THE IMPACT OF THE INTELLECTUAL STYLE

In closing I share a letter written to Lee Strobel that illustrates both the importance and the tremendous potential of the intellectual style of evangelism. I hope it inspires you and your team to do everything you can to release this vital style in your own church and community:

> I have always been the kind of person who felt a need to know and understand "Truth." In college I majored in philosophy and minored in comparative religion. By the time I was in my thirties, I was thoroughly steeped in nihilism and cultural relativism. On some level I probably still wanted to know Truth, but essentially I had given up. Besides, it didn't seem that important to my everyday life.
>
> Then midlife hit and I realized that you (probably) only get one chance to figure all of this out. So I started on what I came to call my mildly manic midlife spirit quest. I started reading philosophy again. I started studying the new physics. I started exploring Buddhism and reading New Age materials. I went to every weird event I could find, like healing workshops on Mount Shasta and past-lives seminars in Maine.
>
> While I was doing this, my nineteen-year-old daughter became a Christian. She began trying to drag me to Christ, and I would occasionally go to church with her just to humor her. But something about what I heard moved me deeply. My spirit felt called, but my intellect was convinced that we were being suckered by the greatest hoax in history.

I felt split in two, so eventually I just started to pray this prayer: *Dear God, show me your truth. I need to know what you want me to believe. I need you to hear me and answer my prayers. I* need *to know—and, by the way, you can't really want me to be a Christian, can you? I mean, who can believe this stuff?*

I had been praying about this for a few confusing months when I went to a service at Willow Creek Church. You spoke there about your own search, and then you said: "Maybe you're someone who has taken the opinions of your professors in college as facts. But I invite you to really seek out the facts, to search out the truth for yourself."

I went to a bookstore, and there was your book, *The Case for Christ*. I took it home, read it that afternoon, and bought several of the other books you'd referenced—and read them cover to cover. For the first time in a long time I began feeling like my head and my heart might be able to sign a truce.

I can't exactly say that when I opened your book I was a skeptic and when I closed it I was a Christian, but that comes close to capturing the truth. It lit the path toward resolving deep conflicts between my intellect and my spirit. Before reading it, I didn't think they could be reconciled. After reading it, I knew they could be.

So thanks, Lee.

Rebekah

To Consider and Discuss

1. What is your church doing to identify and encourage those in the congregation who have the intellectual style of evangelism? What could you begin doing?
2. What kinds of training could you offer people who want to enhance their knowledge and skills in this vital area?
3. Do you have somebody in your leadership circle, staff or volunteer, who would be qualified and impassioned to start and lead a Defenders-like ministry?
4. What outreach events or activities, whether listed in this chapter or new ones just waiting to be implemented, could you begin in order to reach seekers in your community who need answers to their questions?

12

MAXIMIZING OUTREACH AROUND THE TESTIMONIAL STYLE

My name is Lori. I was born and raised in New York in a middle-class family, with kind, hardworking parents. Junior high was a real turning point in my life. I got into all kinds of trouble vandalizing the neighborhood. A guy named Rob became my first boyfriend. Rob started stealing cars from a car lot, and another friend and I were the lookouts. We all felt invincible until one night Rob and I got pulled over by the cops. He decided to try to lose them, and it turned into a high-speed pursuit across two towns, hitting cars and fences, and finally ending up in a cul-de-sac. Rob got away on foot, leaving me to take all the blame.

When school started again, I was famous! I began to hang out with the popular crowd, and I started drinking, trying to drown all of my fear and guilt. My grades dropped drastically, and I lost all interest in school. So my parents decided we would move to California, hoping this would solve my out-of-control behavior!

Within the first week of attending my new school, I began hanging around with the kids who were into drugs and alcohol. I started smoking pot on a daily basis, drinking heavily on the weekends, and eventually I even started using acid and crystal meth. And because of my low self-esteem, I jumped from one abusive relationship to another, looking for the love and attention I craved.

On my nineteenth birthday I went to San Pedro for the weekend with a few friends to attend a "Grateful Dead" concert. Right before

I left I stopped by a friend's house. His father was a dedicated Christian, and he told me he was worried about me going to the show. I was touched by his concern, but I stayed with my plans. He said he would be praying for me.

At the show I took a few hits of acid. Later the crowd started rushing the field where we were sitting. It seemed we'd be trampled, and I was so scared. A voice inside me told me to pray. Overcome with emotion I prayed, "God, help me. I am so sorry!" Somehow we got out of the concert safely, and the next day I drove back to my friend's house to tell him what had happened. His father led me in the sinner's prayer, and I received Christ.

But in spite of being a new believer, I continued having sex outside of marriage, and I became pregnant. My daughter, Cassie, was born shortly after my twentieth birthday. Even though Cassie's father and I were having relational difficulties, I soon married him. I actually believed marriage would cure everything, but eventually we separated. That only added to my guilt.

When I moved into my own apartment, my drinking and drug use got drastically worse. I engaged in brief, meaningless flings based solely on sex and partying. I smoked pot all day to cope, and after my daughter fell asleep at night, I would drink in order to pass out.

One day I went in the bathroom to get high, and I heard a clear voice in my mind say, "Do you really want to keep living this way?" I cried out, "God, I can't stop. I want to, but I can't. Please help me."

The next day I attended Christmas Eve services here at Saddleback Church. I was all alone, and I cried through the whole service as Pastor Rick spoke of God's love. It was amazing to hear that God loved me in spite of all I'd been through. Through the tears I told God to take my whole life—not just a part of it—and that I wanted to live his way.

That Christmas I accepted the greatest gift of all: God's gracious forgiveness. It was a small step of faith, but I would never be the same again. At that moment I experienced a freeing sensation accompanied by an incredible sense of peace. For the first time in my life I could actually feel God's unconditional love for me.

All my obsessions began to lose their grip on me at the moment I gave into God's grace and power. Over time I realized that my heavenly Father truly did love me, and that he would change the painful and shameful things in my life if I would ask him to. He also brought people into my life to encourage me in my spiritual growth.

By far the greatest blessing in my life is my relationship with Jesus Christ. I wish I could fully explain to you how grateful I am for his loving grace in my life. By accepting his unconditional love, I've

> been enabled to extend that same kind of love to others. And by his grace, one day at a time, I've been able to maintain sobriety and purity for the past three-and-a-half years.
>
> You probably haven't struggled with the exact same issues that I have, but all of us have been broken and hurt in some areas. It doesn't help to hide your hurt, whatever it is. If you are new to this church, understand something very clearly: This is a safe place. You will find love, acceptance, help, and the grace you need in this place. That's why God brought you here. So I urge you to let down your defenses, and let God love you.

Out in the church auditorium thousands of people felt both moved and challenged, and many were wiping tears from their eyes. They applauded warmly as Lori sat down. Then Pastor Rick Warren continued his message, which he'd started prior to Lori's testimony:

> What are you most ashamed of? What is that secret sin, that skeleton in the closet, those choices that you wish you'd never made and you hope nobody ever finds out about? It probably came to mind the moment I started talking about it, and you could feel yourself tensing up. Some of you are caught up in a lifestyle that you can't go on with, but that you can't get out of either.
>
> *That is what the grace of God is for!*
>
> There is no therapy in the world, no pill, no book, no seminar that can make the kinds of changes that have happened in Lori's life. Only the grace of God can do that—and you need it. God wants to take the things you are most ashamed of, and he wants to forgive them, wipe them out, wash them away, and give you a fresh start.
>
> Your past is not your present. You don't have to be the same anymore. You can start over—a new life, a new look, a new love with the Lord. It's all available, not by earning it or working for it. It's just a gift, if you will accept it.

The testimonial style, when appropriately put to work in a church, is nearly unbeatable. In *The Purpose-Driven® Church,* Rick Warren says,

> People want to go where lives are being changed, where hurts are being healed, and where hope is being restored. At Saddleback, you see changed lives everywhere. In almost every seeker service, we include a real-life testimony from a person or couple who have been dramatically changed by the power and

> love of Christ. This weekly parade of "satisfied customers" is hard for skeptics to argue with.[1]

That was certainly true for those who listened to Lori earnestly telling her story. Couldn't you sense its compelling power?

AN OLD APPROACH IS "NEW"

It's ironic that one of the new weapons in the arsenal of many highly evangelistic churches is having people tell their stories of how they met Christ. The ages-old testimony meeting has gone twenty-first century!

How old is this approach, really? Well, it goes back at least as far as the blind man Jesus healed in John 9. Immediately after this man received his sight—almost before he had the chance to blink—he found himself looking into the eyes of a gathering of hostile Pharisees. These enemies of Jesus pressed this man for details and doctrinal explanations, but he didn't comply. Nor did he confront them the way Peter soon would or reason with them as Paul later did. Instead, he stared them down and said to them, in effect, "Listen, guys, here's what I know: I *used* to be blind, *now* I can see. *Deal with it!* I mean, what are you going to do, argue with my experience? You know I was blind, and now you know I can see. It seems to me that maybe you ought to add up the facts and look into Jesus for yourselves!"

It's ironic that one of the new weapons in the arsenal of many highly evangelistic churches is having people tell their stories of how they met Christ.

As you're probably aware, the man's short speech was not highly appreciated. The Pharisees didn't nominate it for any awards, print it in the *Pharisaic Times,* or post it on their Web site. But this didn't mean it lacked impact. They got upset because it had so much impact! They were simply unable to deny the work of God—and, in particular, the work of *Jesus*—in this situation. A miracle had happened right in front of their eyes, and they were left grappling with its practical implications for their lives.

The question for us is how we can best put this testimonial style into action on a church-wide level so that more and more seekers will hear about—and grapple with the meaning of—God's miraculous work in our lives. How can we take a personal testimony and leverage it for a wider public impact?

A Parade of "Satisfied Customers"

If God is really changing lives, then let's tell people about it! Saddleback has done this for many years. As Rick Warren indicated, virtually every weekend he pauses somewhere in the middle of his message and lets somebody from the church testify to how God has worked in his or her life in ways related to the topic being talked about. This is something any church can do, whether weekly or on a less frequent basis, but it takes planning and preparation. At Saddleback, one person's ministry is to collect the stories of people throughout the congregation and catalog them by theme. Many staff and volunteer leaders in the church also keep up their antennae, looking for new stories to add to the file. These stories are found virtually everywhere. They come in letters to the staff, in testimonies written prior to baptisms, in hallway conversations, and through interactions in the church's various recovery ministries.

When Rick or one of the other teachers describes to his team the topic of an upcoming message, the leader of this ministry is able to look up stories in the archives that will best fit this particular service. This leader then contacts and meets with the person or couple to make sure their story will really be a fit and to ensure they're at a point personally where it would be wise to put them on such a public platform.

Assuming those things are okay, the leader then works with them on getting their testimonies written down clearly. Care is taken to make sure that all of the right elements are put down on paper and that nothing extraneous or inadvisable is included. Finally, this leader coaches them on how to best present their stories using their written scripts, as well as what to expect in the rest of the service. This last part is important because it helps take away the fear of the unknown for these people, many of whom have never spoken in front of groups of people. They need to know in advance what to wear, where and when to meet, at which point in the service to come up front, how to use the microphone, and so forth.

This all takes effort, but the results are well worth it. When you combine dynamic Christian music; an enthusiastic congregation; clear, biblical preaching; and regular testimonies from sincere church members who, perhaps even with trembling voice, say to the crowd, "Everything you're hearing here today is true, and God has used it to change my life," the impact potential is amazing! The results at Saddleback speak for themselves; thousands have trusted Christ through this powerful ministry.

THE SEVEN

At Willow Creek we've recently been experimenting with a dynamic, interactive alternative to our other weekend seeker services. We call it "The Seven" because it takes place every Saturday night at 7:00 P.M.

The Seven taps into the testimonial style of evangelism in a couple of ways. First, we have a weekly feature called "My Story," where a church attender stands up and reads his or her testimony. These are selected to fit that night's service. But rather than being positioned in the middle of the message, these testimonies are usually presented earlier in the service as a single element. Then, during the teaching time, the speaker almost invariably refers back to something the person has said.

The role of the person who collects and then selects the stories to be used—and then preps the people who will tell the stories—is vitally important. It's the kind of function that goes almost completely unnoticed until it's not done well; then everybody in the church realizes how vital it is! It's very important to appoint someone to this position who has great discernment and a proven ability to encourage and coach as well as to challenge and redirect.

One of the most powerful stories at The Seven was one from a spiritual seeker named Mel, who stood and told the congregation about his still-in-process journey toward Christ. He described how the people and the ministries of the church were helping him move forward spiritually and urging him to finally trust in Christ—a step he wasn't yet ready to take.

People sat on the edge of their seats as they listened to Mel. (Watch for his story in a later chapter.)

The other way The Seven utilizes this testimonial style is through a question-and-answer time at the end of each service. Every week the audience has the opportunity to ask the speaker any questions they'd like to raise concerning the message topic. This part of the service usually draws out more of the speaker's own experience in terms of struggles endured, lessons learned, or victories gained in that particular area. This adds an authentic, personal element to the biblical principles that have already been discussed. This combination seems to communicate particularly well to the later boomers, Gen-X, and even younger people.

ONE-ON-ONES

Another thing we've tried at Willow Creek that has proven effective is what we call "One-on-Ones." These are weekend services at which we replace the sermon with an interview of a prominent man or woman whose story would interest and inspire attenders—especially spiritual seekers who are already coming or who might consider coming to hear this person. An example: Bill Hybels interviewed the Super Bowl–winning football star Mike Singletary. Before the two men came up on stage, we showed some game-highlight videos featuring some of Mike's incredible tackles. This went over in a big way, since Mike had played for our own Chicago Bears. But in the interview things got much more serious when Mike interacted with Bill openly about the hard lessons he had learned about being a man of God and a godly husband. The impact on people was obvious.

Another time, Lee Strobel interviewed Debbie Morris for a One-on-One we titled (in keeping with her book of the same title) "Forgiving the Dead Man Walking."[2] Debbie had been abducted prior to the brutal attack of the couple portrayed in the acclaimed movie *Dead Man Walking*, and it was primarily her testimony that led to the man's conviction. In a frank and gripping way, she gave an account of her horrifying ordeal. She told how God had protected her and later helped her forgive this man. Once again, the telling of a story of God's grace had a powerful effect.

You can deploy the testimonial style in similar ways by interviewing respected Christians in your community or people you bring in for an event. The interview format allows you to draw out powerful stories from people who may not be dynamic public speakers but who will be effective in a dialogue with a skilled interviewer. It also allows you to have a measure of control over what is said and, therefore, over the impressions with which the listeners will be left.

A Powerful Picture

At Hudson Community Chapel in Hudson, Ohio, the testimonial style is used in worship services once each month. In a time called "A Snapshot of Grace," a church member stands before the congregation and tells about the events that eventually led him or her to faith in Jesus Christ.

"Changed Life" Communication Channels

At Ginghamsburg United Methodist Church in Tipp City, Ohio, the testimonial style is used widely. Almost every weekend a church member tells his or her story of a Changed Life through a video used during the service, or in some cases through the person actually telling the story from the platform. They also reproduce many of these stories in their church bulletin.

Video Stories

Pantego Bible Church in Arlington, Texas, is also committed to helping church members tell their stories of finding faith—on video. Randy Frazee, senior pastor at the church, describes their strategy:

> The Home Group is the soul of our evangelism strategy. Video testimonies are a way to express the spiritual transformations and growth that emerge from the relationships in those small groups. The videos are often used for outreach right there in the groups, though they also fit well in other contexts. We often use them in our worship services, along with live testimonies and drama. We use a video when it can be enhanced by images of the places where the story actually happened or by clips of other people who were involved and have seen this person change. Using videotaped testimonies also controls the time in our fast-paced, tightly planned services. (The programming team tells me they're also considering video sermons to control my sermon lengths!)
>
> Our mission is to transform people into fully developing followers of Christ. Nothing inspires and moves people like seeing a real life transformed. When we show a video testimony that presents a life radically changed by the grace of God, it acts as a catalyst for further life change—including new conversions. We strongly believe that this ministry, which combines high-tech with high-touch, will be a dynamic element for effective evangelism in the future.

Testimonies in a Multicultural Context

The church is Southern Baptist, but its name is one simple word—Mosaic—a word that reflects both the community they reside in and the community they are building. The church is a kaleidoscopic mosaic of people from all over the world who have settled in the Los Angeles, California, area. The church's leaders describe their audience as multicultural, postmodern, pluralistic, and global culture seekers.

The Christians in this congregation earn the right to be heard by listening to and learning from the people in their neighborhood. In their unique context, they've developed numerous opportunities for interaction. For example, the church holds forums with members of the Syrian Muslim community. These include panel discussions on beliefs and culture while an audience of both Christians and Muslims observe and then talk to each other about the topic at hand. And, on a monthly basis, some of the members of Mosaic also serve in a ministry to Buddhists.

This is a time of interaction and learning for those who have come from mainland China. Mosaic's members are not afraid of engaging people who have different religious beliefs. They know that Jesus Christ is the Truth and are confident that through trust-filled, honest dialogue, the testimony of Christ will prevail.

Also, in an effort to connect with people from the art community, Mosaic members have begun to express their faith through multifaceted artistic expressions. On a regular basis they hold what they call "Velocity," a two-hour creative arts explosion highlighting original work from Christians involved in fashion design, film, drama, music, and other media. Members have discovered that a testimony can be expressed not only in words but also in dance, painting, drama, and many other ways.

Straight Talk

Menlo Park Presbyterian Church in Menlo Park, California, offers monthly breakfasts designed to reach people in the marketplace. Says Jay Mitchell, the church's executive pastor, "My heartbeat is reaching men and women in the business community. It's my passion. I can't *not* do it."

These events, known as "Straight Talk," have been sponsored by Menlo Park, with some participation from other area churches, for more than a decade. They usually feature local guest speakers who give their personal testimonies. "We strive to provide a nonthreatening place to bring unchurched friends, neighbors, and coworkers in order to show them how faith in Christ can affect their daily lives," Jay explains.

The breakfasts, which are held at a local hotel on the second Friday of the month from October through June, are averaging around three hundred attendees but have had as many as five hundred. Speakers have included Gordon MacDonald, John Ortberg, Lee Strobel, Tony Campolo, Bill Butterworth, Ravi Zacharias, Debbie Morris, Charlie Duke, Richard Swenson, Stanford provost Condoleeza Rice, and former Irvine mayor David Baker.

Although the format varies, a typical Straight Talk session consists of opening remarks and a brief prayer, breakfast, a short testimony by a local person, a forty-minute talk by the featured speaker, and ten minutes of table discussion guided by table leaders. "I used to think that table discussions would be intimidating to seekers, but I've discovered they are a great way to allow people to respond to what they've heard," Jay says. "Depending on the speaker, we may also show a video, do a question-and-answer session, or provide take-away materials."

The results? According to Jay, "Some seekers who might feel uncomfortable attending a church service are finding the Lord through these breakfasts."

Strategic Saturdays

Similarly, Manito Presbyterian Church in Spokane, Washington, holds a large Saturday morning men's breakfast twice each year. They extend a broad invitation through flyers sent in the mail, radio spots, and personal contacts. At the breakfast a professional communicator as well as church members give brief testimonies of how God is working in their lives. They find this partnership of a trained speaker and regular church members very effective.

Breakfasts and Luncheons

A wide variety of well-planned events wrapped around a shared meal and a clearly presented testimony can be highly effective. The theme can be very broad and aimed at a wide audience, or it can be focused on reaching a particular niche of society, such as teachers, lawyers, mothers of small children, foreign students, or one of a thousand other options.

Your church may want to organize and sponsor a breakfast or luncheon on your own or in cooperation with other area churches or with a ministerial association. You could also partner with one of the ministries that have excelled in this approach for many years, such as Christian Business Men's Committee (CBMC International), Campus Crusade's Executive Ministries, or the Fellowship of Christian Athletes (FCA). Rather than viewing the activities of these groups as competing with the church, see them as tools that can benefit everyone involved—particularly the spiritual seekers who will be reached in the process.

Winging It

The followers of Christ at Faith Evangelical Free Church in Manitowoc, Wisconsin, are also committed to going where the people are. They hold an outreach service at a local air show once a year. They bring in a speaker who is well known and has credibility in the aviation world and have this person present his or her testimony. This has become a great way for the church to connect with the aviation community and to bring a clear testimony through a voice this group will listen to.

Dramatic Moments

The leaders at Walnut Hill Community Church in Pittsford, New York, are convinced every believer has a story to tell. They've also realized that sometimes people are at a time or place in life where their story strikes a cord in an extra-powerful way. So when the chief of police became a believer, it made sense to feature his story and let him testify to the work of God in his life. Another story that drew citywide attention was a mother's testimony of God's power and faithfulness following a car accident that left her little girl in a coma.

MULTIPLE FRONTS

A lesson learned by the members of Blythefield Hills Baptist Church of Rockford, Michigan, is that multiple approaches to presenting testimonies are better than the one-size-fits-all plan. They use testimonies at a variety of events, including Super Bowl parties, dinner dramas, women's banquets, and father-son breakfasts. Sometimes the testimonies are from church members and sometimes from special guests (like a sports figure at the father-son breakfast). The church has also experimented with developing "Life Story" tapes. Church members develop their story of faith, and the church records it and provides copies to give to their friends.

THE POTENTIAL OF BAPTISM SERVICES

Baptisms at Kensington Community Church in Troy, Michigan, are a prime occasion for testimonies, because many of those who have made commitments to Christ and are being baptized have invited family members and friends to the service to celebrate with them. The church prepares and plays a brief video testimony of each person who is being baptized. Since many of the visitors are not believers, this is a perfect way for them to hear how Jesus has made a difference in the life of their friend.

At Willow Creek we have done something like this for many years, but instead of showing videos, we read in random order the testimonies of those being baptized. The combination of hearing how God's love has touched these lives and seeing these people follow Christ in such a public way has a powerful effect on those who observe.

One time Lee Strobel was about to baptize a woman whose husband was standing with her. Lee sensed God leading him to ask the man where he stood spiritually. When he did, the man instantly burst into tears. Lee, sensing the man was ready, prayed with him to receive Christ in front of the whole congregation. Then he baptized him and his wife together, right there on the spot!

One other way we try to maximize the impact of baptism services is by producing and offering to our people, free of charge, printed invitations that include the name of our church, a map of how to get there, and a telephone number to call to get more details. People pick these up at our baptism information classes, fill in the details of when the service will be, and then give them to people they want to invite. We believe this simple step can make all the difference in having a family member, friend, or coworker show up. It may also serve to attract these people to a service at a later date.

Read All about It!

The members of the Church of God in Rolla, Missouri, are putting their testimonies in print for everyone to read. Because this congregation is committed to having as many people as possible tell their story of faith, they regularly use their church newsletter as a means of getting the word out. Reading testimonies on a steady basis reminds people that God is at work and that he is still changing lives. One advantage of this approach is that seekers can go back and read the testimonies over and over again.

It is wonderful to hear about ministries that are utilizing media such as church bulletins and newsletters for outreach by telling stories of people in their congregations. Often these tools get locked into routine formats and subject matter. I don't know what could better spice them up or put them to strategic use than some well-placed and skillfully communicated testimonies of people in the community.

An Online "Life Change Library"

The Internet is at present an underutilized ministry tool. Most churches, if they have a presence on the Web at all, have a rather uninspiring home page that contains a picture of their building, a telephone number, perhaps an e-mail address, and the times of their worship services. This is, of course, a good first step—but it's a weak representation of what the church is all about. We're in the *people* business, after all, so let's put this amazing communication tool to work by using it to tell stories of how God is working in people's hearts, their lives, and their families.

For an example of a church that features testimonies on the Internet, check out the "Life Change Library" at www.willowcreek.org. Some of the stories that have been posted there include:

- "I Was Raised in a Christian Home"
- "I've Lived My Life Denying Christ Since I Was Eighteen"
- "My Family and I Came to the United States When I Was Seven"
- "For Many Years I Had Been Filled with an Emptiness I Could Not Explain"
- "The Hardest Thing Was Accepting a Free Gift"
- "I Always Felt I Didn't Measure Up"
- "Seeking Answers After I Lost My Mother to Cancer"
- "I Wanted So Much to Have a Close Group of Friends"

- "I Did Not Know There Was a God"
- "Now That I'm Going Off to College"

APPLYING THE TESTIMONIAL STYLE

Every believer can get in on the action using the testimonial style—which is why we teach it to all of the participants who go through basic evangelism training in the *Becoming a Contagious Christian* course. Sure, it's the area of specialization for a smaller segment of us. But everyone whose life has been touched by God's amazing grace has a story to tell—even if it isn't highly dramatic.

"Now That I'm Going Off to College" hardly has a ring of mystery or intrigue; I can't imagine John Grisham using it as a title for a new novel. But for someone who's at a similar stage in life it's certainly relevant. In fact, it's typically the "ordinary" story that ends up relating best to ordinary people. So if your background is one of being religious for most of your life until one day you discovered what it meant to have a real relationship with Jesus Christ, this is an account your friends need to hear. How many of them, like you did, go to church on a regular basis, are trying to live a relatively moral and upstanding life, and think they'll end up in heaven some day based on their impressive track record? They need to find what you found!

There is power in the telling of God's work in your life. Talk about it and watch God use it! Moreover, do everything you can to help others in your church circulate their stories too. This effort will have an exponential kingdom impact.

To Consider and Discuss

1. How could your church better utilize the testimonial style of evangelism in its public services?
2. What new kinds of services or events could you add to feature this high-impact approach to outreach?
3. What other opportunities have you thought of where your church or ministry could maximize your members' stories of life change?
4. Do you have a system for collecting and cataloging people's testimonies for future use? If not, what volunteer might have the vision and the necessary skills to start and run such a system?
5. In what ways are you equipping your people so they will be ready and confident to communicate their testimonies concisely and clearly? How might you better do this in the future?

13
MAXIMIZING OUTREACH AROUND THE INTERPERSONAL STYLE

I'm what they call around here a "seeker." I believe there's a God, but I've never had a strong understanding of or relationship with him.

I was married and divorced and then tried marriage again. Shortly after my daughter's birth, I became aware of a big void in my life—feeling like a lost child and not knowing where to seek out answers. I was abusing alcohol on a regular basis, a habit I picked up early in life. For several years I felt stuck in my own depression. I was lost inside myself. I felt distant from my wife, my family, my friends, and most certainly from God.

In the midst of my pain, my wife and I happened upon an ad in the newspaper for a new series starting at Willow Creek called "Surviving the Storms of Life." They say pain is a great motivator, and things were bad enough that I was willing to try anything. That pain got me here. Well, at least it got me to the last row way up in the balcony—I didn't want to be converted or anything, I just wanted to listen!

What I heard that Saturday night moved my wife and me to tears. It opened up a flood of emotion unlike anything I'd ever felt in my life. We came back the next weekend, and I remember thinking, *I hope that happens again.* And it did—for the rest of the series. I began to think that God might actually be answering my meager prayers. I felt welcomed, not pressured. I felt accepted for who I was and not judged for being spiritually inept.

I had a Bible at home with a lot of dust on it, and I didn't know exactly how to read it. It was kind of overwhelming, so I thought a seeker group would be a great place to start. But how do you do that? I mean, how do you go there and say, "I know absolutely nothing. I'm a real basic beginner at this, and I need a lot of help"? I was worried the group would be too diverse, too far ahead, or even too far behind me. After much discussion, a lot of hesitation, and some fear of the unknown, my wife and I decided to take the plunge, make the commitment, and see where it would lead. We filled out the card requesting information about seeker small groups and put it in the collection basket, trusting that God would lead us and that he might have a plan for us.

We got hooked up with Ted's small group, and it has been a wonderful experience. We showed up the first time at 5:00 P.M. on a Saturday in the atrium, and Ted had a big sign on his table that said, "Ted's Small Group." I thought, "This is the place!" We sat down with some people who were roughly our age and who came from all over the area. It was a whole conglomeration of people with different thoughts and ideas and philosophies and backgrounds. It's really gelled over the last couple of months. I find myself looking forward to the meeting and thinking, *What questions am I going to bring to the group?*

At first I had a lot of questions I thought were so basic that I was in the wrong place. I've gotten them out slowly over the two months we've been attending. It's all out there in the open now, and that feels great. And my wife is at the same place I am.

Every day of this journey we have experienced something new. I'm finding that every time we meet as a group we learn a little more. So spiritually I've come a long way. I'm not there yet, but I want to keep on going. I'm in the process of accepting Jesus into my life, but I don't know quite how to do that and how to formalize that and actually cross that line and make the connection. I'm learning, and I realize it's a process.

What I lack in knowledge, I make up for in willingness. I'm reading the Bible for the first time now. I'm finding answers there to questions I've asked my whole life. Our group is growing together with the help of a very patient leader. I'm finding that I'm not alone. While each person in our group is there for different reasons, we have a common goal. We're learning together.

I see in our group leader, and in so many people I've encountered here, a peace and a serenity I can only hope I will one day find for myself. Each day as my journey unfolds, I am learning and trying to put my trust in Jesus and discern God's will for me. I'm closer than I've ever felt before to finally filling that big, empty void in my life.

> If you happen upon me in the hallways around here with a lost look on my face, I'm really not lost, just seeking! And that's my story.

Mel courageously told his story in front of the congregation at The Seven service at the end of a summer series at our church. People were encouraged to hear how God was working in him and through the ministries of our church, especially in this ministry of seeker small groups.

REDEMPTIVE RELATIONSHIPS

Seeker small groups provide a place for relationships to form and deepen and for spiritual conversations to flow. It's an approach that builds on the example of Matthew (also known as Levi), who wanted to reach out to his former work associates. Luke 5:29 says, "Levi held a great banquet for Jesus at his house, and a large crowd of tax collectors and others were eating with them."

When you read between the lines, you begin to see what Matthew was doing. He was deepening his relationships with his old friends, and he was helping them form new friendships with Jesus and the other disciples. Jesus later defended Matthew's interpersonal approach to the Pharisees, saying in verses 31–32, "It is not the healthy who need a doctor, but the sick. I have not come to call the righteous, but sinners to repentance."

Matthew knew what you and I know—that people listen best to new ideas in the context of friendship and in an environment of trust. This is why at Willow Creek and in the *Becoming a Contagious Christian* training, we teach and encourage Christians to spend time forming and nurturing relationships with those who are outside God's family. Like Jesus, we want to become "a friend of sinners."

Seeker Small Groups

Seeker small groups, as we discussed briefly in chapter 9, are designed to intentionally bring people together in trust-filled relationships enjoyed in a secure environment. Sometimes these relationships begin in the group, as was the case for Mel. Other times the groups are built around relationships that already exist.

The beauty of seeker small groups really shines through in the second half of their function: They facilitate continuing discussions about spiritual topics and questions. Garry Poole, the innovator behind this ministry at our church, says,

> One of the things I love about leading these groups is that they provide an ongoing excuse to talk to people about God, the

> Bible, and what it means to put our faith in Christ. Without a group, it's hard to sustain that kind of a dialogue on your own. We've all had that experience when we share our faith and our friend says something like, "Oh, that's nice for you," or "That's interesting; you've given me some things to think about," and the conversation comes to a halt. But a seeker small group provides a natural place for both you and your friends to bring the subject up again and again.

Garry teamed up with Willow Creek small group ministry expert Judson Poling to put together and publish their seeker small group curriculum *Tough Questions*[1] to help spiritual dialogue happen more frequently and strategically. These discussion guides were built on the most frequent and pressing questions seekers have been asking in these groups for years, as well as on some of the newer questions. The materials are not designed to spoon-feed the answers. Rather, they draw group members into a discussion, give them the chance to talk about their own ideas and issues, and then gently guide them toward logical and biblical conclusions.

The fruit of these seeker groups has been remarkable. In fact, most of the people who join and stay in a group have become Christians within about a year.

The fruit of these seeker groups has been remarkable. In fact, most of the people who join and stay in a group have become Christians within about a year. Time after time I'll hear of a group starting with, say, two leaders and seven seekers. Then, eight or ten months later, I'll find out that five of these seekers have put their trust in Christ and are about to be baptized. At that point, it's usually only a matter of time for the other two who haven't yet crossed the line. They now have not only the group leaders pulling for them, they also have the overwhelming influence of their five other friends who are saying, with all the zeal that comes with being freshly redeemed, "Look, I had the guts to do this—what's holding you back? Come on, it's way better over here with Jesus!"

Speaking of the way God uses these groups, last week at our midweek worship service a man was asked to stand up on the stage—a guy named Mel—to tell the entire congregation some great news:

> A couple of months ago my wife decided to give her life to Christ. I was a little bit slower than her—I had a few more questions. But the day after Christmas was when I decided to take that plunge. If it weren't for guys like Ted, I certainly

> wouldn't be here. But a lot of people get a lot of credit, because I did ask a lot of questions. I really am grateful....

There's another celebration going on at our church! And, according to Luke 15:10, "There is rejoicing in the presence of the angels of God over one sinner who repents."

The seeker small group idea is one of the most powerful and transferable concepts available to churches today. Wherever you are, you have the resources you need, because it doesn't have to cost anything and you can meet in homes or restaurants. You have the leaders available, because it only takes one to get started—maybe *you*. You can start a group and then add more groups as you find and equip people to lead them. And you may even have forums already set up that lend themselves to the establishing of these groups, whether through a current small group ministry, a cell group or home church network, a visitors' orientation class, or even Sunday school. I like the sound of this one—"seeker Sunday school classes"! Or, how about what some churches in the United Kingdom have started—"Agnostics Anonymous" groups?

As I've warned before, however, don't put a fresh label on something that really hasn't changed. Make sure you've thought through how to design the groups to welcome, relate to, and assist seekers in their spiritual journey. The *Tough Questions* curriculum can help you do this, as can training tapes produced by Garry Poole, which can be ordered through the Willow Creek Association. Also, many churches have found encouragement and help for these kinds of groups through the *Living Proof—Evangelism* curriculum, a video series for small groups that teaches the principles of lifestyle evangelism.[2]

Matthew Parties

At Willow Creek we've long used the phrase "Matthew parties" to refer to social events designed, in the tradition of Matthew's great banquet, to be times that facilitate the forming and deepening of relationships between Christians and non-Christians. These events help us get to know people we can befriend and to whom, over time, we can extend the love and truth of Christ.

These may be formal banquets, giant block parties, sports-oriented events, private dinners, or dessert times with the neighbors next door. They may be highly organized or very loosely structured. You may make them "by invitation only" or declare that "the ticket for admittance is bringing a friend." They are often low-intensity on the Evangelistic Intensity Scale, but they may also be placed further toward the other end of the spectrum and include testimonies and a presentation of the gospel. They may be put together by a small band of believers or sponsored by the entire church. Other than adherence to basic biblical guidelines, your imagination is the limit to the things you may try.

The main idea of Matthew parties is to draw people who don't yet know Jesus into social settings where they'll rub shoulders with committed Christians—especially those with the interpersonal style of evangelism. The impact will be maximized if you tell the believers ahead of time what your greater intentions are so they can be praying with you in advance and watching for God's leadings during conversations at the event.

You can find further ideas and guidelines for doing these kinds of events in *The Joy of Hospitality: Fun Ideas for Evangelistic Entertaining* by Vonette Bright and Barbara Ball,[3] and in *Parties with Purpose: Laying the Groundwork for Discipleship and Evangelism* by Marlene Lefever.[4]

THE INTERPERSONAL STYLE EMPOWERED

Let's look at other ways churches use the interpersonal style of evangelism. As with the other styles, you may see specific ideas you'll want to pick up and run with. Or these examples may simply stimulate creativity and provide energy to try other fresh ideas.

Fastbreak

Park Cities Baptist Church in Dallas, Texas, has found a way to build on outreach-oriented relationships in the business community and create new ones. John Henson, the church's evangelism pastor, explains it this way:

> Fastbreak is a weekly business luncheon that offers a "fast break" during a lengthy business day. A businessperson can enjoy good food, interesting topics, and positive friendships. Each week we have drawings for giveaways to local restaurants, theaters, and sporting events. Then there's the famous "Hoop Shot." A name is drawn, and the person attempts to shoot two points in order to win free lunch at Fastbreak for the year. Contemporary music and skits are also performed, and then an inspirational and often challenging message is given. The Fastbreak message is work-related, offering biblical principles to apply at the office. By 12:45 P.M. they're on their way back to the office, feeling encouraged and perhaps challenged for the rest of the day.

I asked some specific questions about Fastbreak:

Q: What are some of the topics you tackle at Fastbreak?
A: We've looked at topics such as

- balance between work and family
- spirituality and work
- work and rest
- being purpose driven at work
- biblical principles of purpose and personal identity

Q: How do you let people know about Fastbreak?
A: We send a card or an e-mail message to prior Fastbreak attenders, to small businesses around the vicinity of the church, and to the entire church membership. More than anything else, we encourage members to bring coworkers who may not know Christ or who may never attend worship services.
Q: Why does Fastbreak work?
A: A seeker is likely to walk through the doors of our traditional-looking church and have a nontraditional experience. They find people like themselves who are enduring a week of hustle and bustle. Their stress is relieved as the emcee creates laughter and fun with things like the drawings and "Hoop Shot." The skits and songs are similar to the music and drama they would find elsewhere, except they bring a biblical perspective.
Q: What are the results?
A: We often hear feedback that people are learning more about Christ, and some have come into a relationship with him. A few have even taken his message back to their workplace by beginning Bible studies in their offices. We find Fastbreak to be a natural way for members to connect seeking friends with the church and ultimately with Christ.

Small Group Outreach

The leaders at Pantego Bible Church in Arlington, Texas, are dedicated to building the church around small groups that foster deep community, authentic relationships, true accountability, and intentional evangelism.

Each group member commits to identifying three neighbors for whom they will pray and to whom they will reach out as the relationship allows. When the unchurched neighbor sees members of the small group caring for each other and reaching out compassionately into the community, seeds for evangelistic conversations are planted. Jesus said, "Love one another. . . . By this all men will know that you are my disciples, if you love one another" (John 13:34–35). Something important is lost when evangelism is separated from the ongoing life of the body.

One of the important by-products is the natural assimilation of the new convert. Where do new believers go to experience discipleship and biblical community? Naturally, they go into the small group that so diligently prayed for and reached out to them.

"How to Be a Better Neighbor"

West Broad Church of the Nazarene in Columbus, Ohio, employs a creative approach to helping church members reach out to their neighbors. They use videos to bridge relationships and present the message of the gospel. Pastor Bob Butler answered some questions about this unique ministry:

Q: What generated the idea to use videos in the first place?

A: I was previously a pastor in Westchester County, New York, living in a very affluent community called Bedford Hills, which was difficult to reach through the more traditional means. Given our setting, we were open to ideas that might help us connect with our neighbors. One day when I came home from church, I found some videotapes on my porch, which had been dropped off by the Moonies. This group has their headquarters in Westchester County, so they do a lot of work in the area. I thought, *If these people can get into my home through free videos, why can't we do something similar?*

Q: So tell me about the ministry that resulted from this.

A: We go into the homes of our church members and interview them. We ask, "How long have you lived here? Could you tell us a little about your family? Who are your neighbors?" We also ask them what practical things they could do to be a better neighbor to the person who lives on their left and on their right. They give specific responses to questions about how they might serve and care for them. We record their responses on video. Then we provide them with copies of this short videotape to give to their neighbors.

Q: How does this help connect them with their neighbors?

A: Well, on the video they might say, "My neighbor has been having some back pain, so I could rake leaves in the fall or shovel snow in the winter." We had one person tell us that he knew the little boy next door was having some struggles with math class and that he happened to be a mathematics teacher. He said, "I could tutor him once a week and help him grasp the basics." This led to deeper friendships.

Q: How does this become an evangelistic tool?

A: In each video there is a critical transition time. We coach our church members to say something toward the end of the recording like, "You know, I would not be a good neighbor if I didn't say something about an important discovery I've made. I discovered that I needed help in my life. I came to realize I was walking down a pathway that was not bringing joy or real meaning." Then they tell what Jesus has done in their life. Or sometimes they'll say, "Well, I came to the realization that I had to get back to basics and do the ABCs. I had to *(A) Admit* my sin; *(B) Believe* Christ died for me; and *(C) Confess* my sin." This is not an extended sermon, but a simple and clear presentation of the gospel.

Q: How do they get the video to their neighbors?

A: They just go over and say, "We have this program at our church called 'How to Be a Better Neighbor,' and we each said a few words about how we think we could do this. I'm not big on speaking in front of a camera, but I gave it a try. Now I'm on record saying how I'm going to try to be a better neighbor! Here's the tape; it's yours to keep. I hope that you enjoy it and that we can get together sometime to talk about it."

Q: How has this approach worked?

A: It has been highly effective. Even if the neighbor rejects the message of salvation, he does not usually reject the messenger. Almost everybody is glad to hear that another person is committed to being a good neighbor and to caring for them. It also avoids the problem of interruptions. Often when we try to share the gospel in conventional ways there seem to be 101 distractions. With the video, if the phone rings, they just hit the pause button on the VCR. Also, if they didn't fully understand what you said, they can watch it again.

Q: This sounds like an exciting approach to outreach. But what would you say to the church member who is fearful of getting in front of the camera or who is nervous he or she won't say things just right?

A: We actually avoid making videos that seem slick and rehearsed. If the phone rings or the dog barks, or they need to clear their throat, we usually keep right on recording. We find that the more spontaneous it is, the better. We want natural, real-to-life interviews. Anyone can do this!

Friendship Group

Walnut Creek Christian Reformed Church in Walnut Creek, California, has developed a Friendship Group for more than thirty mentally and physically challenged young adults. The relationships, which often grow deep over time, provide natural opportunities for communicating the love and message of Jesus.

A New Home

Orchard Hill Church in Cedar Falls, Iowa, has developed a "Home Away from Home" ministry for college students. It provides a way for church families to invite a college student who is far from home to be a part of their family—which can lead to the young person also becoming part of the church family and maybe even part of God's family.

Food for Thought

The members of Northside Christian Church in New Albany, Indiana, took creativity to "appeeling" new lengths. They made a banana split thirty feet long, and church members invited enough friends to devour the entire dessert—acquainting them with the church at the same time.

Half-and-Half

Pantano Christian Church in Tucson, Arizona, has formed sports teams as a way for people to connect and build relationships. But they enforce what they call their 50/50 rule: All of their teams must be made up of believers and seekers in equal numbers. As the players become a cohesive team, opportunities to share the gospel often begin to flow naturally.

Fit for Faith

Grace Church in Racine, Wisconsin, has a ministry called "Fitness Victorious," an aerobics class that creates a place where women in the church and in the community can join for exercise, relationship building, and interpersonal contact. It has attracted many from outside the church and has become a springboard for a number of deep conversations.

Dessert Outreach

Couples at Christ Presbyterian Church in Edina, Minnesota, have a unique way to connect. They've developed what they call "Couples' Gardens." Six times a year the church hosts a dessert on a Saturday evening. Only couples who have gone out for dinner that evening can come to the event. The ticket to get into the "Couples' Garden" is their receipt from the restaurant where they ate.

During the dessert time a speaker talks about how to strengthen a specific area of the marriage relationship. This becomes a strong point of contact for the spouses who are not yet committed to Christ. It's also a way to bring a nonchurched couple (through "double dating") into a church gathering that is relationally based and nonthreatening.

Punch or Tea?

Woodmen Valley Chapel in Colorado Springs, Colorado, has designed two very creative and very different opportunities for interpersonal evangelism—one for the men and the other for the women.

The one group invites friends over to watch a pay-per-view boxing event on a big-screen TV, and they use the time to get to know each other and to deepen their relationships. The other group has a fancy Victorian tea party to which church members can bring their nonchurched friends. There's time for interaction and discussion, and they sometimes invite an evangelistic speaker.

Moving Out

The members of First United Methodist Church in Smyrna, Georgia, are using a program called "Lifestyle Relational Evangelism"—where church members witness to others within the context of personal relationships. The program involves teams of two to three people who pay a visit to those who have visited the church—in an effort to begin genuine relationships. They've drawn these principles from a book called *Beyond the Walls* by Rev. James W. Hollis of Proactive Evangelism Ministries.[5]

Giving a Break

The women of Kelloggsville Christian Reformed Church in Kentwood, Michigan, use the Coffee Break Bible Study program. It's a relaxing time to share coffee, to study the Bible, and, for those who have small children, to enjoy a much-needed break! In tandem with the Coffee Break program is the Little Lambs Story Hour for children, who have a Bible story time of their own. A prepared curriculum teaches them Bible lessons and presents the gospel in a way they can understand.

Needed Support

Westlake Church, an English-speaking church based in Nyon, Switzerland, discovered the need among visiting au pairs from other countries for an au pair support group. They provide a place for these nannies to connect with others who are living away from home in a foreign culture. Church members offer friendship and assistance for these women as well as an opportunity for Bible study. As a result, many au pairs have understood the gospel for the first time.

WELCOME CENTER

Another interpersonal outreach ministry we have at Willow Creek is our Welcome Center, designed for visitors and seekers. During our seeker services each weekend, we invite anyone who has questions about the church or spiritual matters, or anyone who would just like to talk to somebody after the service, to stop by the Welcome Center.

The Welcome Center can be found in an open area that is inviting and centrally located (it was previously located in an enclosed room, where we put in wide doors and a lot of windows so people could look in and see that it was safe to enter). We play Christian music to help people relax and feel comfortable to talk freely; coffee and cookies are available for any who stop in. Visitors can stay for a minute or two—or for as long as they'd like. Bibles and some basic information on Christianity are available, although we have a separate "Info Booth" to serve people who are looking for general literature, newsletters, and ministry calendars.

We live in a culture that increasingly distrusts spiritual authorities and religious institutions, but thankfully friends still listen to and trust friends.

The room is staffed after every service by teams of friendly, upbeat church members who love people and have been trained through the *Becoming a Contagious Christian* course to communicate their faith. Those with the interpersonal style of evangelism fit this ministry particularly well. We teach the team to try to answer whatever questions arise but especially to look for opportunities to talk about spiritual matters and to share the gospel if the person seems open. We also have smaller rooms available if the need develops for a more private conversation, and the team knows how to reach pastoral staff members who are available should any serious problems or needs arise (although that rarely happens).

The theme verse I've used in training this team is Colossians 4:5–6: "Be wise in the way you act toward outsiders; make the most of every opportunity. Let your conversation be always full of grace, seasoned with salt, so that you may know how to answer everyone."

The results of this ministry have been exciting. In addition to the fact that many newcomers meet new friends here, a number of people have prayed—in the Welcome Center or in an area nearby—to receive salvation.

THE VITAL NATURE OF THE INTERPERSONAL STYLE

I hope you've picked up some ideas in this chapter that you will be able to use in your church—and thought of some new ones as well.

We live in a culture that increasingly distrusts spiritual authorities and religious institutions, but thankfully friends still listen to and trust friends. Let's do all we can to organize ministries and events in our churches around this wonderful approach called *the interpersonal style of evangelism.* As more and more of our members start relationships and build friendships with unchurched people, we'll see increasing numbers of people who give the gospel a fresh hearing and who eventually come to Christ.

To Consider and Discuss

1. What can you do to lift up the value of building relationships with unchurched people among the members of your church?
2. Does your church's weekly schedule allow members to spend unhurried time with those who are not part of your congregation? If not, what meetings or activities could be trimmed back to allow more time?
3. What church ministries or events do you already have that lend themselves to the interpersonal style of evangelism? What adjustments could be made to make them more effective at helping spiritual seekers deepen friendships with Christians and take steps toward trust in Christ?
4. What other ministries could be started to further utilize the interpersonal approach to outreach?

14
MAXIMIZING OUTREACH AROUND THE INVITATIONAL STYLE

"It's going to be an awesome production with live vocalists, a full orchestra, a complete cast of actors, spectacular multimedia, and state-of-the-art lights and sound. I'm sure you'll enjoy it from a pure musical standpoint alone—plus you'll see a creative and powerful portrayal of the story behind Easter.

"But here's the deal. You can't go to this musical without buying an advance ticket, and all the best seats are already sold. So you'll be glad to hear I called in early and bought enough tickets for you and the rest of the choir, as well as for your brothers and sisters, and your parents too! I'd love it if you'd all come to the event as my guest, and then stop by the special reception I'm hosting for our group afterward. We'll have refreshments and desserts and just have a good time hanging out together. So, what do you think—can I count you in?"

Becky tailored beautifully her invitations to her eighth grade choir students. She talked to them individually or in small clusters after school. She didn't pressure them in any way, and she made it very clear that this was an extracurricular activity she was inviting them to as their friend—not something she as their teacher was requiring them to do. It was completely up to them, although she'd hate to have them hear all about it from their friends later and have to live with the regret of not having experienced it! She also called each of her choral students' parents to personally invite them, give them details as to when and where to meet, and answer any questions they might have.

But Becky didn't stop there! She also brought a group of former students who had gone to events in the past and shown interest over the years in these kinds of opportunities. In addition, she invited her own family members, coworkers, and people with whom she interacted in the course of everyday life and business. In fact, she told me that for this and similar outreach events, she goes through her personal address book, starting with the "As" and working through to the "Zs," calling and inviting people to join her and a few friends for the evening. "I figure if they're involved enough in my life to be in my address book," Becky said, "then they're close enough to invite to a high-quality event they'll enjoy and where they'll learn about God."

Can you see the incredible power in unleashing this invitational style of evangelism on a grand scale? The potential is sky-high!

For each group Becky brings to these events, she tries to hold a reception or informal gathering afterward where she and her friends can relax, get to know one another better, and talk about what they've just experienced together. Some of these gatherings have been in a room she's arranged to use at the church; some have been in homes. In the case of the Easter event, she actually went to the trouble of borrowing a friend's house one of the nights, since it was much larger than her own town house.

For this one holiday event, this individual church member invested five hundred dollars on one hundred tickets, as well as spending additional money to host receptions. When the final count was in, she had used ninety-six of those tickets, allowing many students, friends, family members, and acquaintances to see, experience, and then talk about this stirring dramatic portrayal of the life, death, and resurrection of Jesus Christ. All of this resulting from one music director on a teacher's salary!

Can you see the incredible power in unleashing this invitational style of evangelism on a grand scale? The potential is sky-high! This is one of the primary evangelism styles that Willow Creek and many other rapidly growing seeker-oriented churches have been built on. And, as I pointed out earlier, it's also the one that fuels attendance at most of the classic evangelistic crusades, including those of Billy Graham, Franklin Graham, Luis Palau, and many others.

HISTORICAL EXAMPLES OF THE INVITATIONAL APPROACH

Like the other evangelism styles we've discussed, this approach has precedence in the Bible. In John 4 we read about the woman drawing water at the well who had the good fortune of encountering Jesus. She was shocked by his knowledge of her background and lifestyle, and she soon realized that he was a prophet of God. But then he really surprised her with the news that he was more than a mere prophet; he was the long-awaited Messiah!

This Samaritan woman wasted no time. She ran back to her town and told all of her friends—and anybody else who would listen—whom she had just met. Then she quickly invited them to go to the well with her in the hope that they too could meet Jesus and hear what he had to say. They did, and through this invitational style of evangelism, many of them trusted Christ, and the church in Samaria was launched.

It's interesting that this is also an approach D. L. Moody used in his own evangelistic efforts soon after he moved to Chicago. Here's what Lyle Dorsett says in his book *A Passion for Souls,* quoting in part from *The Life of Dwight L. Moody* written by his son William R. Moody and published in 1900:

> He "at once hired a pew, which he undertook to fill every Sunday." He hailed idle young men off street corners, he beckoned early risers from rooming houses, and he even went into saloons and called forth young inebriates who were getting drunk in the ubiquitous watering holes that were open on Sundays. "Whether the novelty of the invitation or the irresistible earnestness and cordiality of the young man [was the reason, he] induced a large number to attend." William Moody pointed out that "the object was at any rate attained, and before long he was renting four pews, which he filled every Sunday with his strangely assorted guests."[1]

PUTTING THIS APPROACH INTO ACTION

The question in our churches today is this: What kinds of events and opportunities can we provide that will make it easy for our people to employ this style of evangelism and bring their friends to places that will help them in their spiritual journeys?

As I teach about the styles of evangelism all over the United States and around the world, I'm discovering that the invitational style is the least utilized among local churches. In many places members can't even understand or relate to it. Why? Because styles flourish where there's opportunity. And in many church settings the opportunities for utilizing this approach are few or none.

Members may be encouraged to invite their friends to church, but they know better. They can see that the services are really designed for the already convinced. In fact, like me and perhaps like you, many attendees have already been through the painful experience of cringing through a service or event, friend in tow, knowing it is not even coming close to relating to his or her world. Once you've endured that uncomfortable experience, fresh doses of encouragement, pressure, or even guilt won't convince you to bring people to this kind of event again.

The challenge for us is to design services or events that will hit the mark and provide strategic places for our people to bring their friends. I'm not saying *every* activity a church does should have that goal. But in many churches almost all of the programs or services fail to provide that kind of place—so why not begin by providing at least something, and then expand from there as God leads?

At our church we provide a place to which our people can invite their friends every weekend at our seeker services, as well as to occasional special events, including the Easter outreach to which Becky brought her friends. We also offer ongoing opportunities on a much smaller scale through our seeker small groups, which we discussed in chapter 13. But as I've tried to make clear, each church needs to discover and develop approaches that will fit them and the people they're trying to reach. You may not want or need to do events each week, or you may want to but not be ready to do so yet. In chapter 9 we talked about starting with less frequent events, doing only what you can do with relevancy and excellence (for further help in empowering this style, you may want to go back to chapter 9 to review the ten principles for high-impact outreach ministries and events).

THE POTENTIAL IN THE INVITATIONAL STYLE

Pollster George Barna's studies have shown, as we saw earlier, that one out of four adults in the United States would go to church if a friend would only invite them—which is exciting on two levels: First, if we'll provide appropriate opportunities and help our people invite their friends, we will start many of these friends on journeys that will lead them to trusting in Christ. Each time you execute an effective event, some of the new people should "stick," get involved in the church, and take a next step spiritually.

Second, something important also happens with the three out of four people who are invited but unwilling to attend: Their curiosity is piqued, and, in many cases, spiritual conversations begin to flow right then or will take place in the near future. For example, I might invite a neighbor to a series at our church called "Making Life Work," based on the book of Proverbs. He may respond with a "thanks, but no thanks," as the majority will do. But rather than becoming annoyed, I can smile and say something like, "That's fine, but the series will last for the next several weeks, so let me know if you decide you want to check it out later. I'll tell you what—it has been fascinating to see how a three-thousand-year-old book can offer so much practical help for my daily decisions at work and for my relationships with Heidi and the kids." This kind of approach may elicit from him a question about what I mean or a request for specifics on how the teaching has been helpful.

Outreach events and ministries can become engines that drive evangelistic discussions around your church and throughout your community.

Another thing we can say if people turn down our invitation is, "That's fine—but I'm curious about your spiritual background. Did you go to church as a child?" Even if they reply, "No, and to tell the truth, I try to stay as far away as I can from organized religion!" you can still say something along the lines of, "Wow, it sounds like you've had some bad experiences! What happened?" In most cases they'll be more than happy to give you an earful about their religious misadventures!—which is good, because you'll now be talking about spiritual things and have an opportunity to show them that what Christians and the church *can* be like and that what Christ *really* offers are far different than what they've experienced in the past.

These kinds of opportunities present themselves as we unleash the invitational style of evangelism. Outreach events and ministries can become engines that drive evangelistic discussions around your church and throughout your community.

MINISTRIES AND EVENTS THAT FUEL THE INVITATIONAL APPROACH

Let's look at some examples of ministries and activities built around the invitational style.

The *Alpha* Experience

Emmanuel Reformed Church in Paramount, California, began its ministry in 1925 as a somewhat inwardly focused and traditional church, but as their community changed through the years, they felt the need to change as well. Their battle cry became "From Tradition to Mission!" One of the programs they've recently implemented in order to reach their community is the *Alpha* course, a multiple-session practical introduction to the Christian faith. *Alpha* relies on the invitational style to get people to attend, the interpersonal style to help them relax and feel at home (they share a meal and enjoy interacting and laughing together), and the intellectual style to explain and defend biblical truth. Emmanuel's outreach pastor, Bill White, explains:

> We started the *Alpha* course, which originated at Holy Trinity Brompton Church in London, to reach those who were curious and had questions about Christianity. We wanted to create a nonthreatening atmosphere in which we could invite nonchurched people to be exposed to biblical Christianity and then draw their own conclusions.
>
> We gather over a ten-week period, meeting mostly in homes. After enjoying a meal, we present a talk, either live or from the *Alpha* video, which gives reasons for believing, the basic gospel message, as well as humorous stories and relevant illustrations. These talks provide the content for the small group discussions that happen afterward. They allow the guests to explore at their own pace.
>
> Our policy is not to answer people's questions for the first five weeks. Instead, the group leader will say, "Wow, that's a great question. What do other people think about that?" or "Tell me more about where that question comes from." What ends up happening is that the guests start working out some of their own answers—and those answers mean a lot more to them than the ones we could give. Plus, this allows time for them to get to their real core issues. Eventually when we say, "What do other people think about that question?" the guest will call us on it and ask what *we* think. At that point, *Alpha* has really begun, because they have sorted through the issues enough to find their major questions—and they are serious about finding answers. That's when the group leader speaks, both from the Scriptures and from experience, and seeks to teach and persuade the *Alpha* guest.
>
> About halfway into our most recent course, a guy named Gary asked whether he was going to heaven or hell. "That's a

good question" was all the group leader got out before Gary turned to him with pointed finger and said, "Don't give me that! What do *you* think? Where am I going when I die?" The leader knew it was time to take the group through a series of verses in Romans explaining how we can make sure we're going to heaven. For the first time, every guest took out a pen and anxiously scribbled down the verses!

In our first year we saw twenty-two people accept Christ through the *Alpha* course, and the majority of those have been plugged into the church because of the relationships they've built in the group. And about half of them go through *Alpha* a second time to beef up their knowledge of the faith so they can more intelligently share the gospel with their friends and family.

A Synergistic Combination

An exciting pattern that is developing in churches in the United States and around the world is the synergy of repeating the *Alpha* course and the *Becoming a Contagious Christian* training back-to-back. From The Peak Community Church in downtown Denver, Colorado, to Trinity Baptist Church in Kelowna, British Columbia, Canada, to Crossroads Church in Ferney-Voltaire, France, just over the border from Geneva, Switzerland, to a church called *Ryttargardskyrkan* in Linköping, Sweden—the reports are much the same. According to these and a growing number of other churches, these two programs are mutually supportive weapons in a church's outreach arsenal. *Contagious* helps raise evangelism awareness, values, and activity all across the church. Then the *Alpha* course gives a specific, targeted place to focus and apply these values as friends are invited into the course and led to Christ. The *Contagious* course, in turn, provides a way to further ground those new believers in the gospel and to equip them to share their faith with other friends and invite them back to strategic places like seeker services and outreach events—as well as to the next round of the *Alpha* course.

Derek Rust from The Peak Community Church in Denver, Colorado, wrote that, "as an area regional adviser for *Alpha,* I regularly talk to churches about doing *Becoming a Contagious Christian* as a prep to running *Alpha.* If this is done, in our limited experience, *Alpha* should gain far more unchurched participants for whom the course is designed." Craig Twiford of this same church echoes this comment when he says, "My sense is that the two complement each other. As a church that does both, I can't imagine doing it any other way." They recently ran their eleventh *Alpha* course—this one in partnership with nearby Vineyard and Presbyterian churches—and have seen many men and women turn to Christ.

A Delayed Service

Another method Emmanuel Reformed Church, in Paramount, California, uses to reach its changing community is to offer a service on Sundays at noon! The church's multicultural pastoral team reports the following:

> A few years ago we surveyed the area to get a read on the spiritual climate. Next we prepared a new multicultural service to match people's desires in ways that would be appropriate (for example, we set the service time for 12:00 noon so seekers could sleep in and still make it!).
>
> Then we started inviting. We called 26,000 households in the immediate area. One of the elders of the church alone made over a thousand of those phone calls! We put thousands of door hangers on doorknobs. We made countless personal invitations to friends and coworkers.
>
> We invited the neighborhood, and the neighborhood came. The day Emmanuel's noon service began, over three hundred people showed up!
>
> One of those who came as a result of the phone calls was a woman named Debbie. With no real church background, she was amazed to hear about this God who loves her. At the very first opportunity, she walked down the aisle to the prayer team and gave her life to Christ. Now Debbie leads one of the teams that cares for new people at the church, making sure that those who are invited are also nurtured in the faith.
>
> Someone who visited as a result of the door hangers was Alicia. She came from a troubled family but found a new family at the noon service. After a few months she gave her life to Christ, and he began changing her from the inside out. But it didn't stop there! She wanted others to have the same experience, so she started inviting too. She brought her two children to the church, and they became Christians. She brought her neighbors, and two of them came to faith. Then she started reaching out to the children in the neighborhood. She couldn't wait for the church to find space for the neighborhood kids in their children's programs, so she started her own Bible club—in her garage! Today she gathers fifty kids in her garage each week, sharing with them the good news of Jesus Christ.

F.R.A.N.K. Services

Bridgeway Community Church, in Columbia, Maryland, is a nondenominational, seeker-sensitive, multicultural church of about five hundred members. A couple of years ago it held its first F.R.A.N.K. service (which stands for Friends, Relatives, Associates, Neighbors, and their Kids). A few weeks prior to the service, the pastors had begun encouraging members to bring their non-Christian friends.

At F.R.A.N.K. services seekers experience dynamic worship, a drama, special musical presentations, a biblical sermon related to some aspect of modern life, and a powerful gospel presentation and invitation. Seekers who cross the line are encouraged to meet with an assistant pastor after the service in order to receive a booklet the church has produced entitled, "Now What? How to Begin the Christian Life."

Senior Pastor David Anderson makes the following observation:

> The results of the F.R.A.N.K. services have been encouraging. During our first year, forty-five individuals received Christ during these services. And our entire congregation has been energized to invite more people to church. Seeing people stand up or come to the front to receive Christ has had a tremendous impact on our whole church family as we have seen God's power at work. We have continued our F.R.A.N.K. services, with one designated service per sermon series. We challenge our entire congregation to send out or to personally hand out our printed invitation cards to coworkers, neighborhood friends, and family members.

A Weekend for Eternity

Menlo Park Presbyterian Church in Menlo Park, California, has been holding men's outreach events for more than a decade. They recently invited Lee Strobel as their guest speaker.

"We called it a 'summit' rather than a 'retreat,'" says lay leader Bill Skibitzke, "because the word *retreat* conjures up negative thoughts among many men who are afraid they're going to be forced to sit around and bare their souls to each other for two days! We also developed an attractive, four-color brochure using themes from Lee's book *The Case for Christ,* and handed it to two thousand men prior to our services. We knew we had to do this right, because businessmen in our community are used to dealing with impressive-looking printed pieces."

"The men in our church used these brochures to make hundreds of personal invitations," notes executive pastor, Jay Mitchell. "In addition, we went to a meeting of the women's ministry and asked them to help us by inviting and encouraging their spouses to attend—especially those who didn't yet know Christ. As a result of these efforts, the summit was a sellout."

Those who attended the event at a Monterey hotel heard Lee relate his personal journey from atheism to Christianity, provide evidence for *The Case for Christ,* answer questions from the group, and present the gospel. "We designed this summit to reach people at different levels," says Jay. "We knew that some would be more influenced by personal stories and others by factual information, so we made it a blend of the two. Choosing Lee as the speaker was a no-brainer. In addition to the impact his personal story has, his credentials—graduate of Yale Law School and a reporter for the *Chicago Tribune*—are important to people in our setting."

"We had purposely targeted new believers, seekers, and those who hadn't considered the possibility that God might be reaching out to them," Bill Skibitzke says. "We knew that these people might be skeptical of an event like this, so we did everything we could to make them feel comfortable. Music was key in terms of creating energy, and we had some very lively songs performed by a couple of young guys from the church to set up each session. We've found that guys don't tend to like sing-alongs, so this was much more effective. We also used a room that could handle our group of 180 but not many more, because if the room's too big, it gives the impression that a lot of people didn't show up."

The results of this summit: Eighteen men became Christians, forty promised to begin earnestly seeking the truth, and eighty recommitted their lives to Christ.

Promiseland for Kids

Promiseland, the children's ministry at Willow Creek, is like a combined seeker service and small group experience designed especially for children, from infants through grade five. It combines the power of God's Word, taught in relevant and creative ways, with the power of loving, discipling relationships. It incorporates drama (often including kids as actors), video and multimedia segments, puppets, large group teaching, and small group activities that help kids apply the Bible lessons in their daily lives—as well as a lot of fun along the way.

Promiseland meets at the same time as our adult seeker services on Saturday nights and Sunday mornings, and thousands of children enjoy attending each week. Because they love interacting with one another and learning about Jesus, kids have an ideal opportunity to invite other kids they know from school or their neighborhood. It also opens the way for them to invite their parents to "big church."

Many adults who don't attend church have a nagging sense that they really ought to—especially for the sake of their kids, who "could use a little religion."

Many adults who don't attend church have a nagging sense that they really ought to—especially for the sake of their kids, who, as they often put it, "could use a little religion." When your church has an exciting program that attracts and impacts children, it becomes a powerful magnet that can draw whole families to the church. It's the effect on which McDonald's has built an empire.

The fruit of Promiseland over the years has been phenomenal. In fact, in the last year hundreds of families came to our church for the first time because of Promiseland—and over 500 kids made the decision to trust in Christ! Sue Miller, director of Promiseland, received a letter not too long ago that beautifully illustrates the potential of a dynamic children's ministry:

> Dear Sue:
>
> Why does an irreligious person come to Willow Creek? Why do they come back? What can help them commit their lives to Christ and begin to become fully devoted followers of Christ?
>
> Well, I have the answers—at least from my perspective.
>
> Close friends invited our family to a Mother's Day service. We were somewhat overwhelmed but very impressed with the whole experience. Our friends kept inviting us, so occasionally we would go to the weekend services. As we became more familiar with the church, one thing became clearly evident: *Our kids loved going to Promiseland!*
>
> We were reluctant to go to Willow. It was our kids' insistence that turned us into weekend seekers. The rest of the story is a God thing. It wasn't long before we started going to New Community. Christ and the church became important parts of our lives.
>
> Now for the "Good News." My wife and I have accepted Jesus Christ as our Lord and Savior. Our son accepted Christ in the church's junior high ministry, Sonlight, and our daughter did the same in Promiseland! Wow! Yeah, God! And thank you to Willow Creek and most especially to the Promiseland ministry!
>
> My wife and I were baptized at the church and are now participating members. We both have found ministries we are serving in and feel passionate about. And today our daughter

is part of Sonlight and serves as a student helper in Promiseland with the four-year-olds.

I hope you can share this with your Promiseland staff and all the volunteers that make Promiseland such an awesome place for kids to go and grow, for without it we would probably still be lost, irreligious people with no real church home.

Thanks again—we are *eternally* grateful.

The Braniff Family
(Jim, Chris, Jimmy, and Brianna)

How can you beat stories like this? We are thrilled and blessed to hear them regularly. And, I'm happy to say, the Promiseland curriculum, including high-quality videos, leader's guides, instructions for volunteers, reproducible handouts, and much more, is now available for your church to use as well.[2]

RainbowLand Week

In an interview Debi Filippi, a leader at Chesapeake Church in Huntingtown, Maryland, shared about an exciting outreach for children called RainbowLand Week.

Q: What is RainbowLand Week?

A: It's a high-energy, high-impact week of fun, music, learning, and friendships—all designed for children. We meet with the kids from 9:00 until noon each day. We have group learning through drama (with adults in full costume in the cast), music written by our church members, learning in small groups, and time to build real friendships with other children and the leaders.

We hold RainbowLand Week in June. The first one was held for one week on a beach in Southern Maryland with about a hundred people. This last time we ran the program for two weeks, and we had about 800 children and 250 volunteers. More than half of the people involved were seekers, and many were not yet church attenders.

Q: Does this mean that some of the volunteers are not yet Christians?

A: Yes, we find that this outreach touches both the kids and the volunteers. That's in part why we have mandatory training for all volunteers, which includes adults, college age people, and even junior and senior high school students. All of them go through a program that includes learning the Bridge illustration and a simple presentation of the gospel. Also, the theme of the week always sticks close to the core message of the gospel. This allows us to reach the children, but it also places the message of God's love and salvation directly before each of our volunteers.

Q: How do you tie this event into the life of Chesapeake Church?

A: We are very intentional about this. We have a big picnic at the end of the event with amusements, music, food, and a lot of fun. We encourage the children to bring their family members and friends. This becomes a time of natural and nonthreatening contact with leaders and church members. We also hand out invitations to our Sunday services.

Q: What kind of fruit have you seen from this outreach?

A: Many stories could be told. For example, one of our youth volunteers saw the Bridge illustration, and he accepted Christ that very day. He then investigated baptism. Accompanied by his parents he attended an interview with one of our elders. After the interview his father privately went back into the room and asked the elder to show him the Bridge illustration. The elder did so—and the father accepted Christ; sometime later both he and his son were baptized together.

An Integrated Approach

Because reaching out to and inviting unchurched people is so important to Ginghamsburg United Methodist Church, in Tipp City, Ohio, they work hard to make themselves visible in their community. Here are some of the ways they get the word out:

- *Television commercials*—they develop award-winning commercials designed to grab the attention of TV viewers with compelling visuals and soundtracks.
- *Radio commercials*—they record radio spots that complement the TV commercials and give a clear and positive invitation to the church.
- *Newspaper ads*—they put high-quality, attention-grabbing ads in the local paper to attract potential churchgoers.
- *Direct mail postcards*—they reach into homes by using colorful postcards that carry the theme of their various holiday celebrations.
- *Invitation cards*—they customize invitations for special services and give them to church members to hand-deliver to family and friends.

"We've discovered that this kind of comprehensive and diverse approach reaches many people," says Tammy Kelley, "and it makes it clear to people that they're always welcome at Ginghamsburg

Church." The church has also developed a media guide to help other churches customize all of the above tools for their own context. (See the Church and Ministry List at the back of the book for more information on how to contact Ginghamsburg Church.)

Going Public

The members of Crossroads Community Church in South Lyon, Michigan, have also gone public with their invitations. They participate in a citywide parade every year and bring their children's ministry puppets. They hand out 500 balloons and 650 water bottles that advertise their church's name, location, service times, and Web address.

Entering Students' World

The chapel ministry team at Hope College in Holland, Michigan, has found that it has to be creative in inviting students to chapel services. There is no requirement for students to attend, so when a student shows up, it's because he or she chooses to be there. Although the music and communication style are very contemporary, the chapel building itself is very traditional in appearance. So the challenge was how to get new students into the building to discover that what happens there really is for them.

Dean of the Chapel Ben Patterson and the team responded to this challenge by using a different style of invitational outreach. Rather than first inviting the students into the chapel, they simply invited themselves into the world of the students. Their team sets up a "stage" in a pine grove right in the middle of the campus. Complete with sound system and a full band, they wake up the grove—and the whole campus—with energetic Christian music. In this way many students have been attracted to the chapel ministry.

Now the challenge has shifted from trying to get students *to* the chapel to finding room *in* the chapel for all of them to sit! The historic Dimnent Memorial Chapel, complete with stained glass windows and pipe organ, now has standing room only. Hundreds of students attend three times a week.

Christmas Pageants and Matthew Parties

Some outreach events are small and intimate; others are big and blow back your hair! University Baptist Church in Coral Gables, Florida, has found a dynamic way to combine both. For more than two decades they have held an annual Christmas pageant. They now have more than 20,000 people attend over a four-day weekend.

The first half of the pageant tells the story of how Christmas is celebrated all over the world; the second half presents the birth, death, and resurrection of Jesus Christ through music and the creative arts. The purpose of the pageant is to allow people to experience the joy of Christmas and to see the real meaning of the holiday. This is the "big event" aspect of the outreach.

At the same time, church members are encouraged to hold Matthew parties by inviting their guests to dinner following the program. During the meal they can discuss the pageant and reflect on what they have seen and heard. This also provides a wonderful opportunity to invite their guests to attend the church's Christmas Eve service.

Love Thy Neighborhood

Cherry Hills Community Church in Highlands Ranch, Colorado, has encouraged its members to put the invitational style to work in their homes during the Christmas season, using a plan called "Love Thy Neighborhood." The approach, innovated by Neighborly Evangelism Ministries in Littleton, Colorado, helps church members build relationships with neighbors and communicate to them the life-changing message of Christ. The parties range from events designed simply to break down walls and get to know the people next door, to ones where testimonies and the gospel message are sensitively shared. The hosts prayerfully determine the appropriate goal for their own event, and the Host Party Kit provides them with what they need to launch this outreach and invite their neighbors.

"I've been amazed at how excited our members have become about reaching out to their neighbors through these parties," said Steve Fernalld, director of outreach at Cherry Hills. "Many of them come back with reports of their neighbors not only attending but later thanking them for discussing the true meaning of Christmas. And I heard about one party that led to the wife holding an evangelistic study with six to eight women and the husband organizing a study for the men. God has used these easy-to-do events to open a lot of doors for the good news of his Son. As a result, the lives of the party hosts and those who attend are being radically changed!"

The Host Party Kit and other resources are available through Neighborly Evangelism Ministries.[3]

Internet Invitations

Members of Mecklenburg Community Church in Charlotte, North Carolina, have begun using the Internet as a tool for inviting people to church. They've set up a Web page (www.mecklenburg.org)

designed to be an invitational tool. It provides what they call a "Nicodemus Experience" for those who are reluctant or afraid to say yes when a friend invites them to church. It aims to give them a new perception of "church" and to highlight how other unchurched people like them have found value in doing this. Their friends can simply say, "If you want to know more, just check us out on the Web."

At Willow Creek we've done the same thing and have also experimented with posting invitations on our site that members can then forward to their friends by means of an e-mail message. As the technology advances, it's becoming easier to do this kind of thing not only with text-based invitations but also by including color pictures or video clips of the church or of an event similar to the one you're inviting them to attend.

Postal Potential

Direct mail has proved to be an effective tool for Palm Beach Community Church in Palm Beach, Florida. During the Easter and Christmas seasons they send invitations to more than 10,000 homes in their community as a simple way to get an invitation into many hands.

Seizing a Strategic Opportunity

The members of South Hills Community Church in San Jose, California, like many other churches in the area, cooperated with the Billy Graham Evangelistic Association and its crusade in that region. Hundreds of people attended the event as a result of invitations extended by church members. Many who might not be willing to visit the church were open to attending the crusade of an internationally known evangelist—and some of them have now joined the church.

No Tickets Needed

New Heights Church in Madison, Wisconsin, meets in a movie theater. This congregation uses its location as an opportunity to boldly invite family, friends, coworkers, and even total strangers to "discover what church is like when your feet stick to the floor and it smells like popcorn, but God still shows up!" Many accept the invitation, amazed that God is active in a place other than a church building!

In Good Taste

The "Bring-a-Friend BBQ" has become a regular event for the Vineyard Community Church in San Luis Obispo, California. This event features a tantalizing chicken barbecue and a carnival for kids. Church members are provided with tickets to give to their friends, neighbors, and coworkers. Members invite friends to attend the last Sunday service on the morning of the barbecue and to stay for the meal and fun afterward. During the service visitors are given the opportunity to fill out a response card; church members report that consistently five to ten people make commitments to Christ at each of these events.

A Sweet Idea

First Assembly of God Church in Des Moines, Iowa, got creative and challenging at the same time. They planned a Valentine's Day banquet and encouraged church members to attend and bring a nonchurched couple with them. The tickets were sold in sets of four. On the honor system, each church couple had to agree that they would invite only couples who were not regular attenders at any church. The first time they held this event seven people gave their lives to Christ.

A Sporting Chance

Crossroads Christian Church in Lexington, Kentucky, has discovered that sporting events can be a natural point of entry through the use of the invitational evangelism method. So they now sponsor basketball, volleyball, and baseball leagues, most of which take place on the church grounds. Invitations are extended to local groups and friends in the community.

From Jazz to Jesus

Crossroads Christian Church has also developed a coffeehouse where it has made arrangements with a local jazz band to come in and play music. This nonthreatening atmosphere has become a natural place for church members to invite unchurched friends. For them, there's a real difference between, "Hey, do you want to go to church?" and "Can you join us for coffee, dessert, and some great jazz?" For many the coffeehouse becomes a first step into deeper involvement at the church.

Maximizing the Season

Mountain Park Community Church in Phoenix, Arizona, connects with its community by presenting a live nativity scene each Christmas season; along with the live nativity the church offers a petting zoo, hot chocolate, cookies, and music from carolers. Flyers are sent into the community inviting everyone to come to the manger. The same flyers are given to church members so they can use them to personally invite friends and family.

Invitational Options

Blythefield Hills Baptist Church in Rockford, Michigan, offers multiple invitational opportunities. Church members are encouraged to bring friends to events such as a soccer camp, a basketball camp, a blood drive, a dinner theater, an Easter drama, a "Video Bowl" for teens (video competitions on a large-screen TV), a Super Bowl party, and a seeker-sensitive gospel presentation at the church. They carry out their ministry with a constant eye toward inviting others to connect to the life of the church.

Super Bowl Outreach

One of the events sponsored by Blythefield Hills Baptist Church deserves further mention, namely, a Super Bowl outreach. Through a partnership between Sports Outreach America, *Sports Spectrum*, and Athletes in Action, a Super Bowl Outreach Kit has been made available for use in homes, churches, or anywhere a group gathers to watch the National Football League's annual Super Bowl football game. The kit includes a simple training and resource booklet, several *Sports Spectrum* magazines that can be handed out, and a high-quality video with testimonies of professional football players who have put their trust in Christ. Portions of this video can be played at various points during and after the game as a way to help people think about their standings in a much more important league.

Tom Felton of *Sports Spectrum* told me, "Over the last eight years we have seen over 50,000 people make decisions for Christ through Super Bowl Outreach parties."[4]

Budgeting Seminar

One of the invitational events at Willow Creek that has really taken off is our annual budgeting seminar held in our activity center near the beginning of each calendar year. Participants learn important biblical principles about budgeting, saving, giving, and practicing good stewardship. While the event is not overtly evangelistic, the biblical principles tangibly help people and in the end often help to draw seekers to the Bible and to the church. This event has been so well received, with hundreds of people attending each year, that we now offer it two times each winter.

Summer's End

Saddleback Valley Community Church in Lake Forest, California, sponsors an outdoor extravaganza on their property to which church members invite their friends and neighbors. Summer's End is held on

Labor Day weekend, when many people seem to have a lot of free time and there isn't much else going on in the community. The event includes food from a variety of local restaurants that have booths scattered around the church grounds, live music from multiple stages, and all sorts of games and activities for adults and their children. As many as 40,000 people have visited the campus to experience Summer's End, which has a low-intensity evangelistic feel. Visitors get an opportunity to interact with church members and socialize with them in a casual and fun environment. For many it doesn't take long before their curiosity brings them back for a weekend service at the church; to encourage this, each person attending Summer's End is given a brochure highlighting the church's upcoming weekend services.

PUTTING THE INVITATIONAL APPROACH TO WORK

I hope you're forming a vision for the incredible potential of the invitational style of evangelism. When you combine a congregation that possesses warm hearts toward lost people with events designed to bring these people into the church and introduce them to the Savior, there's no telling how God might work!

To Consider and Discuss

1. What events or ministries does your church already have that could be maximized by envisioning and encouraging those with the invitational style?
2. What could be done to remove unnecessary obstacles in order to make your worship service more understandable and accessible to the non-Christians you and other members might bring?
3. What kinds of tools, like printed invitations or Internet postings, might you be able to start providing to people in your church to make it easier for them to invite their friends to outreach services and events?
4. What could you do to provide and promote strategic next steps into the life of your church—and into the life that Christ offers—for those who are drawn to your outreach events?
5. What else could be done to raise the vision among your congregation to "make the most of every opportunity" like Becky did (the schoolteacher mentioned at the beginning of the chapter)?

15
MAXIMIZING OUTREACH AROUND THE SERVING STYLE

You have no idea how much joy it gives our family to provide your family with this car.—A Fellow "Creeker"

That was all the note said. What it was attached to said the rest. The note was in an envelope taped to the dashboard of a late-model Honda Accord! Not only that, but included in the envelope was a gift certificate to our church's food service, along with coupons for five free car washes and five free oil changes.

This gift, which was given by an ordinary, middle-class family in our church to a single mom and her kids, sent an unmistakable message: You matter to God, and you matter to us too. It exemplified 1 John 3:18: "Dear children, let us not love with words or tongue but with actions and in truth." When we do that—when we let people *see* that we care about them and not just *hear* that we do—it models what Christ is like and becomes a powerful magnet that pulls people to him.

We've seen this "pull" time and time again through Willow Creek's exciting CARS Ministry—CARS stands for Christian Auto Repairmen Serving. It was started by a few automobile mechanics who wanted to reach out and care for others in ways that fit them. They reasoned that if the church would provide the parts, they would volunteer the labor, and together as the body of Christ we could repair cars for families and individuals in need. Later this vision was expanded to include asking people to donate used cars to the church rather than trade them in at car dealerships. Many people have accepted this challenge down through the years. The

CARS team fixes up the donated cars and gives them to those with the deepest needs—like the family that received the Accord. Any donated cars not worth fixing are sold, and the proceeds are applied to the cost of operations, which has resulted in making it a completely self-supported ministry.

Today the CARS Ministry takes in, refurbishes, and gives away over a hundred cars each year. This ministry obviously serves and blesses those on the receiving end, and it has been used by God to warm and open the hearts of many recipients. But it also captures the attention of those in the community who have heard about this unique ministry. Bill Hybels recently reported, for example, that when he invited his neighbor to one of our Christmas Eve services, the man said, "I hear you distribute used cars to needy people in the community. Other than the traffic jams I see on the roads around your church," he continued, "that's all I know about Willow Creek. So sure, I'd be willing to come to your Christmas service."

A BIBLICAL EXAMPLE OF THE SERVING STYLE

Against the backdrop of the world's hardship and pain, any individual Christian or church fellowship that offers selfless help and service stands out in stark contrast. This certainly was true of the efforts of Dorcas, the woman in Acts 9 who made articles of clothing as an act of loving service done in the name of Christ. She served in ways that must have made people look heavenward and ask, "Why? Why would you do this for me?" People couldn't ignore the love of God that was manifested in her efforts to tangibly bless them.

God didn't ignore Dorcas either. When she died, God sent an apostle to pray over her, raise her back to life, and put her back into service. God must have really valued her service! Why? At least in part because this kind of activity, when combined with a clear Christian witness, forms one of the most powerful styles of evangelism. Yes, this approach is usually at work behind-the-scenes and sometimes takes a long time to have an observable spiritual impact, but it also tends to reach the hardest-to-reach people.

A CONTEMPORARY COUNTERPART

A friend of mine named Dick grew up with an alcoholic father who was often controlled by drink and by anger. One night his dad was riding a bus after spending time at the tavern, but in his drunken stupor he couldn't figure out where to get off or how to find his way home. But a stranger saw his predicament and lovingly reached out to assist him. This man not only helped him find his bus stop, he even got off with him and walked him to his house.

Dick remembers hiding behind the door that night with his two brothers as they listened to these men talk. The boys were trembling in fear of their dad and, worse, they thought he had brought home another drunk from the bar. But much to their surprise this stranger, a man named A. J. Gray, turned out to be the pastor of a small neighborhood church—and he was kindly inviting their father, along with the rest of the family, to visit a Sunday worship service.

Dick's father never forgot this selfless act of service. And although he wasn't ready for church yet himself, he encouraged the rest of the family to attend, and they began doing so frequently. As a result of hearing the gospel message there, Dick, his mother, and his two brothers all trusted in Christ within the next couple of months. And years later, Dick's father found salvation too!

The impact Dick has had since then on extended family members, friends, neighbors, coworkers, and people in our church is immeasurable. In fact, Dick was one of the founding elders of Willow Creek Community Church, and both of his brothers serve as elders in their own churches as well. And it all started with compassionate, no-strings-attached service done in the name of Jesus Christ—or service-style evangelism.

OUTREACH OPPORTUNITIES UNLIMITED

There's certainly no shortage of situations in which we can reach out to people by serving them. In fact, many effective organizations have been built on this combination of serving the tangible needs of people while pointing them to the truth of Christ—organizations like the Salvation Army, World Vision, World Relief, Compassion International, Prison Fellowship, Samaritan's Purse, Habitat for Humanity, and many others. Many mission agencies also have this approach at the heart of their mission.

For every situation and varied need, we can offer service that will reveal God's love.

This style of evangelism is as broad as human need. For every situation and varied need, we can offer service that will reveal God's love and give us an opportunity to express the compassion of Jesus, who "did not come to be served, but to serve, and to give his life as a ransom for many" (Mark 10:45). The important thing is that we serve the way Jesus did—selflessly, with no strings attached. Naturally we'll hope people will be influenced to come to Christ, but we should never serve in a way that manipulates or forces them to do so.

There's no limit on who can become involved in this high-impact approach. I heard recently, for example, about a woman who ran an ad in the "Personals" section of her local newspaper. It said, "If you're lonely, hurting, or just need someone to talk to, please give me a call. I can at least listen. . . ." What's interesting is that the woman who placed this ad was an elderly shut-in who uses a wheelchair. She had a heart for people and a desire to extend the love of Christ in whatever way she could, and she refused to be bound by her circumstances.

Do you suppose she had any takers on her offer? Try thirty callers a week! With very little effort, this dear lady started an active encouragement and evangelism telephone ministry—a ministry God has used to point all kinds of people toward his love and grace. Just imagine the impact she'll have if she discovers the world of e-mail and chat rooms!

Intentional Acts of Kindness

Steve Sjogren and the Vineyard Community Church in Cincinnati, Ohio, have turned the service style of evangelism into a veritable art form. In his book *Conspiracy of Kindness,* Sjogren says, "God is looking for people who are willing to participate in acts of love and kindness to those outside their present circle. He is looking for people who believe that a humble demonstration of love plants a seed of eternity in the hearts of others that will blossom into faith in Christ."[1]

Conspiracy of Kindness chronicles story after story of Christians reaching out through simple relational acts of kindness—and God using these acts to draw people to himself and to his church. It also presents a host of ideas churches can employ to serve people free of charge, no strings attached. In fact, it ends with a chapter called "Servant Evangelism Projects That Work," which lists more than a hundred ideas and then charts out fifty-eight different project possibilities. These include things like a "Single Mom's Free Oil Change," a "Neighborhood Windshield Washing," and even a "Doggie Dirt Cleanup of Neighborhood Yards"—apparently for the most committed corps of servant evangelists! The chart lists what will be needed for each project in terms of equipment, number of people, required skills, and costs, and it even gives the optimal weather conditions around which to plan the outreach. (For more information, be sure to check out the Servant Evangelism Web site at www.servantevangelism.com.)

Sjogren ends his book with a story that illustrates the potential of the servant approach:

Last Labor Day we held a free car wash. We have tried car washes at different locations—gas stations, malls, grocery stores, and even bank parking lots on holidays. Our favorite spot is a place on the north side of Cincinnati called Jenny's Sportsbar. Best known for their country music and "meanest man" contests, this bar advertises on several popular FM radio stations.

We had washed several dozen cars on this particular day when a man cruised in at the wheel of a flashy new import. He hopped out of the car and we went to work. As the "designated evangelist" at the moment, I began to explain why we were washing his car for free. This man smiled, nodded in approval, and then said, "So who do I make out my check to?"

"You don't understand, sir. We aren't taking money for this car wash. We just want to show you God's love in a practical way," I said. I repeated this explanation three times before he finally got it. I could tell because his expression changed: he lit up, his eyes got big, and his mouth was hanging open. By my fourth explanation, he was all ears.

Then he did something that I have seen several times when doing servant evangelism. This man began to confess his failures to me right there in the parking lot of Jenny's Sportsbar. He told me about his sexual escapades, his lack of church attendance, and yet his awareness of God's presence over the years....

This was an amazing turn of events. In just a couple of minutes, I had encountered this man at a very deep level. He had just shared several intimate secrets of his heart with a total stranger. Our kindness had paved a road of love and acceptance for this man. His response spoke of a sincere desire to reconnect with this God who had taken time to seek him out.[2]

Marilyn Manson and Mountain Dew

The scene is downtown Grand Rapids, Michigan. As you walk up to the large arena, you see a mass of young people in line for a concert. The headline act is shock-rocker Marilyn Manson (named after Marilyn Monroe and mass murderer Charles Manson). The crowd is noisy and energetic, ready to see a show unlike any they'd ever seen.

As you get closer, you notice a group of people engaging the concertgoers in lively discussion. The protesters are Christians with signs expressing their disapproval of Marilyn Manson and all those who would attend his concert. These zealous protesters are yelling at the crowd, and the Manson fans are shouting back with equal intensity.

No physical blows are exchanged across the battle lines, but verbal missiles and assaults are being launched back and forth.

Soon another group of Christ-followers enters the mix. It's a band of nineteen- to twenty-nine-year-olds from a ministry called "the groUp," sponsored by Corinth Reformed Church in Byron Center, Michigan. They unload bags of ice, coolers, and cases of Mountain Dew. They walk up to the pulsating crowd of anxious rockers and begin giving away soft drinks. No signs condemning anyone, no strings attached—just free drinks, a smile, and a sincere, "Have a good evening."

Some of the young people going to the concert simply accept the free drink and move on. Others say thank you and ask, "Why are you doing this?"

The answer comes naturally and without any shame attached, "We love God, and we love you!"

Some snicker and walk away. Others linger and talk a bit. One young man begins to interact more deeply and even decides to throw his ticket away and help members of "the groUp" hand out more drinks! Out of this simple act of service, lives were touched, and the love of Jesus was communicated to people who might have had no other positive contact with Christians.

From the Heartland

Another church, Heartland Community Church in Lawrence, Kansas, had the same vision, but they had the advantage of being located directly across the street from the Granada Theater, where Marilyn Manson was slated to play. Earlier on the day of the concert, Pastor Paul Gray spoke on the fact that Jesus Christ came to earth and took all of the sins of everyone—including Marilyn Manson and his followers—upon himself on the cross. Although Manson bills himself as "Anti-Christ Superstar," Gray urged the congregation to view Manson as a fellow sinner in need of the Savior and to love the person without condoning the actions and attitudes.

According to the church's press release,

> That evening, while patrons were waiting in line for the concert, the Heartland band and vocal team provided praise-and-worship music from the church with speakers in the open doorways pointing toward the crowd. Members inside the church participated in praise and worship and in praying for Marilyn Manson and his fans. An hour before the concert doors opened, they gave away 400 cans of cold soda to those in line. Concert attenders were told, "We knew you'd be waiting in line and thought you might be thirsty." When asked, Heartlanders replied, "We're from the church next door."

During the hour-long interaction there was no negative response from the concertgoers, and many positive comments were made, such as, "This is the kind of thing Christians ought to be doing. . . ."

Heartland members felt that many seeds for Christ were planted.

Prayer Evangelism

One of the most fundamental and important ways we can serve people is to pray for them. The Mission America coalition of Christian denominations and ministries and their Lighthouse Movement encourage individuals and entire congregations to reach others by praying for them first. They advocate a simple but effective three-part approach: *prayer, care,* and *share.* They describe this approach on their Web site (www.lighthousemovement.com):

> *Prayer* calls God's Spirit into action to meet the physical, emotional, and spiritual needs of others—in neighborhoods, schools, the workplace. There are creative ways to pray, including:
>
> - Group Prayer: Claiming Jesus' promise from Matthew 18:20, "For where two or three have gathered together in My name, I am there in their midst."
> - "Prayerwalks": A way for individuals, couples, or groups to pray for people by name as they walk together past their homes.
> - Privately: Making use of a journal to track prayers and answers.
>
> *Care* for people on the prayer list is a living witness to the love of Jesus Christ. Through warmhearted words and deeds, ways are opened to share His good news. Ideas include:
>
> - Perform acts of kindness that demonstrate the love of Jesus Christ.
> - Build personal relationships as God provides natural opportunities.
> - Reclaim a sense of community by bringing people together for coffee or backyard barbecues.
>
> *Share* the gospel as opportunities arise. Open the way by:
>
> - Displaying a Lighthouse Movement window decal, thereby identifying your home as a Lighthouse and opening the door for questions.

- Sharing hope, prayer, and faith through conversations.
- Embracing the opportunities God gives to let your light shine in a sensitive, natural way.

The Rocky Mountain Christian Church in Longmont, Colorado, has applied this approach. Pastor Allen Alhgrin challenged his church members to pray for someone and present Christ in loving ways. "If you will pray and present, God will take it from there," Alhgrin assured his congregants.

Alan Boyd, a businessman and church member, said, "I've never considered myself an evangelist. It seemed like a big job reserved for ministers and serious Christians." But when he heard Pastor Alhgrin's challenge, it broadened his horizons. "This I could handle," recalls Boyd. "No selling involved!"

Initially Boyd was able to pray for five minutes before running out of thoughts. "Then an interesting thing happened. My prayer time kept expanding. Just as any exercise plan expands, so did my prayer time. I prayed, asking God to use me. I placed my life in his hands. More of my thoughts and actions turned toward God."

Within one week of Boyd's renewed commitment to prayer, three individuals initiated personal conversations with Boyd about problems in their personal lives. "I found myself talking about Christ and how my priorities were changing. It was easy! I hadn't prepared or studied for this. I simply had prayed," he says. Soon Alan Boyd's three friends told other friends, and Boyd discovered other unexpected opportunities to share Christ.

Backpacks and Angels

The members of Mountain Park Community Church in Phoenix, Arizona, have discovered a way to serve people in their own backyard. A small community in Phoenix called Guadalupe is filled with people who face the daily challenges of poverty, substandard housing, and limited access to electricity and plumbing.

At the beginning of each school year the members of the church fill backpacks with school supplies and clothing and give them to children in Guadalupe. After the congregation began this ministry over a decade ago, it became clear that they could meet some of this community's greater needs. Many church members have now forged relationships with individuals and families in Guadalupe and are helping in a variety of ways to offer hope, a better quality of life, and a relationship with Christ.

Another seasonal evangelistic program at Mountain Park is the Angel Tree Ministry. Each Christmas members of the church join with

Prison Fellowship to provide Christmas gifts to children who have a parent who is incarcerated. These gifts are collected over the course of several Sundays and then hand-delivered to the homes of the children, and they're given in the name of the parent who is in prison. Just seeing the looks on the children's faces when they receive these gifts makes it worth all the effort. The church members have discovered that simple acts of compassion really do stand out in our world, and that people are drawn to the love of God by this kind of service.

The Last Call

In a small resort town hugging the eastern shores of Lake Michigan a group of churches has forged a partnership to serve those with a particular need. Their ministry is aptly named "Last Call."

Q: What is Last Call?

A: Last Call is a ministry to those who spend Friday or Saturday evenings in the bars around the Grand Haven area. If they drink too much and don't have a designated driver to take them home, we offer to drive them.

Q: How do they find out about this service?

A: The bar owners allow us to come in on Friday and Saturday evenings and put notes on each table that announce this service and give a phone number patrons can call. We are available from 10:00 P.M. to 2:00 A.M., or until the last call for drinks. We wait at a coffee shop in the area until our passengers arrive or call for a ride.

Q: Do many people use this service?

A: Absolutely! Not only do we drive them home, but we even have one of our team members take their car home and park it in their driveway. People are thankful for this service—including those who own the bars.

Q: Do you have any special training for the people in your ministry?

A: We offer the *Becoming a Contagious Christian* course two to three times a year to train all of our drivers.

Q: How does this ministry open doors for communicating the message of Christ?

A: A big part of what we are doing is offering a very specific and needed service that keeps these people and others on the roads safe. At the same time, we are willing to listen, talk, and share the gospel when it seems appropriate. We try to communicate the Good News through both our actions and our words. We also give each person printed material and let him or her know about the churches that support this ministry. We want people to know they are welcome.

Q: This is a creative ministry. How did it get started?

A: It began with a man named Zack Lahring, who came out of a background of abusing alcohol in bars in Grand Haven. After Zack became a Christian, God called him to go back into the bars and offer people a ride home. Others got word of what he was doing and asked if they could be part of what was becoming an emerging ministry. Before we knew it, we had a cross-denominational, multichurch ministry with more than a dozen drivers sharing the care and love of Jesus.

Redemptive Recovery

Melody Coutts, pastor of adult ministries at Beulah Alliance Church in Edmonton, Alberta, Canada, describes how their recovery ministries have been effective evangelistically while meeting people's immediate needs:

> We began our recovery ministries eight years ago with a twelve-step program, "Christians Victorious," for those with addictions and codependencies. We use *The Twelve Steps: A Spiritual Journey* workbook in a small group setting. Through this ministry, people are gaining freedom from their habits and are beginning personal and spiritual growth journeys.
>
> The next recovery group we established was Overcomers, which is designed to help survivors of sexual abuse. This group, though small, has become a safe place for individuals to overcome past abuse and live in the freedom Christ offers. The relational context, and the focus on gathering with other people who have similar experiences, has created a place that is both supportive and healing.
>
> Later we started a divorce recovery program that uses the DivorceCare video curriculum. We reach out to the wider community by advertising this program in the local newspaper. The supportive small group environment of this ministry is what ultimately gets people involved in the community of Beulah.
>
> We also added a ministry called "Boundaries," and then another, "Safe People," both based on the books and materials written by Henry Cloud and John Townsend. In addition, we started a grief/loss recovery group.
>
> All of these programs help people find support for dealing with their specific struggles, a safe place to connect at the church, and, for a number of those involved, a relationship

with Christ. When we first began these groups, we discovered that about a third of the attenders were seekers. Some of these same people are now serving as leaders in these ministries, reproducing themselves in others.

Rebuilding Lives and Eternities

One of the most evangelistically effective ministries at Willow Creek Church is our divorce recovery ministry called Rebuilders. It is designed to strengthen and save troubled marriages as well as to help recently divorced people rebuild their lives. While the ministry serves them in their area of pain, it also leads many to the place where they can address their greatest need—a relationship with Christ.

One woman who was helped in both of these ways by Rebuilders makes this observation:

> I liked the teaching because it was by real people who had gone through situations similar to mine. I liked the people there because they didn't want to be spiteful or out for revenge (my other friends wanted my husband to pay for what he had done to me and wished bad things to happen to him). I appreciated being in an environment where people were truly focused on supporting one another through what I consider to be the most difficult thing I will ever go through. I also wanted to do anything I could to help my kids get through it. I felt terribly guilty for making a decision that was going to throw their whole lives into turmoil.
>
> At one of my first sessions I got in a group and started to feel some bonding with the other members. Our leader, Pam, really believed in the ministry and had "been there" herself once and wanted to help. She also wanted me to become a Christian, but she wasn't pushy about it. Sometimes I was afraid I was disappointing her because I wasn't totally convinced that God existed. But I just couldn't honestly say I believed, even though by that time I really wanted God in my life. I prayed and prayed for him to show himself to me. I was waiting for a sign or some kind of proof. That didn't happen, and I just couldn't understand why God didn't want me. I thought maybe it was because I wasn't perfect. I thought if I just fixed some things in my life, then he'd show himself to me. I was so jealous of those who knew God. I wanted the inner peace they had. It made me explore it even more.

This was the point where I became an active seeker. I started reading books on Christianity. The more I read the more I understood. Finally it clicked for me. I realized without a doubt (no sign from God, flash of light, or anything like that) that what I was reading was the truth. I realized that I didn't have to be "fixed" before God would accept me. God loves me despite my imperfections. I accepted God right then and there, and I will never go back.

Social Assistance

The Family Resource Center of Revere is a ministry of the First Baptist Church of Revere, Massachusetts, and is designed to demonstrate God's love to the Revere community. It originated out of two basic beliefs: first, to win a hearing for the gospel, the church must respond to the needs of people in tangible, effective ways; second, social service programs alone do not bring the complete changes needed in people's lives. Interestingly, many social service agencies are also starting to recognize the need for something more. They're seeing that churches offer an atmosphere of love and community they can't provide. Consequently, some of these agencies now refer people to the church's resource center. Also, the center has developed a database of, and working relationship with, most of the area social service agencies, counseling programs, shelters, food pantries, and other community resources.

The center's staff works hard to create a warm and safe environment for individuals and families referred to them. Their goal is to offer encouragement, resources, ongoing support, and additional referrals that will empower families to create secure, loving, and self-sustaining home environments. They also encourage those who receive their help to explore their relationship with God, and they look for natural opportunities to introduce the message of Christ. This may come initially in an offer to pray for the client or in a response to one of his or her questions. A developing relationship may lead to counseling with the church's pastor or other church members as well as an invitation to a worship service or special church event. The goal is to help clients develop credible relationships with believers who can point them to Jesus Christ.

Pastor Chuck Oblom says the church is also "moving in three new ways to expand its evangelistic reach: (1) developing upbeat, seeker-friendly services; (2) creating small groups where people can gain a sense of belonging, love, and compassion; and (3) running the *Alpha* program so people can learn about Christ in a nonthreatening, systematic way."

Serving "Sin City"

Tom Mahairas was the least likely person to make an impact on any community, let alone New York City. A casualty of the '60s hippie movement and heavily involved in experimental drug use, Mahairas's downward spiral came to an abrupt end when he met Christ in 1968. Soon Tom and his wife, Vicky, started meeting in the living room of their apartment with a small group of other believers in hopes of starting a church. The group grew at an amazing rate and has become a shining model of the service style of evangelism.

Today Manhattan Bible Church is located in two buildings in the Washington Heights/Inwood section of Manhattan, one of the city's toughest neighborhoods. Because of the community's large Hispanic population, Mahairas quickly realized that if the church was to be a true light in its community, it needed a way to reach the neighborhood Hispanics. Today the church has a vital Spanish ministry that utilizes one of their two buildings. Hundreds have found salvation there.

A year later the church began the Manhattan Christian Academy, a fully accredited grade school for the neighborhood kids. What began as a "safe haven" for the kids quickly turned into an effective evangelistic outreach to their parents. In the ensuing years, entire families have come to know Christ because of their association with the school.

But Mahairas knew this wasn't enough. As more and more of his childhood friends died drug-induced deaths, he realized that the church also needed to serve those who were trapped in addictive lifestyles. In 1982 the church founded their Transformation Life Center, a one-year rehabilitation and discipleship program that God has used to alter the lifestyles and eternities of many.

But one other group of people was neglected in the Washington Heights area—the homeless. As the church began to pray and ask God for a practical way to reach them, finances were miraculously provided to open the Manhattan Love Kitchen, which feeds hundreds of homeless people every day of the week—and in the process has led many of them to Christ.

Ministering to Immigrants

The Chinese Community Church of Washington, D.C., has created the Chinatown Service Center that serves immigrants and helps them in their transition to American life. It also offers tutoring to Chinese young people. This connection with both adults and students during their time of dramatic transition effectively extends the love of God and opens the door for life-changing ministry.

SUPPORTING REFUGEES

During the influx of Indo-Chinese refugees a few years back, Cedar Ridge Community Church in Spencerville, Maryland, developed a way of serving these people who were coming into the United States. Church members helped them deal with the wide variety of issues involved in getting settled and on their feet, and in the process built relationships that often lasted over time—and in some cases that will even last for eternity!

BUILDING TRUST

Northside Christian Church in New Albany, Indiana, serves its community by means of a construction ministry. When people—most of whom don't have a church background—ask for help with work projects, the church evaluates the need and, in many cases, steps in and serves. Church members estimate costs, purchase materials, and work together to get the job done. They've discovered that the people they serve—and these people's neighbors—are amazed and moved by this generous, no-strings-attached approach to serving-style evangelism. As a result, many are open to invitations to church services and events and to conversations about Christ.

SMALL GROUPS SERVING BIG

The members of Blythefield Hills Baptist Church in Rockford, Michigan, have challenged all of their small groups to look for creative ways to serve their community. In response, one group fired up chain saws and helped neighbors cut up and haul away fallen trees after a major storm. Another group brought food and clothing to a family who had lost their possessions in a fire. As the church's small groups serve people in many different ways, they're seeing more and more people open themselves up to the love and influence of Christ.

A FULL-SERVICE FELLOWSHIP

The members of Three Rivers Christian Fellowship in Three Rivers, Michigan, have made themselves available for a variety of practical acts of service. They clean up yards and rake leaves for the elderly, plow snow after storms, and offer food from their food pantry. These simple acts become powerful reminders of God's love.

A FOUNDATION FOR TRUTH

The members of Crossroads Community Church in Cincinnati, Ohio, have joined many other congregations in the United States and around the world in partnering with Habitat for Humanity to help build houses for those in need. Those who receive new homes long remember this tangible expression of Christ's love.

Threads of Love

Some of the women at First Presbyterian Church in Baton Rouge, Louisiana, have developed a ministry they call "Threads of Love." They get together and sew gowns for women who have experienced miscarriages. This simple act of compassion has touched many people at a painful time in their lives. The women in the group keep a scrapbook of letters of appreciation they receive from gown recipients. Some of these women have even become part of this ministry, showing care for others in the same way. Out of this ministry the church has also developed a special Christmas service for parents who have lost a child. In this setting the hope found in Christ is lifted up, the meaning of Christmas is illustrated, and a clear presentation of the gospel is given.

THE LIST GOES ON

Many more examples of the serving style could be given—simply out of my own context at Willow Creek alone! I hear stories regularly about people who come to Christ through our grief support ministry, which helps survivors deal with the loss of a loved one; our Good Sense ministry, which assists people in bringing order to their financial world; our food pantry, which feeds both urban and suburban individuals and families who have fallen on hard times; our ministry for the homeless; and our extension ministries, through which hundreds of our members serve and reach out to people with all kinds of needs in all kinds of places, from the inner city of Chicago to the outer reaches of the world. I'm sure you could add many more examples from your own church or circle of contacts as well.

What's ironic is that often seekers are drawn first *to help us in serving* and then *to faith in Christ.* My friend Terry Toro, who directs our conference team at the Willow Creek Association, recently shared an example. She and her small group were hosting a Matthew party. Each member was to invite a non-Christian friend, and everyone was to bring small toys, school supplies, hygiene items, and a shoe box. They packed their shoe boxes with the toys and other supplies to send to needy children around the world via Operation Christmas Child, an annual outreach ministry sponsored by Franklin Graham's ministry called Samaritan's Purse.

Terry told me that Cathy, the friend she had invited, was initially very skeptical about Christians and about the church. But this party and the activity of serving kids in need began to soften her heart and change her perceptions. Eventually, as a result of this experience, a number of invitations to services, multiple conversations and explanations of the gospel, and a lot of prayer from Terry and other small group members, Cathy opened up to the love of Christ. In fact, she came to our Good Friday service and, along with her two daughters, received salvation that very night. Today they are active participants in our church who are finding fresh ways to share the love of God with their other friends. And it all started with her being asked to help meet the needs of others!

The serving style of evangelism positively impacts both the servant and the one being served.

The serving style of evangelism positively impacts both the servant and the one being served. It does wonderful things inside of us as believers, it blesses and draws those it touches, and it can even pull in outsiders who would love to join us in helping those in need. The important thing is that we see the potential of this powerful style and unleash it in as many ways as we can. The possibilities are endless. We just need to be sensitive to the needs of people and willing to be creative and take some God-honoring risks.

LIBERATING PEOPLE AND MINISTRIES

Some of us—especially those who are impassioned about evangelism—have a tendency to project our own particular approach on the people we lead. Implicitly or explicitly, we send signals that say, "If you really loved Jesus, you'd be doing what I'm doing. You'd be reaching people the way I'm reaching them." What we don't realize is that we are burying people in guilt and condemnation and making them want to run when they hear the word *evangelism*. Many of these people love Jesus as much or more than we do, but they weren't gifted or designed by God to do outreach the way we do it.

A personal story will illustrate this. A friend of mine named Tony came to Christ a few years ago through the outreach efforts Heidi and I were involved in at the overseas church I mentioned in chapter 3. The change in his life was immediate and obvious to those of us who knew him. He was filled with joy and excitement about the new life ahead of him.

A couple of years passed, and I decided to look up Tony when I was visiting his part of the world. But before I had a chance to see him, I ran into some people from his church. "Oh, Tony," they said, "he doesn't seem to be doing very well spiritually." I was disappointed to hear this, but since I was going to have dinner with him that night, I knew I'd have a chance to talk to and encourage him.

That evening I asked Tony directly how he was doing in his relationship with Christ. With a bit of sadness in his voice, he said, "I guess it's not going very well."

"Tell me about it," I said.

"Well, I know that if I were really committed the way I ought to be, then I'd be out there with the visitation team each week sharing the gospel with people," Tony confided. "But I just can't bring myself to do it. I've tried, but it's just so hard for me."

Trying to look past the shame Tony was obviously feeling, I asked him to tell me about his walk with Christ other than in the area of outreach. "Oh, it's going pretty well, I guess," he replied, "although I did miss a couple of quiet times this week. I'm really trying to follow Christ, but I just wish I didn't have such a lack of courage when it comes to telling other people about him."

Are you starting to get the picture? This sensitive young Christian, who loved God and wanted to serve the church, was buried by guilt and the belief that he was spiritually deficient—all because he didn't fit his church leaders' predominant style of evangelism.

I finally asked him, "Tony, if you could serve Christ in any way you wanted to, and there were no limitations or barriers preventing you from doing so, what would you like to do?"

Without hesitation Tony said, as his eyes brightened a bit, "Oh, I have such a passion for hurting and needy people. I'd love to start a soup kitchen in the inner city and feed people and show them how much God cares about them."

"Tony, that's fantastic!" I assured him. "I'll bet God planted this desire in you. It's something we call the serving style of evangelism! You don't have to feel bad for not going out with the visitation teams; God wired you up to do evangelism in ways that will reach people the visitation teams will probably never reach. And," I added emphatically, "you have to stop letting the differences between you and other Christians convince you that you're not doing well spiritually! You have to get comfortable following Christ in the ways *he* leads you, reaching people in a style that fits the personality he has given you."

You have to get comfortable following Christ in the ways *he* leads you, reaching people in a style that fits the personality he has given you.

It's crucial for us as leaders to liberate our people in the same way and to make sure we never lay guilt trips on them for not being like us. We need to say to them, "I'm not like you, and you're not like me, and that's a good thing!" Think about it—if anyone else in your church was exactly like you, one of you would be unnecessary! This truth bears repeating: It takes all kinds of Christians to reach all kinds of non-Christians.

To Consider and Discuss

1. You already have people in your church who are helping meet the tangible, physical needs of others. What can you do to motivate and train them so they'll move from just being servants to being full-fledged service-style evangelists?
2. What ministries in your church could be given an added evangelistic component, making your members agents of not just relief but of salvation as well?
3. Are there creative ministries or events you could initiate that would provide outlets for those in your church who have the serving style of evangelism? List three or four ideas.
4. Are you being intentional about pointing people who have been assisted by your church's various serving ministries toward faith in Christ and broader involvement in the church? Where are some opportunities to accentuate current efforts?
5. The serving style of evangelism tends to work behind the scenes. What stories and members could you highlight in order to honor and thank these people for their efforts and to raise this value and activity further in your church?

PART 4

CONTAGIOUS MINISTRY

We've seen the critical need for establishing our evangelistic mission, values, and strategy (part 1). We've unpacked the 6-Stage Process for putting these into play and increasing our church's overall evangelistic effectiveness (part 2). And we've explored a vast array of outreach examples and opportunities expressed through the six styles of evangelism (part 3).

The elements seem to be in place. What's left to discuss?

Two things: *courage* and *action*.

Courage—to shamelessly preach the message of the cross of Christ. We live in a culture—in the world and sometimes even in the church—where we're tempted to tone down what we say about biblical topics like sin, judgment, and hell. There's a powerful pull—one that can affect leaders of both traditional and contemporary churches—toward substituting uplifting stories and positive platitudes for the pride-shattering, eternity-altering truth of the gospel. Chapter 16 reminds us that if we do everything else right but fail on this one, we've failed entirely. In the church, relevance apart from revelation is reprehensible. We must faithfully and courageously preach the gospel message, remembering that it is today and always "the power of God for the salvation of everyone who believes."

Action—which is the outward expression of courage. We must go beyond just understanding the evangelistic needs and opportunities that surround us. We must begin taking the steps, making the changes, and initiating the activities necessary to reach more and more lost people for Christ. Chapter 17 pulls together all of the principles in this book, adds a few other important thoughts, and urges us to move forward confidently in God's power to build a contagious church.

16

COMMUNICATING THE GOSPEL WITHOUT COMPROMISE

It was bold, hard-hitting, direct. It was even borderline dangerous. It certainly wouldn't be given favorable mention in the *Journal of Political Correctness*.

The setting: *Easter Sunday.*

There were multiple services with a combined attendance of tens of thousands of people. Many visitors were present, including a high percentage of seekers and skeptics. The music was celebratory. The people in the seats were joyful and smiling, and they were wearing their Sunday best—clothes that in many cases hadn't been out of the closet since, well, last Easter. Families were together to enjoy a nice church service and then go out for a good brunch. The sun was even shining!

You get the picture. If ever there was a day for pleasantness and a toning down of the teaching a bit to keep the people happy, *this was the day.*

Enter the pastor. He walks quietly to the podium looking a tad serious. He welcomes the crowd, says a short prayer, and then, after a short introduction, launches into his sermon: "I want to start right out by saying this: If Jesus was who he said he was, and if he really did come back from the dead, then biblical Christianity is true and every other religion in the world is false!"

Start there? And then what—really get serious?

What was Bill Hybels thinking? Did he get up on the wrong side of the bed? Did he have a fight with his wife the previous night or have too much caffeine that morning? Didn't he realize that it was Easter—the day everybody comes to church to feel good?

Well, I didn't have to ask Bill what he was thinking. I already knew. He was standing in front of these people with an acute awareness that some of them would never have the chance to hear the gospel again. He was saying to himself, "This is my one shot for the entire year to jolt some of these people out of spiritual complacency, fuzzy thinking, and false hopes, and get them focused on where they stand before a just and holy God."

"But," some might ask, "was that really *seeker sensitive?*" It all depends on how you define the term. It was certainly an in-your-face approach—and further evidence that Bill has the confrontational style of evangelism we discussed in chapter 10! To answer the question, though, let me share something Mike Slaughter, senior pastor of Ginghamsburg United Methodist Church in Tipp City, Ohio, said to me: "A lot of people have the mistaken idea that being 'seeker sensitive' means watering down the truth so that our listeners won't be offended. But that's not what it means at all. What it really means is that we learn to speak the language of the people we're trying to reach so clearly and effectively that when we're done talking to them, they'll *know* they've been offended!"

The most "seeker *in*sensitive" thing we can do is withhold from people any part of the life-giving message of the gospel.

Mike was referring, of course, to the inescapable "offense of the cross" the apostle Paul refers to in Galatians 5:11. It offends every unrepentant person's pride and sense of self-righteousness.

The most "seeker *in*sensitive" thing we can do is withhold from people any part of the life-giving message of the gospel. Bill was simply attempting to do that day what all of us as Christian leaders should want to do every day: "Be wise in the way you act toward outsiders; make the most of every opportunity" (Colossians 4:5). And he was trying to honor the biblical command that says:

> Preach the Word; be prepared in season and out of season; correct, rebuke and encourage—with great patience and careful instruction. For the time will come when men will not put up with sound doctrine. Instead, to suit their own desires, they will gather around them a great number of teachers to say what their itching ears want to hear. They will turn their ears away from the truth and turn aside to myths. But you, keep your head in all situations, endure hardship, do the work of an evangelist.
>
> 2 TIMOTHY 4:2–5

THE EVANGELISTIC BOTTOM LINE

We've talked about many things related to building effective evangelistic churches. We've looked at how the evangelism priority must permeate our mission, values, and strategy. We've examined the 6-Stage Process for raising and expressing this priority. We've fleshed out the practical expression of this process by describing numerous outreach ministries and events built around each of the six styles of evangelism. I'm convinced—and I trust you are too—that these are all highly important elements for attaining our goal and reaching more and more lost people in our communities.

But let's be very clear: None of these plans or approaches will make our church truly contagious if the core concept we're proclaiming—at both the personal and public levels—is not *the unadulterated gospel of Jesus Christ* and his blood shed to pay for our sins.

If you think it takes a modern message to reach modern people, I think you're wrong. However, it may take a modern *method* to effectively communicate the age-old gospel message, as we talked about in chapter 2 under the heading of cultural relevance. Paul said in 1 Corinthians 9:22–23 (NRSV), "I have become all things to all people, that I might by all means save some. I do it all for the sake of the gospel, so that I may share in its blessings." But we, like Paul, must be extremely cautious in how we apply this relevancy principle, always making certain that neither the mode of speaking nor the desire to influence is allowed to distort or soften our biblical content. As Bill Hybels and I said in the *Becoming a Contagious Christian* book, "Contagious churches have learned that they must communicate *to* their culture without compromising *with* their culture. They know that if the message of the cross of Christ is ever diluted or hidden, then the battle has already been lost. What good is it to speak the language of secular people if we lose our message in the process?"[1]

Paul made clear his own commitment to proclaim the unaltered gospel message in 1 Corinthians 2:2: "I resolved to know nothing while I was with you except Jesus Christ and him crucified." He intentionally focused on that simple yet central truth, refusing to add or subtract any elements. He also challenged us, under the inspiration of the Holy Spirit, to follow his example: "But even if we or an angel from heaven should preach a gospel other than the one we preached to you, let him be eternally condemned! As we have already said, so now I say again: If anybody is preaching to you a gospel other than what you accepted, let him be eternally condemned!" (Galatians 1:8–9).

This is a stern warning about a grave issue. Scripture does not mince words for anyone who claims to be a teacher of the gospel yet meddles with the message. If you or your church are ever tempted to modify or soften this message—even a little—in the hopes of gaining acceptance and admiration from an unbelieving audience, think again. To do so would be to compromise with the culture, to forget the mission Jesus gave us, and to disobey the very God we claim to serve.

The ironic thing is that most real seekers are looking for a leader who has the courage to look them in the eye and tell them the truth about their spiritual predicament.

After Paul gave his admonition in Galatians 1:8–9, he concluded in verse 10 with these strong words: "Am I now trying to win the approval of men, or of God? Or am I trying to please men? If I were trying to please men, I would not be a servant of Christ."

We have a mandate to please God alone by preaching the pure gospel message alone—whether people like it or not. The ironic thing is that most real seekers are looking for a leader who has the courage to look them in the eye and tell them the truth about their spiritual predicament—and then show them the way to the One who can help. And even when people don't want to hear about the cross—and some truly won't, as the Bible predicts—we need to preach Christ anyway, asking him to use our efforts, bless his message, and draw people to himself.

Scripture assures us that's God's desire, and Romans 1:16 tells us that the gospel is "the power of God for the salvation of everyone who believes." We have a message that is backed up by the highest power in the universe, so we can and should proclaim it boldly!

SHORING UP YOUR CONFIDENCE

Fresh Experience

Perhaps you like the sound of what I'm saying but lack confidence in the power of the gospel. Maybe you need to spend some time around other ministries or churches once in a while to have your faith expanded. If the fruitfulness factor in your particular setting has been low for a long time, it might do you and your team a world of good to go across town or across the country to a place where you can hear stories and see evidence of ongoing life change. Attendees at our Willow Creek Association conferences—especially the Contagious Evangelism Conference—tell us that hearing these kinds of stories is often one of the biggest benefits of being on our campus or on the grounds of other churches where we hold our regional training events. They not only pick up practical ideas, but they also gain a fresh hope and vision for the redemptive potential of their own churches.

Fresh Facts

Consider also the possibility that somewhere along the line your trust in the Bible has been shaken—perhaps because of the cynical words and attitudes of a university teacher or even a seminary professor. Maybe an articulate but skeptical friend threw challenges in your path you didn't know how to handle. It could have happened recently or perhaps many years ago, but if you've never taken the challenge and done the work of finding the answers, these things can daunt your faith and rob you of confidence in the reliability of the Bible and in the power of the gospel.

If this is your situation, I can relate! In college I took a philosophy class in which the teacher—who was an ordained Protestant minister—systematically assailed the Christian students' unsophisticated trust in "traditional theology" and "literal interpretations of the Bible." When these kinds of attacks come from eloquent, highly respected teachers with impressive credentials and a lot of letters behind their names, they're hard to ward off. You might keep a poker face and pretend your faith is unfazed, but it will very likely affect your level of conviction and assertiveness when you look a seeker or a congregation in the eye and tell them why they need to trust and follow Christ.

But remember this: Smart people have been wrong before—including your wise old professor! And other smart people disagree with these smart people, and everybody can't be right! Truth can't be ascertained by adding up the number of degreed professors or even learned preachers who take a certain stand. You have to do your homework for yourself. Get to the root issues. Listen to the arguments and be alert to the assumptions and biases. Read the defenses of the faith by some of the leading apologists of our day. Pray for wisdom and for genuine answers as you study. Seek and you will find. And you'll feel your confidence climbing by the moment!

This is the process I had to go through in college. Along the way I found out that my skeptical professor had never even read the expert evangelical works that defended biblical orthodoxy. He was too busy perusing his liberal theology books and journals to trifle with the texts that might have put his suspicions to rest. I began to read what he wouldn't and found bracing answers to the challenges he'd been presenting. The more I studied the higher my confidence quotient went—to the point where I had much more faith in the facts of historic Christianity than ever before. In fact, I felt so emboldened that

I went to the leaders of the InterVarsity chapter on our campus and asked to teach at two of their large group meetings. I wanted to share my discoveries with the other students whose theological cages had also been rattled.

What about you? Do you need to reinforce your foundation of facts and evidence? If so, do your homework. Really commit to it. For your own sake and the sake of those you will help in the future, go after it with vigor. Read the books, listen to the tapes or radio programs, have the conversations, go to the seminars, and do everything necessary to bolster your faith. If you don't know where to start, try books like *The Case for Christ* and *The Case for Faith* by former-skeptic-turned-defender-of-the-faith Lee Strobel.[2] Also, classic primers like *More Than a Carpenter* by Josh McDowell[3] and *Know Why You Believe* by Paul Little[4] can be a tremendous help, though they're geared to a beginner's level. Start there, and then go on to the more advanced works by thinkers like J. P. Moreland, William Lane Craig, Gary Habermas, and Norman Geisler. Reading cover to cover the textbook by Norman Geisler and William Nix, *A General Introduction to the Bible,*[5] did wonders for my faith during my era of questioning in college. The deeper you look into the basis of Christianity's beliefs, the more confident you'll become.

FRESH FAITH

One principle for strengthening your trust in the Bible—a principle often overlooked because of its simplicity—is to *read it daily.* Doubts can easily creep in when we aren't staying in the Book and opening ourselves up to fresh shots of inspiration, insights, and instructions from the God who inspired it.

If it feels like I'm "preaching to the choir," you need to know that, according to Tom Youngblood of International Bible Society, the vast majority of Christians do not read their Bibles every day. What bothered me most when Tom first told me this was the painful realization that I had slipped into patterns of irregular Bible reading and needed to re-up my own commitment.

While I don't want to turn legalistic about it, I do need to at least aim to read God's Word every day, knowing that "faith comes by hearing, and hearing by the word of God" (Romans 10:17 NKJV). I need—and so do you—to "let the word of Christ dwell in [us] richly" (Colossians 3:16). We have to become so saturated with the truths of Scripture that, over time, we gain "the mind of Christ" (1 Corinthians 2:16), and begin, as John MacArthur puts it in his radio programs, "to see the world through chapter and verse eyes." That's why my longtime friend and accountability partner, Brad Mitchell, and I have agreed to ask each other regularly if we've "read yet today." We want to reinforce Bible reading as a daily—and lifelong—pattern. Staying in the Book increases our spiritual confidence and courage, making us bolder in proclaiming its message to others.

COMMUNICATE THE GOSPEL WITHOUT COMPROMISE

With our confidence level strengthened, how can we then communicate the uncompromised message of Christ in ways that are clear and that really connect with people who live on the far side of the secular spectrum? Well, we've talked about it, and now I want to present an example of it. One of the best ways to learn how to communicate the gospel clearly to seekers is to see it done well.

The following is a message called "The Core Idea," delivered by Bill Hybels at one of Willow Creek's weekend seeker services.[6] I hope you'll be encouraged by its content and inspired by its approach to communicating a complex set of biblical truths in a relevant fashion and at a clear, introductory level.

Whenever I'm learning something new, I usually feel a bit confused until I can wrap my arms around the core idea of whatever the subject is. But once I get that idea under my belt, I can usually relax and enjoy the learning process.

When I was sixteen and first taking flying lessons, I remember sitting in a side room of a hangar in Kalamazoo, Michigan, wondering if I was the only person in the class who didn't understand how airplanes stay in the air. I was anxious about this until the instructor took out a flip chart and started drawing some diagrams. He said the twin enemies of flight are *gravity* and *drag.* Gravity pulls the plane down, and drag holds the plane back. "But," he said, "a properly designed airframe and wing and a properly powered engine will enable a plane to defeat those enemies with two things called *lift* and *speed.*"

Once I saw that, I got it: *the core idea of flight.* Then I was able to settle in and enjoy the rest of the flight training. I've been flying ever since, and even to this day I operate with that core idea in mind.

The same is true in academics. If you're studying political science in college and you hear terms being tossed about like *fascism, socialism, communism,* and *democracy,* you probably feel nervous until an instructor boils down each complicated governing process to just a core idea. Then you say, "Oh, that's not all that complicated. I get it!"

Now, today, before you walk out of this place, it's my goal that you will understand the core idea of Christianity. I really hope that you walk out the door with the full assurance that you get it—that you understand the basic idea of what Christianity is all about.

For some of you, this is going to be review. It will reinforce what you already know, and that's a good thing. For others, this is going to be clarifying. The haze is going to dissipate somewhat and you're going to see the core idea with new sharpness and definition. And for still others, this is going to hit you like a bolt of lightning. You've never heard Christianity boiled down to its very core in terms you could understand. Today might just change everything in your life now, and in your whole eternity.

To get us headed in that direction, have you heard about the videotape that was discovered of Richard Speck? He's the guy who assaulted and murdered eight young Chicago nurses in 1966. This was one of the first mass murders of my generation, and it traumatized the entire city of Chicago for months. Every day, the cry went out for Richard Speck to pay for his crime. I remember the outrage all over the city.

Well, he was tried and convicted. And then he was locked away in Stateville Prison, near Joliet, for eight consecutive life sentences. So that was that! Then he died in 1991.

But recently a videotape was released showing how Richard Speck spent the final years of his life living like a little king in prison. He had free access to drugs and alcohol whenever he wanted it. He had numerous homosexual lovers who would come in and out of his cell. He had carved out a country club kind of life in Stateville Prison.

But it was all recorded on videotape and got into the hands of a news reporter, and it's been a big deal. People are outraged all over again. Why? Because it seems like he didn't make appropriate payment for his crime. And there's just this thing about society—it can't put a crime behind it until there has been an appropriate payment made.

Appropriate payment. Hold on to that concept. In fact, let's call it *atonement*—because it's the same concept, essentially. Atonement is satisfying the demands of justice when a crime has been committed. And we all carry an intuitive understanding of this notion in our heads.

So do you have the idea of atonement now? It's satisfying the demands of justice when a crime has been committed.

The second half of the core idea of Christianity comes out of another word we're quite familiar with—*substitution.* We use this a lot in our culture. It's whoever comes into the basketball game when Dennis Rodman gets kicked out!

Substitute. Taking the place of another. I think we understand this. Remember what we used to do to substitute teachers? I still carry a little guilt about that!

Now put those two words together. *Substitutionary atonement*—it's somebody taking the place of someone else and satisfying the demands of justice when a crime has been committed.

I want to clarify this concept further by taking you for a little walk through the Bible and showing you how this pertains to Christianity and to your life. We're going to start all the way back in the book of Genesis. Shortly after God created Adam and Eve, he said to them, "I've breathed life into you. You can make all kinds of decisions, you're smart, and I love you. We'll commune together, and it's going to be a wonderful experience. But I am a holy and just God. If you start sinning and violating my laws and shaking your fist at me, I've got to let you know something: This wonderful gift of life that I breathed into you is going to come to a screeching halt. You're going to die."

He made it all very clear. But as you know, Adam and Eve bought into a lie from the evil one and flagrantly disobeyed God. So now all of creation holds its breath wondering, What is God going to do? Will he strike them dead on the spot for their rebellion? Or maybe the whole death warning was just a hoax and

God's going to wink and say, "Just kidding! Apple eating is hardly a crime deserving capital punishment. Boys will be boys; girls will be girls. No problem. I'm going to walk away from this one."

What's going to happen? Do you remember what God does? He doesn't strike them dead on the spot, but he doesn't wink and walk away either.

First, he explains that the whole universe is going to be sin-tainted because of what they did. They've opened the door, and now sin is in the world. Human labor is going to be affected, childbearing is going to be painful, human relationships will be complicated by ego, and human bodies will grow old and eventually die.

And God explains that people who continue to live in patterns of rebellion and resistiveness to him will pay. They'll atone for their crimes against God in this life and all throughout eternity in hell.

Sin is a serious thing. But at the end of God's explanation of the consequences of sin, we read in Genesis 3:21 that God does something that must have knocked the wind out of Adam and Eve, who were cowering in shame and guilt for what they had done. The text says that God covered their shame and nakedness with an animal skin. Most people just read right over that and say, "Okay, no big deal." But it *is* a big deal. I think it's our first glimpse of the arrangement that God is designing to provide sinners with an alternative way to have their sins atoned for.

Picture again God's dilemma. He's the absolutely holy and righteous God. He cannot allow sin to go unatoned for—it's got to be paid for. At the same time, he's a tender, loving God whose heart has been captured by these two people and all the others who will follow. The thought of Adam and Eve atoning for their own sins for the rest of their lives and in eternity in hell just breaks the heart of God. It moves him to take upon himself the responsibility for providing an alternative way that sin can be legitimately paid for, without the sinner having to spend an eternity atoning for his own sin, and without God's holiness being compromised.

So look what God does—all the way back in the Garden of Eden. He takes an animal—an innocent animal—and he kills it. Can you imagine Adam and Eve gasping in horror as they see death for the very first time? They hear the screech of the animal that's being killed. They see its awkward movements in its death throes. There's the bleating, the wrenching, the quivering, and then the stillness. And then God takes the skin of the animal and covers the shame and guilt and nakedness of Adam and Eve as if to say, "In order for your sinfulness to be covered, in order for your wrongdoings to be atoned for, an innocent party is going to have to bear the penalty that was rightfully yours."

And, friends, this was kind of a sneak preview. It was the beginning of the playing out of this idea of substitutionary atonement—the arrangement by God for an innocent party to stand in the place of the sinner and absorb the penalty due to that sinner, thereby satisfying the demands of justice. And the guilty party, then, is set free.

Later on in the history of God's people, we read the story of the Exodus. Remember that? You've seen it on old TV movies! God's people, the Israelites, have become a faithless people, and they're being held captive by the Egyptians, who are slowly working them to death. The Egyptians are sinning against the Israelites, and the Israelites are sinning against each other and against the Egyptians—and the whole thing turns into a colossal, sinful mess.

This pushes God's patience to the breaking point. Scripture shows us that God is slow to anger, but if you push him long enough his righteous wrath finally kicks in. That's what happens in this situation. God says, "Enough is enough!" God announces to all of the Israelites and the Egyptians that he's going to bring judgment. He's going to bring it to bear on everyone for their sin. He announces that an angel of death is going to circulate on a given night and take the life of every firstborn son in every household in the land. The wages of sin is death. There would be no exceptions.

But, God adds—almost as a P.S.—"I will offer one option. I will make one provision for any interested party. Anyone who gets an unblemished, prize-of-the-herd male lamb and slaughters it, sheds its blood, and sprinkles a bit of the blood over the door-frame of the front of the house—the angel of death, on that appointed night, will honor the blood of that lamb and pass over that house. The eldest son in that house will not be killed." God says, "That's my arrangement. So all of you can decide—what are you going to do on that given night?"

Well, as it happens, most people just ignore the whole thing. They say, "I don't think God's going to bring judgment. I don't think he's that kind of God. I think we can steamroll right over him and live however we want, and he's not going to lift a finger."

But there were a few people who decided otherwise. They said, "You know, I think if God is God, he is loving *and* just and holy. I think from time to time he'll bring judgment." So they go out and get the lamb.

I imagine a fifteen-year-old kid watching his dad search around in the herd. He finds the best lamb and he's just lifting the knife to kill it when his fifteen-year-old says, "Hey, Dad! What are you doing killing our prize lamb? What did the lamb do?" only to have the father respond, "Well, son, it's the lamb, or you. It's atonement time. Sin is going to be paid for tonight. A holy God has said, 'Enough is enough.' It's the lamb, or you."

We read that the next day every household that had offered up an innocent lamb and sprinkled the blood on the doorframe was spared the judgment. The lamb died, and the sons went free. But the households that didn't offer up the lamb paid with the life of the firstborn child.

Sin is serious. And when it's atonement time, sin gets paid for.

Do you see the substitutionary atonement principle in the story of the Exodus? An innocent lamb takes the hit for the wrongdoing of others, and guilty parties go free.

Later on in the Old Testament, you see the sacrificial system. It foreshadows the substitutionary atonement idea as well. Whenever a person sinned grievously, an animal sacrifice would be made; an innocent lamb would be slain. Only after the death of the lamb would the priest give the guilty sinner the assurance that his or her sin had been atoned for, and then that person could go free.

Then a prophet named Isaiah announces something that makes people's heads spin and hearts stop. In one of his prophecies he says: "But he was wounded for our transgressions, he was bruised for our iniquities. . . . And the Lord will lay on him the iniquity of us all." People didn't know how to handle this prophecy because it sure sounded as though someday, somewhere, God was going to send a human sacrifice to make an ultimate atonement for the sins of the world.

And then, later on, Jesus is born. And he's born amid all of the miraculous circumstances of his birth. He grows up, and there are all of these indications that he's God's Son.

When he's about thirty years old, he goes out one day to where another prophet is preaching. This guy's name is John the Baptist, and a large crowd of people is listening to him. Jesus stands on the fringe of the crowd, and John the Baptist sees him, stops preaching, and says, "Look, everybody!" And he points right at Jesus and says, "Behold, the Lamb of God who takes away the sin of the world."

Here he is, John was saying, the one we've all been thinking about, the one Isaiah prophesied was coming. He's God's ultimate provision for atonement. He's the unblemished prize lamb that will be offered as the ultimate substitute for sin. He's the one that tens of thousands of sacrificial lambs have been foreshadowing all these years.

The people strained to understand, just like many of you who are seekers are straining to understand what I'm saying right now. You're thinking, *Can it be so? How does it all fit together?*

When Jesus began his teaching ministry, he began to refer to himself in these sacrificial terms. He'd give a great talk and people would be applauding. Then he'd add, "But you've got to know something. Not too long from now, I'm going to be sacrificed for all of your sins." And the people said, "No, no, no!"

Then he'd teach another message, and people would go, "Oh, that's great. We love to hear you preach, Jesus." Then he would say, "I'm going to lay down my life for you," and "I am the Lamb of God who's going to take away the sin of the world." And I'm telling you, people just couldn't take it in.

But, sure enough, after leading a sinless, unblemished life, he was arrested and falsely convicted. He was beaten and battered. All the saints and angels in heaven looked on in horror as Jesus was nailed to a cross outside the city of Jerusalem. You think Adam and Eve cringed when they saw death for the first time? You think the fifteen-year-old boy at the time of the Exodus got a little nauseated when he saw his father kill a lamb in the backyard? Imagine what was going on in heaven as Jesus, the innocent second member of the Trinity, slowly bled to death in front of a group of gawkers who—instead of bowing low to worship Jesus for what he was doing—were busy auctioning his robe to the highest bidder. You can bet there was some major cringing and crying going on in heaven when Jesus, the innocent Lamb of God, finally cried out, in effect, "It is finished! I have made atonement for the sins of the world." It just didn't seem right in heaven. The price seemed too high. Guilty sinners don't deserve a substitute like the one God provided. They ought to pay for their own sins.

And you know what? *We should! I* should because I'm the one who does them. *You* should because you're the one who does them. We're the foul-ups. We're the ones who know God's rules and break them. We're the ones who lie when we ought to tell the truth. We're the ones who hate when we ought to love. We're the ones who will hold back when we ought to give. We're the ones who put down when we ought to lift up. We are the ones who ought to include everybody. You know, all people matter to God. But some of us exclude some people for the sheer perverse pleasure of freezing them out of our circles. That's the kind of people we are. And we should atone for those kinds of crimes. I should, and you should.

But the Bible says, in those words you've heard since you were kids, "God so loved the world." You know, as holy, righteous, and just as God is, he has this thing about you. You matter to him. He knows your name. And whenever he thinks about you, his heart is moved with love. So the Bible tells us that God so loved the world that even though we ought to pay for our own sins, he sent his only begotten Son to stand in our place, to pay the penalty we should pay, to make substitutionary atonement for our sin.

Do you see the core idea of Christianity? Jesus Christ taking your place and mine, satisfying the demands of justice so guilty parties like you and me can go free. We can be forgiven and stand blameless before God on the merits of the Lamb of God who paid our price. What an idea! Every other religious system is based on a different core idea. Every other religious system establishes some kind of performance expectation. If you try hard and struggle and wrestle and give money and do all kinds of things, well, they say, you *might* raise your status enough to make it.

And people who do work at it hard often get proud and look down their self-righteous noses at those who aren't doing as well. And then people who don't do as well finally give up and say, "I might as well just take the heat for whatever I've gotta take the heat for."

Christianity is the only religion in the world whose core idea is based on substitutionary atonement—where guilty sinners go free on the merits of the provision God has made in Jesus, his Son, who pays the price on our behalf. It's an amazing thing. Some people have asked me, "How do you get so fired up and stay so fired up about Christianity?" I'm telling you, friends, this is the third time I've given this message. Whenever I talk about it, I can't get over it. There's nothing else like this in the world.

The Bible says that on the Day of Judgment, you're going to stand before a holy God, and there will be no argument whatsoever about whether or not you're a sinner. That's going to be the shortest discussion in history! You're going to know it right away.

In the early eighties, when I was a much younger man, I enjoyed playing park district football. I used to watch the Chicago Bears on television on Sunday afternoons, and I'd say, "You know, I could play with those guys. I really could! I could line up across from a couple of those guys and hold my own."

Then I was invited to be the chaplain for the Bears. I remember driving to Lake Forest for the first time to give my Bible study. I walked around a corner and saw Richard Dent. I was looking right at his navel! I looked at the size of all these guys, and I realized something: When you watch it from afar you can start thinking all kinds of strange thoughts that aren't true at all. But when you get up close, *reality* strikes!

From afar some of us say, "I'll hold my own when I stand before God. I've led a pretty good life." But stand five seconds in the blazing, brilliant holiness of God and you're going to say, "Oh my, I'm in trouble!" You're going to know who the Holy One is and who the sinner is that fast. On the Judgment Day the issue is not who's the sinner—the question is, who makes the atonement? Because in God's economy, sin will be paid for. It's just a question of who pays the tab.

The Bible says that between now and that day, you've got to make a decision. If you're going to take the hit and do your own atoning, then you'll do it forever—separated from God in a place called hell. It's your choice. But there's another option available to you: substitutionary atonement. It's Jesus Christ, out of love, saying, "I'll take your rap. I'll take the hit. I'll pay the penalty. And you, as a guilty party—on my merits—can be free, forgiven, adopted into God's family, blessed in love, and taken to heaven forever. Your choice!"

When you came in, in your bulletin there was a little card. Would you take that out for a minute? Everybody—not just seekers, because we're going to do something all together.

It says the core idea of Christianity is substitutionary atonement—Jesus Christ willingly shouldering the weight of my wrongdoing so that I could be set free. Now, here's what I'd like to have you do. I'd like to have you initial or write your name under that first blank where it says, "I understand the core idea of substitutionary atonement. *I get it.*" Also, where were you and when was it when you first got it?

I put, "August 1968." I was seventeen years old and at a Bible camp in southern Wisconsin when someone explained it to me. I said, *"I get it!"*

Now, if you don't get it yet, don't sign anything. Some of you might say, "Well, I get it right now. It's just been explained to me." Then put down today's date and "Willow Creek Community Church."

You can all talk about it afterward and show each other your cards and say, "That's where I was." And a lot of people, the last couple of hours, have put today's date or last night's date. It's a really exciting thing!

Here's the second part, equally important. The Bible says you can understand the core idea of Christianity and still wind up having to atone for your own sins for yourself in hell forever, because just *understanding* it is not enough. You have to, in humility and with a repentant spirit, say, "Not only do I understand it but I need it, I want it, and I reach out for it. I ask that what Jesus did be applied to my life and my sin. I place my trust solely in his substitutionary atonement for my hope of heaven."

The Bible says in John 1:12, "as many as received him. . . ." You have to invite him into your life as your Savior and Friend. It says in Romans 10:13, "Whoever will call on the name of Lord. . . ." You've got to do that.

So the second thing I'm asking you to do is to initial when and where that happened. When did you appropriate it? Just initial it if you've received the substitutionary atoning death of Christ. Put it down.

For me, "August 1968." About fifteen seconds after I got it, I said, "I need it!" I reached out for it. Jesus Christ's atoning work became real in my life, and I got off the treadmill of trying to earn my way to heaven. I said, "I can't earn it. Christ bought it for me. I receive it as a gift"—and it changed everything in my life.

When was it that this happened for you? If you're thinking, "Uh, oh—I don't know," it might be that you've never really appropriated the substitutionary work of Christ.

The great news is that you can get it squared away right now. If you're ready, just write down your initials to say, "I ask for Christ's atoning work to take effect in my life. I need it. I want it. I reach out for it by faith. I ask for it." And Christ will do that for you today. He *died* to do that for you.

For some of you this is all hitting you too fast. You're thinking, *Whoa, my head's spinning! I don't know what I'm doing here!* Then don't do anything right now. You've got to understand it. It's got to be genuine for it to be meaningful. Just keep coming back, keep seeking, keep asking questions. It might be a week from now, a month from now, or whenever. But some of you are ready right now. So let's just take a minute to do that and then we'll close in prayer [pauses briefly].

Now, do you know what a lot of folks did the last couple of hours? Right after we closed in prayer, they showed their cards to each other. We had a fun time. We said, "If anyone said 'I got it and I appropriated it today,' then whoever they showed their card to had to buy them brunch!" And there's a whole lot of people saying, "Gladly—that would be the greatest thrill in the world!"

Before we close in prayer, I want to say one more thing. When you "get it"—the core idea—and Christ comes into your life, and if you have clear vision about life and eternity, it only seems appropriate that you would reorder your whole life around worshiping the God who provided you with an atonement substitution so you wouldn't have to pay. It only makes sense that you would proclaim this scandalous message of grace to almost everybody you know, and that you'd spend large amounts of time figuring out ways to say thanks to God for what he's done. We're having a baptism service in a couple of weeks. For those of you who've done this recently, you can stand up here and give public witness to the fact that there was a time when you were going to have to atone, but now Christ has done this atoning work on your behalf. What a day of celebration that will be!

Let's pray:

> *Father, your love is so high, so deep, so wide, so pure, and so strong that you offered up your only Son as the substitutionary atonement for the likes of us guilty sinners. We ought to pay, but through Christ we've been set free. What a deal! What a God! What a Savior! What a faith!*
>
> *I pray that as we dismiss today we will do so amazed by grace and committed to spreading it all over the world.*
>
> *For Jesus' sake, Amen.*

BRINGING THE MESSAGE HOME

It has been said that if a preacher ever gives an audience the chance to misunderstand the message, the people will grab it with both arms and run with it! In no case is this more true than with the central message of the gospel. You can preach it, preach it, and preach it again—and some of the people who've heard it a hundred times will look you in the eye and say, "Well, I think I'm a pretty good person," or "I'm pretty sure God will approve of my track record and let me into heaven." You can explain God's free gift of grace, and they'll say, "Thanks . . . I guess I'll have to work harder to earn it."

People seem bent on not "getting it"! That was certainly true in Jesus' day. Just look at Nicodemus's confusion in John 3—a religious leader and teacher, and he was one who just didn't get it. And do you know what? It's true in our day too. Scores of people are part of the church crowd and considered to be real Christians, but their attitude says, "I've done the religious drill, been through the classes, said the right words, gotten the papers. I'm OK and you're OK—so let's just accept each other and live our lives."

These people can look and talk like they've got their spiritual act together, at least when they're around the church, but in their heart of hearts many of them are not true followers of Christ. Paul warned in Titus 1:16 that there would be those who "claim to know God, but by their actions they deny him." In fact, a recent *Barna Report* said that, based on their surveys over the course of more than a decade, "close to half of the people who fill the pews on a typical Sunday are not Christians . . . [and many are actually] atheists or agnostics."[7] For the most part these are not outside visitors. They're regular attenders everyone thinks are on board—and half of them don't "get it." They're churchgoing non-Christians who are often wonderful people—and they certainly matter to God—but they're snared in religious games and mistaken thinking that can actually inoculate them to the truth of the gospel.

Have we gone out of our way to make it clear that it's possible to be in a good church—our church—but not be in Christ?

The important question is this: Have we warned them? Have we gone out of our way to make it clear that it's possible to be in a good church—our church—but not be in Christ? Have we urged our people to examine themselves to see whether they're really in the faith (see 2 Corinthians 13:5)? Have we loved them enough to risk offending them by proclaiming that we *all* need to humble ourselves and kneel, empty-handed and brokenhearted, before the cross of Jesus Christ—and that this is an attitude that marks his true followers throughout their lives?

In some church traditions this is a difficult message to deliver—everyone assumes everyone is okay and doesn't expect anybody to question that assumption. But these are the settings where the danger is the greatest and the need for a warning the highest.

I lived much of my life in an area where almost everyone was moderately "religious" and at least occasionally went to church. But from my observation, relatively few of them manifested changed hearts by being serious about following and serving Christ in their daily lives. Yet their churches had convinced them they were alright the way they were.

This problem really hit home when a teenager who was known for his wild, ungodly lifestyle was killed in an accident. As far as any of us could tell, his life showed no signs of a relationship with Christ—and plenty of evidence to the contrary. Yet at his funeral the pastor reassured everyone that because this young man had been through their church's traditional rites of passage as a child, he was now in heaven enjoying God's presence and rewards. This, of course, encouraged friends and family members to breathe a sigh of relief—and it prevented most of them from looking at their own hearts and making certain they were really "in the faith." I can't help feeling that on that day an opportunity was missed for heaven and all of hell laughed.

For many of us, evangelism needs to start in our own pews. Your church needs to become contagious *inside* before it'll ever become highly contagious *outside.*

Paul warned Timothy about the danger of timidity (2 Timothy 1:7). Evangelistic leadership is not for the faint of heart. It takes courage and requires spiritual and evangelistic guts. My greatest fear as a teacher of the gospel is to allow anyone I influence to keep on living with false religious security—to let them go on, day after day, year after year, thinking everything is all right, only to later suffer the greatest shock and disappointment imaginable on the Day of Judgment. Jesus was very clear about this danger in Matthew 7:21–23: "Not everyone who says to me, 'Lord, Lord,' will enter the kingdom of heaven, but only he who does the will of my Father who is in heaven. Many will say to me on that day, 'Lord, Lord, did we not prophesy in your name, and in your name drive out demons and perform many miracles?' Then I will tell them plainly, 'I never knew you. Away from me, you evildoers!'"

Jesus said in no uncertain terms that you can be a highly religious man or woman, say the right things, address him in the right ways, engage in the right activities—and still not know him or his salvation, and, as a result, end up separated from him for all eternity.

Will you have the courage to break tradition and ignore ecclesiastical correctness in order to lovingly give your people the unadulterated truth—knowing that some will be offended while others will be redeemed? May God give you and those who serve with you the boldness and wisdom to do whatever it takes to overcome spiritual confusion, confront sin, and point people to Christ and his amazing grace. For many of us, evangelism needs to start in our own pews. Your church needs to become contagious *inside* before it'll ever become highly contagious *outside*.

NOTHING BUT THE BLOOD

The gospel message—the core idea of Christianity that says Christ died to pay for my sins and for yours—is needed by everybody, inside and outside the church walls. We have to proclaim this message clearly, without apology, and trust God to empower and apply it in ways that will change lives and build his church.

I end with the words of one of my favorite songs, "Nothing but the Blood." It expresses in a simple way what we've been talking about—the truth the whole world needs to hear:

> What can wash away my sin? Nothing but the blood of Jesus;
> What can make me whole again? Nothing but the blood of Jesus.
> O! precious is the flow that makes me white as snow;
> No other fount I know, nothing but the blood of Jesus.
>
> This is all my hope and peace—nothing but the blood of Jesus;
> This is all my righteousness—nothing but the blood of Jesus.
> O! precious is the flow that makes me white as snow;
> No other fount I know, nothing but the blood of Jesus.

To Consider and Discuss

1. How clearly is the "core idea" of Christianity understood among the core attenders of your church? Are there some steps you need to take to broaden and deepen their grasp of the substitutionary atonement of Christ?

2. Have you ever had your spiritual "cage rattled" by challenges to your faith that you could not easily answer? What happened, and how did it affect you?
3. Have you ever really resolved those issues in your mind? Are there steps you need to take or is there any "homework" you need to do in order to restore your confidence in the Bible and the gospel message?
4. What are some steps you'll commit to and prioritize in order to strengthen the foundations of your faith (review the section "Shoring Up Your Confidence," page 346, for ideas).
5. Do the people in your congregation need more teaching in order to shore up their own confidence in the reliability of the Bible and the power of the gospel? If so, what can you do to remedy this situation?

17

THE VISION: CONTAGIOUS CHURCHES AND A CONTAGIOUS EPIDEMIC

Broken relationships, broken families,
broken promises, broken values, broken hearts,
broken lives in a broken-down world.

In the midst of this mess, allow the local church to function as the Church envisioned by Jesus Christ—a thriving, radiating center of Christian love reaching out in self-sacrificing concern toward the needs of contemporary women, men, and children. Let the church be really the Church and watch it exert a supernatural power of attraction that will irresistibly draw our secular, community-starved contemporaries within its sphere of influence, bring them to Christ in the most natural manner, and integrate them into its life.

The best shot at evangelism is to encourage churches to become and to live as authentic, biblically defined communities so that the Lord Himself can become their Master Evangelist.

DR. GILBERT BILEZIKIAN

What makes a church *truly* contagious?

What kind of church does the Holy Spirit use to not only attract outsiders but to bring them to faith and enfold them into God's family? As I'm sure you're aware, it's more than just an *evangelistic* church! We've focused mostly on evangelistic strategy and activity, both of which play the vital role of helping us make connections, open doors, and expose people to the truth.

But once these people show up, they need to experience a living, vibrant, fully orbed, biblically functioning church—the kind that genuinely worships God, teaches and submits to his Word, is faithful in prayer, enjoys authentic community, deals forthrightly with problems and interpersonal conflicts, practices generous stewardship, and expresses selfless love and service to those inside and outside its walls.

It's the kind of combination we see in the contagious church of Acts 2:42–47:

> They devoted themselves to the apostles' teaching and to the fellowship, to the breaking of bread and to prayer. Everyone was filled with awe, and many wonders and miraculous signs were done by the apostles. All the believers were together and had everything in common. Selling their possessions and goods, they gave to anyone as he had need. Every day they continued to meet together in the temple courts. They broke bread in their homes and ate together with glad and sincere hearts, praising God and enjoying the favor of all the people. And the Lord added to their number daily those who were being saved.

A DISPROPORTIONATE INVESTMENT

The early church had all of the right elements in place, but let's not miss the fact that it also had *an extraordinary commitment to outreach.*

The church had been born out of evangelism, as recorded in the verses immediately preceding the Acts 2:42–47 passage, and evangelism was its top priority. This can be seen in the next couple of chapters as well, where Peter and John healed a man and then used the platform this provided to proclaim the gospel (see Acts 3:11–26). When this action led to their detainment by the authorities, they again made the most of the situation and presented the message of Christ to the rulers and elders (see Acts 4:8–12). Then, after being warned to stop preaching, they were released, and they shared with the other believers what had happened. The church's response? Acts 4:29 tells us they prayed together, saying: "Now, Lord, consider their threats and enable your servants to speak your word with great boldness," and verse 31 says "they were all filled with the Holy Spirit and *spoke the word of God boldly*" (emphasis mine).

But it didn't stop there! After Stephen, one of the church's leaders, was put to death, "a great persecution broke out against the church in Jerusalem, and all except the apostles were scattered throughout Judea and Samaria" (Acts 8:1). So how did all of these rank-and-file church members, most of whom were new converts, respond to this threatening situation? Acts 8:4 tells us that "those who had been scattered *preached the word wherever they went*" (emphasis mine).

This early church was unstoppable! And evangelism was the primary fuel it ran on.

Wow! This early church was *unstoppable!* And evangelism was the primary fuel it ran on. I believe reaching lost people was the first among equals in terms of the church's values.

Likewise, if we want to build a contagious church, I think evangelism needs to be our top priority. Not our *only* priority—again, there needs to be a biblical balance—but the one that gets a higher portion of our creativity, energy, and resources. This has been an important lesson learned at my own church. Consider what Bill Hybels said recently:

> We put together our strategic plan and said, "We're going to assign equal amounts of energy and resources and prayer into each of what we call our *5 Gs* [Grace, Growth, Groups, Gifts, and Good Stewardship]. We're going to knock ourselves out for the next five years to become a biblically balanced New Testament-style church." But a couple of years into the plan, the area where we were having the hardest time making the gains we had hoped and prayed for was the first G—*Grace,* or *evangelism.*
>
> We thought we should put a twenty percent effort into each G. Now that we've done that for a while, we've figured out that this is faulty thinking. *The reality is that we need to make a forty percent investment in the grace G,* and then give about fifteen percent of our efforts to each of the other ones.

Why should we do this? In part, as I've said earlier, because this is the value that tends to slip the fastest—it's that pervasive age-old problem of evangelistic entropy. This disproportionate investment in evangelism also makes sense because this is the area that feeds all the other areas. Do you want to have a worshiping church? Evangelism provides new worshipers! Want to be a discipling church? Evangelism fills your ranks with fresh recruits who need to be discipled. Want to become a sending church? Reach a broad pool of people out of which you can do the sending. Want to be a missions-oriented church? Live out the mission at home in ways that will prepare your people to take that mission to other places. Want to be a Christ-honoring church? Help all your people become friends of sinners, like Jesus was, and to work like he did "to seek and to save what was lost." If evangelism is stymied or shut down, it will directly or indirectly affect every other aspiration and arena of the church.

Moreover, Bill Hybels points out the following:

> The Bible says in Ephesians 6, "We're not just fighting against flesh and blood." If there were one place that the evil one wanted to attack, to make sure that none of this would happen, where would he place his shot? In the area of grace, or evangelism! Why? Because once people come into the family and they have the Holy Spirit inside of them, now it's an unfair fight because "greater is he who is in us than he who is in the world." These people with the Holy Spirit in them—they're going to want to grow and worship and get into a small group. Next thing you know, they're going to want to become members and serve the poor and give of their resources.
>
> Unless we reorient our minds toward this emphasis on grace, we're probably not going to reach our church's redemptive potential.

If this is true of my church, I'd venture to say it's probably true of yours as well—which is why we all need to make a disproportionate investment in the area of evangelism, and why we need to keep making it consistently over time.

A BENCHMARK

As I've spoken with church leaders about the elements needed to build a highly evangelistic church, I've discovered a serious problem: What is considered "highly evangelistic" or "contagious" varies greatly from leader to leader and from church to church. Some church leaders have huge, and perhaps unrealistic, expectations of what their church should accomplish with respect to reaching lost people. This can lead to frustration when they consistently fall short of their lofty goals.

But more often I find the opposite problem: Leaders who have been long accustomed to seeing few or no people put their trust in Christ sometimes begin to consider this situation to be a more or less normal state of affairs. So they can be easily satisfied with only incrementally improved results. But we must not give up striving to attain our church's full redemptive potential, disastrously resulting in our reaching even *one* less man, woman, boy, or girl than we could have reached.

Throughout these pages I've said very little about "church growth"—not because I'm against it, but because it's so tempting to overemphasize the numbers side of the equation. When we focus too much on numeric growth, we tend to start pursuing surface-level solutions rather than doing the deep spadework of examining and strengthening hearts, changing values, and aligning mission and strategy. So we've spent most of our energy on the 6-Stage Process designed to help us address these deeper issues, and then to train, organize, and deploy our people according to their particular God-given styles of evangelism.

But guess what—when we do these things, it generally shows up on the numeric charts as well. The natural question is, what should these charts look like? And how many people should a church of our size reasonably expect to see coming to Christ in a year? And what would be a good benchmark to at least give us some idea of what we should shoot for?

I've thought long and hard about these questions. I've also prayed earnestly about whether to put a specific measure in this book, and if so, which one. I only wanted to do so if it would be helpful, which in my mind means it would be high enough to stretch us and realistic enough to motivate us.

We've all heard scenarios like this: If you reached one person today, and then you and this person reached two more tomorrow, and the four of you reached four more the next day, and so on, a city like Chicago would be reached in twenty-three days, a country the size of the United States just five days later, and the entire world population—all six or eight billion people—in a total of only thirty-three days. The math works! The problem is that this kind of model fails to motivate any of us! It's hard enough to *reach the one person tomorrow,* let alone the increasingly unreasonable requirements on each successive day thereafter.

So it's tempting to throw up our hands and say, "Then let's not look at numbers at all. Let's just keep on doing what we're doing, and let the results take care of themselves." But I think that would be a mistake. These "numbers" are not mere statistics—they're *changed lives!* They're human beings with names and faces, hopes and dreams, families and futures. They're people who matter to God. They're your husband or wife, father or mother, son or daughter, niece or nephew, neighbor or coworker—individuals you love and want to have with you in heaven for all of eternity. And if you have four or five of these people in your life—people your heart aches to reach—then you don't mind counting them and keeping track of which of them have come to faith. We're simply talking about doing this on a church-wide level.

By the way, do you know what they did in New Testament times? *They counted!* Look at a few excerpts from the book of Acts (emphases mine):

- In those days Peter stood up among the believers (a group *numbering about a hundred and twenty*).—(1:15)
- Those who accepted his message were baptized, and *about three thousand were added to their number that day.*—(2:41)
- And the Lord *added to their number daily* those who were being saved.—(2:47)
- But many who heard the message believed, and *the number of men grew to about five thousand.*—(4:4)
- Nevertheless, more and more men and women believed in the Lord and *were added to their number.*—(5:14)
- In those days when *the number of disciples was increasing* . . . —(6:1)
- So the word of God spread. The *number of disciples in Jerusalem increased rapidly*, and *a large number of priests* became obedient to the faith.—(6:7)
- Then the church throughout Judea, Galilee and Samaria enjoyed a time of peace. It was strengthened; and encouraged by the Holy Spirit, *it grew in numbers,* living in the fear of the Lord.—(9:31)

This list goes on, including nearly a dozen additional references just in the book of Acts alone. The leaders of the early church were not shy about looking at, talking about, and recording actual results—and neither should we be shy about it.

As I prayed about the kind of benchmark that would serve churches in fulfilling God's mission, I believe he led me to one that is simultaneously challenging and realistic, yet simple enough to be easily understood and measured. (And what's interesting is that I had "come up with this new model" months before discovering that Dann Spader and Sonlife Ministries have been teaching and helping churches for a long time by means of this model,[1] and that Donald McGavran had proposed it years earlier! Here's the measure:

> *Every church, in cooperation with the work of the Holy Spirit, reaching and retaining one non-Christian per year for every ten Christians who are regular attenders.* In other words, a church of 100 leading 10 people to Christ this year, adding

> them to their fold, and then next year that church of 110 reaching and enfolding 11 more, and so forth. Or, if you have a team of ten people who are planting a church together, reach at least one seeker this year. When you get up to thirty, try to reach at least three. And some day if you reach 1,500, pray and ask God to help you bring 150 non-Christians to Christ.

Remember, this is a *goal*, not a *limit*—God may bless your harvesting efforts way beyond this, at least for seasons at a time. Also, note that a church with this kind of exciting activity will also attract additional Christians who want to be in on the action (as discussed at the end of chapter 5). That's okay, but don't count them as part of the ten percent benchmark!

What I love about the model is that it's doable; 100 people really can reach 10. (One way to achieve this would be for each Frontline Team member—the ten percent with gifts or passion for evangelism—to simply reach one person per year. But you may want to communicate this only to that team; you don't want to keep the rest of the church members from doing their part!) Yet it's also stretching—even for a megachurch of 10,000 attenders, which would be striving to reach 1,000 in a year's time.

The real challenge is to retain the people who come in through evangelism and build on this growth year after year (or redistribute it into newly planted congregations, which will likely reach even more people for Christ). But what's exciting is that if you do this consistently, *your church will double in size every seven years*—through lost men, women, and children coming to know and follow Christ!

And what really motivates me is the fact that if the evangelical churches in the United States would attain and sustain that level, we'd reach the entire nation in about thirty years—which is within the life span of most of us reading this book. (What's more, the situation would be similar in many other countries.) *Talk about a contagious epidemic!*

Now, let's put our feet back on the ground for a moment. Looking at a wide range of studies and statistics, the average rate—what church statisticians call "conversion growth rate"—for churches in America is between two and three percent (and many churches show no gain at all, but are just staying even or perhaps even losing ground). Obviously, this number falls far short of what is needed in order to fulfill the Great Commission—in fact, two to three percent barely stays ahead of the current population growth rate! And this average is only about a fourth of what we're aiming for—the ten percent rate—which dramatically reveals how much work remains to be done.

The importance of this kind of benchmark was reinforced a while back when I spent some time with a group of evangelism leaders from outreach-oriented churches all around the country. I shared this ten percent evangelism growth model in order to get feedback and reactions from these ministry peers. While we had a lively discussion—a couple of them thought the rate was too low and others weren't sure they wanted to count conversions at all—one guy who had been active in most of the earlier discussions had become noticeably quiet.

If we really want to achieve our church's redemptive potential, we've got to change our whole way of thinking. In fact, we're going to have to revolutionize the way we view and do evangelism.

Finally this man, who is a committed evangelism leader at an increasingly evangelistic church, spoke in sober and vulnerable tones. He said, "You know, our church consists of 2,500 believers, and you're telling me we ought to be reaching 250 non-Christians this year. The truth is, we've only been trying to reach about 35. If we were to really try to reach 250, *we would have to change our whole way of thinking!*"

He was right! If we really want to achieve our church's redemptive potential, we've got to change our whole way of thinking. In fact, *I think we're going to have to revolutionize the way we view and do evangelism*. We're going to have to declare war on every front, push back evangelistic entropy, and make reaching and retaining lost people for Christ our top priority. If we'll do this, I believe we can move toward, and in many cases even go beyond, this ten percent evangelistic growth rate.

My sincere hope is that this model motivates you and your team to at least begin to measure, as best you can, how many people are genuinely coming to faith each year through your church's individual and collective efforts. If the number is just one percent of your congregation's present size, then start there. The important question is, what would it take to get it up to two or three percent and then to five percent? *Every* incremental gain is worth celebrating, regardless of whether or not you ever hit the ten percent benchmark!

I recently spoke to a group of church leaders from various places at an all-day workshop at our church, and I ended the day by saying, "Now, I don't want to turn this into a numbers game. If this model helps you, great; if not, just apply the 6-Stage Process and the other principles we've been talking about throughout the day, and let God direct the results."

I was about to close in prayer when Jim Ockenfels, a key volunteer who had been in the room helping with the administrative aspects of the workshop, spoke up. "Mark, before you end I'd like to say something to everybody, if that's okay." Jim had come to faith just a few years earlier through the efforts and invitations of a contagious Christian at our church. Knowing his heart for lost people, as well as his passion to serve church leaders, I gladly agreed to let him say a few words to the group. Standing in the back of the room, his eyes filling with tears, Jim spoke with trembling voice and an obvious conviction:

> *I'll* turn it into a "numbers game" for you.
>
> I'm the youngest of eleven children. There are seven of my brothers and sisters still living. None of them knows Christ. Out of the families of these seven, I've got twenty-one nieces and nephews, and fifty great-nieces and nephews. But of the seventy-eight people I just named, only *three* know Christ as Savior.
>
> I've been praying all day for your churches, because they're spread out all over the country. I've been praying because I want a contagious church to be out there for each of them. That way, if they walk through your doors someday, they'll hear about Christ the way I did when I came to this church.
>
> That's my challenge for you: Build contagious churches and give these loved ones of mine the same kind of chance I had here at this church.

Jim's words helped us all gain a heightened awareness of the importance of the task at hand. I hope they serve you in the same way.

ELEMENTS FOR BUILDING A CONTAGIOUS CHURCH

In this closing section, I want to pull together the elements we've been talking about, and offer a few important new ones, to get a handle on what we need to do in order to build highly contagious churches. These elements stand alongside the broader components of a biblically functioning church discussed at the beginning of the chapter.

LEADERS FULLY COMMITTED TO THE CHURCH'S EVANGELISTIC MISSION (STAGES 1–3)

Jesus, our ultimate Leader, said he came "to seek and to save what was lost" and to "give his life as a ransom for many." Jesus was laser-focused on his evangelistic mission, and he was willing to give it all—and he *did* give it all—to fulfill his mission.

Paul said, "I consider my life worth nothing to me, if only I may finish the race and complete the task the Lord Jesus has given me—the task of testifying to the gospel of God's grace" (Acts 20:24). For Paul too there was no price too great to pay in the effort to complete the task of reaching people for Christ.

We've seen the sacrifice and the evangelistic dedication of the leaders in the New Testament church, recorded in the book of Acts. There's also the example of the church fathers, as well as countless early believers who laid down everything to serve and follow Christ and to strive to fulfill his redemptive purposes.

There was Martin Luther, who risked his life to nail the ninety-five theses to the door of the Wittenberg Cathedral and to translate the Scriptures into the language of the German people. And John Calvin, who sent missionaries into France and Brazil and pioneered the work of evangelism training at his Geneva Academy. And John Wesley, who rode all over the British Isles so he could bring the Good News to the people there, and sailed across the Atlantic so he could send preachers throughout the New World. There was William Booth, who fought the status quo to start his mission of reaching people not just with words of love but also with tangible expressions of help and service. And Dwight Moody, who gave of himself tirelessly to preach the gospel on both sides of the ocean, to print literature, to start schools, and to train younger ministers. And Hudson Taylor, who risked and gave up everything to reach unchurched people in one of the most intimidating mission fields of the world.

I believe that all these heroes of the faith, and countless other men and women who had warm hearts and clear vision, understood what the church was about and saw what it could become—not just a warm company of committed believers but a contagious community ready to enfold, teach, and influence the nonbelievers all around them. They were leaders who gave of themselves to reach lost people with the life-changing message of the cross and then to disciple and grow them up into coworkers who would, in turn, give of themselves to reach still more. And I couldn't agree more with George Hunter when he says in his book *Church for the Unchurched,* "We do not honor our founders by blindly perpetuating in a changing world what they once did . . . we honor them by doing for our time and culture what they did for theirs."[2]

It all starts in the hearts of leaders—those who will own and model evangelistic values (stage 1), tirelessly work to instill those values in those around them (stage 2), and eagerly empower more leaders who will join them in the task of building increasingly contagious churches (stage 3).

Willingness to Try Fresh Approaches

In Existing Churches

Way back in the time of the prophet Jeremiah, God said he would "create a new thing on earth" (Jeremiah 31:22)—and it seems like

God's people have been bent on keeping things the same ever since! We just naturally gravitate toward the safety of sameness. But building a contagious church will require a new way of thinking, as well as a willingness to put these new thoughts into action.

The great evangelist Billy Graham once wrote about what it will take "for the evangelistic imperative to be lived out in the future so that the twenty-first century becomes the greatest century for Christian evangelism in history." Dr. Graham observed that we need the following:

> *A willingness to explore new methods and new fields.* Methods that have worked in the past to make people aware of the church and draw them into its programs will not necessarily work in a media-saturated age. It is no coincidence that those churches that are most often effective in reaching their neighborhoods and cities for Christ are often those that are the most flexible and adaptable in their methods.... The main point is that we need to stand back and be creative.[3]

It's not that we need to become anti-tradition; we just need to ask whether each tradition or practice is optimally serving the biblical purpose for which it was originally created. If it is, keep it. If it's not, and if the Scriptures give us freedom to explore how to best accomplish this purpose—in this case, the purpose of evangelism—then let's find a better way.

Lee Strobel often quotes the stinging words of Winston Crawley, the Southern Baptist missionary, who said, "If our efforts to share the gospel in today's world are limited only to the traditional model, then we have decided in advance on limited outreach and limited growth."

In New Churches

The need for flexibility and creativity does not apply merely to existing churches. Leaders who plant new churches must consider up front what they're trying to build, and why. Beware of the temptation to simply perpetuate old models and put a clone of the mother church in a new neighborhood for the mere reason that there isn't yet a franchise of this particular church "brand" in that area (whether there are other evangelical churches around the corner or not).

This can be a huge waste of kingdom resources! I'm in favor of planting new churches. We just need to plant them *where they're really needed* and make sure we design them to fulfill the greatest need: *reaching and enfolding lost people.*

When you begin a new church, you've got an incredible opportunity to locate it, focus it, and build it in ways that will have a powerful evangelistic impact. And applying the 6-Stage Process—especially the first three stages—will help set the right trajectory and propel it forward:

Stage 1 (Applied to Church Planting): If the leaders of the planting team will *own and model the values of evangelism* from the very beginning, they'll establish these values in the DNA of the new church body. To do so will affect every decision and pattern of development of this church now and into the future. If, on the other hand, these values are set aside to be incorporated after the new church is "a bit more established," then existing patterns will be set, and it will be extremely difficult to later restructure the church's spiritual genetics and establish evangelism as one of its core values.

Stage 2 (Applied to Church Planting): If the church planting leadership team works hard to *instill the values of evangelism* from the beginning, it will serve to form a strong outreach culture and to attract the right people who will contribute to furthering this culture. (It will also repel the unsuitable ones while it's still fairly painless.) There will be a clear sense that this new work is part of a redemptive mission from God and that nothing else in the world could be more important!

Stage 3 (Applied to Church Planting): The church planting team should look and pray from the very beginning for *the right person to empower as its evangelistic point leader* who will protect and promote these evangelistic values from the inception of the church. This will most likely be a key layperson, but it could someday become this person's adventure-filled career! I like what Rick Warren said about this in *The Purpose-Driven® Church*:

> If I were starting a new church today I would begin by recruiting five volunteers for five unpaid staff positions . . . [including someone to] oversee our evangelism and missions programs in the community. As the church grew I would move these people to part-time paid staff and eventually full-time.[4]

Following stages 1–3 prepares the culture and the leadership—both in new church planting ministries and in older established churches—to then do the training, team building, and outreach activities of stages 4–6.

PARTICIPATION OF THE ENTIRE CHURCH BODY (STAGES 4–6)

Effective, sustained evangelism is always a team activity. Jesus recruited twelve disciples and sent them out in pairs (Mark 6:7). Later he commissioned "seventy-two others and sent them two by two ahead of him to every town and place where he was about to go" (Luke 10:1). After Jesus' death and resurrection, he gave the now-famous directive to his followers, "But you will receive power when the Holy Spirit comes on you; and you will be my witnesses in Jerusalem, and in all Judea and Samaria, and to the ends of the earth" (Acts 1:8). Within a matter of days, God miraculously used this team to speak to the crowds of people in their own languages (see Acts 2:6).

What impresses me about the powerful outreach and exponential growth of the early church is the broad participation of the entire group of Christ-followers: "After *they* prayed, the place where *they* were meeting was shaken. And *they were all filled* with the Holy Spirit *and spoke* the word of God boldly" (Acts 4:31, emphasis mine). This was a contagious movement, and it involved *all* of the members of the church.

Every Christian is part of the church to which Jesus gave the Great Commission, and we each have a vital role to play. The task is too huge to be done on the backs of a few pastors, church leaders, or evangelism enthusiasts. We need nothing less than to *liberate and equip all of our believers—one hundred percent of them—to communicate Christ* to their friends (stage 4). I think an important key to this liberation—a key I've tried to weave throughout the book—is the transformational teaching that comes from the Bible and is incorporated into the *Becoming a Contagious Christian* evangelism course, which says you can be yourself and communicate Christ in ways that fit you. We'll all be much more effective when we discover our own natural style of evangelism, and then go on to develop and use it.

Because of this emphasis, the *Becoming a Contagious Christian* course is now being used in churches around the world, not only to train their people for relational evangelism but also as a recruitment tool to open up to people a number of other outreach programs and opportunities. In effect, it functions like the operating system that then utilizes these other specialized software packages.

For example, once someone has gone through the *Contagious* course and has discovered that they have the confrontational style of evangelism, it's a relatively easy next step to get them involved in an *Evangelism Explosion* or *Continuing Witness Training* visitation program. The same holds true for those with the interpersonal style and involvement in the seeker small group ministry, or the invitational style and involvement in the *Alpha* program, or the service style and involvement in a *Servant Evangelism* ministry—and the many other examples that have been given.

Your people will see these as natural next steps once they realize that they, as unique individuals, were designed by God to employ these approaches. The key for us as leaders is to discard either/or thinking and adopt a both/and mentality that initiates and supports multiple approaches. To win the war the church must use *all* of its God-given weapons.

Next, while training all of our believers to share their faith, we dare not neglect those to whom the Holy Spirit has given special gifts and passion to reach lost people with the gospel! This is a divine entrustment from God to the church, and we must carefully manage it as such. That's why, as we've discussed, many churches are beginning to catch the vision for starting *diverse, multistyled, and cross-departmental evangelism ministries*—Frontline Teams—to nurture, encourage, instruct, and empower their key outreach enthusiasts from around the church (stage 5).

Once you have organized this diverse team of evangelism specialists, *watch out!* You've got the ingredients of a high-activity, multipronged offensive unit that can do battle for the kingdom on numerous fronts, from individualized outreach, to small group and classroom structures, to any level or shape of large evangelistic event or ministry (stage 6). And when you put gifted leadership behind that kind of energy and personnel and express it on a church-wide level through the conduits of the six styles of evangelism (as illustrated in chapters 10–15), the results can be spiritually explosive. At this point, let the Holy Spirit take you to creative new places where the gospel can bear fruit as more and more lost people become found.

A final word on the 6-Stage Process: The sequence of the stages is intentional and important. Don't imagine you can really empower a point person until the pastor and many of the other leaders exhibit a heart for lost people. Don't expect to be able to maintain an ongoing, high-quality evangelism training program without a leader having been designated. Don't try to start a Frontline Team without a baseline of basic training that establishes the values and a common language; by the same token be careful not to start a seeker service or a bevy of outreach events until there's a critical mass of people who own the value of evangelism, a unified leadership core of people who are actually building relationships with lost people, and plenty of members who are trained and ready to jump in with both feet.

This last caveat illuminates a common mistake—what some have termed the "build it and they will come" approach (picking up the phrase from the classic baseball movie "Field of Dreams"). Countless outreach services and events have been presented in churches around the world—but nobody came. Why? Because almost no one built bridges of trust to unchurched people and personally invited them to come. We're all tempted to latch on to programs and methods without building the kinds of foundations and structures that can sustain them. But now that we've been properly warned, let's not make this same mistake. Let's go back to stage 1, and start with the heart!

Alignment of the Ministries to the Church's Evangelistic Mission

It's highly possible, even probable, that while there is a strengthening of evangelistic values and culture in your church, various pockets of ministry will be unaffected and even disinterested. These independent silos of activity will want to run unconstrained by the leadership and mission of the broader church. We can't afford to let this happen.

Many of these ministries and functions are fulfilling other parts of the church's purposes, which is a good thing, but as leaders we need to look at each area to make sure it's also being maximized for the *outreach* side of the church's mission. We need to make certain that in every case we're applying the principle articulated in Colossians 4:5: "Be wise in the way you act toward outsiders; make the most of every opportunity."

So, our church's senior leaders meet twice a year with the directors of the various ministries to look at each ministry's goals and plans. They do this in order to make certain that every ministry is staying focused and in sync with the overall direction of the church—or, if it isn't, is agreeable to making adjustments in order to do so. Plans are approved and resources allocated for the ones that are on track. In some situations, strong redirection is applied to help a ministry better fulfill the mission for which it was originally created (or, if it has outlived its usefulness, perhaps to begin the process of bringing it to an end).

Some of these leadership calls are difficult but crucial if we're to steward our limited opportunities and fulfill our redemptive potential. These meetings also provide a forum for encouraging and affirming the aligned leaders and ministries, a place where synergistic interaction and idea-sharing can happen, and an opportunity to join in times of prayer.

This kind of thinking and process needs to be applied not only to individual ministries but also to the church as a whole. Throughout this book I've talked primarily about the activities of individual leaders, teams, and ministries. But sooner or later, as the evangelism mission, values, and strategy take root, the larger structures and events of the church must be examined. If you do this too early, it'll cause a mutiny. But eventually, when the time is right and God's leading is clear, hard questions need to be asked and answered.

If we're really convinced that evangelism is central to the purpose of the entire church, we need to start looking at everything we do through an evangelistic lens. What about the main public services?

Are they making "the most of every opportunity"? If not, what needs to change? Do we need to start a separate seeker-oriented service? Can we get by with retuning our current worship service, making it more accessible to outsiders? (Think carefully about the answer, though; this might ultimately be the right way for you, but far too many churches hide behind the idea of just being "a bit more seeker-sensitive," using it as an excuse to change little or nothing. Many "seeker-sensitive worship services" are in reality the same old fare, with superficial cosmetic fixes and face-lifts that fail to address or relate to a truly unchurched visitor.)

What about the music? What about the messages? What about the sound and the lights? What about the appearance of the building, the accessibility of the auditorium, and the times of the services? What about the tone and persona of the people who stand up front? What about the sign out by the road and the sayings or slogans on it? Does the name of the church serve to open doors to seekers rather than close them?

The redemptive mission of the church is simply too important to let fear and traditional strongholds keep us from examining everything in light of our biblical, God-directed vision.

I'm fully aware I'm treading on dangerous ground! But guess what? Building a contagious church will require you to do the same. The redemptive mission of the church is simply too important to let fear and traditional strongholds keep us from examining everything in light of our biblical, God-directed vision. We *must* align the entire church to accomplish its mission of reaching lost people for Christ. We need to be wise about what to address when, but we must be courageous to move ahead as the Spirit leads.

Strategic Coordination of all Outreach Activities

Throughout these pages we've talked about a number of strategic evangelistic activities and events, but there's a danger that we will think of each of them in isolation. When we do this, we fail to see the exponential gains that would have been possible with a more integrated approach, both with respect to planning and promotion.

For example, why not schedule Frontline Team events a week or two after the completion of one of the *Becoming a Contagious Christian* training courses? To do so will allow you to explain and promote Frontline (and hand out flyers) to fresh groups of people at the very point when they'll be the most motivated to attend. In fact, I often have a Frontliner come with a fresh story and tell it briefly to the group going through the training course. Their enthusiasm is infectious, and it serves to draw many of these trainees to the team!

Why not schedule evangelistic subministry meetings, like seeker small group training or Defenders gatherings, as well as outreach events, to follow on the heels of Frontline Team meetings? To do so will allow you to build vision and excitement for these ministries at each team meeting. You can also pray together about these initiatives with the people who will most naturally be motivated to lift them up to God.

At Christmas or Easter services, what well-placed printed or spoken invitations could be presented that would point holiday visitors to strategic next-step opportunities? What weekend sermon series could be announced? What special event for the children or students should be launched? If the fall season is a time when a number of people return to the church, or if January is a time when well meaning seekers make New Year's resolutions to come to more services, how do you then seize the moment to build momentum? If you're teaching a series on questions skeptics ask, what could you do to encourage guests to seek information about a seeker small group immediately after the service or later in the day?

I can't answer these questions for you, but I can challenge you and your team to begin to think this way and to realize that *every* class, service, and event is a natural opportunity to point people toward strategic next steps.

By example, here's a sequence our church followed during a recent ministry season:

- January 10: Frontline Team, with Garry Poole, Lee Strobel, and me speaking to the team, with the primary purpose of turning up the evangelistic temperature for this particular year's run
- January 28: Vision Night at our worship service, with Bill Hybels challenging the church to deepen its evangelistic intensity
- February 4–March 4: Lee, Garry, and I taught a five-week series at our worship services called "The Unexpected Adventure," designed to heighten the evangelistic readiness of all of our believers and to whet their appetites for the *Becoming a Contagious Christian* training course
- March 13–22: "Stuff," an outreach musical and dramatic production on life and relationships, is presented in ten performances
- March 29–April 26: *Becoming a Contagious Christian* course is taught over four consecutive Sunday nights, in part to prepare people to maximize the Easter season and teaching series to follow

- April 10–12: Good Friday and Easter, expanded to ten services, with clear invitations given to newcomers to follow Christ—and to attend the series that begins the following week
- April 18–May 2: The three-week seeker service series "What Money Can't Buy" is taught (covering the subjects of "Conviction," "Humility," and "Loyalty")

I hope this helps illustrate the kind of integrated, strategic thinking that can build synergy and momentum in your own setting. The specifics may differ, but the desired outcome is the same: the church united around its evangelistic mission, and increasing numbers of lost people coming to faith in Christ.

Sustained Effort

Building contagious churches does not come naturally or easily, even for the most evangelistically committed leaders. There will be internal struggles and external resistance. The commitment will be costly in terms of time, finances, and pain-inducing change. Without question, the noble intention of prioritizing lost people will be challenged and your motives questioned.

Jesus constantly faced these kinds of problems, as did Paul and Peter. As I read my Bible this week, it struck me that after Peter obeyed the vision from heaven and courageously went into the house of Cornelius and led to Christ all who had gathered there, he was then chastised by his fellow Christ-followers! Acts 11:1–2 says, "The apostles and the brothers throughout Judea heard that the Gentiles also had received the word of God. So when Peter went up to Jerusalem, the circumcised believers criticized him." This would be utterly shocking were it not such a familiar pattern in both the pages of Scripture and the experiences of risk-taking evangelists throughout history!

Within a few days of reading that passage, I received an e-mail message from a pastor friend in Australia who is leading his church toward greater evangelistic fruitfulness. He wrote:

> Why didn't you tell me that a church committed to reaching the unchurched was so hard to build? The only criticism so far is from Christians. Pretty sad.
>
> However I'm pumped—it is so good to see people bringing their friends, and then telling us how much their friends enjoyed it. It cannot get much better.
>
> Your mate,
> (his name)

I wrote him back and quoted from Luis Palau's booklet, *Heart for the World:*

> From the least to greatest, all true evangelists have been criticized, attacked, and even persecuted. That shouldn't surprise us, for "everyone who wants to live a godly life in Christ Jesus will be persecuted" (2 Timothy 3:12).... Most people who evangelize create waves. And when you create waves, a lot of people get upset.... Nevertheless it's a sign that you're doing something right when certain people begin to get upset because of what you represent and preach.[5]

It's often said that pioneers are the ones who get shot at the most. This is never fun, and most of us never get used to it. But we must remain faithful to the mission to which God has called us. We have to remember that our marching orders are from Jesus himself and that he is able to sustain us.

Stay the course. Acknowledge setbacks and the mistakes you will inevitably make. Recast your biblical vision. Along the way, tell lots of stories of the ways God is using these endeavors.

So stay the course. Acknowledge setbacks and the mistakes you will inevitably make. Recast your biblical vision. Regroup your resources. Re-up your efforts. Along the way, tell lots of stories of the ways God is using these endeavors. Have people share fresh testimonies. Celebrate even small successes. Let the people in the congregation get a taste of the fruit that their prayers and hard work are producing.

Unswerving Devotion to Christ and His Message

I'll only mention this element briefly because I dealt with it at length in the last chapter: Beneath every evangelistic effort there must be a pure love for Christ and a wholehearted devotion to his gospel, which is "the power of God for the salvation of everyone who believes" (Romans 1:16). Incidentally, it's interesting to note that, as a general rule, the churches that are really growing around the world are those that have a high view of the Bible and place a strong emphasis on the message of salvation and the need for every person to trust in Christ—demonstrating that God uses those who work with him, in his way, for his purposes.

COMMITMENT TO PRAYER AND THE ROLE OF THE HOLY SPIRIT

We've talked a lot about evangelistic mission, values, and the 6-Stage Process. But let me remind you one more time about the Power behind the process.

- No one seeks God unless he first seeks them (Romans 3:11).
- No one loves God except that he first loved them (1 John 4:19).
- No one comes to the Father except that he draws them (John 6:44).
- There would be no salvation but for the cross of Jesus Christ (Hebrews 9:22; 1 Peter 3:18) and the power of the gospel message (Romans 1:16).
- God is the ultimate evangelist, and we are simply servants in his redemptive enterprise (John 16:8–11).

Billy Graham puts it this way in the article I quoted earlier:

> We are commanded to be faithful in proclaiming the Word—and yet, at the same time, every success, every advance, no matter how slight, is possible only because God has been at work by the Holy Spirit. The Spirit gives us the message, leads us to those he has prepared, and brings conviction of sin and new life. . . . When we understand that truth, we also will realize the urgency of prayer in evangelism. My own ministry, I am convinced, has only been possible because of the countless men and women who have prayed.[6]

As I began working on this book, I struggled to determine just where prayer fits in this process. Should it be stage 1? Prayer always seems to precede effective evangelism. I quickly realized, however, that prayer cannot be relegated to one step in the process—no, it must permeate every part of it! So I've tried to weave it in *at every stage.* It intersects and invades every step and gives it life. It is essential to the whole enterprise!

Billy Kim, the director of the Far East Broadcasting Company (FEBC), recently made this observation to over 6,000 leaders at the Baptist World Congress in Melbourne, Australia: "Prayer is my first advice. Prayer is my second suggestion. And prayer is my third suggestion. . . . If I had to do it all over, I would do more praying and less preaching."

Evangelism professor Lewis Drummond, in his book *The Word of the Cross,* says: "Prayer is probably the final answer to effective evangelism. It is a tremendous resource of power. . . . Prayer is essential to spiritual power in one's life and ministry, not to mention its centrality in revival. . . . Every great spiritual movement has been conceived, born, and matured in intercession."[7]

And Pastor Jim Cymbala of The Brooklyn Tabernacle says in *Fresh Wind, Fresh Fire,* "If we are courageous enough to go on the spiritual attack, to be mighty men and women of prayer and faith, there is no limit to what God can accomplish through us. . . . What counts is bringing God's power and light into a dark world, seeing local communities touched by God as churches turn back from perilous apathy to become Holy Spirit centers of divine activity."[8]

GOD IS STILL BUILDING HIS CHURCH

In the first chapter I told the story of "The Little Church that Could," Mount Carmel Community Church in Glennville, California—the town with an entire population of 130 people! God has done exciting things through the leaders and members of this once-tiny congregation.

At the other end of the spectrum, it's exciting to report what God is doing in places like Central Christian Church in Las Vegas, Nevada—a town with no shortage of lost people! A little more than a decade ago this church was clicking along quite comfortably with about 500 members. But Pastor Gene Appel and the leaders around him caught the vision for building a church to reach unchurched people, and, by God's grace, today they're averaging about 5,000 attenders at weekly services—a great number of whom came to Christ through the ministry of Central. In the ensuing period they've also planted a second church on the other side of the city, Canyon Ridge Christian Church, which is already averaging about 3,000 attenders per week. The two churches are now planning to start a third one—and a contagious movement is afoot!

Another thrilling story comes from New Hope Christian Fellowship in Honolulu, Hawaii. This church was planted by Wayne Cordeiro and a handful of people in 1995—and in five years it has already grown to over 6,000 attenders, and people are coming to faith so quickly the church can barely keep up with the requests for baptism. Good thing they have a big body of water nearby—the Pacific Ocean—so they can baptize a lot of people all at once!

These kinds of stories could be multiplied many times over, including the ones about Ginghamsburg United Methodist Church in Tipp City, Ohio; Mecklenburg Community Church in Charlotte, North Carolina; Mountaintop Community Church in Birmingham, Alabama; Orchard Hill Church in Wexford, Pennsylvania; Woodmen Valley Chapel in Colorado Springs, Colorado; and Mars Hill Bible Church in Grandville, Michigan—not to mention the well-publicized accounts of God's activity in Saddleback Valley Community Church in Lake Forest, California; and Willow Creek Community Church in South Barrington, Illinois.

There can be no doubt that God is up to something! More and more churches are becoming contagious! I recently received an e-mail message with this story from a newer church in the Chicago area:

> The baptism was incredible! 158 participants and packed services. The mom of one of our leaders came to watch her niece be baptized, and then accepted Christ herself at the first service. She then reconciled with her two daughters and asked to be baptized at the next service by her daughter with whom she had just reconciled! There are many more stories like this. We were all in *awe*! Praise God!

I hope your heart rejoices with mine over these exciting reports of God's activity in churches around the country—and we've barely mentioned the phenomenal work he's doing in other parts of the world!

Ultimately this book is not about any of these other churches; it's about *your* church and about what you and your team will do in cooperation with the Spirit to make it a more contagious place.

But ultimately this book is not about any of these other churches; it's about *your* church and about what you and your team will do in cooperation with the Spirit to make it a more contagious place. I'm convinced that this is what God wants to do. Jesus declared, "I will build my church" (Matthew 16:18). He explained that "this is to my Father's glory, that you bear much fruit" (John 15:8). And he told us to "go and make disciples" and promised that he would be with us, helping us at every step along the way (Matthew 28:19–20).

So, in light of what *God wants to do,* I can tell you with confidence that *you can do this!* With him by your side, you can build a highly contagious church that reaches increasing numbers of lost people. Act now; start with the heart, take the necessary steps, lean on God at all times, *and watch him use you!*

A daunting task? Yes, in some ways—but don't be frightened! Let me conclude by reminding you of the resources we have to back us up. We have:

- *The Father*—who "so loved the world that he gave his one and only Son"
- *Jesus Christ*—who came "to seek and to save what was lost" and "to give his life as a ransom for many"

- *The Holy Spirit*—who is right now convicting the world of sin, drawing people to Christ, and empowering us in our efforts
- *The Gospel*—which is "the power of God for the salvation of everyone who believes"
- *Prayer*—with the assurance that God "is able to do immeasurably more than all we ask or imagine"
- *The Church*—which, when it is working right, is a powerful magnet that attracts people into the new community
- *Spiritual Gifts*—with which God equips every member of his church for a strategic role in this great redemptive drama
- *The Word of God*—which is "sharper than any double-edged sword" and which will not return to God empty
- *The Promises of God*—which assure us of his protection, power, and provision
- *The Great Commission*—which reminds us that evangelism is God's idea and command and which promises Christ's presence with us, to the very end of the age, as we seek to fulfill his mission

God's divine power truly has given us "everything we need for life and godliness" (2 Peter 1:3)—and, I might add, for *ministry* as well! So I ask you, in the question posed by the apostle Paul, "If God is for us, who can be against us?" (Romans 8:31). God *is* for us. He's made that abundantly clear! And as we seek to build contagious churches that expand the borders of his kingdom, he'll be *with* us to help us complete the work.

To Consider and Discuss

1. Looking at the broader picture of a contagious church, are there areas *other than evangelism* where you think your church could use some shoring up in order to better reach and retain outsiders?
2. What could you do personally to help make the things you listed happen?
3. Reflect on the evangelistic growth rate for your church. Take an estimated number of people who trusted in Christ through the ministry of your church in the last year and who now attend, and divide it by your number of weekly attenders (for example, nine new believers, divided by 150 attenders, would come out as .06, or a six percent rate).

   ____ (came to Christ and attend), divided by _______ (average attendance) = ____%

If you'd like to see that number move up, what incremental gain will you pray and work toward, and by what date would you hope to reach it?

Desired rate: ____% by date: ____________

4. Skim through the headings in this chapter under the major section labeled "Elements for Building a Contagious Church." Identify the areas where a concentrated effort is most needed in your church, especially to reach your desired evangelistic growth rate. Rank by priority.

____

____

____

5. How can you best help your church make progress in these areas?
6. Take time to pray right now, alone or with your group, for the efforts of your church to reach increasing numbers of lost people for Christ.

As you take steps to build a contagious church, you'll undoubtedly have interesting and exciting stories to tell along the way. We'd like to hear them! Contact us at:

ContagiousChurch@willowcreek.org

Also, for information on our annual fall **Contagious Evangelism Conference**, which is designed to inspire and equip pastors, evangelism directors, and entire church leadership teams, contact the Willow Creek Association at 1–800–570–9812 (outside the United States call 1–847–765–6208), or visit us on the Web at www.willowcreek.com.

CHURCH AND MINISTRY LIST

CHURCHES MENTIONED

Willow Creek Community Church
67 East Algonquin Road,
South Barrington, IL 60010
Phone: (847) 765-5000
Fax: (847) 765-9222

Calvary Church Newport Mesa
190 East 23rd Street,
Costa Mesa, CA 92627
Phone: (949) 645-5050
Fax: (949) 645-1106

Canyon Ridge Christian Church
6200 West Lone Mountain Road,
Las Vegas, NV 89130
Phone: (702) 658-2722
Fax: (702) 658-9622

Mars Hill Bible Church
3501 Fairlanes Avenue SW,
Grandville, MI 49418
Phone: (616) 249-3337
Fax: (616) 249-3308

Mount Carmel Community Church
19 Dunlap Road, Glennville, CA 93226
Phone: (661) 536-8238
Fax: (661) 399-0188

Mt. Olivet Baptist Church
8501 North Chautauqua Boulevard,
Portland, OR 97217
Phone: (503) 240-7729
Fax: (503) 285-4668

New Hope Christian Fellowship O'ahu
290 Sand Island Access Road,
Honolulu, HI 96819
Phone: (808) 842-4242
Fax: (808) 842-4241

Orchard Hill Church
2551 Brandt School Road,
Wexford, PA 15090-7931
Phone: (724) 935-5555
Fax: (724) 935-6805

Southeast Christian Fellowship
3140 Q Street S.E.,
Washington, DC 20020
Phone: (202) 581-3387

CHURCHES DISCUSSED UNDER THE SIX STYLES OF EVANGELISM

Chapter 10: The Confrontational Style

First Baptist Church
Story Title: A Synergistic Combination
506 Legacy Drive, Smyrna, TN 37167
Phone: (615) 459-3311
E-mail: sharejesus@eeinternational.org
Contact: Shelby Smith

New Hope Baptist Church
Story Title: A Synergistic Combination
551 New Hope Rd., Fayetteville, GA 30214
Phone: (770) 461-4337
Fax: (770) 460-9933
E-mail: megg@newhopebc.org
Contact: Meg Groce

Tabernacle Church of Norfolk
Story Title: Variations on Visitations
7000 Granby Street, Norfolk, VA 23505
Phone: (757) 440-8224
Fax: (757) 423-8941
E-mail: Barbking2@aol.com
Web: www.TABChurch.org
Contact: Barbara King

First Presbyterian Church
Story Title: Variations on Visitations
P.O. Box 2006, Baton Rouge, LA 70821
Phone: (225) 387-0617
E-mail: Ferguson.td@fpcbr.com /
tdoug34@aol.com
Contact: Doug Ferguson
See Also: *Serving Style*

South Hills Community Church
Story Title: Variations on Visitations
36 W. Springer Dr.,
Highlands Ranch, CO 80126
Phone: (303) 346-9200
E-mail: sohills@ecentral.com
Contact: Ken Bartlett
See Also: *Intellectual Style*

Corinth Reformed Church
Story Title: A Mugging Ministry
129 - 100th St. SE,
Byron Center, MI 49315
Phone: (616) 477-4652
Fax: (616) 877-0327
E-mail:
kevinharney@corinthreformed.org
Contact: Kevin Harney
See Also: *Serving Style*

Victory Point Ministries
Story Title: Reaching Crowds at Home
11598 E. Lakewood Blvd.,
Holland, MI 49424
Phone: (616) 738-1800
Fax: (616) 393-0093
E-mail: ninal@vpm.org
Contact: Matt McMann

Northeast Christian Church
Story Title: Reaching Crowds at Home
9900 Old Brownsboro Road,
Louisville, KY 40241
Phone: (502) 426-6668
Fax: (502) 426-9974
E-mail: ronkastens@necchurch.org
Contact: Ron Kastens

Mountain Top Community Church
Story Title: Reaching Crowds at Home
2221 Old Columbiana Rd.,
Birmingham, AL 35243
Phone: (205) 823-7090
E-mail: office@mountaintopchurch.com
Contact: Nancy Macrina

Eastview Christian Church
Story Title: Back to Basics
P.O. Box 1687, Bloomington, IL 61702
Phone: (309) 451-5000
Fax: (309) 888-9903
Contact: Ken Osness

CrossWinds Church
Story Title: Advancing on a Retreat
6444 Sierra Ct., Dublin, CA 94568-2692
Phone: (925) 551-3300
Fax: (925) 551-3739
E-mail: mcutrone@crosswindschurch.org
Contact: Marty Cutrone

Park Cities Baptist Church
Story Title: A Strategic Student Thing
P.O. Box 12068, Dallas, TX 75225
Phone: (214) 860-1500
E-mail: jchenson@pcbc.org
Contact: John Henson
See Also: *Interpersonal Style*

1st Assembly of God
Story Title: In Dramatic Fashion
2725 Merle Hay Road,
Des Moines, IA 50310
Phone: (515) 279-9766
E-mail: mailus@dsm1ag.org
Contact: Richard Hardy / Rick Junkins
See Also: *Intellectual, Invitational Styles*

First Assembly of God
Story Title: In Dramatic Fashion
10700 - 75th St., Kenosha, WI 53142
Phone: (262) 694-3300
E-mail:
postoffice@kenoshafirstassembly.org
Contact: David Duncan

CHAPTER 11: THE INTELLECTUAL STYLE

Windsor Crossing Community Church
Story Title: Utilizing Weekends
P.O. Box 6456, Chesterfield, MO 63006
Phone: (636) 532-1212
Fax: (636) 225-8627
E-mail: gregholder@primary.net
Contact: Greg Holder

Scottsdale Family Church
Story Title: Utilizing Weekends
10135 East Via Linda, Suite 224,
Scottsdale, AZ 85258
Phone: (480) 614-0001
E-mail:
alann@scottsdalefamilychurch.org
Contact: Alan Nelson

Chesapeake Church
Story Title: Utilizing Weekends
6201 Solomons Island Road,
Huntingtown, MD 20639-0936
Phone: (410) 257-0700
Fax: (410) 257-0296
E-mail: sch7@chesapeake.net
Contact: Sandy Holmbo
See Also: *Invitational Style*

Kensington Community Church
Story Title: Discoveries Made Here
1735 E. Big Beaver, Suite B,
Troy MI 48083
Phone: (248) 689-3200
E-mail: gary4an@yahoo.com
Contact: Gary Foran
See Also: *Testimonial Style*

Mosaic
Story Title: Better than a 2 x 4
715 S. Brady Ave.,
Los Angeles, CA 90022
Phone: (323) 728-4850
E-mail: info@mosaic.org
Contact: Erwin R. McManus
See Also: Testimonial Style

Central Christian Church
Story Title: Hot Topic Zone
1000 Marks St., Henderson, NV 89015
Phone: (702) 735-4004
E-mail: ptrainor@centralchristian.com
Contact: Paul Trainor

Evergreen Baptist Church of LA
Story Title: A Guided Journey
1255 San Gabriel Blvd.,
Rosemead, CA 91220
Phone: (626) 280-0477
Fax: (626) 280-3892
E-mail: kfong@ebcla.org
Contact: Mike Nakajima

Hudson Community Chapel
Story Title: Student Skeptics Forum
46 E. Ravenna St. B-3,
Hudson, OH 44236
Phone: (330) 650-9533
E-mail: jacoffey1@aol.com
Contact: Joe Coffey
See Also: *Testimonial Style*

Wooddale Church
Story Title: Friend to Friend
6630 Shady Oak Rd.,
Eden Prairie, MN 55344
Phone: (952) 944-6300
Contact: Ken Geis

Christ Presbyterian Church
Story Title: Christianity 101
6901 Normandale Rd., Edina, MN 55435
Phone: (612) 920-8515
E-mail: kevin@cpconline.org
Contact: Kevin Sharpe
See Also: *Interpersonal Style*

Crossroads Community Church of Hyde Park
Story Title: The Ultimate Quest / Harnessing the Potential of Books
3500 Madison Road,
Cincinnati, Ohio 45209
Phone: (513) 731-7400
E-mail: bwells@crossroadscommunity.net
Contact: Brian Wells
See Also: *Serving Style*

South Hills Community Church
Story Title: The Written Word
36 W. Springer Dr.,
Highlands Ranch, CO 80126
Phone: (303) 346-9200
E-mail: sohills@ecentral.com
Contact: Ken Bartlett
See Also: *Confrontational Style*

Woodmen Valley Chapel
Story Title: The Wisest Word
477 Woodmen Road,
Colorado Springs, CO 80918
Phone: (719) 599-8652
Fax: (719) 592-9305
E-mail: info@wvchapel.org
See Also: *Interpersonal Style*

1st Assembly of God
Story Title: "That's a Good Question"
2725 Merle Hay Road,
Des Moines, IA 50310
Phone: (515) 279-9766
E-mail: mailus@dsm1ag.org
Contact: Richard Hardy / Rick Junkins
See Also: *Confrontational, Invitational Styles*

Windsor Crossing Community Church
Story Title: Innovating on the Internet
P.O. Box 6456, Chesterfield, MO 63006
Phone: (636) 532-1212
Fax: (636) 225-8627
E-mail: gregholder@primary.net
Contact: Greg Holder

Central Christian Church
Story Title: Sound Reasoning
1000 Marks St., Henderson, NV 89015
Phone: (702) 735-4004
E-mail: ptrainor@centralchristian.com
Contact: Paul Trainor

Xenos Christian Fellowship
Story Title: The Crossroads Project
1340 Community Park Drive,
Columbus, OH 43229
Phone: (614) 823-6500
Fax: (614) 823-6530
E-mail: leffelj@xenos.org
Contact: Jim Leffel

CHAPTER 12: THE TESTIMONIAL STYLE

Saddleback Valley Community Church
Story Title: A Parade of "Satisfied Customers"
1 Saddleback Parkway,
Lake Forest, CA 92630
Phone: (949) 609-8700
Fax: (949) 609-8702
See Also: *Invitational Style*

Hudson Community Chapel
Story Title: A Powerful Picture
46 E. Ravenna St. B-3,
Hudson, OH 44236
Phone: (330) 650-9533
E-mail: jacoffey1@aol.com
Contact: Joe Coffey
See Also: *Intellectual Style*

Ginghamsburg United Methodist Church
Story Title: "Changed Life" Communication Channels
6759 S. Country Rd. 25A,
Tipp City, OH 45371
Phone: (937) 667-1069
Fax: (937) 667-5677
E-mail: tkelley@gum-net.org
Contact: Tammy Kelley
See Also: *Invitational Style*

Pantego Bible Church
Story Title: Video Stories
2203 West Park Row,
Arlington, TX 76013
Phone: (817) 274-1315
E-mail: clyde@pantego.org
Contact: Clyde Hodson
See Also: *Interpersonal Style*

Mosaic
Story Title: Testimonies in a Multicultural Context
715 S. Brady Ave.,
Los Angeles, CA 90022
Phone: (323) 728-4850
E-mail: info@mosaic.org
Contact: Erwin R. McManus
See Also: *Intellectual Style*

Menlo Park Presbyterian Church
Story Title: Straight Talk
950 Santa Cruz Avenue,
Menlo Park, CA 94025-4682
Phone: (650) 323-8600
Fax: (650) 323-8645
E-mail: virginia_woodson@mppc.org
Contact: Virginia Woodson
See Also: *Invitational Style*

Manito Presbyterian Church
Story Title: Strategic Saturdays
401 East 30th, Spokane, WA 99203
Phone: (509) 838-3559
E-mail: saltandlight@pcartisan.com
Contact: David Smith

Faith Evangelical Free Church
Story Title: Winging It
4727 Broadway St.,
Manitowoc, WI 54220
Phone: (920) 684-7208
E-mail: bzahn@lakefield.net
Contact: Barb Zahn

Walnut Hill Community Church
Story Title: Dramatic Moments
395 W. Bloomfield Rd.,
Pittsford, NY 14534
Phone: (716) 383-0670
E-mail: whcc@frontiernet.net
Contact: Chip Toth

Blythefield Hills Baptist Church
Story Title: Multiple Fronts
6727 Kuttshill Dr., Rockford, MI 49341
Phone: (616) 688-9597
E-mail: thoytbhbc@aol.com
Contact: Tim Hoyt
See Also: *Invitational, Serving Styles*

Kensington Community Church
Story Title: The Potential of Baptism Services
1735 E. Big Beaver, Suite B,
Troy MI 48083
Phone: (248) 689-3200
E-mail: gary4an@yahoo.com
Contact: Gary Foran
See Also: *Intellectual Style*

Church of God, Rolla
Story Title: Read All About It!
400 Olive, Rolla, MO 65401
Phone: (573) 364-1025
E-mail: joncarol@fidnet.com
Contact: Carol Hudler

CHAPTER 13: THE INTERPERSONAL STYLE

Park Cities Baptist Church
Story Title: Fastbreak
P.O. Box 12068,
Dallas, TX 75225
Phone: (214) 860-1500
E-mail: jchenson@pcbc.org
Contact: John Henson
See Also: *Confrontational Style*

Pantego Bible Church
Story Title: Small Group Outreach
2203 West Park Row,
Arlington, TX 76013
Phone: (817) 274-1315
E-mail: clyde@pantego.org
Contact: Clyde Hodson
See Also: *Testimonial Style*

West Broad Church of the Nazarene
Story Title: How to Be a Better Neighbor
52 Woodlawn Ave.,
Columbus, OH 53228
Phone: (614) 878-3829
E-mail: boxman13@aol.com
Contact: Bob Butler

Walnut Creek Christian Reformed Church
Story Title: Friendship Group
860 Bancroft Rd.,
Walnut Creek, CA 94598
Phone: (925) 934-2099
E-mail: jdykstra@wccrc.com
Contact: Jerry Dykstra

Orchard Hill Church
Story Title: A New Home
1215 Elmridge Dr., Cedar Falls, IA 50613
Phone: (319) 266-9796
E-mail: orchardh@aol.com
Contact: David Bartlett

Northside Christian Church
Story Title: Food for Thought
2801 Grant Line Rd.,
New Albany, IN 47150
Phone: (812) 945-8704
E-mail: george.ross@ncc-in.org
Contact: Vince Garmen
See Also: *Serving Style*

Pantano Christian Church
Story Title: Half-and-Half
10355 E. 29th St., Tucson, AZ 85748
Phone: (520) 298-5395
Fax: (520) 885-7182
E-mail: kerygma101@aol.com
Contact: Kurt Berger

Grace Church
Story Title: Fit for Faith
5731 Northwestern Ave.,
Racine, WI 53406
Phone: (262) 632-2111
E-mail: grace@wi.net
Contact: Rusty Hayes

Christ Presbyterian Church
Story Title: Dessert Outreach
6901 Normandale Rd., Edina, MN 55435
Phone: (612) 920-8515
E-mail: kevin@cpconline.org
Contact: Kevin Sharpe
See Also: *Intellectual Style*

Woodmen Valley Chapel
Story Title: Punch or Tea?
477 Woodmen Road,
Colorado Springs, CO 80918
Phone: (719) 599-8652
Fax: (719) 592-9305
E-mail: info@wvchapel.org
See Also: *Intellectual Style*

First United Methodist Church
Story Title: Moving Out
1315 Concord Rd., Smyrna, GA 30080
Phone: (770) 436-4108
E-mail: ljc576@aol.com
Contact: Linda Carroll

Kelloggsville Christian Reformed Church
Story Title: Giving a Break
610 - 52nd St. SE, Kentwood, MI 49548
Phone: (616) 534-0085
Contact: Diane Dykgraaf / Maury De Young

Westlake Church
Story Title: Needed Support
rue Juste-Olivier, CH 1260,
Nyon, Switzerland
Phone: (011) 41-22-990-24-50
Contact: Becky Luedtke

CHAPTER 14: THE INVITATIONAL STYLE

Emmanuel Reformed Church
Story Title: The Alpha Experience
15941 Virginia Ave.,
Paramount, CA 90723
Phone: (562) 531-6820
E-mail:
bobjohnson@emmanuel-church.org
Contact: Robert Johnson / Bill White

The Peak Community Church
Story Title: A Synergistic Combination
900 Auraria Parkway Suite 227A,
Denver, CO 80204
Phone: (303) 620-0085
Contact: Derek Rust / Gary Wilkerson

Emmanuel Reformed Church
Story Title: A Delayed Service
15941 Virginia Ave.,
Paramount, CA 90723
Phone: (562) 531-6820
E-mail:
bobjohnson@emmanuel-church.org
Contact: Robert Johnson / Bill White

Bridgeway Community Church
Story Title: F.R.A.N.K. Services
10451 Twin Rivers Rd. #251,
Columbia, MD 21044
Phone: (410) 992-5832
E-mail: info@bridgecom.org
Contact: David Anderson

Menlo Park Presbyterian Church
Story Title: A Weekend for Eternity
950 Santa Cruz Avenue,
Menlo Park, CA 94025-4682
Phone: (650) 323-8600
Fax: (650) 323-8645
E-mail: virginia_woodson@mppc.org
Contact: Virginia Woodson
See Also: *Testimonial Style*

Chesapeake Church
Story Title: RainbowLand Week
6201 Solomons Island Road,
Huntingtown, MD 20639-0936
Phone: (410) 257-0700
Fax: (410) 257-0296
E-mail: sch7@chesapeake.net
Contact: Debi Filippi / Sandy Holmbo
See Also: *Intellectual Style*

Ginghamsburg United Methodist Church
Story Title: An Integrated Approach
6759 S. Country Rd. 25A,
Tipp City, OH 45371
Phone: (937) 667-1069
Fax: (937) 667-5677
E-mail: tkelley@gum-net.org
Contact: Tammy Kelley
See Also: *Testimonial Style*

Crossroads Community Church
Story Title: Going Public
594 North Lafayette,
South Lyon, MI 48178
Phone: (248) 486-0400
E-mail: markfreier@crossroads-sl.org
Contact: Mark R. Freier

Hope College Chapel
Story Title: Entering Students' World
141 E. 12th St., Holland, MI 49422-9000
Phone: (616) 395-7966
E-mail: speese@hope.edu
Contact: Cheri Speese

University Baptist Church
Story Title: Christmas Pageants &
Matthew Parties
624 Anastasia Ave.,
Coral Gables, FL 33134
Phone: (305) 448-4428 ext. 251
E-mail: riveraubc@yahoo.com
Contact: Robert Rivera

Cherry Hills Community Church
Story Title: Love Thy Neighborhood
3900 E. Grace Blvd.,
Highlands Ranch, CO 80126
Phone: (303) 791-4100
E-mail: sfernalld@chcc.org
Contact: Steve Fernalld

Mecklenburg Community Church
Story Title: Internet Invitations
8335 Browne Road, Charlotte, NC 28269
Phone: (704) 598-9800
Fax: (704) 598-1115
E-mail: lreeb@mecklenburg.org
Contact: Lloyd Reeb

Palm Beach Community Church
Story Title: Postal Potential
3970 RCA Blvd., Suite 7009,
Palm Beach Gardens, FL 33410
Phone: (561) 626-5683
E-mail: liz@pencilandpixel.com
Contact: Liz Heart

South Hills Community Church
Story Title: Seizing a Strategic
Opportunity
6601 Camden Ave.,
San Jose, CA 95120-1998
Phone: (408) 268-1676
Fax: (408) 997-8324
E-mail: markw@south-hillschurch.org
Contact: Mark Weimer

New Heights Church
Story Title: No Tickets Needed
2601 Crossroads Dr., Suite 165,
Madison, WI 53719
Phone: (608) 244-3400
Fax: (608) 244-0645
Contact: Bill Rushing

Vineyard Community Church
Story Title: In Good Taste
4029 South Higuera,
San Luis Obispo, CA 93401
Phone: (805) 543-3162
Fax: (805) 543-5369
E-mail: info@slovine.org
Contact: Thom O'Leary

1st Assembly of God
Story Title: A Sweet Idea
2725 Merle Hay Road,
Des Moines, IA 50310
Phone: (515) 279-9766
E-mail: mailus@dsm1ag.org
Contact: Richard Hardy / Rick Junkins
See Also: *Confrontational, Intellectual Styles*

Crossroads Christian Church
Story Title: A Sporting Chance / From Jazz to Jesus
4190 Todds Rd., Lexington, KY 40509
Phone: (606) 263-4633
E-mail: mssmlove@aol.com
Contact: Mark S. Love

Mountain Park Community Church
Story Title: Maximizing the Season
2408 E. Pecos Rd.,
Phoenix, AZ 85048
Phone: (480) 759-6200
Fax: (480) 759-9686
E-mail: mpcc@mountainpark.
Contact: Carma Wood
See Also: *Serving Style*

Blythefield Hills Baptist Church
Story Title: Invitational Options
6727 Kuttshill Dr., Rockford, MI 49341
Phone: (616) 688-9597
E-mail: thoytbhbc@aol.com
Contact: Tim Hoyt
See Also: *Testimonial, Serving Styles*

Saddleback Valley Community Church
Story Title: Summer's End
1 Saddleback Parkway,
Lake Forest, CA 92630
Phone: (949) 609-8700
Fax: (949) 609-8702
See Also: *Testimonial Style*

Chapter 15: The Serving Style

Vineyard Community Church
Story Title: Intentional Acts of Kindness
11340 Century Circle East,
Cincinnati, OH 45246
Phone: (513) 671-0422
Fax: (513) 671-2041
Contact: John Sinclair

Corinth Reformed Church
Story Title: Marilyn Manson and Mountain Dew
129 - 100th St., Byron Center, MI 49315
Phone: (616) 877-4652
Fax: (616) 877-0327
E-mail: kharney@corinthreformed.org
Contact: Kevin Harney
See Also: *Confrontational Style*

Heartland Community Church
Story Title: From the Heartland
619 Vermont Street, Lawrence, KS 66044
Phone: (785) 832-1845
Fax: (785) 832-9521
E-mail: hartlandcc@sunflower.com
Contact: Paul Gray

Rocky Mountain Christian Church
Story Title: Prayer Evangelism
9447 Niwot Road, Niwot, CO 80503
Phone: (303) 652-2211
Fax: (303) 652-8072
E-mail: jmiller@rmcc.org
Contact: Judy Miller

Mountain Park Community Church
Story Title: Backpacks and Angels
2408 E. Pecos Rd.,
Phoenix, AZ 85048
Phone: (480) 759-6200
Fax: (480) 759-9686
E-mail: mpcc@mountainpark.org
Contact: Carma Wood
See Also: *Invitational Style*

Second Christian Reformed Church
Story Title: The Last Call
2021 Sheldon Ave.,
Grand Haven, MI 49417
Phone: (616) 842-0710
Fax: (616) 842-2097
Contact: Pastor Rob Byker
See Also: *Interpersonal Style*

Beulah Alliance Church
Story Title: Redemptive Recovery
17504 - 98A Ave.,
Edmonton ALTA. Canada T5T 5T8
Phone: (780) 486-4010
E-mail: ktaylor@beulah-cma.org
Contact: Keith Taylor

First Baptist Church
Story Title: Social Assistance
209 Beach St., Revere, MA 02151
Phone: (781) 284-4550
E-mail: fbcrevere@juno.com
Contact: Charles Oblom

Manhattan Bible Church
Story Title: Serving "Sin City"
401 W. 205th St., New York, NY 10034
Phone: (212) 567-2276
Fax: (212) 567-5218
E-mail: mbcny@hotmail.com
Contact: Pastor Willie Bobe

Chinese Community Church
Story Title: Ministering to Immigrants
900 Massachusetts Ave. NW,
Washington D.C., 20001
Phone: (204) 647-9858
E-mail: tengpresby@aol.com
Contact: Rev. Bill Teng

Cedar Ridge Community Church
Story Title: Supporting Refugees
2410 Spencerville Rd.,
Spencerville, MD 20868
Phone: (301) 384-7444
E-mail: briancrcc@aol.com
Contact: Brian McLaren

Northside Christian Church
Story Title: Building Trust
2801 Grant Line Rd.,
New Albany, IN 47150
Phone: (812) 945-8704
E-mail: george.ross@ncc-in.org
Contact: Vince Garmen
See Also: *Interpersonal Style*

Blythefield Hills Baptist Church
Story Title: Small Groups Serving Big
6727 Kuttshill Dr., Rockford, MI 49341
Phone: (616) 688-9597
E-mail: thoytbhbc@aol.com
Contact: Tim Hoyt
See Also: *Testimonial, Invitational Styles*

Riverside Church
Story Title: A Full-Service Fellowship
207 E. Michigan Ave.,
Three Rivers, MI 49093
Phone: (616) 273-8723
E-mail: trcf1@net-link.net
Contact: Rev. Darren Maracin

Crossroads Community Church of Hyde Park
Story Title: A Foundation for Truth
3500 Madison Road,
Cincinnati, OH 45209
Phone: (513) 731-7400
E-mail: bwells@crossroadscommunity.net
Contact: Brian Wells
See Also: *Intellectual Style*

First Presbyterian Church
Story Title: Threads of Love
P.O. Box 2006, Baton Rouge, LA 70821
Phone: (225) 387-0617
E-mail: ferguson.td@fpcbr.com / tdoug34@aol.com
Contact: Doug Ferguson
See Also: *Confrontational Style*

MINISTRIES MENTIONED

Willow Creek Association
67 East Algonquin Road,
South Barrington, IL 60010
Phone: (847) 765-0070
For Willow Creek Resources (800) 570-9812
Fax: (847) 765-5046

Alpha International Office
Holy Trinity Brompton,
Brompton Road,
London SW7-1JA, England
Phone: 44-20-7581-8255
Fax: 44-20-7584-8536

Alpha North America
109 East 50th Street,
New York, NY 10022
Phone: (212) 378 0292
Fax: (212)-378-0262

Answers In Action
P.O. Box 2067,
Costa Mesa, CA 92628-2067
Phone: (949) 646-9042
Fax: (949) 646-0603

Athletes In Action
P.O. Box 588, Lebanon, OH 45036
Phone: (513) 933-2421
E-mail: aiacom@aol.com

Barna Research Group, Ltd.
5528 Everglades Street,
Ventura, CA 93003
Phone: (805) 658-8885
Fax: (805) 658-7298

Billy Graham Center, Wheaton College
500 College Avenue,
Wheaton, IL 60187-5593
Phone: (630) 752-5918
Fax: (630) 752-5916

Billy Graham Evangelistic Association
1300 Harmon Place,
Minneapolis, MN 55403
Phone: (612) 338-0500

Campus Crusade for Christ
100 Lake Heart Drive, Orlando FL 32859
Phone: (407) 826-2000

Christian Business Men's Committee (CBMC)
1800 McCallie Avenue,
Chattanooga, TN 37404
Phone: (423) 698-4444
Fax: (423) 629-4434

Compassion International
3955 Cragwood Drive,
Colorado Springs, CO 80918
Phone: (719) 594-9900
Fax: (719) 594-6271

Evangelism Explosion International
5554 N. Federal Highway,
Fort Lauderdale, FL 33308
Phone: (954) 491-6100
Fax: (954) 771-2256

Faith Studies International
PO Box 786, Chanhassen, MN 55317
Phone: (952) 401-4501 or (800) 964-1447
Fax: (952) 401-4504
E-mail: FSMN@faithstudies.org

Fellowship of Christian Athletes
8701 Leeds Road,
Kansas City, MO 64129
Phone: (816) 921-0909

Habitat For Humanity International
Partner Service Center,
121 Habitat Street,
Americus, GA 31709
Phone: (912) 924-6935, ext. 2552
E-mail: public_Info@Habitat.org

Intercristo
19303 Fremont Ave. North,
Seattle, WA 98133
Phone: (206) 546-7330
Fax: (206) 546-7375

International Bible Society
1820 Jet Stream Drive,
Colorado Springs, CO 80921
Phone: (719) 488-9200
Fax: (719) 488-0870

InterVarsity Christian Fellowship
6400 Schroeder Road, Madison, WI 53711
Phone: (608) 274-9001
Fax: (608) 274-7882

Luis Palau Evangelistic Association
1500 N. W. 167th Place,
Beaverton, OR 97006
Phone: (503) 614-1500
Fax: (503) 614-1599

Mission America / Lighthouse Movement
5660 Lincoln Drive, Suite 100,
Edina, MN 55436
Phone: (612) 912-0001
Fax: (612) 912-0002
E-mail: info@lighthousemovement.com

Moody Broadcasting Network
820 N. La Salle Boulevard,
Chicago, IL 60610
Phone: (312) 329-2034

The Navigators
3820 North 30th Street,
Colorado Springs, CO 80904
Phone: (719) 598-1212
Fax: (719) 260-0479

Neighborly Evangelism Ministries
9824 W. Girton Drive,
Lakewood, CO 80227
Phone: (800) 838-4368
Fax: (303) 969-8689

Network Ministries International
25108 B Marguerite Pkwy, Suite 217
Mission Viejo, CA 92692
Phone: (949) 588-1533
Fax: (949) 768-8076

New Tribes Mission International Headquarters
1000 E. First Street, Sanford, FL 32771
Phone: (407) 323-3430

Prison Fellowship
1856 Old Reston Avenue,
Reston, VA 20190
Phone: (703) 834-3675
Fax: (703) 834-3658

Proactive Evangelism Ministries
P.O. Box 1251,
Douglasville, GA 30133-1251
Phone: (770) 949-9674
Fax: (770) 949-5181
E-mail: Proact1@aol.com

Probe Ministries
2025 Guadalupe, Suite 248,
Austin, TX 78705
Phone: (512)505-0105
Fax: (512) 505-0110

Purpose-Driven Ministries
Saddleback Valley Community Church,
1 Saddleback Parkway,
Lake Forest, CA 92630
Phone: (949) 609-8700
Fax: (949) 609-8702

Salvation Army International Headquarters
101 Queen Victoria Street,
London EC4P 4EP, United Kingdom
Phone: 44-20-7332-0101
Fax: 44-20-7236-4981

Salvation Army USA Headquarters
615 Slaters Lane, Alexandria, VA 22313
Phone: (703) 684-5500
Fax: (703) 684-3478

Samaritan's Purse
801 Bamboo Road, Boone, NC 28607
Phone: (828) 262-1980
Fax: (828) 266-1053

Servant Evangelism
Vineyard Community Church,
11340 Century Circle East,
Cincinnati, OH 45246
Phone: (513) 671-0422
Fax: (513) 671-2041

Sonlife Ministries
526 N. Main, Elburn, IL 60119
Phone: (630) 365-5855
Fax: (630) 365-5892

Sports Outreach America
P.O. Box 3566,
Grand Rapids, MI 49501-3566

2100 Productions
c/o InterVarsity Christian Fellowship,
6400 Schroeder Road,
Madison, WI 53711
Phone: (608) 274-9001
Fax: (608) 274-7882

World Relief
450 Gundersen Drive,
Carol Stream, IL 60188
Phone: (630) 665-0235
Fax: (630) 665-0129

World Vision, Inc.
34834 Weyerhaeuser Way South,
Federal Way, WA 98001
Phone: (253) 815-1000

Youth for Christ
7670 S Vaughn Ct.,
Englewood, CO 80112
Phone: (303) 843-9000
Fax: (303) 843-9002

NOTES

Chapter One

1. Cited by George Barna in his seminar and handbook "What Effective Churches Have Discovered," 1996. Very recent studies, however, indicate an encouraging upward trend in churches providing evangelism training.

2. Bill Hybels and Mark Mittelberg, *Becoming a Contagious Christian* (Grand Rapids: Zondervan, 1994); Mark Mittelberg, Lee Strobel, and Bill Hybels, *Becoming a Contagious Christian* evangelism course (Grand Rapids, Zondervan, 1995).

3. Henry Blackaby and Claude King, *Experiencing God: Knowing and Doing the Will of God* (Nashville: LifeWay Christian Resources, 1990).

Chapter Two

1. Ruth A. Tucker, *From Jerusalem to Irian Jaya: A Biographical History of Christian Missions* (Grand Rapids: Zondervan, 1983), 173.

2. This expanding drawing is built on the classic "Bridge Illustration" originally developed by the Navigators. The Bridge illustration has been used by God to reach countless non-Christians over the last several decades. We teach a personalized version of the Bridge illustration, with permission from NavPress, in the *Becoming a Contagious Christian* evangelism training course (Session 5) and book (chapter 11).

3. For details on Lee's story and the facts that convinced him, I highly recommend reading, and then giving to others, his groundbreaking book, *The Case for Christ* (Grand Rapids: Zondervan, 1998).

4. Tim Celek and Dieter Zander, with Patrick Kampert, *Inside the Soul of a New Generation* (Grand Rapids: Zondervan, 1996).

5. Rodney Clapp, *A Peculiar People: The Church As Culture in a Post-Christian Society* (Downers Grove, Ill.: InterVarsity Press, 1996), 167.

6. Clapp, *A Peculiar People,* 194–95.

7. Billy Graham, "Recovering the Primacy of Evangelism," *Christianity Today,* 8 December 1997, 27.

8. To see a listing of these elements by subject, log on to the Willow Creek Web site at www.willowcreek.com and click on "ServiceBuilder."

9. Don Richardson, *Eternity in Their Hearts* (Ventura, Calif.: Regal, 1984).

10. George Barna, *The Habits of Highly Effective Churches* (Ventura, Calif.: Regal, 1999), 109.

11. *Equipping for Evangelism* (Minneapolis: World Wide Publications, 1996), 362.

Chapter 3

1. George Barna, *The Barna Report,* vol. 1, no. 1 (1996), 1. This bimonthly newsletter for church leaders is full of the latest in American demographic research. To order, call 1-800-933-9673, ext. 2037.

2. Mark Mittelberg, Lee Strobel, and Bill Hybels, *Becoming a Contagious Christian* evangelism course (Grand Rapids: Zondervan, 1995).

3. This message is adapted from Bill Hybels, "Philosophy of Ministry," Seeds Tape #C9102. We are discussing only the first three steps of this seven-step strategy because they are the ones that relate directly to evangelism. The others, which come after a person has trusted in Christ, are as follows: (4) participation in our midweek worship services, (5) involvement in a small group, (6) service in the church according to spiritual gifts, and (7) stewardship of resources to build the kingdom. From there a person should spiritually reproduce by going back to step 1, building relationships with others who are outside the family; 2, sharing a verbal witness with them; and 3, bringing them to outreach events—and so the cycle continues. Tapes of Bill Hybels presenting the seven-step strategy are available through the Willow Creek Association. Call 1-800-570-9812 (outside the United States call 1-847-765-6208) or log on at www.willowcreek.com.

4. Sterling Huston, *Crusade Evangelism and the Local Church* (Minneapolis: World Wide Publications, 1984), 52–53.

Chapter 4

1. Sam Walton, *Sam Walton, Made in America: My Story* (New York: Doubleday, 1992), 188.

2. George Barna, *Evangelism That Works* (Ventura, Calif.: Gospel Light, 1995), 90.

3. Robert Coleman, *The Master Plan of Evangelism,* 2d ed. (Grand Rapids: Revell, 1993).

4. Rebecca Manley Pippert, *Out of the Saltshaker & into the World* (Downers Grove, Ill.: InterVarsity Press, 1979, updated 1999).

5. Joe Aldrich, *Lifestyle Evangelism* (Portland, Ore.: Multnomah, 1999).

6. Jim Cymbala, *Fresh Wind, Fresh Fire* (Grand Rapids: Zondervan, 1997), 182.

7. George Gallup, Jr. and Jim Castelli, *The People's Religion* (New York: Macmillan, 1989).

8. Jim Petersen, *Evangelism as a Lifestyle* (Colorado Springs: NavPress, 1980); *Living Proof—Evangelism,* 12-session video curriculum (Grand Rapids: Zondervan, 1996).

9. D. James Kennedy, *Evangelism Explosion,* 4th ed. (Wheaton, Ill.: Tyndale, 1996).

10. Luis Palau, *Say Yes: How to Renew Your Spiritual Passion* (Grand Rapids: Discovery House, 1995), 145.

11. Robert Coleman, *Singing with the Angels* (Grand Rapids: Revell, 1998), 65.

12. Bill Hybels, "One Life at a Time," Seeds Tape #C9901 (available through the Willow Creek Association at 1-800-570-9812).

13. Lee Strobel, Mark Mittelberg, and Garry Poole, "The Unexpected Adventure," Seeds Tapes #C9805–C9809 (available through the Willow Creek Association at 1-800-570-9812).

14. "When We Move Out," Moody Cassette Ministry. For information call 1-800-MBN-1224.

15. The *Jesus* film (Inspirational Films, Inc.) is available on video from Campus Crusade for Christ at 1-949-361-4425, or online at www.jesusfilm.org.

16. *The Harvest* video is available through Venture Media, 100 Sunport Lane, Orlando, Florida 32809, telephone 1-800-729-4351, or online at www.theharvest.com.

17. The "*EE-TAOW*" video is available from New Tribes Mission, 1000 E. 1st St., Sanford, Florida 32771-1487, telephone 1-800-321-5375

18. Lyle Dorsett, *A Passion for Souls* (Chicago: Moody Press, 1997).

19. Billy Graham, *Just As I Am: An Autobiography of Billy Graham* (San Francisco: HarperSanFrancisco, 1997).

20. Rick Warren, *The Purpose-Driven® Church* (Grand Rapids: Zondervan, 1995).

21. Bill Hybels and Lynne Hybels, *Rediscovering Church* (Grand Rapids: Zondervan, 1995).

22. *The Journey (NIV): A Bible for Seeking God and Understanding Life* (Grand Rapids: Zondervan & Willow Creek Association, 1996).

23. Charles Swindoll, *Come Before Winter and Share My Hope* (Grand Rapids: Zondervan, 1994; originally published by Multnomah, 1985), 160–62.

Chapter 5

1. Rick Warren, *The Purpose-Driven® Church* (Grand Rapids: Zondervan, 1995), 82.

2. Sam Walton, *Sam Walton, Made in America: My Story* (New York: Doubleday, 1992), 173.

3. Walton, *Sam Walton, Made in America,* 221.

4. Walton, *Sam Walton, Made in America,* 223.

5. Wayne Cordeiro, *Doing Church as a Team* (Honolulu, Hawaii: New Hope Christian Fellowship O'ahu, 1998), 163–64.

6. John Kotter, *Leading Change* (Boston: Harvard Business School Press, 1996), 36.

7. These six styles of evangelism were presented previously in the *Becoming a Contagious Christian* book and the *Becoming a Contagious Christian* evangelism training course.

8. Mark Mittelberg, Lee Strobel, and Bill Hybels, *Becoming a Contagious Christian Leader's Guide* (Grand Rapids: Zondervan, 1995), 82.

9. Everett Rogers, *The Diffusion of Innovations,* 4th ed. (New York: Free Press, 1995).

10. For more information, call the Willow Creek Association at 1-800-570-9812 (outside the United States, call 847-765-6208), or log on to the Willow Creek Web site at www.willowcreek.com.

11. George Barna, *Evangelism That Works* (Ventura, Calif.: Gospel Light, 1995), 84.

12. For more information on this process, I recommend the book *How to Change Your Church (Without Killing It),* by Alan Nelson and Gene Appel (Nashville: Word, 2000).

13. Barna, *Evangelism That Works,* 100.

Chapter 6

1. Bruce Bugbee, *What You Do Best in the Body of Christ* (Grand Rapids: Zondervan, 1995).

2. Greg Ogden, *The New Reformation: Returning the Ministry to the People of God* (Grand Rapids: Zondervan, 1990).

3. Bruce Bugbee, Don Cousins, and Bill Hybels, *Network: Understanding God's Design for You in the Church* (Grand Rapids: Zondervan, 1994).

4. Robert S. McNamara, *In Retrospect: The Tragedy and Lessons of Vietnam* (New York: Time Books, a division of Random House, 1995), 332.

5. George Barna, *Evangelism That Works* (Ventura, Calif.: Gospel Light, 1995), 97. Emphasis added.

6. Barna, *Evangelism That Works*, 97.

7. Barna, *Evangelism That Works*, 136–37.

Chapter 7

1. John Kotter, *Leading Change* (Boston: Harvard Business School Press, 1996), 156.

2. Steven A. Macchia, *Becoming a Healthy Church: 10 Characteristics* (Grand Rapids: Baker, 1999), 139.

3. J. Oliver Buswell, *A Systematic Theology of the Christian Religion* (Grand Rapids: Zondervan, 1962), Part III–Soteriology, 75–76.

4. Mark Mittelberg, Lee Strobel, and Bill Hybels, *Becoming a Contagious Christian Youth Edition,* revised and expanded for students by Bo Boshers (Grand Rapids: Zondervan, 2000).

Chapter 8

1. Bill Hybels, *Defining Moments,* "Catalyzing a Corps of Evangelists," Seeds Tape #DF9809 (available through the Willow Creek Association at 1-800-570-9812).

2. *Pursuit* magazine, published four times a year by Evangelical Free Church of America. For information, call 1-952-853-1750 / 1-800-995-5360, or e-mail <pursuit@efca.org>.

3. *The Life@Work Journal,* published bimonthly by The Life@Work Co. For subscription information, call toll free at 1-877-543-9675, or e-mail <subscriptions@lifeatwork.com>.

4. *Sports Spectrum* magazine, published bimonthly by RBC Ministries. For information, call 1-215-781-8779 or 1-800-283-8333, or visit RBC's Web site at www.rbc.org.

5. *The Journey (NIV): A Bible for Seeking God and Understanding Life* (Grand Rapids: Zondervan & Willow Creek Association, 1996).

6. Lee Strobel, *The Case for Christ* (Grand Rapids: Zondervan, 1998).

7. Lee Strobel, *The Case for Faith* (Grand Rapids: Zondervan, 2000).

8. Bill Hybels, *The God You're Looking For* (Nashville: Thomas Nelson, 1997).

9. Ken Blanchard, Bill Hybels, and Phil Hodges, *Leadership by the Book* (Colorado Springs: WaterBrook, 1999).

10. James Emery White, *A Search for the Spiritual: Exploring Real Christianity* (Grand Rapids: Baker, 1998).

11. Josh McDowell, *More Than a Carpenter* (Wheaton, Ill.: Tyndale House, 1977).

12. Robert Laidlaw, *The Reason Why* (Grand Rapids: Zondervan, 1970).

13. Gary Poole and Judson Poling, *Tough Questions,* series of seven study guides for seeker small groups (Grand Rapids: Zondervan, 1998).

14. George Barna, *Evangelism That Works* (Ventura, Calif.: Gospel Light, 1995), 100.

15. Bill Hybels, "The Evangelism Gift," Seeds Tape #C9903 (available through the Willow Creek Association at 1-800-570-9812).

16. Lee Strobel, *The Unexpected Adventure,* "If Jesus Lived in My House," Seeds Tape #C9805 (available through the Willow Creek Association at 1-800-570-9812).

Chapter 9

1. George Barna, *Marketing the Church* (Colorado Springs: NavPress, 1988), 111.

2. Garry Poole and Judson Poling, *Tough Questions,* series of seven study guides for seeker small groups (Grand Rapids: Zondervan, 1998).

3. Stan Telchin, *Betrayed!* (Grand Rapids: Chosen Books, 1982).

4. Rick Warren, *The Purpose-Driven® Church* (Grand Rapids: Zondervan, 1995), 157–58.

5. Phillip E. Johnson, *Darwin on Trial* (Downers Grove: InterVarsity Press, 1993).

6. Philip Doddridge, "O Happy Day!" *Praise! Our Songs and Hymns* (Grand Rapids: Singspiration Music, 1979), 275.

7. Lee Strobel, *Inside the Mind of Unchurched Harry and Mary* (Grand Rapids: Zondervan, 1993), 159.

Chapter 10

1. Dann Spader, *The Everyday Commission* (Colorado Springs: WaterBrook, 1994), 56.

2. For more information on this and the other churches discussed throughout these pages, turn to the Church and Ministry List at the back of the book.

3. FAITH is a strategy combining evangelism and Sunday school. It originated at First Baptist Church in Daytona Beach, Florida, through the efforts of Bobby Welch and Doug Williams. It has been introduced to Southern Baptists by the LifeWay Sunday School Group, who partnered with First Baptist Church in developing materials and launching a national training plan. For more information contact the FAITH Sunday School Ministry Department at 1-615-251-2477, or visit the LifeWay Web site at www.lifeway.com.

Chapter 11

1. Garry Poole and Judson Poling, *Tough Questions,* series of seven study guides for seeker small groups (Grand Rapids: Zondervan, 1998).

Chapter 12

1. Rick Warren, *The Purpose-Driven® Church* (Grand Rapids: Zondervan, 1995), 247.

2. Debbie Morris, *Forgiving the Dead Man Walking* (Grand Rapids: Zondervan, 1998).

Chapter 13

1. Garry Poole and Judson Poling, *Tough Questions,* series of seven study guides for seeker small groups (Grand Rapids: Zondervan, 1998).

2. *Living Proof—Evangelism,* twelve-session video curriculum (Grand Rapids: Zondervan, 1996).

3. Vonette Bright and Barbara Ball, *The Joy of Hospitality: Fun Ideas for Evangelistic Entertaining* (Orlando, Fla.: NewLife Publications, 1996).

4. Marlene Lefever, *Parties with Purpose: Laying the Groundwork for Discipleship and Evangelism* (Colorado Springs: Cook Ministry Resources, 1998).

5. James W. Hollis, *Beyond the Walls: A Congregational Guide for Lifestyle Relational Evangelism* (Nashville: Discipleship Resources, 1993).

Chapter 14

1. Quoted in Lyle Dorsett, *A Passion for Souls* (Chicago: Moody Press, 1997), 59.
2. The Promiseland curriculum is published by Willow Creek Resources and can be ordered by calling the Willow Creek Association at 1-800-570-9812 (from outside the United States call 1-847-765-6208).
3. To contact Neighborly Evangelism Ministries, call 1-800-838-4368, or visit their Web site at www.neighborlyevangelism.org.
4. For more information on the Super Bowl Outreach Kits, call 1-800-BOWL-PARTY (1-800-269-5727), or log on to www.gospelcom.net/rbc/ss/outreach/sb/.

Chapter 15

1. Steve Sjogren, *Conspiracy of Kindness: A Refreshing New Approach to Sharing the Love of Jesus with Others* (Ann Arbor, Mich.: Servant Publications, 1993), 11.
2. Sjogren, *Conspiracy of Kindness*, 209–210. Story used with permission.

Chapter 16

1. Bill Hybels and Mark Mittelberg, *Becoming a Contagious Christian* (Grand Rapids: Zondervan, 1994), 209.
2. Lee Strobel, *The Case for Christ* (Grand Rapids: Zondervan, 1998); Lee Strobel, *The Case for Faith* (Grand Rapids: Zondervan, 2000).
3. Josh McDowell, *More Than a Carpenter* (Wheaton, Ill.: Tyndale House, 1977).
4. Paul Little, *Know Why You Believe,* 2nd ed. (Downers Grove, Ill.: InterVarsity Press, 2000).
5. Norman L. Geisler and William E. Nix, *A General Introduction to the Bible,* rev ed. (Chicago: Moody Press, 1986).
6. Bill Hybels, "The Core Idea," Seeds Tape #M9621 (available through the Willow Creek Association at 1-800-570-9812).
7. George Barna, *The Barna Report,* bimonthly newsletter, October 1999, 4.

Chapter 17

1. For information on Sonlife's ministry, call them at 1-630-365-5855, or visit them at their Web site at www.sonlife.com. Also, their mailing address can be found in the Church and Ministry List in the back of the book.
2. George Hunter, *Church for the Unchurched* (Nashville: Abingdon, 1996), 67.
3. Billy Graham, "Recovering the Primacy of Evangelism," *Christianity Today,* 8 December 1997, 29–30.
4. Rick Warren, *The Purpose-Driven® Church* (Grand Rapids: Zondervan, 1995), 147.
5. Luis Palau, "Heart for the World" (Portland, Ore.: Luis Palau Evangelistic Association, 1989), 9–10.
6. Graham, "Recovering the Primacy of Evangelism," 30.
7. Lewis A. Drummond, *The Word of the Cross* (Nashville: Broadman & Holman, 1992), 330–32.
8. Jim Cymbala, *Fresh Wind, Fresh Fire* (Grand Rapids: Zondervan, 1997), 181–82.

Willow Creek Association

FOR PREVAILING CHURCHES

This resource was created to serve you and to help you in building a local church that prevails! It is just one of many Willow Creek Resources copublished by the Willow Creek Association and Zondervan Publishing House.

Since 1992, the Willow Creek Association (WCA) has been linking like-minded, action-oriented churches with each other and with strategic vision, training, and resources. Now a worldwide network of over five thousand churches from more than eighty denominations, the WCA works to equip Member Churches and others with the tools needed to build prevailing churches. Our desire is to inspire, equip, and encourage Christian leaders to build biblically functioning churches that reach increasing numbers of unchurched people, not just with innovations from Willow Creek Community Church in South Barrington, Illinois, but from any church in the world that has experienced God-given breakthroughs.

Willow Creek Conferences

In the past year, more than 65,000 local church leaders, staff, and volunteers—from WCA Member Churches and others—attended one of our conferences or training events.

Conferences offered on the Willow Creek campus in South Barrington, Illinois, include:

Prevailing Church Conference—Foundational training for staff and volunteers working to build a prevailing local church; offered twice each year.

Prevailing Church Workshops—More than fifty workshops cover seven topic areas that represent key characteristics of a prevailing church; offered twice each year.

Promiseland Conference—Children's ministries; infant through fifth grade.

Prevailing Youth Ministries Conference—Junior and senior high ministries.

Arts Conference—Vision and training for Christian artists using their gifts in the ministries of local churches.

Leadership Summit—Envisioning and equipping Christians with leadership gifts and responsibilities; broadcast live via satellite to sixteen cities.

Contagious Evangelism Conference—Encouragement and training for churches and church leaders who want to be strategic in reaching lost people for Christ.

Small Groups Conference—Exploring how small groups can play a key role in developing authentic Christian community that leads to spiritual transformation.

Prevailing Church Regional Workshops

Each year the WCA team leads seven, two-day training events in cities across the United States. Workshops are offered in topic areas including leadership, next-generation ministries, small groups, arts and worship, evangelism, spiritual gifts, financial stewardship, and spiritual formation. These events make quality training more accessible and affordable to larger groups of staff and volunteers.

Willow Creek Resources

Churches can look to Willow Creek Resources for a trusted channel of ministry tools in areas of leadership, evangelism, spiritual gifts, small groups, drama, contemporary music, financial stewardship, spiritual transformation, and more. For ordering information, call 800-570-9812 or visit www.willowcreek.com.

WCA Membership

Membership in the Willow Creek Association as well as attendance at WCA Conferences is for churches, ministries, and leaders who hold to a historic, orthodox understanding of biblical Christianity. The annual church membership fee of $249 provides discounts for your entire team on all conferences and Willow Creek Resources, networking opportunities with other outreach-oriented churches, a bimonthly newsletter, a subscription to *Defining Moments* monthly audio journal, and more.

WillowNet (www.willowcreek.com)

This Internet service provides you with access to hundreds of Willow Creek messages, drama scripts, songs, videos, and multimedia suggestions. The system allows you to sort through these elements and download them for a fee.

Our Web site also provides detailed information on the Willow Creek Association, Willow Creek Community Church, WCA Membership, conferences, training events, resources, and more.

Willow Creek Association
P.O. Box 3188
Barrington, IL 60011-3188
Phone: (800) 570-9812
Fax: (888) 922-0035
Web: www.willowcreek.com

Becoming a Contagious Christian

Communicating Your Faith in a Style That Fits You

MARK MITTELBERG, LEE STROBEL, AND BILL HYBELS

We all want to reach lost people for Christ. But the truth is, most Christians never lead another person to Christ.

Becoming a Contagious Christian is designed to help change that. This best-selling course provides all the tools you'll need to help your church's members discover their own personal styles of evangelism. In only eight 50-minute sessions, you can help people learn to comfortably and confidently communicate their faith. Taught in twenty languages around the world, this course is designed especially for people who think that evangelism is not for them.

Now help every member of your church develop the heart and skills for reaching lost people. They can't all be Billy Graham—but they can be exactly who God designed them to be!

The Groupware kit (0-310-50109-1) includes:
Leader's Guide (0-310-50081-8), one Participant's Guide (0-310-50101-6), Overhead Masters (0-310-50091-5), and the Drama Vignettes Video (0-310-20169-1)

Also available:
Becoming a Contagious Christian, Youth Edition (see page 409).
The entire curriculum has been rewritten for high school students, complete with a new Drama Vignettes Video containing situations and actors they can relate to.

Becoming a Contagious Christian
The original book by Bill Hybels and Mark Mittelberg
Hardcover 0-310-48500-2
Softcover 0-310-21008-9
Audio Pages 0-310-48508-8

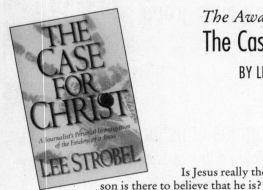

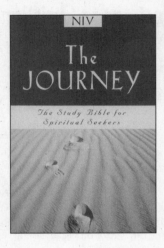

We want to hear from you. Please send your comments about this book to us in care of the address below. Thank you.

ZondervanPublishingHouse
Grand Rapids, Michigan 49530
http://www.zondervan.com